ARTICULATE FLESH

ARTICULATE FLESH

MALE HOMO-EROTICISM
AND MODERN POETRY

Gregory Woods

1987
Yale University Press
New Haven and London

Set in Linotype Sabon by Alan Sutton Publishing Ltd, Gloucester and printed and bound in
Great Britain by The Bath Press, Avon.

Library of Congress Cataloging-in-Publication Data

Woods, Gregory, 1953–
  Articulate flesh.

  Bibliography: p.
  Includes index.
  1. English Poetry—20th century—History and
criticism. 2. Homosexuality, Male, in literature.
3. Erotic poetry, English—History and criticism.
4. Erotic poetry, American—History and criticism.
5. American poetry—20th century—History and
criticism. I. Title.
PR605.H65W66 1987   821'.91'09353   87–10646
ISBN 0–300–03872–0
ISBN 0–300–04752–5 (pb)

CONTENTS

ACKNOWLEDGEMENTS

I owe a particular debt of thanks to Guido Almansi, who supervised my doctoral research at the University of East Anglia, on which this book is based. Others who commented on early drafts include J.B. Broadbent, Valentine Cunningham, A.E. Dyson, Ann Geneva, Thom Gunn, Eric Homberger, Franco Moretti, and Lorna Sage. I am also grateful for the patience and good humour of Robert Baldock and Mary Carruthers, my editors at Yale.

The short section of Chapter 2 called 'Three Battles' was first published as 'Tre battaglie: archetipi di omoerotismo nella letteratura di guerra', translated by Maria Rosaria Carpentieri and Carmen Brancatelli, in *Sodoma: rivista omosessuale di cultura*.

Many sections made their first appearances as lectures at Keswick Hall College of Education, the University of East Anglia, and the University of Salerno. Some of my ideas on elegy and friendship were modified by my students at Salerno.

INTRODUCTION

Eros pitches his house in the human body. It is here that all declarations of love, poetic or otherwise, have their origin; and it is hither that, even after their dizziest flights of spirituality, they must return. The verbal flourish of erotic candour — the song or sonnet, graffito or *billet doux* — is an echo of the body's signs, an articulation of the flesh. Since this book is about poetry written by men in either passing or lasting moods of erotic attraction to other men, the body in question is male.

Male homo-eroticism is not the exclusive preserve of however small a minority you believe homosexual men to be. It is a major, self-referential part of male sexuality as a whole. The themes I am dealing with exist not at the periphery of general interest (within a category labelled 'homosexual', containing only those authors known to have been homosexual, and shunted to a corner of the library with other 'side issues') but at the very centre of the mainstream. I have therefore chosen to use the expression 'homo-erotic' as a way of moving beyond the notion of a restricted 'homosexual' tradition.

The most problematic aspects of my subject are implicit in its very existence. To what extent is one justified in separating the homo-erotic from the hetero-erotic, and both from the erotic as a whole? After all, one conclusion which will insistently force itself on our attention is that male, homo-erotic themes in literature share many of the characteristics of the wider (hetero-erotic, but male-dominated and phallocentric) tradition: the same alliances between sex and violence, for instance, or between sex and discourse.

One answer to this question is simple enough. The two traditions (or, perhaps, the two aspects of the same tradition) are already separate because they have been separated. Science, Church, and State have taken the liberty of dividing homo- from heterosexuality; so, how can one think of them as anything but divided? One was declared insane, immoral, and illegal; the other sane, moral, and legal. These circumstances pitted the consequent insecurity of the writers in one group against the complacency of those in the other. Who could blame homosexual writers for not wishing to be associated with heterosexual, when the latter had already anathematised them?

To speak of love between men is always a violation of tact. Such things should be left unexpressed: for are they not, by common consent, *unspeakable*? The mouth of the man who loves men, fouled by his sexual acts, duly fouls the words he speaks. At once both secretive and garrulous, his tongue is an apparatus of heresy and treachery: to begin to speak is already to have said too much. It follows, therefore, that the literary expression of male love, however succinct, will invariably be considered excessive.

Since it was first driven underground, the love that dare not speak its name has assumed many aliases. Different groups and individuals adopted different solutions to the articulation of the unspeakable. But what such writers all had in common were restrictions on their sexuality. Near the start of his book on *The Homosexual Tradition in American Poetry*, Robert K. Martin asks the crucial question, 'What would homosexual poetry be like without oppression?'[1] His rhetoric excuses him from providing a reply; but two are available to us. The first is that the strength of the literature of homosexuality lies in obliquity, arising from the need to resort to metaphor to express sexual meaning. The end of oppression would result in an outspoken and affirmative erotic literature, with rather more pricks than phallic symbols. Homosexual poetry would be nothing — or little more than pornographic description — without its scaffolding of oppression.

The second reply to Martin's question is, on the contrary, that homosexual writers would, at last, be able to explore their sexuality and its connotations with a degree of freedom, without having to pack their texts with the imposed irrelevancies of someone else's notion of tact. The case of a poet like Hart Crane is illustrative. In order to conceal his sexuality, Crane hid relatively straightforward emotions under an ornate carapace of difficulty. Thereafter, he suffered a critical response which denied, or ignored, any contribution of his sexuality to his poetry, other than by the indirect means of aggravating his alcoholism and hastening his suicide. Baroque with the stratagems of the oppressed, his work was read as being gratuitously overwrought. If such poets were free to write as they chose, their poetry could quickly outdo the successes of its own tradition.

An eminent adherent to something like the former view is George Steiner, whose essay on 'Eros and Idiom' laments lapses into outspokenness by such modern writers as Proust and Genet. Their freedom to speak of men who love men has, somehow, damaged their work. (Steiner does not explicitly use this claimed disadvantage of liberty to excuse oppression, any more than one would unflinchingly cite Paul Celan's 'Todesfuge' as a positive consequence of its subject, the extermination of six million European Jews.)[2]

More bluntly on the side of discretion is Jeffrey Meyers, in his book on *Homosexuality and Literature, 1890–1930*. The novels of Genet, Burroughs, Rechy, and Selby, he writes, 'concern the homosexual's acts and not his mind, and appeal to sensation rather than to imagination'. These four very different novelists lead him to conclude that 'The emancipation of the homosexual has led, paradoxically, to the decline of his art'.[3] That Meyers speaks of the 'emancipation of the homosexual' in the past tense, clinches the self-destruction of his argument: for the more sordid elements of the works to which he refers, and of which he complains, are the direct issue of continuing social, legal, and political oppression. (If an emancipated Genet exists, I should be glad of the page references.)

Given such objections to the explicit statement of homosexual desires and acts, it is not surprising that the audience of these texts has gradually divided into sympathetic and unsympathetic readers: those who are either embraced or repulsed by the mere fact that such things have appeared in print at all. This division, crudely mapped, tends to coincide with the prejudged battle-lines of sexual orientation itself.

Should I, then, have begun by saying 'I am homosexual'? Or must I act out the strabismus of bisexuality? I could always, of course, ape the 'objectivity' of being straight, if such ideological complacency had not been discredited by at least a decade of European literary theory. In any case, it should be one of the roles of a critic to minimise the effects of divisive categories: to agitate for (not simply to *assume*) an undifferentiated readership. If there is such a thing as a literature of gay men (and I think there is), it is not a collection which only those readers who have more or less explicitly acknowledged their own exclusive homosexuality can appreciate: gay books for gay readers (though there is plenty of room for these). On the contrary, if we are to recognise the proper place and function of this book's themes, we have to avoid any tendency to separate them off. We must try to integrate perception of them into the currency of critical discourse. These themes exist within a context of others, and their meanings are open to the common reader, straight or gay or neither.

I do not mean to spend time attempting to prove, in a biographical sense, that any of the poets mentioned in these essays is or was 'a homosexual' (a word I shall use only as an adjective). Some will have formed only homosexual relationships, others only heterosexual relationships, others both, and the rest neither. Their physical couplings are not really my concern. All appear here, simply, because their poetry expresses, to a lesser or greater extent, a reaction to others of their own gender, which seems to have its place in the broad field of erotic literature. If I quote only one line of a poet's work, it is not to claim that he is 'a homosexual'. Likewise, if I were to quote his whole output; which I shall not.

A brief account of my original reading for this book should clarify the question of orientation. I began, of course, with the works of male poets I knew to be, or to have been, homosexual or bisexual, regardless of whether they wrote in foreign languages or before the First World War, matters which would later exclude them from my main concern. From these, I was able to deduce a number of common homo-erotic themes. I then moved to the works of poets whose sexual orientation was unknown, or known to be heterosexual. In these, I isolated many examples of the same themes: 'homosexual' poetry by 'heterosexual' poets.

Thus, for example, while I would not seek to claim that T.S. Eliot was, by any significant definition, homosexual or even bisexual — I believe and concede that he was probably not — I am still convinced that *The Waste Land* is, at least in part, a consummate love poem whose object is (most of the time) male. It makes sense to identify this figure as Eliot's beloved friend Jean Verdenal, who was killed in the First World War; but to suggest, without evidence, that these two men were lovers, in a sexual sense, would be idle intrusion, since it could contribute nothing more than we already know to the reading of the love poem. (The same can be said of Tennyson, Hallam, and *In Memoriam.*)

This matter of an author's sexuality is continually bringing me back to a remark Bonnie Zimmerman makes on lesbian literature: 'If a text lends itself to a lesbian reading, then no amount of biographical "proof" ought to be necessary to establish it as a lesbian text'.[4] Exactly. A gay text is one which lends itself to the hypothesis of a gay reading, regardless of where the author's genitals were wont to keep house. The biography of the author may be little more than a signpost, indicating both where one is most likely to find texts open to certain readings, and what kind of reading a given text is most likely to reward. To pretend that the sign is pointing in the opposite direction, or actually to turn it to face the wrong way, is, of course, mischievous and futile.

Having confirmed, at least to my own satisfaction, that homo-erotic themes were common to so many male poets, whatever their stated/assumed orientation, I managed to move beyond having to consider who had slept with whom. Much of this book, therefore, is about poetry by men in general; and about male sexuality in general.

But the most outspoken and enthusiastic versions of homo-erotic themes remain likely to come most often from men who regard themselves as homosexual. I have concentrated on them. In other words, my reading took me on a circular course from and to known homosexual poets. (Of the five I chose to study in detail in the second half of the book, only one, Lawrence, would have regarded himself as heterosexual.)

Since there are areas other than the erotic that separate homo- from heterosexual writers, I cannot claim to have given a full account of the distinguishing features of a literature of homosexuality. I have barely begun to mention the verbal iconography of rooms, doors, keys, masks, performances, foreign languages, eavesdroppers, gossip, and so on, which are as characteristic of the work of male, homosexual poets as are their reactions to male flesh. It would take another volume at least as long as this to deal with the full effects oppression has had on this literature. Such a book would be about lesbians as well as gay men: for, if there is such a thing as a 'Gay Sensibility' shared by members of both sexes, it is a response to discrimination, rather than a unanimity of desire.

The first half of the present book deals with what seem to me the main *topoi* of male homo-eroticism: firstly, by dismantling and reconstructing the male body itself; secondly, by observing it in and after energetic action, either at war or in sports; and thirdly, by considering it as an instrument of creativity — as the author, text, and subject of its own futures. In the second half, I show how such themes are adopted and adapted to different ends by five poets: Lawrence, Crane, Auden, Ginsberg, and Gunn. Whilst my central concern is with male poets writing in English between 1914 and 1984 — the writers who appear in the first section of my bibliography — I have also treated myself to a wide variety of background texts from earlier periods, in other languages, and by women. The reader should infer from this pliancy of limits that my argument is meant to be, not exhaustive and definitive, but exploratory and suggestive.

PART ONE

THEMES

1 THE MALE BODY

THE AGES OF MAN

Three types of male physique, three distinct ideals, occur in Western art: the adolescent pliancy of Narcissus, Apollo's firm but graceful maturity, and the potency of Heracles, tacitly poised on the verge of deterioration. 'They could almost be seen as the same body at different stages of its development.'[1]

The three physical types correspond with sexual types. The adolescent may be endowed with an indefatigable penis,[2] but is chiefly admired for the delightful promise of his backside. Shakespeare is not interested in his boyfriend's penis (sonnet 20). The Earl of Rochester's page, who 'Does the trick worth forty wenches', is thus praised for the anal, rather than the phallic nature of his prowess. And when Marlowe describes the 'heavenly path' of Leander's spine (*Hero and Leander* I, 68), he means the dream-ladder *down* which a Jacob might climb to reach Paradise.

Heracles is the opposite type, unequivocally phallic. When he lays down his club, he is still heavily armed. His musculature seems designed for the pinning down of loved ones, while the phallus does its work. He and the adolescent, as sexual opposites, together form the perfect couple: Heracles and Hylas, Hadrian and Antinous.

Between the two lies the adaptability of Apollo, the single couple: a dual sexual nature in one physique. He is best depicted in three dimensions: for we must be able to wander at will from penis to buttocks to penis, gazing at his statue as though in his bed, making love with each aspect of him in turn. He has no one point on which to focus, and must be sculpted or described as the body, complete. (In his reincarnation as Jesus, however, He tends to be seen mainly from the front, tied to the pillar, nailed to the cross, or addressing the viewer. His Sacred Wounds and Heart are frontally exposed.) In the versatility of his manhood, Apollo is, perhaps, the ideal ideal.

In literature, where a boy's date of birth can be specified, the types of body are best studied chronologically, at first, according to age. Our most experienced guide in this matter is the eminent geographer and seismologist of human landscape, the Marquis de Sade. His book *Les 120 journées de Sodome*, intended as a kind of *Summa pornographica*, had to contain as many types of body as could be combined to perform the sum of the sexual acts he could imagine. Although Sade is not the most reliable witness to the ordinary man's sexual tastes, his division of male beauty between adolescent and adult is still useful. The *dramatis personae* of his book include eight boys, aged between 12 and 15 and chosen for their facial and bodily appearance of innocent delicacy, and eight men, aged between 23 and 34 and chosen solely on the basis of phallic enormity.[3]

Sade's main point is that boys are best suited to being penetrated, and men to penetrating. A boy's beauty lies in his face and behind; a man's, in his penis and musculature. The boy is soft and malleable; the man, solidly powerful. So, we do not expect to find Sade stating the length of a boy's penis. Likewise, he tends not to describe a man's buttocks; and he allows a man to have the ugliest of faces, providing his penis is correspondingly large. Modern writers may disagree. But just as, in the Italian Renaissance, male beauty could be polarised to such extremes as Donatello's and Michelangelo's versions of David, so today the basic idea of the separate types still applies. For the sake of argument, let us liken Sade's boys to William Burroughs' or Tony Duvert's, and his men to Jean Genet's.

The two main points of difference between Sade and the modern writers in general are worth noting, here, before our survey begins. For a start, boys penetrate and men are penetrated. The rigidity with which Sade treats sexual roles, at least in the early outline of his characters' functions, is not to be taken literally. Secondly, he omits from this initial list of characters any youth between the ages of 16 and 22, inclusive. In fact, this is generally considered to be the most desirable age, particularly the late teens. I shall consider it in a moment; but I must begin closer to puberty.

What few references there are to boys aged 12 are not to those relatively late developers who have not, by this age, begun to pass through puberty; but, rather, to boys whose secondary sexual characteristics are partially in evidence, and who have reached a stage of experimentation and self-discovery, which is itself of some interest. Such boys tend not to be explicitly considered as sexual partners. However, they have begun to acquire certain features which foreshadow and include sexual beauty. Also, for the first time, they are coming to think of themselves in sexual terms, particularly as they start to experience the pleasures, and sometimes the anxieties, of masturbation.

In Felice Picano's poem 'Cinema Verité', a 12 year-old repeatedly plays truant from school to watch Alan Ladd in a cowboy movie. His hero-worship runs, at least, to noticing the colour of Ladd's eyes, and a certain shot in which Ladd gently caresses himself 'next to his holster'. One day, no doubt, if not today, he will go home and, picturing the same celluloid gesture, discover masturbation. Kenward Elmslie recalls this milestone in his own life very clearly: it was in Washington, on a Sunday, and he was 12.[4]

When Charles Henri Ford writes that 'A 12-year-old cock / looks lovely by candlelight', he contravenes Sade's unwritten rule about the concentration of pubertal beauty in the buttocks. From his remark, we can derive a final observation: that the beauty of the 12 year-old is only seen, and seen in a romantic light. His penis is observed, but not touched or tasted. His sexual activity, such as it is, is conducted either on his own, or with others of his own age, Sade notwithstanding.[5]

It is in reference only to his 13 year-olds that Sade goes against his own tendency, by paying some attention to boys' genitals. One of the three is conventionally handsome with a pretty bottom. But the second has a penis which is said to be well advanced for his age; and the slight effeminacy of the third is belied by the unmistakeable virility of his penis. Such boys seem to be at the stage where genital development outstrips that of the rest of the body, and the penis seems out of proportion with the boy. This imbalance leaves an inordinately sexual impression of what beauty the boy possesses.

Hero-worship and masturbation are no less the erotic activities of the 13 year-old than of the 12 year-old. Harold Norse's 'Let Me Love You All at Stillman's Gym' covers both activities. He remembers himself at 13, with an embarrassingly girlish face, but also with newly grown pubic hairs, the secret sign of his actual maturity. From a window, he watches a group of older youths changing in the open air after a swim. When they notice their young voyeur, apparently imagining him a girl, they shout and wave their penises at him, before carrying on with their games. In curtained safety, the boy masturbates. An extended reference is now made to Walt Whitman's voyeur (in 'Song of Myself', 11), who watches a group of young men bathing, and imagines herself out into their midst. In Norse's piece, desire is the watchword of the boy's age, spoken with all the extravagance of Whitman himself: 'I am 13. I want to love America.' But, at 13, the self is the lover. Appropriately, the piece ends with the boy performing the sophisticated feat of autofellatio.[6]

Like that of their younger counterparts, the beauty of 13 year-olds tends, merely, to be observed; but, because of the imbalance I have mentioned, between boyish bodies and more manly genitals, such observation may be drawn to the groin. In 'Swan River', Paul Goodman watches a boy bathing: 'His body is gold, / his penis taut of age thirteen, / his eyes are lapis, his teeth are square, / he is laughing'. It is the penis, not the boy himself, that betrays his age. Furthermore, because the penis is mature enough, voyeurism is no longer its own reward. The insistent problem the poet puzzles over is 'how to get / to kiss this river boy'. Sexual intercourse is no longer such a distant proposition.[7]

14 year-olds fall into two types: the rapidly strengthening boy, who is already a youth; and the slower developer, softer and more gentle. In Thomas Mann's *Death in Venice*, Tadzio, first described as a long-haired boy of about 14, is of the latter type, with a hairless and pale body, soft to the point of frailty. Generally, however, the 14 year-old is portrayed beginning, or old enough to begin, his sexual life-span. In Ian Young's poem 'Chinese Boy, 14', the boy is a ripe fruit, tasty and juicy, which has just been prised open and probed by a thirsty tongue. Whether the image is phallic or anal, or both, is of no consequence. What matters is that fruit should be eaten when ripe. Otherwise, it will rot.[8]

Of Sade's two 15 year-olds, one is likened to Adonis (after whom he is named), and the other is said to be the most delicious of all eight. The peak of pubertal development has been reached. The boy is now a youth. The next few years will see the transition into manhood. 15 is no longer a time of innocence: by now, the boy is thought to be entering the sexual world to which his body has introduced him. Call him, rather, semi-innocent. Nor is this an age particularly suited to love. The boy's sexual momentum allows him no pause for such refinement. Granted, Harold Norse records a sleepless but sexless night with a 15 year-old; but the lack of sex was Norse's, not the boy's fault.[9] According to other such accounts, from the *Satyricon* onwards, when there is pleasure to be had, a boy will comply with his partner's wishes, as long as, for propriety's sake, he can pretend to be asleep.

The sexual characteristic of the 15 year-old, then, is his eagerness — as E.A. Lacey records, in his poem 'Oneiromancy'. Also at this age (in some cases, even earlier), the boy may begin to feather his nest, or add to his family's income, by combining business and pleasure in the gentle arts of prostitution. In the poem 'Veracruz', Lacey goes out at night, 'looking for Paulinho or Dario or Betinho or any other 15- or 16-year-old chicken to share my sheets and flesh with: / pick out, pick up, pick on, pick over, pick apart – throw away'. Finally, to contradict my remark about love, in Ian Young's 'Honi Soit Qui Mal Y Pense', we do find a 15 year-old who is the younger half of a homosexual couple. But he is the exception to a fairly general rule.[10]

16 is the most popular of the specified ages. In the *Satyricon*, Giton, the boyfriend over whom Encolpius and Ascyltus come close to blows, is 16. In more recent literature, Frederick Rolfe's pet story-teller, Toto, is 16, looks like Cellini's Perseus, and is both as 'smooth as a peach' and as 'noble as a god'. John Giorno's 'Johnny Guitar' and Dennis Kelly's updated version of Thomas Mann's Tadzio, are both 16; as is the subject of Darío Galicia's 'Blues for a Portrait of a Working-Class Boy', who, despite being 'scrawny' is even 'more beautiful than Che Guevara'.[11]

Being both boy and man in one body, the 16 year-old is liable to appear as a beautiful youth, a fresh influence in an adult world, whether that world is cast as a gay bar, a cruising area, or a poet's bed. Paul Goodman's poem 'For G., Aet. 16' is an account of finding such a boy-man, serving behind the bar at a party; and of falling in love with him for the half hour in which they are together. This youth's attraction lies in his 'blue eyes and flowing hair'. In 'Sweet Sixteen', Salvatore Farinella marvels at the thigh muscles of a youth, as they are tensed and displayed for his benefit; and at the 'juicy and pliant' touch of the boy's balls as he moves closer. The poem ends in anticipation of their taste. In bed with Ian Young, a 16 year-old displays the sexual enthusiasm associated with his youth; and his balls, too, promise a delicious taste: 'his penis / swelled / so big and thick / I thought it would / split / like a ripe pod . . . and spill / white sugar dust / over us both'.[12]

Characteristic of all these youths is the sense of wonder they instil in their older observers or lovers. Every movement seems choreographed by a genius. Every orgasm approaches the conditions of miracle. But how is it with the youths themselves? It may be that they have other pleasures in store, as have the two in E.A. Lacey's 'Puerto Montt'. Aged '16 or 17 perhaps, at the most', they are following two girls, while Lacey follows them. Harold Norse also distinguishes between the man's vision of the youth, and the youth's of himself, in a poem called 'Green Ballet'. On a muddy bank of the Tiber, a man is fellating a youth, presumably having paid to do so. The youth is 16, and dressed in rags. The only physical detail we know of him is that he has 'red lips'. The man 'sees god as he looks up / at the boy', but the boy sees no such thing. He is thinking of a local whore. That distance is the price one pays for a hustler — in addition to his fee.[13]

A final point about 16 year-olds is made by Allen Ginsberg, in 'New York to San Fran', when he writes of himself 'murmuring what a beautiful / big pecker you got to a / pimply 16 year old boy / with his pants down on / my pallet, / who talked all night about his / intellectual disorders'.[14] The pimples are a minor drawback. What counts is the intellectual puberty, which could interfere with the most ingenious of sexual plans. These youths can no longer be patronised with smiles. Some of them actually demand to be listened to.

17 suffers by being sandwiched between two of the most popular ages, and is referred to infrequently. To Harold Norse, it was a year of boredom, during which 'reading made matters worse', because 'the Russian nihilists almost destroyed me'. Again, intellectual puberty interferes with sexual contentment. Not that, at school, there was any lack of sexual activity: 'my notebooks grew damp with sperm / in the boys' room I masturbated / and was masturbated by other boys / I fell in love with their asses'. But schoolboy games of mutual masturbation seem no longer sufficient to the 17 year-old. I take the last line quoted to mean that Norse's mind had moved to anal intercourse, in advance of his experience. His radical solution to the problem was to catch a train out of town. Later, in Tangier, he met 17 year-old Mohammed Rifi, who became his boyfriend and to whom he addressed a series of poems.[15]

In 'Chicken', Norse writes of a younger boy, who by running and playing football is carefully exercising his sinewy body, of which he is justifiably proud. He says to the poet, 'I oughtta / be big / all over when / I'm 17'. He probably will be: for, at 17, our subjects combine the suppleness and stamina of youth with the strength of adulthood, and their physiques take on the appearances of power. Ian Young meets a 17 year-old on a bus, and arranges to see him later; but the youth's hands make him slightly uneasy: 'Strong. A punk's hands. / Those hands would take me. / In the end, / I would have to come to terms / with those hands.' In an untitled poem, James Mitchell, only in his thirties at the time of writing, calls himself 'a tired / old fucker', and begs his 17 year-old boyfriend to be gentle with him. He complains that he can no longer come three times in half an hour, and that he needs the occasional rest from the 'rabid lungings' of the youth's 'insatiable cock'. From 17, begins the descent into adult sexuality.[16]

Athenian young men were liable for military service at 18, the beginning of manhood. 18 is the current age of majority in Britain – except where male, homosexual intercourse is concerned. In modern literature, it is usually the lowest age of those great favourites, sailors – unless they be mere cabin boys or galley slaves. This is an age of much deeper experience – of a worldly, if not necessarily a sexual sort – than its predecessors. E.A. Lacey recalls having made love to an 18 year-old naval cadet, 'in the throes of sex and life', who was due, the following week, to sail for the Antarctic. Ed Cox writes of being in the navy at 18, and of the hand of a friend touching a thigh; but of masturbating in the bathroom, for lack of a better alternative.[17]

At this age, we encounter hustlers more frequently. As John Rechy often points out, the professional life of a hustler is extremely short. It is probably at its most active and successful in the late teens, becoming less and less so in the twenties. Dennis Cooper writes of a less than perfect 'Eighteen Year Old Whore', on whose flesh, when he 'flexes what he's built, / one mousey tattoo / comes alive like a cartoon'. We are left with the rather pathetic impression that he is marked with a likeness of Mickey Mouse. In 'Fishboy', Harold Norse gives a more hopeful description of an 18 year-old hustler, whom he fellated in Paris for a 'loan' of five francs. He never got round to this youth's 'white, smooth, flaring, voluptuous, perfectly calipered' arse, but contented himself with what must have been 'the world's most desirable' thighs. For these marvels, the boy invariably undercharged his astonished suitors, the number of whom, alone, seems to have kept him solvent.[18]

Allen Ginsberg remembers groaning with desire 'to be kissed on the mouth & held close / to the breast of the fair boy's body I / desired then & there but it wasn't done / so I talked all night explaining my / delicate condition as hurt-voiced as I felt / in my crying throat & sad warm 18 yr. old breast.' He sounds just like the 16 year-old whose night-long self-examination he complained of, in the poem quoted above. Notice that what he desired at 18 is worded, not as one of the frankly sexual urges so common to his poetry — and which he would not have avoided, had that been what he meant — but as the need to be held and kissed. This is in keeping with the general view of 18 as an age at which lasting relationships can be begun. Physical development has slowed down, and with it sexual surprise. The mind can be concentrated on love. John Wieners records that at 18 he began a long affair with an older man. E.A. Lacey spent a year with a 'crazy' 18 year-old, whose penis was 'pale and urgent', but who had the knack of spending Lacey's money. But the greatest problem in loving a youth of this age has external causes. It is described in Harold Norse's poem 'Blood of a Poet', named after Cocteau's film. The poet in question is jailed for five years 'for making love / to a boy of 18 / who wanted it'.[19]

19 is an age without any characteristic peculiar to itself. It suffers, like 17, from the popularity of its two neighbours. But it must have some charm of its own, since Walt Curtis gives, as the first of '29 Reasons I Luv Him': 'He's 19 years old'. Jack Spicer writes about the 19 year-old Rimbaud, in *A Fake Novel about the Life of Arthur Rimbaud*. 'The Exterminator' in Will Inman's prose piece of that name, fellates another man for the first time when 19, and then begins to weep at the sudden thought that he may be homosexual. Finally, Harold Norse describes a 19 year-old French youth as 'an

adolescent of the type makes you water to devour the muscles, devour him whole'. Even now, the finer qualities of adolescence have not been left behind.[20]

Norse and Lacey are the poets of the age of 20. In 'Last Night at the Party', Norse becomes jealous when a 20 year-old he has taken to a party picks up another youth. In 'This Beautiful Young Man', he is annoyed by another 20 year-old, who takes pleasure in rebuffing the sexual advances of older men, except those of an unnamed 'famous poet'. Otherwise, he claims to be heterosexual. One significant point about him, an aspiring poet himself, is that his looks are superior to his poetry. The only sphere in which youthful confidence does not outweigh achievement or ability is the physical.[21]

In 'Survivor', Norse writes of a skinny, battered youth, who has survived the death of his parents, the beatings his brother gave him, and the general horrors of 'a Nazi camp in the suburbs'. Now, at 20, he has come out, had one of his ears pierced, and grown his hair. But the memory of his childhood and adolescence also survives, sexually, in 'a need for chains / and the stinging strokes of a strap on your rear'. Norse's one concern is to make this 'Poor little rich boy' laugh. On the other hand, in the poem 'To a Hustler', Norse describes a youth who is exasperatingly full of 'the sheer joy of being 20 years old', to the ridiculous extent of masturbating while watching a Boris Karloff movie on television. His sexiness is caught in the one line, 'We could bottle the perfume of your crotch and make a bundle'. But he is, sexually, too energetic for the poet, who was 60 when the poem was written.[22]

In a long poem called '101' (after a temperature, then an age), E.A. Lacey also complains half-heartedly about the antics of a 20 year-old hustler. This youth, he writes, 'takes half the money I make because he too / Feels that half his life has gone or is going by and he must enjoy it while he can'. Lacey himself was a mere 31 when he wrote the poem. For the hustler, old age follows closely upon youth; and a hustler's old age is liable to bring him, before he has lived out much more than a couple of his twenties, back into society – in the present case, 'as a clerk or salesman or waiter, which he'll settle down to being in his own good time, no doubt, though he still deludes himself that he'll be an actor, a singer, a somebody'. What makes him somebody at 20 is his body.

Lacey's other 20 year-old has made a name for himself by murdering fifteen people and giving a title to the poem, 'Carlos Eduardo Robledo Puch.' The photograph of him in a newspaper reveals 'a child's small sensitive mouth', and a body, Lacey writes, 'just like so many boys I've had here, there and elsewhere'. This youth, tried and sentenced, is spared the hustler's problem, of growing old on the streets. He will be 'well fucked and at home in prison'. His desirability is not lessened by the horror of his crimes. Looking at the photograph, Lacey 'cannot suppress the urge toward masturbation'.[23]

On the edge of adulthood, young men become so much more than mere sexual entities, and their styles of life lead them off in various directions. The teens are amenable to some kind of classification; the twenties, much less so. For this reason, we can expect to find ages in the twenties less frequently specified than those in the teens. When each year saw so much growth and development, it was sometimes necessary to pinpoint the stage the lover had reached. In his twenties, development will be steady, but slow.

After all we have seen and read, it comes as something of a shock to remember – if we had ever forgotten – that in the United Kingdom and many of the United States, 21 is the male homosexual age of consent (lesbians having been paid the fortunate insult of not being recognised by the law).[24] Perhaps it is in tacit recognition of the absurdity of 21 as a lower age limit, that not one of the poems I have read refers explicitly to a 21 year-old.

Constantine Cavafy's interest in the effects of time on love leads him to specify, more often than most poets, the ages of the young men he describes. All are in their twenties, the youngest being 22, the eldest 29.[25] Here, the specification of age is concerned less with particular erotic qualities than with the imminence of premature decline. In the twenties, according to Cavafy's sad vision, passionate love shifts from present tense to past. The poet over thirty can write only elegies on passion. In 'Before Time Should Change Them', he seems to count it fortunate that circumstances come between two young lovers: for, in separation, 'The one for the other / Will seem to stay ever / Twenty-four years old / The handsome boy still'. His version of decline has two aspects, physical and mental. Physical beauty and passionate willingness, both at their peaks in the twenties, decline as the years pass. It is better, therefore, to retain a beautiful memory of this age than to hang on to the fading reality of a later age. Love is not a lasting presence. It belongs to a single decade.

But Cavafy's vision is more appreciated than shared. In 'Lexington Nocturne', Jonathan Williams uses a night in bed with a 22 year-old as the basis for a statement on the love of men for boys. So the qualities of the teens are not entirely lost. In 'The Platonic Blow', W.H. Auden's 24 year-old reminds us of those mere 13 year-olds with apparently disproportionate genitals: for, although the young mechanic tells his life story 'Like a little boy', his penis is unquestionably manly, being not only long and thick, but also 'ineffably solemn and wise'. Such young men have seen only the beginnings of love's development. Adulthood may bring strength and responsibility, but does not eradicate inexperience at one blow. Harold Norse writes of a scarred, 26 year-old Vietnam War veteran who, despite his experience of combat, is still 'a nice blond kid' with plenty to learn, and plenty of time in which to learn it.[26]

The specification of age serves a purpose only in reference to years in which there is appreciable development, and only to those in which generalisations of type have a hope of accuracy. To write that a man is 40 would be saying nothing particularly detailed about his physical or mental characteristics or capacities. It is important to remember that in this brief survey of the ages of man, I have cited only those works in which an actual number of years is mentioned. Only Cavafy and Norse make regular use of this shorthand device. Most poets leave the lover's age implicit in the wider description.[27]

I should add, by way of conclusion, that age is not a concern specific to homosexual desire. The reader can be sure that for every Hyacinth there is, somewhere in Western literature, a Beatrice, Little Nell, Alice, or Lolita; and that Maurice Chevalier never thanked heaven for little boys. At the same time, while it is widely believed that homosexual men are irrationally fearful of ageing and bitter in old age, this myth can always be countered with a heterosexual Yeats, ever resentful of his physical decline, and a homosexual Whitman, revelling in the renewal of his vigour as each year passes. This seems to be a matter of personality or mood, rather than sexual orientation.

NARCISSUS

Of the adolescents already classified as the Narcissus type, in whom a chiefly receptive sexual beauty is discerned, there are many in literature, history, and myth; but, of these, two receive far more attention than the rest, thereby meriting our concern. They function as standards of beauty and as the archetypes of distinct sexual sorts. Both are creatures of the Greek myths: Narcissus himself, and Ganymede.

Narcissus is most often referred to in a simile, when some boy's beauty is likened to his. In one of Raymond Radiguet's poems, a boy is described as a 'Future fleur comme Narcisse'. In *Death in Venice*, Tadzio's smile is likened to that of Narcissus. Cavafy's Iases, used to this convention, complains posthumously – in his poetic epitaph – that he was too often loved less as himself than as a reincarnation of

Hermes or Narcissus. Because his myth is less overtly carnal than Ganymede's, Narcissus offered himself as an ideal subject for those Uranian painters and poets whose love of boys' bodies had to masquerade as an interest in matters mythological and aesthetic. Indeed, the July 1889 issue of the *Artist* recommended the boy's 'pale, sweet face' and 'sleepy, liquid eyes' as a suitable case for artistic treatment. S.S. Saale obliged, by providing for the September 1890 issue a sonnet in which he is reminded of Narcissus by the sight of some modern boys bathing.[28] But the myth has connotations which render it unsuitably full of meaning to be merely picturesque.

Narcissus was a teenager without a lover, absorbed in the languor of his own unchannelled desire. At the same time, he was a boy who fell in love with another boy, who happened to be himself.[29] The myth is homosexual, even if male homosexuality (contrary to Freud) only partially and intermittently meets the conditions of the myth. Narcissus' passion for his own reflection can be used as a symbolic portrayal of the love of one male for another – that is, for a human being whose physical appearance is superficially closer to a woman's than his own – but it is too explicit to represent definitively all the manifestations of the sexual orientation. We must, therefore, distinguish between two literary uses of the myth: the broadly symbolic, with the approximate equivalence of two male bodies (relating to male homosexuality in general); and the narrowly analytic, with the individual man who is motivated by self-esteem (relating to narcissism in particular). Two men face each other; or one faces his own reflection. The latter use is as well suited to a hetero- as to a homosexual subject. In some cases, both approaches occur at once. In 'Narcissus Hermaphroditus: Variations on a Theme by Ovid', James Kirkup shows how 'The universal meets the individual case', as the two sexes of the reflected narcissist desire and are desired by each other and themselves, weaving all possible patterns of human sexuality within one auto-erotic fabric.[30]

Consider the man with the mirror. It is evident that a limited number of sexual acts is available to a man who is in love with his own reflection, since every move he makes is followed precisely and simultaneously by his image. When their bodies meet, on the mirror's surface plane, each part must meet its counterpart. Source and image can kiss, when lips and tongues meet in exact apposition; but the tips of their tongues cannot pass each other. Nor can the source reach out and stroke his image's cheek or chest: for one hand must stop and be stopped by the other. One of Tony Duvert's 15 year-olds experiences all these difficulties: 'Il se déshabille. Il essaie de s'embrasser dans la glace. Ça réussit mal. On a beau happer, on ne saisit rien. Et puis c'est sa propre figure. Le jeu de remplacer soi-même ce qu'on désire est compliqué et répugnant, quand on ne s'aime pas. Les lèvres laissent un dessin gras et mouillé sur le miroir.'[31] For the same reasons, the more advanced pleasures end comically, before they have begun: anal intercourse, in an intractable apposition of anuses or penises; and fellatio, in a kiss. All that remains is self-masturbation *à deux*, an arrangement which complies with the mirror's strict requirement of distance, sexually realised in mutual exhibitionism and voyeurism. Alex Portnoy masturbates in front of a mirror so as to watch from a new angle the emergence of his semen. The narrator of Susan Sontag's novel *The Benefactor* takes to masturbating in the mirror after the death of his wife. In 'Crouching in the Corrida', Harold Norse writes: 'I face the full-length mirror in the / dark hotel and masturbate / to a flamenco guitar'.[32] Even the semen thus emitted can never wet the loved one's flesh; but must meet his, and slither down the glass. So the man who loves his own reflection must, however reluctantly, discard the mirror, and his image with it; and substitute for his image's flesh his own. Once he has done so, the natural consummation of his desire is reached in an act of self-penetration.

On the subject of autofellatio, Kinsey and his colleagues are uncharacteristically vague. Only about 'two or three males in a thousand', they claim, are capable of this feat. But 'a considerable portion of the population does record attempts at self fellation, at least in early adolescence'; and, in 'three or four' recorded cases, men depended on this sexual technique 'for some appreciable period of time'. Tom Driberg accepted the word of a room-mate of Nijinsky's who testified to the dancer's capability in this respect. Jean Cocteau kept a photograph of a self-fellating man behind that of a woman whose hypothetical son he wanted to father; but the attempt at sympathetic magic, apparently, failed.[33]

In the novel, references to autofellatio are all the more interesting for their rarity. In Brian Aldiss' *The Hand-Reared Boy*, there is a schoolboy whose inventiveness, tender age, and twelve-inch penis inevitably combine, to self-satisfying effect. The adult narrator of Jerzy Kosinski's *Cockpit* adds a further refinement and sucks himself only in the presence of a woman, 'as if the two of them are making love to a third person', thereby rendered quasi-heterosexual this quasi-homosexual act. Alex Portnoy bends over his genitals when masturbating, so that he can catch his semen in his mouth, allowing ballistics to compensate for his physical shortcoming.

Of the poetic references I have been able to find, all are recent and by Americans. Kenward Elmslie recalls 'bending down and touching my dick with my own tongue, fully aware that one day this wouldn't be possible'. It is Harold Norse's opinion that 'real men would rather / bash in your head than suck your cock. / But every man has tried to suck his own.' Another piece by Norse, 'Let Me Love You All at Stillman's Gym' (already cited, above), ends with a convincing portrayal of the sexual eagerness, physical strain, and sense of achievement involved, as a boy fellates himself.[34]

Autofellatio was one of the secret Tantrik methods of acclivity – that is, of redirecting sexual energy from the genitals to the brain, for the purpose of enlightenment.[35] (We can make sense, or one sense, of Proverbs 5.15: 'Drink water out of thine own cistern and running waters out of thine own well'.) Textual analogues are the formally circular stories of Raymond Roussell, which, like some of the journeys their author took, exist in order to begin and end at the same point. However, the literary usefulness of this sexual orobouros is limited to that area of literal narcissism triggered, at least, by the lack of a sexual partner, if not by total self-absorption. When we turn to the use of Narcissus as a symbolic representation of homosexuality, we find mirrors which no longer prevent consummation. This being the territory of such distinguished celebrators of the mirror as Lorca and Cocteau, glass softens, and source and image are able to move into each other's arms.

One might think that the result of entering a mirror, as of the snake's autophagy, would be disappearance. The source, passing behind the reflective plane, would be obscured by all other sources – say, the reflection of the room in which the mirror hangs – and would no longer cast an image. Contrary to the experience of Alice, each part of the source would cancel out that of the image, as though source and image were powers on either side of the equation $x = -x$, where the value of x must be nil.

Not so. The entry of the mirror is a carnal image, in which two lovers enter each other simultaneously. They do not disappear into, but fuse with each other. Although both are likened to Narcissus, the homosexual man escapes the fate of the narcissist, by having chosen a mirror into which he can step. Jean Cocteau understood this distinction, but chose to retain the narcissist element when, representing himself, he created the famous cinematic image of the poet entering the mirror, in *Le Sang d'un poète*. The 'mirror' is a framed pool of water, shot from above. Descending, the poet appears to walk into it; but unlike Narcissus, he later re-emerges from it. Cocteau's mirror is an image of the creative process – a reaching into and reflection on the self – as well as of love. (Indeed, he sees the two as one, there being no creativity without love, and vice versa.) Remember Shakespeare's 'mirror up to nature' and Stendhal's

'miroir qui se promène sur une grande route', as related represent-
ations of the writer's art.

However, representations of nature are not necessarily accurate.
We must entertain the possibility of the flawed mirror. Cocteau's *Le
Livre blanc* employs a pornographic narrative device which epito-
mises the dishonest erotic mirror and symbolises the pornographer
rather than the lover. The narrator, hidden behind a two-way mirror
in the wall of a bathroom, watches youths bathing. Some of them,
imagining themselves unobserved, use their own reflections as mas-
tubatory icons. Of course, from behind the mirror, they look as if
they are gazing at the narrator himself, who, remaining hidden, joins
them in their activity. One youth presses himself up against his
reflection to kiss it, thus unwittingly allowing the narrator to
embrace the other side of the glass. 'Une fois, un Narcisse qui se
plaisait approcha sa bouche de la glace, l'y colla et poussa jusqu'au
bout l'aventure avec lui-même. Invisible comme les dieux grecs,
j'appuyai mes lèvres contres les siennes et j'imitai ses gestes. Jamais il
ne sut qu'au lieu de réfléchir, la glace agissait, qu'elle était vivante
et qu'elle l'avait aimé.'[36] Both ejaculate, with evident satisfaction;
but only the cold glass receives the benefit of their semen. The mirror
has deceived both participants in this rite: the youth, by forcing on
him the illusion of being alone with, and of embracing himself; and
the narrator – who sees himself as an undeceived deceiver – by
allowing him to imagine for one, orgasmic moment, that the youth
can see him and is embracing him. Because both have opted for the
literal mirror (the property of narcissism) rather than the symbolic
(the property of homosexuality), they receive the lesser, merely
orgasmic satisfaction of masturbation, rather than the shared ecstasy
of actual intercourse.

Housman begins the fifteenth poem in *A Shropshire Lad*: 'Look
not in my eyes, for fear / They mirror true the sight I see, / And there
you find your face too clear / And love it and be lost like me'. The
boy to whom the poem is addressed would be, like the youth in the
bathroom, captivated by himself, but erotically involved with the
substance behind the illusion of self: the other. In this case,
however, he can see both himself and the other, as in a plate of
ordinary glass. Taking this symbolic tendency to its conclusion, in
'Mirrors, or Narcissism', Mutsuo Takahashi places two mirrors face
to face, and speaks of the loving energy that flows between them.
Lorca, too, uses mirrors as the image of love. In 'Suicidio',
therefore, when a youth kills himself by smashing his image in the
mirror, an erotic violence is implied. Attempting to enter himself,
Narcissus is drowned.[37]

GANYMEDE

The name of Ganymede, from the Greek *ganuesthai* and *medea*, means 'rejoicing in virility' or 'bright penis'. From it comes the Latin *catamitus* and the English 'catamite'. Ganymede was a Trojan prince who, because he was watching his father's flocks when carried off by an eagle, tends to be described, in later versions, as an Arcadian shepherd boy. He was reputed to be the most beautiful youth in the world. The myth of his abduction to Olympus contains a number of elements which recommend it to our attention.[38] It deals with a homosexual seduction. It affirms the beauty of young men, by which even a god is liable to be distracted. It suggests that in the possession or creation of such beauty lies one way to heaven. It makes a shepherd of a prince, a domestic servant of the shepherd, and a demigod of all three, thereby granting that the boy one picks up (literally, in this case), even if he be a mere mudlark, can make the social leap, up or down, to his lover's level. (In the shepherd boy versions, Ganymede is a little like a Horatio Alger hero, hoisted out of obscurity by a combination of 'Luck and Pluck' and another rhyme of Zeus' devising.) It has the boy serve drinks to the god, as a symbol of the nature of their sexual relationship. In Zeus' metamorphosis, it gives a kind of respectability to animal lust and to the violence of sexual assault. Above all, it provides the example of a god as a homosexual lover.

M. Minucius Felix complained that such tales as this were, merely, 'precedents and sanctions for men's vices' (*Octavius* XXIV.7). Indeed, Zeus and Ganymede are offered as precedents to Socrates' relationships with boys, in the *Phaedrus*; to Orpheus', by Ovid (*Metamorphoses* X, 155–61); and to Edward II's affair with Piers Gaveston, by Marlowe (*Edward II* I.iv, 181–2). The widespread exemplary use of the mythic couple leads to a more general use of their names together, to speak of male homosexual lovers; and of Ganymede's alone, to speak of beautiful boys, ready for homosexual love. So, while *The Affectionate Shepheard* of Richard Barnfield, in conventional pastoral vein, is called Daphnis, the boy to whom he addresses his love songs is Ganymede. John Boswell has shown how the word 'Ganymede', both noun and adjective, came to be a medieval equivalent of the modern word 'gay', used positively within a discernible gay subculture, and sometimes negatively from without.[39]

Modern writers are no less impressed by the boy's fame. J.R. Ackerley applies the myth to his own experience of gay bars: 'Standing at the various bars, with our token half-pints before us, we would eye each other surreptitiously, perhaps registering the fact that with so many eagles about, if any Ganymede did arrive we would have to work fast'. During leave from the Great War, Michael

Davidson encountered 'A Ganymede of a page-boy' in the Savoy. John Lehmann describes a photo he took of one of his boyfriends on a beach: 'he looks, not like Venus but Ganymede Anadyomenos, a semi-divine creature fresh from the waves. If Zeus had been looking that way at that moment he could not have resisted, but would have sent the eagle down as fast as one of his thunderbolts.' Keith Vaughan, after chasing a boyfriend in the sea off Mexico, recorded the event in his diary, as 'a breathless Zeus pursuing fleet-footed Ganymede'.[40] Lacking in any reverberative depth, such elementary references testify to the resilience of the myth's fame. The naming of the boy is a straightforward acknowledgement of homosexual interest, an aspiration to consensual 'rape'.

Any reference to Ganymede implies, before anything else, sexual acts or desires. In the ninth of the *Satires*, Juvenal mentions that Ganymede's shrine at the temple of Peace was a popular place of sexual assignation. Courtesans wore images of his abduction. In Aristophanes' *Peace*, a dung-beetle flies up to Olympus, intending to feed on Ganymede's ambrosial excrement – ambrosial, because it contains both the food of the gods and Zeus' semen (1.724). But the most direct reference to the purely sexual meaning of the myth is made by Meleager, when he calls his left hand, with which he masturbates, a Ganymede (*Epigrams* II.43).

If a beautiful boy is a Ganymede, any part of him may be likened to the corresponding part of Ganymede. In Philip Gillespie Bainbrigge's extraordinary play in verse, *Achilles in Scyros* (1927), Achilles (disguised as a girl) is trying to seduce 'Charmides' (a girl in disguise), and says of the supposed boy's supposed penis:

> God knows
> I'm certain yours is like a budding rose,
> Lovelier than Ganymede's love-blossoming rod,
> Whose thighs inflame the tyranny of God.[41]

In whole or part, Ganymede is an aesthetic and erotic scale, against whom all other young, male aspirants to beauty must be measured. There can be no questioning his sexiness, since it inflamed a god. But this is not to say that the beauty of all other mortal youths falls short of his. In William Browne of Tavistock's *Britannia's Pastorals* (1613), Jove himself mistakes a boy called Doridon for Ganymede (I.2, 417–22). Likewise, in Marlowe's *Hero and Leander* (II, 157–8), while Leander is swimming the Hellespont, Neptune is quite deceived by his beauty:

> Imagining that Ganymede, displeased,
> Had left the heavens; therefore on him he seized.

Only when the youth begins to drown in his embrace, thus revealing his mortality, does the god release him.

Just as any beautiful boy is a Ganymede, and as his parts can be compared with Ganymede's, so one's intercourse with him is comparable to Zeus' with Ganymede. Step by step, each mortal seduction corresponds with the Olympian. Just as Meleager's thirst is quenched when he kisses a boy, so is Zeus', by the kisses and nectar Ganymede provides (XII.133). The famous nectar is, itself, of little consequence, except as a trigger to the metaphor of thirst and satisfaction.

The same is true of the Arabic convention of deep, red wine poured out by luscious youths: it is an eloquent expression of the qualities inherent in the youths themselves. Granted, Shaykh Nafzawi speaks of 'a state of intoxication which induces an awareness of the charms, grace, suppleness and fine deportment of a stripling'; but the much headier intoxicant consists of the charms, grace, suppleness, and deportment themselves. It is in this sense that Abu Nuwas writes: 'Supreme joy was never known to any but the sort of man who takes a drink with catamites'.[42]

Traditionally, the colour, taste, and intoxicant effect of a cup of wine are put to shame by those of a boy's lips. Two Hispano-Arabic poems capture this mood perfectly. The first is by Al-Waqqaši (1017–96). It begins: 'Wonderful, how wine has borrowed from / The character and qualities of him who tortures me / The odor of his breath, the sweetness of his kiss, / The inebriating sugar of his looks, / The brightness of his face, the redness of his cheeks, / The pleasant charm of his colorful robe!' The second is by Abū 's-Salt Omayya (1067/8–1133/4): 'Oh slender youth, whose handsome face does share / The beauty of wine he pours into the cup: / Its effects are those of his eyes, its color is / That of his cheeks, its taste is that of his lips.'[43] These are exactly the characteristics of the wine served by Ganymede on Olympus. (Remember, too, that the Qur'an promises a heaven staffed by 'immortal youths with bowls and ewers and a cup of purest wine'.) Semen, of course, is the best vintage available, taken from the richest grapes. In one of a series of similes describing the male orgasm, Mutsuo Takahashi likens the ejaculating penis to Ganymede pouring nectar from a jug.[44]

The myth's earlier aspect, that of the sudden abduction, is its other obvious metaphor for sexual intercourse. Of this, the clearest modern expression is a sentence in *Miracle de la Rose*. Divers is walking behind Genet, in step, close enough to be pressing against his back.

J'étais comme si, déjà sous lui, il m'eût baisé, m'assommant de tout son poids et aussi me tirant à lui comme l'aigle Ganymède,

comme enfin il devait le faire cette quatrième nuit qu'il passa avec
moi, où mieux préparé, je le laissai entrer en moi profondément
et qu'il s'abattit, de sa masse énorme (tout un ciel me tombant sur
le dos), ses griffes enfouies dans mes épaules, et ses dents mordant
ma nuque.[45]

The eagle's forceful grip, at the same time, penetrates and caresses
the flesh of its prey, leaving no permanent wounds. At first, the bird is
an enormous, breath-taking burden on the prey's back. With the
impulse of flight, both become weightless as they rise from the
ground, aware only of their mutual contact. Beast and human are
joined, belly to back, and their movement is entirely that of the
animal: flight. The more one sees of the myth, the less appropriate
does Rembrandt's version seem (Ganymede as a wailing and
urinating baby), despite the typical benevolence of its concern.

The myth's applicability to more modern times is tested by poets
who explicitly bring it up to date. J.H. Hallard, in *Carmina* (1899),
finds all Ganymede's qualities in a modern boy:

Yes, Ganymede is here among us now,
The gods have lent him for a summer's day.
Behold the carven beauty of his brow,
The mystic eyes that gaze so far away,
The tender lips, the hyacinth hair of him,
And moulded marvel of his every limb![46]

Another version of Ganymede Descended appears in Cuthbert
Wright's short story 'Ganymede' (1922), whose narrator encounters
the Olympian cup-bearer urinating in the Luxembourg Gardens.[47]
No doubt, this is another of the choice wines offered to Zeus.
Apparently taking the boy as a possible substitute for Christ,
Wright's narrator says to him: 'You are beyond art as you are
beyond rhetoric, divine animal, Unattainable One, born to torment,
and, who knows, to save us'.

When William Plomer's naked Ganymede is kidnapped from a
field near Troy, the citizens' reaction takes a form appropriate only
to our own century: 'The next day's headlines were the talk of Troy: /
BIG BIRD SENSATION, MISSING LOCAL BOY'. In Jim Eggel-
ing's 'The Ganymede Equation', the eagle is updated: Zeus sends
down a Cadillac, which scoops up Chicano youths in its gaping
doors. But poverty interferes: the boys are so skinny, it takes two to
make one Ganymede. Jonathan Williams' Zeus is a 'sex / expert',
who cruises the Trojan Coast ('eagle-eyed', of course) in search of
young, male talent. The boy he finds is 'that catamite cat, Kid

Ganymedes,' an 'erstwhile eagle-scout / bed-mate'. These poems waver between appreciative mock-heroic and contemptuous burlesque. Some seem to be dealing with Ganymede, merely, because he is an important figure in the homo-erotic tradition, rather than because he is intrinsically interesting. He seems named for the sake of his name, an indiscreet conceit, included to betray the poem's deeper theme, if any. As an acceptably classical, but transparently homosexual figure, he gives his name to a magazine for gay men, in Leo Madigan's novel *Jackarandy*; and his myth marks the doorway of a gay bath-house in Dirk Vanden's *All is Well*.[48]

From such relatively trivial modern versions, we pass to the more deeply considered. In the ninth of the sonnets from China, Auden uses the apocryphal shepherd-boy tradition, and veers towards the sexless humanity of the Rembrandt. Here is a 'humble boy', bored by Zeus' conversation, who 'yawned and whistled and made faces, / And wriggled free from fatherly embraces'. He spends most of his time with Hermes, who is nearer his age, immortality notwithstanding. Auden's point is about the attractions of violence to human character. Before Zeus set loose his eagle, he sent a dove to Ganymede; but, when the boy was not seduced by this symbol of peace, the god used compulsion instead. Later, when Zeus' mind is on love, Ganymede is learning 'so many ways of killing' from the more attractive Messenger. His innocence is illusory. He was seduced by the violence of his abduction, his rape; not by the loving attention which was to follow. His affections fix on Hermes, in whom aggression is deeply established. The poem was inspired by hostilities in China, not Arcadian revelry. It claims immediate bearing on the modern world.[49]

Paul Goodman's 'Ballade to Jean Cocteau', also, concentrates on the violent aspects of the myth. 'Martyrs of the crimes of sex', Goodman writes, 'are not by Jean and me / blotted out of memory / but wept and named, so all may read / and know ourselves and ye.' Among such crimes the poem includes are the murder of Hyacinth by Zephyr, the abduction and rape of Europa by Zeus, the drowning of Hylas by the nymphs, and the mounting of Pasiphae by the bull. The refrain, throughout, is 'To heaven was raped Ganymede'. Goodman asks us to 'pay respects / of etiquette to outlawry', by reading these myths with care. We should learn about our own sexuality from them, not revere them as some kind of beautiful, functionless edifice like the Parthenon. I take the poem's final point, that the eagle did not draw blood from Ganymede with its talons, to mean that the story's violence exists only in metaphor, the realm of Goodman and Cocteau. If so, the violent crimes listed might represent the harmless aggression underlying everyday sexual acts;

and the heaven to which Ganymede was raped – repeatedly raped, in the refrain – is of an earthly sort.[50]

Our final revision of the myth occurs in William Bell's extraordinary poem 'Bach Improvising at the Organ', towards the end of which, there is a description of the martydom of Saint Sebastian. The saint is pierced by arrows, the arrows of music and love, which enable him to endure the pain they inflict. So far, so orthodox. But his ascent to heaven is in the pagan style. 'Strong pinions of the eagle bear him up / even to the final sphere of heaven', where the other saints recline in Olympian splendour. To them, 'he bears the honeyed cup', while angelic choirs sing Bach's improvisation to its close. The 'cup' is the flaming arrow he has become – his ascent is likened to the flight of one of the arrows which killed him. His beauty, immortal now, is nectar to the pantheon.[51]

Renaissance Neo-Platonists made of Ganymede's abduction an allegory of the soul's ascent to heaven. Others cast Christ as the boy. In Giles Fletcher's poem *Christ's Victorie, and Triumph in Heaven, and Earth, over, and after death* (1610), the Ascension is compared with Ganymede's rape. In William Drummond of Hawthornden's *An Hymn of the Fairest Fair*, God the Father is served nectar by a flower-garlanded youth with curly hair, presumably the Son. The most famous of the spiritualised versions is Goethe's 'Ganymed' (1774), in which the youth yearns to ascend to the loving bosom of the Father. William Bell's combination of the myth's carnal spirit with the allegorical tradition seems to me a lot more successful. The myth's frankly sexual nature is too powerful to be discarded altogether. Ganymede is nothing if not a catamite.[52]

SAINT SEBASTIAN

Of all the figures in the Christian pantheon, apart from Christ Himself, only Sebastian achieves the erotic status of so many boys and men in Greek myth. The patron of archers, he has in modern times taken on certain additional responsibilities in the area of male homosexuality. François Le Targat has summed up the qualities of his martyrdom as follows: 'La beauté de la nudité, la jeunesse, la force supposée due au métier des armes, les amitiés particulières, les flèches symboliques, la douleur, le sang des plaies, le goût de la mort dans l'extase héroïque'.[53] While there are bearded versions of the saint (by, among others, Bernini, Domenichino, Dürer, Gozzoli, Holbein, Titian, Van Honhorst, and in Humphress and Jarman's film *Sebastiane*, and moustached versions by Corot and Van Dyke) he is generally portrayed as a beardless youth. His body tends to be smooth, pale and – even in the shadows of his low-slung loin-cloth – hairless. As passive as Ganymede, but never shown in the dynamic throes of flight or capture, Sebastian is a vertically constrained Narcissus, contemplative and self-absorbed. He does not see his attackers: for his mind is turned inward, reflecting on the perturbation of his flesh.

In the title poem of *Antinous and Other Poems* (1907), Montague Summers said that the boyfriend of Hadrian is still worshipped today, but in Christian form, as Sebastian or Aloysius. Summers may have read Frederick Rolfe's 'Two Sonnets, for a Picture of Saint Sebastian the Martyr by Guido Reni, in the Capitoline Gallery of Rome', which had appeared in the June 1891 issue of the *Artist*. The opening of the second sonnet spells out the attraction of Reni's painting and the martyrdom it depicts:

A Roman soldier boy, bound to a tree
  His strong arms lifted up for sacrifice,
  His gracious form all stripped of martial guise
Naked, but brave as a young lion can be,
Transfixed by arrows he gains the victory[.]

The central character of Rolfe's *The Desire and Pursuit of the Whole* writes a novel about a certain *Sebastian Archer*, the plot of which is summarised with unsubtle references to the martyrdom: 'pierced by archdiaconal arrows', 'A fresh shower of shafts hurtled at him naked', and so on. A similar gesture to the martyr was made in exile by Oscar Wilde, who combined good and evil victims by calling himself Sebastian Melmoth – the latter being the protagonist of Charles Maturin's *Melmoth the Wanderer*, condemned to a peripatetic eternity for having sold his soul.[54]

In the Palazzo Rosso at Genoa there is a more polished version of Reni's picture, to which Yukio Mishima referred in the photographs he had taken of himself as Sebastian, and in *Confessions of a Mask*, where the narrator is aroused by the painting's pagan qualities. He, too, likens Sebastian to Antinous. The saint seems unconcerned by the arrows which pierce his side and armpit, and his wounds are bloodless. While looking at a reproduction of this painting, Mishima's young narrator learns to masturbate. His ejaculation onto his desk and school books is as much a gentle 'flock of arrows' as is Pablo Neruda's semen, in the third of his *Twenty Love Poems*.[55]

The ambiguity of his plight, and of his reaction to it, makes Sebastian the ideal patron saint of the male, homosexual masochist. In Will Aitken's poem 'Park Mont-Royal', the saint is called to mind by the image of a desirable young man, assailed on all sides by the erections of lovers or rapists. And James Merrill has the saint encourage his tormentors, crying out, 'Come! He loves me best who nearest / To my heart hits!' 'He kisses me who kills, who kills me kisses!'[56]

ORPHEUS DISMEMBERED

When the ideal boy becomes the ideal young man, he can no longer be compared with the likes of Narcissus, Ganymede, Hylas, Hyacinth, Antinous, and Sebastian. Seen complete, his physique is that of Apollo, shared repository of beauty and reason. But, since the Apollonian principle opposes with self-knowledge and moderation the creative and passionate values of Dionysus, Apollo proves himself inadequate to the role of erotic archetype. Like a statue of himself, he is an *aesthetic* ideal, undisturbed by the heat and pulse of blood. His beauty is of an immobile sort, requiring in itself a cool dignity which minimises the appearance of movement in its movements. Paradoxically, it is to another champion of spiritual virtues that one turns in search of an alternative adult physique.

The poet Orpheus, whose singing animated the trees and anaesthetised the damned, is a natural subject for poetry. His tragic double loss of Eurydice is well suited to the demands of the hetero-erotic arts; but his later advocacy and practice of the love of boys, and his consequent death at the hands of the vengeful Maenads, lend themselves, also, to the purposes of *homo*-eroticism. Herbert Marcuse compares him with Narcissus, on the grounds that 'The classical tradition associates Orpheus with the introduction of homosexuality. Like Narcissus, he rejects the normal Eros, not for an ascetic ideal, but for a fuller Eros. Like Narcissus, he protests against the repressive order of procreative sexuality.'[57] Orpheus is the homosexual poet, whose skill alone can cause the supposed 'laws' of nature to be broken, and whose assassination fails to still his song. (He is the mythic analogue to Lorca.)

Intact, torn, and scattered: such are the three conditions of the body of Orpheus. The first, being the condition, also, of the Apollo already dismissed, is negligible. But the second and third bear some relation to the nature of sexual appraisal and activity, insofar as looking at and making love to a person may be deeds of dismemberment. 'The true body is a body broken.' So says Norman O. Brown, before quoting Yeats: 'Nothing can be sole or whole / That has not been rent'.[58] Osiris is torn apart and killed, by Seth; then put together and revived, by Isis. The sexual element is never absent: Isis can find all the parts of Osiris except the penis. (Subsequently, statues of him bear detachable genitals, of some material foreign to the whole.) Leucippus is torn apart by nymphs when nakedness betrays his gender. In psychoanalytic myth, the carnivorous vagina castrates.

The focus of desire is narrow and operates obsessively in close-up. As soon as my lover is close to me, he is the sum of his parts. Each hand of mine can touch only a hand's breadth of his flesh. My eyes can see only a part of him at any time. My mind is unable to touch the whole body, but must wander over it from part to part, as though the parts were disconnected, and the whole a hypothesis. My lover disintegrates in my embrace, and I in his. Certain parts – our genitals, for instance – may become the temporary centres of our deeds. But, just as the eyes amass the fragments they have seen into a jigsaw of the whole, and as the blind hands synthesise the feeling of the individual limbs they have caressed, so too, in miraculous equilibrium, the roving mind both scatters and gathers at once.

Nor can the literature of sexuality behave otherwise. From its store of words for parts – 'leg', 'hand', 'chest', 'navel', 'penis', 'buttock', and so on – the poem of the body is constructed, to the purposes of which the word 'body' itself would in its vagueness prove as inadequate as a distant view of my lover's body to my sexual desire. The writing of the love poem is an enactment of the love it expresses. The reading of it is no less of a sexual act, distance notwithstanding.

Robert Duncan's poem 'The Torso' ranks with the most acute love poems of the century.[59] Its shifting focus corresponds with that of a man kneeling to fellate his lover: the collar bone, chest, navel, and pubic hair are examined in turn. But the occasion of the poem involves the two men in reversed roles. While the speaker's mind moves down the torso of the lover, the lover himself is on his knees, fellating the speaker. The fantasy of the one duplicates the deeds of the other. The effect, even if only one man is fellating the other, is of a mutual act, and of simultaneous climax. The parts of each are superimposed on those of the other and the two are, if not identical, indistinguishable. Like the words themselves, which fall over a wide area of the page leaving gaps within as well as between many of the lines, physical fragments are strewn, or seedlike sown, across an undescribed landscape which is nonetheless, in its parts, particular and detailed.

Poem, body, and landscape are one, located directly in front of our reading and kissing lips (the reader shares the speaker's point of view, and is implicated in his sexual act), and in front of and immediately within the locked gates of Paradise, to which the lovers' hands turn genital keys: 'His hands unlocking from chambers of my male body' . . . 'my hand in your hand seeking the locks, the keys'. The features of the poem's gardens, far from being wild, have been carefully landscaped. They include 'the red-flowering eucalyptus, / the madrone, the yew', with which the poem begins; the entrance, associated with the lover's mouth; the 'sleeping fountains' of his nipples; the temple of his belly, at the centre of which lies his navel, possibly associated with the omphalos of Delphi, supposed centre of the ancient world; and the root and flower of his groin. Each part of the body's topography (typography) is associated with a point near the entrance to the spiritual domain. Physical and spiritual consummation are approximate, drawn closer together by love.

Homosexual intercourse knows no such thing as 'foreplay'. There is no imperative of progression from genital apposition to intromission, to emission, to withdrawal. Forbidden intercourse is governed by only one rule – that it not occur – which it breaks. Beyond this fact, all possible forms of sexual act are available to the climactic moment. Any part of the body has potential as an erogenous zone.[60] That which has been scattered is not necessarily discarded. This is not to say, however, that homosexual intercourse is haphazard. Love invariably leads from edge to centre, but via any selected regions of the whole physique. The Muses gather the limbs of Orpheus, to bury them at the foot of Olympus. The head, still singing, adopts the task of prophecy.

Narcissus grows hairier, and becomes Apollo-Orpheus. According to the Greek and Arabic traditions, his new facial and body hair may disqualify him from being the beloved any longer. He should seek, instead, to be the lover, of a beloved of his own. The lover of adult males is distingushed from the lover of women or boys by his acceptance of the beard (or, at least, of stubble in the morning). Hair can be used by the poet as a sign of maleness. Thom Gunn's 'Without a Counterpart' is clearly homo-erotic: for the landscape-body of the loved one, referred to only as 'you', is covered in 'prickly turf'. When Gavin Dillard writes, 'if your chest was a cat / it could be no more furry', or 'our beards embind together', he need not tamper with the vagueness of 'you' in order to specify gender. In another of his poems, the hairiness of a kissed belly reveals, both to the reader and to the drowsy poet, the nature of the nipple which he subsequently sucks.[61]

The richness of the hairy, male body is suggested by Lawrence, in a description of Lady Chatterley's lover, spoken by Connie Chatterley herself: 'You've got four kinds of hair. On your chest it's nearly black, and your hair isn't dark on your head: but your moustache is hard and dark red, and your hair here, your love-hair, is like a little brush of bright red-gold mistletoe. It's the loveliest of all!' Merely to notice this variety – although she fails to speak of his legs and arms – is a liberating experience for one who seems previously to have examined only the formal and socially acceptable, controlled luxuriance of men's heads and faces. What grows on the body is more clearly a remnant of human animality, and of animal sexuality. In two poems, Harold Norse refers to his own black 'fur'. And Jerah Chadwick writes that hair 'is all of the animal / that is left, the nipples' mane / the sparse fleece of our stomachs / carded into so much wool'.[62]

The dismemberment of Orpheus is castration taken to extremes. The puberty of Narcissus involved growth of the genitals as well as of hair. The enlarged penis is a token not only of maleness, but also of adulthood. It is the first part to be torn from Orpheus, both in his death, and in sexual intercourse's re-enactments of it. Its isolation from the rest of the body is customary homage to its importance. In isolation and erect, it is a symbol of pre-dismemberment: it *stands for* the body as a whole.

It is not for me to trace the history of the belief that a large penis grants greater sexual pleasure to the receptive partner than a small. Let us, merely, recall the efforts recommended by the *Kama Sutra* to the man whose lingam does not come up to standard. He should rub it with the bristles of certain insects, or with egg plants, or with buffalo butter, or with a hot oil containing pomegranate seeds, for many nights.[63] Devices of comparable ingenuity continue to be sold for the same purpose today, and probably have much the same effect, of temporary inflammation. The sense of inferiority which drives men to attempt enlargement, no doubt, also gives rise to myths of well-endowed heroes. Dillinger is said to have had a penis twenty-two inches long.[64]

In poetry, penis size tends to be specified only when the poem itself is pornographic (as in Auden's 'The Platonic Blow', in which the organ blown is nearly nine inches long and three thick), or when the poem refers to the conventions of pornography (Harold Norse's 'Adult Bookstore': nine inches), graffiti (E.A. Lacey's 'Oneiromancy': eight inches), or contact advertisements (John Giorno's 'EXHIBI-TIONIST': eight inches).[65] But how can a mere measurement sum up this most protean of all parts of the male body? Erotic literature has countless ways of expanding on the vital statistic. I dare not detail more than one or two such aspects, for lack of space.

One of the most frequent poetic guises of the male genitals is as a plant or flower. (A pun is, often, intended: a flow-er being that which flows.) In *Le Livre blanc*, the penis of one of Jean Cocteau's lovers is a plant, casting its seed about: 'cette fabuleuse petite plante marine, morte, fripée, échouée sur la mousse, qui se déride, se développe, se dresse et jette au loin sa sève dès qu'elle retrouve l'élément d'amour'.[66] In 'The Torso', Robert Duncan described the penis as a 'stamen of flesh', through which seed rises.

Mutsuo Takahashi's poetry is as heady with the scent of flowers as a Ronald Firbank novel or Genet's *Les Bonnes*; and one is tempted to believe that all such blooms have the same genital significance. A man is a rose tree; his penis, the rose. The penis is a 'pale lily', buried beneath a man's shorts; or, again, a 'Budding rose, rose with petals uncurled, dewy rose / My rose-shaped love, my god'. How appropriate, then, is James Kirkup's Japanese 'Short Story' in verse, about a man who chops his boyfriend into tiny pieces:

> His balls
> And his still-trembling prick
> Were artfully arranged
> On the spikes of a flower-holder,
> A flower arrangement
> In the style of the Sogetsu school,
> Decorated only
> With stains ripped from
> His old pair of rayon bikini pants.[67]

The bunch of grapes that swayed so scandalously over Nijinsky's genitals, when he danced *L'Après-midi d'un faun*, reminds us of the other popular, horticultural image, of the genitals as fruit. The title of an anonymous pornographic book, *The Fruit-Shop* (1765), refers to the vagina. 'Deserters of the fruit-shop' are celibates, masturbators, and homosexual men. D.H. Lawrence makes barely more sophisticated use of the ripe fig. Harold Norse describes a boy as having 'balls like ripe, heavy pears'. E.A. Lacey sees 'curved fruit' down the fronts of swimming trunks, and describes a particular penis as a 'lush banana'.[68]

The penis as fruit is eminently edible. The image offers an invitation to the prospective fellator. In its next form, the penis demands to be seen ejaculating, or to ejaculate into the enigmatic darkness of the bowels (rather than the relatively familiar shadows of the mouth). Dylan Thomas speaks of 'A candle in the thighs', which 'Warms youth and seed and burns the seeds of age'. Ian Young writes of cupping his hand 'round the warm / candle of your cock'. E.A. Lacey says, of a lover, 'at night his pale candle consoled me'. As so often, Jean Genet extends the commonplace image, seeming to renew it. When Querelle claims falsely to have a venereal disease, Seblon has a vision of 'le sexe ulcéré, coulant comme un cierge pascal où cinq grains d'encens sont incrustés'.[69] At the end of Helmuth Costard's film *Besonders Wertvoll*, a penis ejaculating into the camera's eye is juxtaposed with a candle blown out by a farting anus.

As the penis emits semen, the phallic candle emits light – an image which should be familiar to readers of Hart Crane. *Orgasms of Light* is the title of Winston Leyland's second anthology of gay verse.

Mutsuo Takahashi refers to semen as 'Darts of Light'. Graham Jackson says to his lover, 'You murmur mutely how you'll enter me again / to scatter moons inside my yielding frame / a milky way to ornament my soul'.[70]

Robert Graves' white goddess, then, becomes a fecundating god: the male moon. Graves himself, in the poem 'Problems of Gender', acknowledges our continuing indecision about the genders of sun and moon.[71] In one ancient tradition, the moon was hermaphroditic, or of alternating gender. Men would make sacrifices to Luna; women, to Lunus.[72] Masculine in German and feminine in French, Italian, and Spanish, the moon in English is happily neither and can be imagined, therefore, as either.

In Arabic poetry, the male moon is an adolescent. Abu Nuwas sings to a baker's boy, 'Your shop is heaven, you are the full moon, / and your nearby loaves are golden stars'. But lunar brightness depends on youth. Abul Hasan Yafar tells his beloved, 'You were the full moon / until that night / when it was your turn to wane. / When the fuzz appeared / I said: / This is the end of love; / the black crow / of your beard / is the signal / for separation.' The moon is a bright, unclouded face or smooth, round buttocks – sexually receptive, in either case. In *The Queen's Vernacular*, Bruce Rodgers lists the phrase 'take a trip to the moon' as modern gay slang for anilingus, where 'moon' refers, of course, to the backside.[73]

But the male moon is best known as a fecundating repository of light. It is the glans penis, or a testicle, or semen, or the genitals as a whole. To Nikolai Klyuev, 'The sun and moon are lion testicles!' In Sylvia Plath's 'Childless Woman', because the womb is void, the moon discharges to no purpose. Edmund Miller writes of his lover, 'he retracts / the foreskin of the stormy sky – / I see the moon'.[74]

Semen in mid-air; the phallus, torn from the body and cast aside, in radiant isolation – in either case, an end to intercourse. The dismemberment of Orpheus is in the same relation to his death, as sexual intercourse to ejaculation and detumescence. Detumescence is implicit in intercourse, as death is in dismemberment. The erect penis, the ultimate in potency, is so prone to fetishistic isolation that it becomes the symbol of the ultimate in impotence, castration.

(With a greater emphasis on fellatio than that of heterosexual intercourse, male homosexual intercourse puts the insertor's penis at risk, not from the metaphorical *vagina dentata*, but from the literal *os dentatus*: the toothed mouth. In both Leo Madigan's *Jackarandy* and Jerzy Kosinski's *Cockpit*, vengeful fellators bite off the organs they suck. Paul Mariah's 'Childe Roland' is about a young man who was imprisoned at the age of 16 for having bitten off his cousin's penis. The cousin had called him a 'queer' at quite the wrong moment. The toothed mouth may also operate in an aggressive kiss, as in Alan Parker's film *Midnight Express*, when, in a fight, one man bites off another's tongue. Furthermore, since *The Queen's Vernacular* lists to 'bite' as modern gay slang for to 'contract and relax the sphincter muscle during anal intercourse', the metaphor of sexual risk is seen to have its exact equivalent in relation to male, homosexual intercourse: the *anus dentatus*.[75])

Of the dismembered fragments of the homosexual male, the second most important, after the genitalia, is the protean eye, mouth, and second sexual organ: the anus. As mouth, it fellates; as toothed mouth, castrates. As either, it demands to be kissed. According to a character in Günter Grass' *The Flounder*, 'The ass is one thing that ideology is afraid to touch. Can't get its claws on it. Can't read any idea into it'. Therefore, he argues, lovers should not fail, be they hetero- or homosexual, to get to know and love that part of each other's anatomy. He recommends a particular sexual act, which he refers to as 'the archetype of Christian charity': anilingus.[76] Once called the *osculis posterioris* or *osculum infame*, anilingus was officially associated with witchcraft, in a Bull issued by Pope Gregory IX, in 1233. The conventional way off doing homage to the Devil was, after all, to kiss him on the buttocks or anus. This was one of the crimes of which the Knights Templar were collectively accused, in the period between their mass arrest in 1307 and their dissolution in 1312.[77] Much as one would like to believe that at least this one part of the body is, as the Grass character claims, free of ideological pressure, the Gregorian Bull, and the widespread tyranny of laws against anal intercourse, suggest otherwise. Mario Mieli has no doubts on this point:

> What in homosexuality particularly horrifies *homo normalis*, the policeman of the hetero-capitalist system, is being fucked in the arse; and this can only mean that one of the most delicious bodily pleasures, anal intercourse, is itself a significant revolutionary force. The thing that we queens are so greatly put down for contains a large part of our subversive gay potential. I keep my treasure in my arse, but then my arse is open to everyone.[78]

One of the best-known of poems on an anilingual theme is the third of Rimbaud's sequence of three, 'Les Stupra'. This sonnet on Paul Verlaine's anus (written, in fact, by both poets) celebrates a land-scape dotted with small clots of red earth ('petits caillots de marne rousse'), where one may wander, fed and watered as in heaven on earth: 'C'est le tube où descend la céleste praline, / Chanaan féminin dans les moiteurs enclos'. In the fourth part of the sequence 'Two Guys', Dennis Cooper describes a boy who, addicted to licking out his lover's anus, decides to test the variety of its taste, by making the lover eat only pizza for a few days, then only Indonesian food. The consequent differences in taste are appreciable, if slight. Jean Genet tries the same restaurant, in *Pompes funèbres*; like Rimbaud, he, too, finds a version of Eden in this act: 'une charmille très fraîche où tout entier je pénétrais en rampant pour m'endormir sur la mousse, dans l'ombre, y mourir'.[79]

Sense of place is particularly keen in descriptions of this most bucolic of sexual acts. The narrator of Leonard Cohen's *Beautiful Losers* finds a fascinating ring of 'minnie hills' to explore. During a 'Night of Sweat', Salvatore Farinella drinks from a spring, while his eyelashes 'sweep / the valleys' of his lover's backside. In 'The Platonic Blow', W.H. Auden wanders into the 'dark parks' behind a young man's genitals, then down 'shaggy slopes' to his goal. But it is to the central character of Larry Kramer's *Faggots* that we must turn for the most extraordinary imaginative feat, as he kisses his lover's backside for the first time: 'He took both cheeks in his hands and he buried his face in it like an elegant pillow in a perfect Italian palazzo overlooking the blue Mediterranean where they could be when they were living happily ever after. If they hadn't moved to England.'[80]

The scattered fragments of the body of Orpheus lose their erotic characteristics to the land. The penis is a mountain, the anus a cave. The body is as large as the land it is scattered over: in one corner lies a hand, in another a foot, in the north the eyes, in the centre the navel ... Petrification, by which the fragments merge with the ground on which they fall, reunifies them through the land. Some individuals are more likely than others to be associated with the land they inhabit. Norman O. Brown has shown how, in certain systems of thought, a nation is the body of its king, with the king himself as phallus-brain.[81]

PHYSICAL GEOGRAPHY

In one of his lyrics, Goethe personifies Love as a landscape painter.[82] The poet is sitting at a craggily picturesque spot, in a crepuscular mist, when a boy appears and, with his finger, 'paints' a sun, some gilt-edged clouds, some mountains, trees, a river next to a flowery meadow, and, finally, at the forest's edge, a beautiful maiden, whose cheeks glow with the colour of the fingertip which painted them. Now, a slight breeze sets the whole thing in motion, and the maiden approaches the poet where he sits. . .

One of the questions the poem raises is more insistent than the others. Why, it goes, should love not have been a portraitist? The maiden is necessary to the picture; but is she not, also, sufficient? Is the scenery not a superfluous backdrop to her crucial presence? Of course, our answer is liable to come from aesthetic history, since it has to do with Romanticism's allegiance to the picturesque. But other issues arise, less local to the specific age. It is clear that loved ones are often associated with particular locations. We think of Eve in Eden, rather than the outside world; of any courted boy or girl in Pastoral, surrounded by sheep or goats, on a slope beside a spring; of a Medieval lady, under siege, in her walled garden; of the naked woman in a *fête champêtre*, the lines of her body repeated in those of the distant hills; and so on. We may even conclude, in the more emphatic instances, that the loved one could not possibly be loved in any other location. Instead of serving as an evocative or decorative background to a portrait of the loved one, the landscape becomes the subject, of which the human figure is but a small, if not insignificant part. (Here, we may have a microcosmic and stylised version of the history of landscape painting itself.) This trend of thought naturally concludes in the concept of the beloved landscape; or of the loved one as a landscape.

How does one paint a landscape? As if it were within reach. That is to say, as if its horizon could be touched with a brush – or, in the case of Goethe's Love, with an outstretched hand. Landscape painting is a way of managing the world, of touching the horizon, while yet deferring to its size; and of creating it anew. What painter has not moved a tree, as if in fact, to suit his composition? In the course of painting it, he reduces his landscape to a human scale. He gathers up its parts, bringing them all into reach; tames its waywardness, by eliminating seasonal change; frames, names, and sells it. One need not say, of the sun, that it smiles, or of a storm, that it frets, to engage the pathetic fallacy. Even without explicit anthropomorphism, the very fact of description is enough.

Goethe's painter is an invention. What his poem actually describes is the spreading light of dawn. But the dawn reveals a landscape in the colours of a boy's flesh. The lyric is a discreet striptease, motivated by the thought of love. The nudity of the landscape teaches the poet nothing about the conservation of nature, and precious little about how to paint. Its lesson is on love. Art does not, in the end, control the matter. A natural breeze is required, to breathe life into the loved one: and when the landscape lives, the poem ends.

The depiction of the loved one's body as a landscape is a common device. Any example would do, but my personal favourite occurs in Shakespeare's *Venus and Adonis (231–4)*, when Venus says to Adonis:

I'll be a park, and thou shalt be my deer;
Feed where thou wilt, on mountain or in dale:
Graze on my lips; and if those hills be dry,
Stray lower, where the pleasant fountains lie.

In this context, the point to note about the literature of male homo-eroticism is undramatic: we have no reason to expect anything but as frequent a use of the body-landscape device as in the wider tradition. A man's body has as many woods and pastures as a woman's, after all. His landscape may be slightly more hyperborean, what with its craggier hard edges and denser arborescence, but is no less varied and breathtaking than hers. So, it is with all the weight of established convention behind them that the following examples operate.

At its simplest, the landscape metaphor occurs in reference to men's body hair, which is said to be like grass. Addressing his leaves of grass, Whitman says: 'It may be you transpire from the breasts of young men.' From this possibility (grass as hair) comes its complement (hair as grass). To Mutsuo Takahashi, a man's pubic hairs are 'downy grasses' and, later, a lawn or neatly cut hedge. But less domesticated scenes are more common. Genet describes Querelle's body as woodland earth covered in pine needles ('son ventre, tendre comme le sol d'un sous-bois couvert d'aiguilles de pin'). From here, our path leads into the wilder, and more mysterious, sacred forest. Lingering over a man's groin, Takahashi writes of a 'forest of highly fragrant hair'. Likewise, Auden, looking up at a man's body from between his legs, looks 'through the forest of pubic hair / To the range of the chest, rising lofty and wide'. As in the Goethe poem, beyond the forest, mountains rise up to the sky. When mosquitoes hover over Peter Orlovsky's head, Allen Ginsberg sees them as 'bloodsucking cannibal transparent vultures / circling over Peter's yellow mountainside of hair'. Stephen Spender sees 'muscles extending / in ranges with lakes' across the limbs of young men.[83]

If his parts are parts of a landscape, the whole of a man's body may be seen as a complete land or world. One of the Scandinavian myths has it that the world was made, by Odin and two of his brothers, out of the body of the giant Ymir. His bones became mountains and rocks; his flesh, soil; his hair, vegetation; and his blood, the sea. His skull was raised up to form the dome of the sky; and what we think of as clouds are, in fact, loose fragments of his brain. The first woman and man were born out of his left armpit. The modern tendency is to think of the earth in vaguely similar terms, but as a woman: Mother Nature and Mother Earth.

However, the male land and world are not forgotten. E.A. Lacey speaks of his lover's body as an 'alien continent'. A more compact image is that of the island, as in these two sentences by Christopher Isherwood: 'When winter returned and Otto revealed himself bit by bit as he pulled off layers of thick clothes, his nakedness aroused both of them even more. His body became a tropical island on which they were snugly marooned in the midst of snowbound Berlin.'[84] Although the lover is spoken of as a landscape, he remains at the same time a man, and can share with his lover the delights of wandering over the countryside he is. If he is, on one hand, an island, he is also, on the other, one of its islanders. One problem with the body-landscape device is that, in most cases, it implies an animate ('active') and an inanimate ('passive') principle which, if they do not necessarily interfere with love's desired unity, do suggest an imbalance of pleasure. So, the device is generally reserved for those quiet moments before or after sexual intercourse, when by sight and touch one lover examines the other, who lies silent and still. (In the hetero-erotic tradition, the examiner is generally the male partner.)

One of the most inviting of the male islands is Greek: Odysseus Elytis' 'Body of Summer'. A man lies, sprawling on his back, with cicadas basking in his ears, ants on his chest. There are lizards in his grassy armpits. Waves lap at his feet, and a light breeze wafts the smell of herbs from his pubic hairs. Offshore, the sirens sing to him, of his beauty. From a description near the start of 'The Fourth Rome', I assume Nikolai Klyuev had visited the same spot: 'There is the shore of nipples, the torrid island of buttocks, / The valley of the groin, the plateau of knees; / Song-filled pebbles and colored seashells / Lure whole gangs of sirens to come swimming this way.'[85]

Once they have observed the landscapes of beloved flesh, lovers must go ashore. That is to say, physical must follow visual contact. In Kirkup's translation of 'A Song of Love', Jean Genet writes to his boyfriend: 'On your hips and your neck my lambs will pasture, / Nibbling a rich grass baked by the sun'. The proximity of this to the Shakespeare, quoted above, underlines my point about the conventionality of the device. That it should come from Genet's, of all pens, is proof. In the same sense, it is according to formula that Aaron Shurin writes a poem called 'Pilgrimage', in which his lover's nipples are hills, and his whole body is 'a geography', over which the poet's hands wander. A more developed adherence to an effective formula comes in Edward Lucie-Smith's 'Asleep', in which, with tongue and fingers, the poet explores his lover's sleeping body. Its sweetly scented flesh is a version of Eden: 'Paradise / of my imagination! / Thickets, bowers, crevices! Paths / twined and retwined, going nowhere!' He ambles through this maze, on a gentle treasure hunt. With a degree of naivety, possibly feigned, he asks,

'What do you mean me to find?' The answer, not provided, is the sexual goal, which forms the centre of the maze: either the Fountain of Youth or the Tree of Life, or both combined. This garden has affinities with the genital garden at the centre of Auden's *The Age of Anxiety*.[86]

Before we leave the garden, it is worth pausing to remember the significance of the plants around us, as suggested by the myths of their origins. Many of them bear human memories: the adonis-flower, of Adonis; the anemone, of Anemone; the cornflower, of Cyanus; the crocus, of Crocus; the daisy, of Belides; the heliotrope, of Clytie; the hyacinth, of Hyacinthus; ivy, of Cissos, the myrrh shrub, of Smyrna, or Myrrha; and the narcissus, of Narcissus. The trees, also, remember human origins: the cypress, as Cyparissus; the laurel, as Daphne; the linden, as Baucis; and the oak, as Philemon.[87] Love, either their own or the gods', motivated all their metamorphoses. Theirs is the landscape of human desire, in floral form. From them, William Burroughs derives his 'flesh garden', in which there grow enormous, genital trees, born from the bodies of dead youths. Each tree has 'smooth red buttocks' and 'a quivering rectum' on one side of its trunk, and, on the other, clusters of 'phallic orchids'. By cross-fertilisation, trees and human being reproduce themselves: a youth penetrates the tree, whose orchids ejaculate semen; which is gathered up by the youth, to 'make flesh' with; which in turn, when dead, provides the seed for a new tree.[88]

Alternatively, flowers are an expression, not of their own, but of the earth's desire. In the sixth part of Roy Campbell's *The Flaming Terrapin*, the following passage occurs: 'Where each young Hercules, tired of the chase, / Has lain, the earth becomes a mess of flowers: / His pleated muscles and his burning face / Are sweeter to the earth than April showers, / And where he slept the flaming corn aspires / To harp the wind along on golden wires.' Man is the potent principle. It is his beauty as much as his toil that activates the soil's fecundity. As the mandrake grew from the semen of the hanged man, so Campbell's flowers grow from the sweat of the beautiful. Man creates the landscape in his own image, to his own glorification. The idea of corn as an Aeolian harp is a timely reference to nature's involvement in the arts. Again, the point of Goethe's landscape painter is affirmed.[89]

There is a point at which the symbolic and the real landscapes coincide, to underline the erotic significance of location. Harold Norse's 'Island of Giglio' ends as follows: 'when I set foot on shore / a youth emerged from the crowd / barefoot and olive-skinned / and we climbed up rocky slopes / till dusk fell and close to the moon / at the mouth of a cave we made love / as the sea broke wild beneath the cliff.' The landing on the island coincides with the meeting of the boy (it olive-treed, he olive-skinned); the exploration of the island, with that of the boy; the reaching of the cave, with that of the boy's anus; and the crashing of the waves, with orgasm. In much the same way, William Burroughs' youths often make love in caves or muddy pools. The whole world seems, at times, to take on the physical characteristics of the place Steven Marcus calls Pornotopia. By now, I think we can safely discard Marcus' definition of the 'essential imagination of nature' in Pornotopia as only an 'immense, supine, female form'. After all, there is no lack of male, homosexual pornography. Let us, rather, think of Pornotopia as a nation divided into two states, female and male.[90]

Having toured these lands, how can we fail to accept the validity of Goethe's description of Love as a landscape painter, rather than a portraitist? Love's art is not concerned to capture a likeness, by faithfully copying appearances: a single expression, a frozen gesture, a characteristic suit of clothes. . . To paint a man's portrait is proof, merely, that one has looked at him for some hours; or at his photograph. But to portray him as his landscape is to capture in symbols the most intimate aspects of one's knowledge of his body and soul; and to revive in paint or words the enchantment of his presence. The viewer can recognise the man in a portrait, without any need to understand him; but the landscape device requires us to profit by our imagination.

JESUS CHRIST

The land is the source of our substance and sustenance. Just as Adam was born from it, so we all die into it. Even our feats of spirituality are envisaged in terms of earthly physique. Our yearning to transcend the body is always compromised by the desire to take it with us when we go. We populate our dreams of heaven with youthful humanoids. So, while Love is a robust urchin with wings, Divine Love is a gang of angels as solid as schoolboys.

According to the chronology of the Christian faith, God made Man [sic] in His [sic] image, and then made Christ in Man's image. So, given that my lover is made in God's image, shall I not find in him a trace of divinity? And, if God is made in my lover's image, shall I not quicken with desire for Him?

This kind of unflawed reasoning lies behind a great body of devotional poetry, most of it written by men, which is identical in its conventions to secular love poetry, and differs from it only in the name of the beloved: Jesus Christ. (Modern versions of such poems have been written by, among others, Gerard Manley Hopkins, Robert Duncan, and Geoffrey Hill.[91]) As in most erotic poetry, the desired goal is bed. A poem attributed to Richard Rolle of Hampole (d. 1349) suggests that, 'though hard the way / Love brings us near that bed of rare delight / Where Christ and soul of man at last unite'. And the moment of union tends to be described in recognisably sexual terms. Here, for instance, is the start of a poem by Saint John of the Cross, as translated by Roy Campbell:

> Oh flame of love so living,
> How tenderly you force
> To my soul's inmost core your fiery probe!
> Since now you've no misgiving,
> End it, pursue your course
> And for our sweet encounter tear the robe![92]

Furthermore, Psalm 23 ('The Lord is my shepherd') and many less famous devotional works are entrenched in the Pastoral tradition. With its visions of a prelapsarian Golden Age, this accommodates a simple polymorphous eroticism, of which homo-eroticism is a prominent part. An interesting amalgam of the pagan and Christian iconographies occurs in a fresco in the Catacombs, on which Christ is portrayed in His role as shepherd, carrying not only in one arm the customary lamb, but also, in the other, a set of Pan pipes.[93]

As Wayland Young says, 'Divine love was always an alternative to sexual love' (or an alternative form of sexual love, which we might, for the sake of brevity, call *theophilia*) 'and was free to appropriate its language'. Young quotes Origen's third-century statement that 'The soul ought to adhere to its spouse and hear his word and embrace him and receive the seed of the word from him'; and Saint John Chrysostom's claim that, 'not only was God a spouse to virgins, but he was also a more ardent lover than men'.[94] He may be bride or groom, to men or women. Digby Mackworth Dolben's 'Brevi Tempore Magnum Perfecit Opus' is an elegy on a 17 year-old youth, who was the otherwise chaste bride of Christ: 'We think the Bridegroom sometimes stood beside him as he slept, / And set upon those virgin lips the signet of His love, / That any other touch but His they never should approve.' Death was their wedding, the ascent to heaven their ascent to bed.[95]

All kinds of theological and iconographic problems arise as soon as desire for Christ intensifies to the point at which we yearn to see Him naked. The Baptism and the Crucifixion are the two moments of semi-nudity we are accustomed to; but they were not always so. In the tenth century, the figure on the cross tended to be portrayed in a long robe which left only His hands, feet, and face uncovered. In the eleventh and twelfth centuries, the robe shortened, its sleeves vanished, and Christ's breast was sometimes uncovered to reveal His wound. In the thirteenth century, the robe became a mere tunic; and in the fourteenth, Christ was left with a scrap of linen wrapped round His loins.[96] But there have been frequent deviations from the sequence of this slow striptease. In the British Museum, there is an Italian ivory carving of Christ crucified in a narrow loin cloth, which dates from as early as the fifth century. According to Gregory of Tours, writing in the sixth century, when an image of Christ in a loin cloth was displayed in a church at Narbonne, Christ Himself put in an appearance, fully dressed, to make His complaint to the priest. Later, Benvenuto Cellini carved a naked Christ crucified, which a scandalised Philip II of Spain had to veil with a handkerchief. There is another such Christ, by Michelangelo, in the Casa Buonarroti in Florence.[97]

Of course, the task of depicting the penis of the adult Saviour could have caused endless wrangles. Should it be bigger than average, befitting Christ's status as God? Should it modestly be smaller, thereby inviting innuendo and ridicule? Or should it be of a universally average length and girth? If so, what *are* the average length and girth? The problem is solved if we recognise that representations of Christ are modelled not on Christ Himself, but on ordinary young men, and it is their sexiness as much as His that remains in the final product. After having an affair with a woman, Tennessee Williams happened to watch a college play, on which he comments: 'The Christ figure . . . was Fleishman, the leading young actor that year. He was elevated nearly naked on the cross – and it was his virile young beauty that drew me back toward my more predominant sexual inclination.'[98] In John Logan's poem 'On a Prize Crucifix by a Student Sculptor', the living flesh of a student, hanging from the bars in a college gym, becomes the still image which represents the living flesh of Christ.

> This Christ's chest heaves with the
> Runner's breath, the legs torqued, the tight,
> Powered thighs not at rest, as though
>
> They jump in contest. The belly caves beneath
> The holy human building of his ribs;
> His thin belly feels the touch of hands,
> Of lance. His navel buds above his loins
> Where lies his genital, secret as a
> Boy's, breeched, denied, terrible with weight
> Of seed and with the supple strength of God.[99]

When such actors take the role of Christ – that is, when He is seen again *in the flesh* – only the most myopic spectator could miss the erotic potential of a narrative in which a beautiful young man allows himself to be mocked, flogged, crowned with thorns, stripped naked, and left to die, publicly, in lasting agony. Logan's concentration on the hidden genitals is central to his purpose. As he asks later, 'Ah God, if Christ has not a body . . . And all of that, what good is He to us?' Sexuality is a necessary party of the myth of a deity who becomes wholly human, and the myth is severely impaired by its excision. The Sacred Heart must be given the full benefit of its phallic associations, as symbol of the loving glans penis of the Lord.[100]

Leo Steinberg has shown the importance of the *ostentatio genitalium* in Renaissance representations of the Christ child. The genitals are proof both of incarnation and of Christ's restoration of sinlessness to humanity. Christ's manhood (maleness) is the sign of His Manhood (humanity). His circumcision foreshadows His crucifixion.[101]

Now, just as sexual intercourse may be reduced to an obsessive conjunction of genitalia, so the idea of a sexually viable Christ may be fetishised to the point where, as Manhood incarnate, He enters the worshipper as a phallus. Pisanus Fraxi's *Bibliography of Prohibited Books* lists *An Essay on Woman*, by 'Pego Borewell, Esq', which contains a parodic prayer to the phallus as Creator, and an illustration of a phallus, entitled (in Greek) 'The Saviour of the World'.[102] Felicien Rops made two etchings of a naked Magdalene, masturbating at the foot of the cross, to which is nailed a giant phallus.[103] Harold Norse's poem 'Allegro Vivace' celebrates John Allegro's book *The Sacred Mushroom and the Cross*, which establishes convincing associations between the mushroom, the cross, the phallus, and Christ. Norse comments: 'Jesus Christ was a prick. /Let all gay men proclaim their holiness. / They've worshiped the sacred mushroom / for millennia. THE COCK IS HOLY!'[104]

If Christ is a phallus, of course, the logical conclusion must be that the Eucharist is an act of fellatio. Norman O. Brown writes: 'Eucharist is the marriage feast; the union of the bridegroom and bride. He gives himself to his bride with the bread. Eat your fill, lovers; drink, sweethearts, and drink deep. The two become one flesh, incorporating each other, by eating. The transubstantiation is the unification; is in the eating.'[105] The Manicheans and the Albigenses are said to have sprinkled semen on their Eucharistic bread.[106] As Wilde wrote, in *De Profundis*, not without double meaning, 'Love is a sacrament that should be taken kneeling, and *Domine, non sum dignus* should be on the lips and in the hearts of those who receive it'.

A more outspoken variation on the same theme appears in Antler's poem about semen, 'To the Seed of the Male of my Species'. The poem ends: 'Not till boycome is served at communion / will I believe the Father of Jesus / is the God of Love'. In 'Son of Man', Will Inman writes, of Christ: 'He entered the bodies-and-souls / of men and women / with words and self. / He touched them, and / more virginal than ever they gave birth / to themselves.'[107]

Although He personifies virility, Jesus generally fails to make the grade in *machismo*. A tradition of the androgynous Christ, with certain supposedly womanly qualities – from His maternal love for us, as divined by Julian of Norwich, to His 'head of woman's hair', as described by Lawrence Durrell – leads Robert Duncan to conclude that 'He was part girl'.[108] Furthermore, the theme of Christ's homosexuality is periodically recurrent. Saint Aelred of Rievaulx called the relationship of Jesus and John the Evangelist a heavenly marriage (*thalami caelestis*) and used it to defend his own sentimental friendships.[109] Christopher Marlowe claimed Jesus and John were bedfellows. In *Justine*, the Marquis de Sade suggested that the same was true of all the Apostles. Edward Prime Stevenson's book on *The Intersexes* (1908) attributed the behaviour of Judas to a 'jealous homosexual passion'. The only book of Uranian verse to appear during the First World War, Cuthbert Wright's *One Way of Love* (1915), contains the suggestion that Christ must have been a lover of boys. Finally, 'The Young Christ' of Frank O'Hara says to Himself, 'I must be a pansy / myself, they say all the Jews are really'.[110]

In his interview for *Gay Sunshine*, Robert Duncan gives credence to one of the gnostic myths, in which 'Christ and Satan are twin brothers and Christ loves Satan throughout, eternally. Unremitting absolute Christ love. And Satan falls in love with Christ.'[111] Perhaps, it is as an unrecognisable remnant of some such belief that the boy (*neaniskos*) in the shirt (*sindōn*) appears so briefly, in Mark 14.51–2. When Christ is arrested, the boy alone follows Him, the disciples having fled. However, when he, too, is about to be arrested, the boy escapes by slipping out of his shirt, leaving it in the hands of the man who tries to stop him. He runs out of the narrative in the nude. Commenting on this incident, in the third chapter of *The Genesis of Secrecy*, Frank Kermode offers as one of many possible interpretations, that the boy was Christ's lover. Kermode also asks whether this boy could not be the same as the youth in another narrative by Mark, quoted by Clement of Alexandria. In this incident, Christ raises from the dead a young man, who loves Him and begs to go with Him. As instructed, the young man visits Christ at night, wearing only a *sindōn* over his naked body. Throughout the night, Christ teaches His young friend something of the mystery of the kingdom of God.[112]

To complement the phallic aspect of Christ's body, there is also a receptive capacity consonant with the passive side of His personality. Digby Mackworth Dolben's 'Homo Factus Est', a love poem to Jesus, includes an expression of the wish to enter and hide in 'the utter stillness / Of Thy wounded Side'. Aleister Crowley is characteristically more outspoken, when he associates the vagina of 'La Juive' with the wound in Christ's side. Robert Duncan, too, connects vagina and sacred wound, in 'As in the Old Days'.[113]

Many of the above themes were brought together in an unusually clumsy poem by James Kirkup, 'The Love that Dares to Speak its Name', and published by *Gay News* in 1976. An openly gay Christ, penetrated in all orifices and fellated by the centurion who takes Him down from the cross, meets death in the last spasms of ejaculation, but rises on the third day to continue proudly to bless homosexual intercourse in all its expressions. The poem is no more discreet than the undistinguished illustration – of Jesus naked – that accompanied it. So, in 1977, *Gay News* and its editor were sent to trial and found guilty of publishing a 'blasphemous libel'. For this reason, I may not quote the poem.[114]

The fact remains that to embrace the faith is to be embraced by Jesus. (Remember Flaubert's Saint Julian, lying naked with a leprous Christ, 'mouth to mouth, breast to breast', and ascending to heaven, ecstatic in His embrace.[115]) The logic with which gay Christians augment the tale of David and Jonathan by adopting the myth of a Christ who would approve of their loves, seems watertight. Mutsuo Takahashi's poem 'Christ for Thieves' is a prayer to this generously loving Christ, asking Him to be 'the father for homosexuals', a role to which He is suited by the breadth of His loving personality. The man-loving Christ is, emphatically, promiscuous.[116]

Walt Whitman followed the myth of Christ quite closely in formulating his ideal of universal comradeship and polymorphous relationships, in visions of which he himself often plays the part of a wandering Messiah:

Come, I will make the continent indissoluble,
I will make the most splendid race the sun ever shone upon,
I will make divine magnetic lands,
> With the love of comrades,
> With the life-long love of comrades.

The basis of this comradeship, both Whitman's and Christ's, is that the human being, made in God's image, and the God, made in human image, are potentially identical and morally equal. Whitman writes: 'What do you suppose I would intimate to you in a hundred ways, but that man or woman is as good as God?'

HERACLES

The nature of the heroism of Heracles corresponds with the nature of his physique. His astonishing muscles are indistinguishable from the armour he wears, of gold and bronze, given him by Athene and Hephaestus. He strangles and flays the Nemean Lion, with his bare hands. Subsequently, wearing its pelt, he augments his own leonine hairiness. His limitless stamina exhausts the Ceryneian Hind, in a year-long chase. By day, he conquers kings with a club of olive-wood; by night, he conquers women with his club of flesh. In fifty consecutive nights, he proves his sexual prowess by fathering fifty-one sons on the daughters of Thespius. He wrestles with and overcomes Eryx, Achelous, and Antaeus. Eventually, as if to demonstrate the similarities of martial, sporting, and sexual competition, he establishes the Olympic Games.

However, Heracles' aggressive supremacy is tempered with ambivalence. His virility is happily compromised, by several homosexual affairs and his unexplained tendency to transvestism. He has sexual relationships with Hylas, Eurystheus, and his own nephew and charioteer, Iolaus. Love takes precedence over heroic endeavour when, in order to search for Hylas, he abandons the expedition of the Argonauts. When he is bought and enslaved by the Lydian queen Omphale, he is dressed in women's clothing; and he appears similarly clad, later, when fighting the Meropians and marrying Chalciope.[117]

The muscles of Heracles seem acquired, as if they were wonderful but superfluous additions to the man's necessary physique. When naked, he still looks clothed. (Surely, his pectorals can be removed, like a quilted vest.) When unarmed, he still looks ready for battle. (Surely, he can lay down his biceps, as a sign of peaceful intentions.) Every position the body adopts gives the impression of a pose, as if its exhibitionistic muscles were constantly demanding spectators. But Heracles himself, as he develops his physique, subjects himself primarily to his own scrutiny. The mirror is offered all the best views. Despite the dissimilarity of their appearances, Heracles and Narcissus are close kin.

In his interview for *Gay Sunshine*, John Rechy mentions a drag queen who once told him, 'Your muscles are as gay as my drag'. Rechy comments: 'Of course many bodybuilders are gay. I love the muscular aspect of myself. Yet, in effect, though different, it's similar in reversed purpose to drag. It's the opposite side but from almost the same source. The queen protects herself by dressing in women's clothes and the bodybuilder protects himself in muscles – so-called "men's clothes".'[118]

Muscles are armour. To a magazine photograph, Harold Norse writes, 'My mouth wanders the muscular ridges of your belly / the breastplates of your pectorals'.[119] Wilhelm Reich's notion of 'character armour', although strictly a psychological metaphor, clearly has roots in physical effect. The man who is psychologically on the defensive tenses his muscles. Continuous tension develops them. The psyche defends itself by erecting defences around the body in which it is lodged. The defender apes the aggressor, lest he be attacked. By doing so, he does, indeed, gain physical strength. On top of the muscles, other uniforms may be worn: breastplate over breast. Leather gear is both literal and symbolic protection to the motorbiker. The military uniform performs its functions even during peaceful skirmishes in the bedroom. The functions of clothing and physique, each a fetishistic representation of the other, overlap.

The final effect of the heavily muscled male body is of hollowness. As the leather and studs of the biker hang motionless in the closet, with little more human about them than the vague shape and stench of their owner, might the body of Heracles not, also, prove empty? With irony as subtle as a fist, Harold Norse refers to the bodybuilders in a gymnasium as 'intellectual giants!' In fact, we can never be so sure of the muscle man's interior. We can react to it, only, with questions. James Kirkup's 'The Body-Builder' ends as follows:

Is the perfect torso that he seeks
Anatomically complete?

We look towards the face to find
The soul behind the pouch's pose.
What heavy handsomeness of mind
Instructs the proud set of his nose?

Is fitness a neurotic bore?
Does muscle-definition hide
A healthy vacancy, or more
Than what appears outside?[120]

The Heraclean realms of warfare and sport (which I examine in detail in the next chapter) are tailor-made to suit the body of their protagonist. With erection and muscular development being so closely associated as to share a common opposite, impotence, even the common soldier can play the part of sexual hero. If he lacks the physique of Heracles, all he need do is slip into his uniform, fasten his boots, and fix his bayonet. The myth is sustained by its fetish. Seen as through a magnifying glass, the soldier's body performs insignificant tasks, enlarged accordingly; and Narcissus, the spectator in the mirror, is impressed.

2 MEN OF WAR

Any study of the function of erotic themes in the literature of war must be based on an appreciation of the complementary function of martial themes in erotic literature. In the *Ars amatoria* (II, 233), Ovid says love is a kind of warfare: 'Militiae species amor est'. Of modern writers, Georges Bataille is the most consistently persuasive, on the interdependency of eroticism and violence: 'Essentiellement, le domaine de l'érotisme est le domaine de la violence, le domaine de la violation'.[1] It remains for us to note that this relationship exists no less in the literature of male homo-eroticism than in that of hetero-eroticism.

The penetrating penis, or *penis aculeatus*, is commonly visualised – and used, indeed – as a weapon. When Aleister Crowley calls it a 'fond ruby rapier' or a 'great sword', and when E.A. Lacey writes of 'slim white cocks that like sharp knives / cut my ass', they merely extend the tradition which was already ancient when Shakespeare called the penis a dart, lance, pike, poll-axe, sword, or weapon. Predictably, a sexual encounter between men will soon become a deadly form of combat, like that shown in certain old Japanese drawings, where 'wrestlers and muscle men' fight, 'with no other weapons save their long, thick, huge-headed, and erect penises'.[2]

Phallic range and influence are further enhanced by the image of the penis as an arrow – the enchanting dart of Eros and subduer of Sebastian – with the body as its bow. Paul Goodman likens a boy's body to 'a gently taut bow'. The title of Robert Duncan's collection, *Bending the Bow*, refers to those erotic manoeuvres, physical and mental, which ready the phallus for firing. Alternatively, as in one of Harold Norse's poems, the penis itself may be the 'stiff curved bow / of anxious meat', which fires arrows of semen.[3]

With the transition to fire-arms, the ballistics of sexual intercourse soon increase in deadliness. In the film *Un Chant d'amour* and the novel *Pompes funèbres*, Jean Genet's famous sexual ritual, of one man forcing his pistol barrel into the mouth of another, sets the pattern others develop. Gavin Dillard says his own penis discharges 'like a rifle'. Mutsuo Takahashi likens the combination of a man's genitalia to 'A cannon with its two wheels'. Harold Norse refers to his own 'heavy artillery', while Frank O'Hara envisages a 'missile' with a 'smoking muzzle'. Finally, Norse calls the penis the 'bomb of love', an image we can pair with Allen Ginsberg's converse classification of the atom bomb as an artificial phallus big enough to pleasure the vanity of a whole nation: 'America when will we end the human war? / Go fuck yourself with your atom bomb'. Clearly, when Jane Fonda, as Barbarella, seeks a holster for her gun, she chooses the most appropriate place: down the front of an angel's loincloth.[4]

The active weapon, if accurate, makes a wound: an image of itself or its projectile, sculpted like a mould in living flesh. The complementary purposes of weapon and wound are analogous, in this context, to those of penis and sexual orifice. Since this is the case, there is no reason why a bandage, or some other form of dressing, need not be as sexy to the fetishist – that is, to anyone – as an item of underwear. It is in this spirit that we should read such poems as Cavafy's 'The Bandaged Shoulder' and some of Whitman's nursing poems from the American Civil War, as well as Wilfred Owen's remark, in the 'Apologia Pro Poemate Meo', that love is 'Bound with the bandage of the arm that drips'.[5]

But we must not forget the curative properties of the sexual act, even if it cures what it caused in the first place. The penis makes a wound into which it fits exactly. Therefore, by entering the wound, it plugs it. The bleeding is stanched, the wound effectively closed. Ejaculation is an injection of balm. An oral caress may have an equally soothing effect, as Norse suggests when he writes, 'you close my wounds with your tongue'.[6]

This tradition of violent love cannot fail to exert an influence on the poetry of war, particularly when that poetry is littered with suggestions, as in Owen's 'Arms and Boy', that bullets yearn, as if with erotic desire, to nuzzle into the vulnerable warmth of boys' hearts.[7] The tradition is more than a literary conceit. It is an accurate representation of the view many men, hetero- and homosexual, have of sexual processes, and of their own relationships with other people, whether women or men. In *Against Our Will : Men, Women and Rape*, her history and indictment of such attitudes, Susan Brownmiller defines rape as 'the real-life deployment of the penis as weapon'. Before proceeding, the reader is advised to turn to the third chapter of Brownmiller's book, where she outlines the incidence of heterosexual rape – often excluded from conventional lists of the 'atrocities' of war – in the First and Second World Wars, and in the wars in Bangladesh and Vietnam. She shows that rape is still, as it has always been, an institutionalised aspect of wars, other than certain types of civil war or popular uprising. The victorious soldier considers it his prerogative – often, indeed, his duty – to rape any woman of the losing side.[8] I am reminded of the ancient Egyptians' ceremonial custom, of buggering defeated troops, thereby asserting sexual and political mastery over them.

It would be satisfying to be able to claim that since the flowering of the Gay Movement the use by male, homosexual poets of the image of the phallus as a weapon has either lessened or ceased altogether, at least in the works of those men concerned with sexual politics and committed to a readjustment of the supposedly natural manifestations of masculinity. There is little evidence to support such a belief. If anything, the tradition is being consolidated, by gay men anxious to reclaim their cultural heritage. (I ought to add the obvious: phallic weaponry still ravages the hetero-erotic literature of male writers, as ever.)

My next concern is to look at the complementary issue, not of war's place in love, but of love's in war.

CARPE DIEM

One of the words most often used in war poetry is 'love'. What hatred war begets is institutional and public, and has the paradoxical effect of intensifying feelings of affection, which remain personal and private. Sooner or later, in fact, every war seems to have become a time for love, memorable more for its proofs of affection than for those of enmity; and, in particular, a time for young men to love each other. Denis de Rougemont writes of the 'explosion of sex which has usually accompanied huge armed struggles' as an adjunct to war's more literal explosions. But, with reference to the First World War, he notes a new feature: in total war, the explosion of sex 'can now only occur among civilians at the rear'. Presumably, he refers to heterosexual acts (and overlooks the issue of rape). André Gide's *Corydon* offers a partial corrective. 'I'm sure', says Corydon, 'that periods of martial fervour are essentially uranian periods, just as one finds warlike races to be particularly prone to homosexuality'. This, he implies, is why the *Code Napoléon* shows a certain leniency with regard to male homosexual acts.[9]

When Marcel Proust writes that 'War, which turns capital cities, where only women remain, into an abomination for [male] homosexuals, is at the same time a story of passionate adventure for [male] homosexuals if they are intelligent enough to concoct dream figures', he is referring, of course, to the Paris of the First World War. But Paris was far from being empty of young men, as Proust knew. His Baron de Charlus, walking through the streets of the city, sees so many soldiers of various nationalities – including Germans, in Zeppelins, overhead – that he does not know which way to look. In Jupien's brothel, clients can demand the services of members of 'every branch of the armed forces, every one of the allied nations'. Charlus' favourites seem to be the English soldiers, whom he compares with Greek athletes, his imagination staying closer to convention than his behaviour.[10] Similarly, Jean Cocteau admired the English troops he saw passing through Boulogne. He commented: 'The English are the proof that marble gives a wrong idea of the color of Greek faces'.[11]

The Second War was no less sexy than the First. According to Harold Norse, 'the war decade of Hitler and Mussolini provided plenty of fuel for erotic fires. Sailors and soldiers were to be had for the asking.' Elsewhere, he says the forties meant to him 'death, sex and war', with 'sailors everywhere'.[12]

The London of the Second War was as enhanced as the Paris of the First. Goronwy Rees has described how Guy Burgess 'brought home a series of boys, young men, soldiers, sailors, airmen, whom he had picked up among the thousands who thronged the streets of London'.[13] According to John Lehmann's autobiographical novel, *In the Purely Pagan Sense*, the public urinals of London became popular points of sexual assignation, particularly during the blackout. 'Heavenly bodies filled them, and it was often quite impossible for anyone who genuinely wanted to relieve himself to get in.' During the Phony War period, before any signs of hostility reached Britain, 'An atmosphere of heightened emotion dominated; kisses were exchanged with those one would never in normal times have reached the point of kissing; declarations of devotion and admiration were made that might never have come to the surface otherwise; vows to keep in touch, to form closer and more meaningful alliances when peace returned, came from upper lips that were usually stiff.'[14]

At the end of 1941, the United States entered the war. In 1942, their troops entered Europe. This had a remarkable effect, not only on the balance of power, but also on the social and sexual balance of the Europeans. According to Keith Vaughan's diary entry for 16 June 1944, American participation had made the whole war more light-hearted, more like a game. 'Wounded soldiers, in spite of what had been seen beneath bombed buildings and in the gutters of burning London, were suddenly good looking young men in attractive head bandages.'[15] Not unlike the ideal warriors of the First World War, in fact. Quentin Crisp records that London had begun to resemble 'a paved double bed' from the very start of the Blitz. But nothing in this earlier period can compare with the impact (at least, as Crisp describes it) of the Americans' arrival.

This brand new army of (no) occupation flowed through the streets of London like cream on strawberries, like melted butter over green peas . . . As they sat in the cafés or stood in the pubs, their bodies bulged through every straining khaki fibre towards our feverish hands. Their voices were like warm milk, their skins as flawless as expensive indiarubber, and their eyes as beautiful as glass. Above all it was the liberality of their natures that was so marvellous. Never in the history of sex was so much offered to so many by so few. At the first gesture of acceptance from a stranger, words of love began to ooze from their lips, sexuality from their bodies and pound notes from their pockets like juice from a peeled peach.[16]

In *I Am My Brother*, the second volume of his autobiography, John Lehmann describes 'the emotion and enthusiasm with which certain members of the American forces stationed in England were taken up' by the social establishment of London.[17] Cecil Beaton, finding them far more attractive than their British counterparts, commented: 'They do not seem to contaminate the gum they chew'.[18] (These effects may date from the American intervention in the First World War, after which, according to Martin Green, the United States were widely felt to have taken over from Britain the monopoly on occidental virility.[19])

Needless to say, the sexual benefits of war were felt, also, in the United States themselves. When fear of Japanese air attacks caused coastal California to be blacked out at night, according to Tennessee Williams, 'The Palisades were full of young servicemen, positively infested with them, I'd say, and when I'd driven by one who appealed to my lascivious glance, I would turn the bike about and draw up alongside him to join him in his spurious enchantment with the view.'[20] Christopher Isherwood's biographer provides a similar picture of California:

Many people found the war years sexually stimulating, in the sense that brief encounters were more frequent. There was an urgency about them too which appealed to some tastes, as did the blackout. Servicemen on leave would hang around the corners of Sunset Boulevard and other Hollywood streets, ready for a party that could easily become an orgy. The beaches north of Santa Monica became regular meeting-places and the scenes of nocturnal gatherings until, several years after the war, there was a big clean-up.[21]

The loving encounter is a common feature, also, in the memoirs of the servicemen themselves. Indeed, T.E. Lawrence's *Seven Pillars of Wisdom* begins with a classic sequence on this theme. Eric Hiscock's *The Bells of Hell Go Ting-a Ling-a Ling* is a virtual catalogue of descriptions of, and speculations on the nature of, the relationships between comrades in the First World War. *The Cage*, Dan Billany and David Dowie's memoir of their lives as prisoners of war in Fascist Italy, turns into an intensely personal account of the one-sided romance between a fellow-prisoner and Dowie himself.[22]

It follows that the fictional and poetic literature of this time of love, war-time, will have an erotic dimension; as will the literature of the institutions of war, cadet schools and armed services, whether depicted at war or at peace. Melville's *Billy Budd* set the bounds of what has since become a convention: the novel about an erotic relationship between an officer or N.C.O. and a younger man in the ranks. *Billy Budd* (1891) is followed by Lawrence's *The Prussian Officer* (1914), Carson McCullers' *Reflections in a Golden Eye* (1941), Loren Wahl's *The Invisible Glass* (1950), Dennis Murphy's *The Sergeant* (1958), David Caute's *At Fever Pitch* (1959), Simon Raven's *The Feathers of Death* (1959), James Purdy's *Eustace Chisolm and the Works* (1968), Simon Raven's *Sound the Retreat* (1971), and Robin Maugham's *The Last Encounter* (1972).[23]

It seems not insignificant that more of these novels were written and published in the fifties than in any other decade. Perhaps, having completed another war to end all wars, the world felt safe to begin to relive them all. Furthermore, during the Second World War and the subsequent decade, the number of prosecutions under the British laws banning male homosexual acts increased alarmingly, in direct proportion with the increasing zeal, not of the men indicted, but of the police.[24] In this way, sexual relationships between men became public property, material for reformers and novelists alike.

THE DEATH OF LOVE

Robert Duncan says we yearn for the comfort of love more acutely during a war than at any other time.[25] But while war can in some senses be seen as a period in which love holds sway, we can never forget the other fact, that war destroys what love it creates or intensifies. War is a war on love; and (in spite of the common theme of the army of lovers, to which I shall return) 'An army is an army against love'.[26] Temporary incarceration in the trenches caused impotence on such a large scale that Denis de Rougemont was prompted to call the First World War 'a kind of vast castration of Europe'.[27] The Second World War had the same effect on some. For instance: 'The shock of the outbreak of war in 1939 was such as to make me sexually impotent' for several years.[28]

In the poetry of Alun Lewis, the mere fact of being in uniform – generally considered such a fillip to a man's sexual appeal – seems to place one beyond the bounds of amorousness. The subject of 'The Sentry', a mere guard in warrior's clothing, complains that he has left the realm in which boys and girls embrace and lovers accompany one another down the 'beautiful lanes of sleep'. Instead, he has to guard the 'Cold shore of thought' on his own. In 'Odi et Amo', where love becomes a pun on the routine abbreviation of 'ammunition', the rifle-aiming soldier feels as if his body were no longer his own, now that fire-arms have taken the place of genitalia. His loins, he complains, are atrophied – 'flat and closed like a child's'.[29]

To be wounded, as much as to be in love, is justification of involvement in war: it gives the whole thing some point – just as orgasm is the aim of desire. Particularly in the First World War, when men seldom knew if the shots they fired had actually hit or killed an enemy, getting wounds was more to the point than giving them. This has something to do with the euphemistic way in which a man can describe his distinguished war record in terms of the number of injuries he sustained, rather than the number of men he maimed or killed. (In the Air Force, the opposite is true, because an aeroplane costs more than its pilot and is therefore worth counting.) Not to be wounded is not to be fully involved. Indeed, ultimately: not to die is not to have been at war. The garlands of praise, therefore, go to the dead: the young men to whom the subsequent volumes of poems and memoirs will be dedicated. In 'Burma Casualty', Alun Lewis takes his theme of war's castrating impulse to the necessary conclusion of death, which he describes in terms of the following tender but dangerous caress:

> The dark is a beautiful singing sexless angel
> Her hands so soft you scarcely feel her touch
> Gentle, eternally gentle, round your heart.
> She flatters and unsexes every man.[30]

In the earlier war, Wilfred Owen came to darker conclusions on similar themes. Death has 'The Last Laugh' when, in the poem of that name, a soldier whose mind is on love is shot and sinks to the ground, until 'his whole face kissed the mud'.[31] That, according to Owen, is the true extent of love's involvement in war: as futile metaphor, ennobling what invites despair. Owen's war does not cause anything so fortunate as impotence. In 'Disabled', he describes a man whose legs have been blown off – probably along with his genitals – and who has returned to England. 'To-night he noticed how the women's eyes / Passed from him to the strong men that were whole.'[32] (Picture Lady Chatterley's eyes, moving from chair-ridden Clifford to the gamekeeper.) During the Second World War, Richard Trudgett referred to such 'Disabled Soldiers' as 'the lost brides'.[33] And the homosexual paedophile in Keith Douglas' 'Gallantry' must be out of reach of his variant of love, now that he is dead: for his fellow soldiers have decided they need no longer gossip about him.[34] Christopher Isherwood, one of a generation which missed having to participate in the First World War, regretted his youth, because the war was an opportunity 'to prove one's masculinity, to show that one was not impotent – or homosexual'.[35] As we have seen in the poetry, no war could serve any such purpose; and no war should be required to do so.

War's final iniquity becomes evident if we couple our two present themes as events, in chronological order: war encourages the establishment of love affairs, only to destroy them. Comradeship is the great advantage of a time of war. The horror is in the death of comrades. War's elaborate malice prepares us for death by thus rendering us most vulnerable to it. John Lehmann describes a young sailor he met, during the Second World War: 'He had an inseparable friend, a sharer in everything he had done, enjoyed, endured; but the army machine had taken this friend away from him. He could hardly express the misery this separation had caused him, and as he dwelt on it, he began to work up to a torrent of outrage and hatred against war: I had never seen a soul in torment so nakedly before me.'[36] The comrade is not even dead yet; just gone to war. Death would have all the more intense an effect. Imagine, then, sustaining such losses as a matter of routine, over a long period of combat, in the conditions of Roy Fuller's 'Autumn 1940', when 'No longer can guns be cancelled by love'.[37]

At Torquay in 1918, Robert Nichols wrote a poem called 'The Secret', which became the second in a sequence of four on the First World War, collectively called 'Yesterday', and dedicated to Siegfried Sassoon.[38] The speaker has returned from the trenches, where many of his comrades remain, drowned and buried in French mud. His secret is that he can no longer love women. Furthermore, since the war has ended, the conditions in which he could love men have been removed. War has deprived him altogether of the ability to love. When a woman speaks, he remembers the voices of dying comrades; and her loving glance is obscured by the memory of 'the turquoise glaze / Fixed in the blue and quivering gaze / Of one whom cocaine cannot daze'. (Blue eyes, here, are as explicit a sign of beauty and nobility as the golden hair which, as Paul Fussell points out, adorns so many of the soldiers in the poetry of the First World War.[39]) Nor can he submit to a woman's kiss – 'I, that have felt the dead's embrace; / I, whose arms were his resting-place; / I, that have kissed a dead man's face'. After a war as savage as this, of course, an armistice is to the fighting men no occasion for great rejoicing, but one of bitter remembrance. Robert Graves says, in *Good-bye to All That*, that on hearing the supposedly good news he went out for a solitary walk, 'cursing and sobbing and thinking of the dead'.[40] Far from bringing peace and a universal availability of love, the end of a war may bring only a silence filled with bad dreams.

THREE BATTLES

Three battles exemplify the connections which exist between male homo-eroticism and war. All three passed beyond the bounds of history when, at different times, they were commandeered by philosophy and art; and all three are known to us today not for their historical significance as much as for their respective places in the folkloric tradition of the beautiful warrior.

At the battle of Chaeronea in 338 B.C., Philip II of Macedon forced what Milton called 'that dishonest victory' over the Sacred Band of Thebes, an army of three hundred Greek lovers and loved ones, which had thitherto seemed invincible. According to Plutarch's *Life of Pelopidas*, when the fighting was over, Philip wept as he surveyed the field, and said of the Greek dead, 'Perish any man who suspects that these men either did or suffered anything that was base'. It is presumably to the Theban Band that Phaedrus refers, in his famous speech on the strengths of an army made up of lovers, in Plato's *Symposium*.

That the Band was defeated, is secondary, the theory being of more interest than its practical outcome. The story of the Theban Band is recurrent is some form or other throughout the written history of war: it is one of the more dramatic enactments of the concept of war as the enemy of love and (perhaps more so) of war as love's ultimate fulfilment – of death as orgasm. Philip saw on the field of Chaeronea not only dead warriors who had warred and lost, but also sleeping lovers who had loved and won.

At Ichinotani in 1184 occurred a single death, which the author of the *Heike Monogatari* turned into one of the most popular anecdotes in Japanese literature. The warrior Kumagai Naozane tears off the helmet of an enemy with whom he is grappling at the edge of the sea, only to be confronted by the beautiful face of Atsumori, a teenaged boy. Several of Kumagai's allies are fast bearing down on him, and he realises that with great reluctance he must kill the boy. He explains his dilemma, and the boy agrees that he must die. Having beheaded him, he strips the boy of his armour, and finds therein a flute in a pouch. This must be the source of the exquisite music which, on the eve of battle, he heard coming from the enemy camp.[41]

In a sequel, the play *Atsumori* by Zeami Motokiyo, the warrior, now a priest, meets the ghost of the boy he had to kill, and the two are united as 'Friends in Buddha's Law'.[42] The necrophile undressing of the corpse and the discovery of its phallic flute and pouch confirm the story as a classic of the type with which we are concerned. By stripping the dead in order to carry off their uniforms and weapons as trophies, the victor demilitarises them, leaving them naked, vulnerable, and sexy: better suited to bed than to grave. Whether they were foe or friend is immaterial.

In 1364, the Florentines beat the Pisans in the battle of Cascina. This was no great strategic victory, but a stroke of luck (for both Florence and the history of art). When the Pisan soldiers were bathing, naked and unarmed, the Florentines made a successful surprise attack, thereby providing Michelangelo with an excuse to depict a crowd of naked male figures in violent action. He executed a cartoon of the battle for the Palazzo Vecchio in 1504. In fact, as Kenneth Clark says, 'in Florence, from about 1480 to 1505, the compulsive subject was a battle of naked men'.[43] This trend appears to have been set by Pollaiuolo, not necessarily with reference to the events of 1364: for a number of antique sarcophagi depicted the subject, and demanded to be copied or outdone. Cascina's strategic significance was nothing, compared with its dramatic resonance. We can forget the Florentine army. It was the Pisans who were naked, who were swimming, and who died as they struggled to arm themselves, half submerged and half dressed. Indeed, Cascina is their victory. Its meaning lies, not in military honours, but in the vulnerability and beauty of male flesh.

From these three battles (Chaeronea, Ichinotani, Cascina) several themes emerge, all to do with the tensions and cohesions between man's two favourite images of himelf: as lover and as warrior. We notice visual preoccupations in all three cases. The central image in the case of Chaeronea is of the field of dead lovers, as surveyed by the weeping victor (in Kenneth Clark's terms, bodies in the state of pathos); in Ichinotani, the unmasked face of the soldier too young to die; and in Cascina, relaxed bodies bursting suddenly into action, but in vain (Clark's energetic nudes). Chaeronea and Ichinotani highlight the tears of the victor, suddenly aware of his crime against beauty, love, and life. Ichinotani and Cascina grant strategic and symbolic meaning to water, in which armour is a superfluous encumbrance, and war an unseemly intrusion. Cascina and Chaeronea plead the cause of comradeship, in their respective crowds of nudes and lovers. Elements of all three will appear again and again in literary material on warfare.

CASCINA

The themes of the story of Cascina have been dealt with in Paul Fussell's essay 'Soldiers Bathing', and I have no wish to duplicate his arguments here.[44] 'The scene of bathing soldiers is common', he writes, 'not because soldiers bathe but because there's hardly a better way of projecting poignantly the awful vulnerability of mere naked flesh.' It is as well, therefore, not to allow an enemy to see one's naked body. In his novel *Kaputt*, Curzio Malaparte describes an encounter with Heinrich Himmler in a sauna bath. 'Naked Germans are wonderfully defenseless', he comments. 'They are bereft of secrecy. They are no longer frightening. The secret of their strength is not in their skin or in their bones, or in their blood; it is in their uniforms. Their real skin is in their uniform. If the peoples of Europe were aware of the flabby, defenseless and dead nudity concealed by the *Feldgrau* of the German uniform, the German army could not frighten even the weakest and most defenseless people. A mere boy would dare to face an entire German batallion.'[45]

Fussell's two other points are: firstly, that in the poetry of the First World War, the bather is invariably a private soldier, watched and described by an officer; and secondly, that such scenes belong to an English tradition of voyeuristic arts, consolidated at the end of the nineteenth century by such painters as Henry Scott Tuke (and in the United States, we might add, by Eakins and Bellows), as well as by most of the poets known as the Uranians.[46] I can make no substantial addition to Fussell's argument, other than by adding to it two further examples of bathing scenes.

During the First World War, Jean Cocteau was a member of an ambulance unit, one of the purposes of which was to provide washing and de-lousing facilities for the troops. What Francis Steegmuller calls 'a certain amount of photographing naked soldiers in the mobile showers' must have inspired the remarkable poem 'La Douche', where white and black limbs set off eachother's beauty and are given an erotic glaze by the constant flow of clean water.[47]

A poem by Lieutenant P.W.R. Russell, called 'Midday Swim –

Mersa Matrŭh', is special for its conformity to type. The officer watches as a tanned and muscular youth, standing in the water, reaches out to the sun and cries out, with utterly convincing banality, 'O God – it's great to be alive'. The implication is, of course, that he will soon be dead.[48]

In the twelfth-century *Roman d'Alisandre*, Alexander the Great and his troops restore themselves to vigour by bathing in the fountain of youth. When our modern soldiers bathe, no such facility is available. Rejuvenation is merely cosmetic – a washing away of the grime that wrinkles young faces – since the naked body of the watched youth announces nothing so clearly as two facts: its potential as lover's flesh is lost, and its future as corpse is assured.

CHAERONEA

In his essay 'A Problem in Modern Ethics', John Addington Symonds supported the assertion that Walt Whitman's poetry recalls the story of the Theban Band, by quoting Whitman's 'I Dream'd in a Dream', the end of 'To the East and to the West', and the beginning of 'For You O Democracy'.[49] Two lines from 'Over the Carnage Rose Prophetic a Voice' would have been as apt: 'Be not dishearten'd, affection shall solve the problems of freedom yet, / Those who love each other shall become invincible', as the boys in the Band were meant to be. But explicit allusions to this relatively obscure moment in Greek history are more likely to be made by the products of British public schools, with their detailed classical education, than by the likes of Whitman. So, it is Symonds himself who spells out the relevance of the Sacred Band, in 'The Song of Love and Death', which was written in Whitman's honour and dates from about 1875. Here, Symonds heralds a new era of comradeship and homo-erotic chivalry, to whose adherents he gives the following promise:

> Stirred from their graves to greet your Sacred Host
> The Theban lovers, rising very wan,
> By death made holy, wave dim palms, and cry:
> 'Hail, Brothers! who achieve what we began!'[50]

The note of holiness is not gratuitous. Where once the monastery of Gembloux took the entire Sacred Band, *en masse*, as its patron saints, Symonds now commandeers them as his own. The army of lovers is used as both patron and precedent for the incipient movement towards the public acceptance of male love. In the mid-1890s, there operated a British group called the Order of Chaeronea, intended, according to Jeffrey Weeks, 'both as a support group for its members and as the focus for homosexual resistance and reform campaigns'.[51] Its members included such notable Uranian poets as Samuel Elsworth Cottam, George Ives, Charles Kains Jackson, John Gambrill Nicholson, and Montague Summers. Laurence Housman was, certainly, a member; his brother A.E. Housman was, possibly, another.

Even the more recent political scene has found it hard to resist the vivid image of the army of lovers. The West German director, Rosa von Praunheim's filmed history of the Gay Movement in the United States is called *Army of Lovers or the Revolt of the Perverts* (1979). On the annual Gay Pride March in San Francisco in 1979, at least one banner read: 'An army of lovers cannot be defeated'.[52] In their column in a gay periodical, Lige Clarke and Jack Nichols gave the following reply to a letter from a G.I. in Vietnam: 'Dig this vision: thousands of soldiers moving – naked – in the steaming jungles, carrying – not guns – but their own genitals, and getting closer to one another in the dark. A saner pattern by far than any war.'[53] The new army of lovers fights, with love, only for peace. In the same vein, Allen Ginsberg writes of 'the joy of armies naked / fucking on the battlefield'.[54]

The story of the battle of Chaeronea relies for much of its effect on the beauty of a field paved with dead young men. This common theme in the literature of war is little more than an illusionistic trick, in which the horror of severed limbs and punctured torsos evaporates. But the trick is none the less effective, for all its shameless gloss. Remember 'The Rime of the Ancient Mariner' (IV):

The many men so beautiful!
And they all dead did lie[.]

The dead must be beautiful, if we are to honour them and do justice to our love for them. If possible, they should be more beautiful than the living. In Wilfred Owen's poems, the dead seem beautified by the need to establish themselves in the security of pleasant memory. In 'Has Your Soul Sipped?' Owen declares that nothing sweeter exists than the threatless smile on the lips of a murdered boy. The fragment 'As Bronze May Be Much Beautified' speaks of the lustre a man gains in death. And the whole of 'Greater Love' is concerned with contrasting the living and the dead, to the disadvantage of the former.[55] Rupert Brooke plays down the carnage of war to an extraordinary extent, in 'The Dead', by making Ganymedes of the newly dead, as they pour out 'the red / Sweet wine of youth'.[56] A sentence from the seventh part of George Macbeth's 'A Poet's Life' is truer to the ways in which war is treated by its recorders than to the actual horror it involves: 'All around the exploding shells / destroy mere boys in attractive / postures that war artists / can make romantic.' Macbeth's pointed comment is: 'The poet is not destroyed'.[57]

More recent visions have not deviated from the accepted pattern. Robert Duncan's poetic essay on the Korean War mentions 'The dead by the roadside /beautifully naked, left over / that the old may grieve'.[58] However, if any corpse of recent years stands out as having particular glamour, it is that of Che Guevara, photographs of which were reproduced on posters to grace bedroom walls throughout the Western world. Andrew Sinclair's study of Che contains two telling sentences on his charisma. Firstly: 'Che was not only one of the more heroic men of his age; he was also one of the more intelligent, more original, more ascetic, more radical, more human and more beautiful men of his age.' And secondly, Sinclair's final sentence: 'For the rich nations of the earth, and for the corrupt governments that rule many of the poor nations, the dead Che is a terrible and beautiful enemy'.[59] The beauty is the rub: it never faded into middle age. Allen Ginsberg's 'Elegy Che Guevara' speaks of a 'young feminine beardless radiant kid / lain back smiling looking upward / Calm as if ladies' lips were kissing invisible parts of the body' in the famous photographs of his 'reposeful angelic boy corpse'.[60]

The beauty of the dead is further enhanced by the special magic of moonlight, which somehow conceals and enables one to forget war's horror. After one of many small victories in his campaign, T.E. Lawrence went down at night to inspect the Turkish dead, and found them stripped of arms and clothing by the Arab victors. 'The dead men looked wonderfully beautiful. The night was shining gently down, softening them into new ivory. Turks were white-skinned on their clothed parts, much whiter than the Arabs; and these soldiers had been very young. Close round them lapped the dark wormwood, now heavy with dew, in which the ends of moonbeams sparkled like sea-spray'.[61] Considering that these men have all been shot or stabbed to death, the scene is remarkably lacking in clotting blood and matted hair, severed limbs and smashed skulls. The new ivory of their flesh is altogether too clean. But, of course, the necessary gore would not be pertinent to Lawrence's mood, and must be left, at most, implicit. Lawrence notices the nakedness and youth of the dead men, and writes as if they were satisfied lovers, merely asleep.

The cosmetic function of moonlight is widely exploited, to this same end. Even the trenches, according to Edmund Blunden's 'Illusions', can seem lovely 'in the moonlight, in the lulling moonlight'.[62] When his own care has proved to no avail, Whitman calls on the moon's greater skills, so that the 'ghastly, swollen, purple' faces of the newly dead may be calmed by its sacred light.[63] However, the moon has many moods, and as many functions, in addition to the cosmetic. Sometimes, it is a detached observer; but, more often, it exerts a sinister control on men, as if in league with death. In Giuseppe Ungaretti's 'Watch', it cruelly illuminates the clenched teeth of a comrade's skull; and in 'The Captain', by the same poet, the moon seems to have stage-managed the events leading to a soldier's death in the First World War.[64] In poems from the Second World War, Keith Douglas feels the moon interfering cynically with lovers and the 'Dead Men' of his title; and John Berryman, examining relationships between 'The Moon and the Night and the Men', describes the intrusive moon as both cold and violent. In 'Christ in the Hospital', Roy Campbell's seems to be a very different moon from Lawrence's: it is now 'a soldier with a bleeding eye'.[65]

Men's memories of war – and, therefore, the art they will make of it in peace-time – concern friendships. It would be hard to find a single memoir which does not do so (if one's inclination were to try). Fear 'gains each David his Jonathan', according to David Jones' *In Parenthesis*.[66] As Dunstan Thompson says in 'Field Music', a series depicting soldiers as lovers, 'whether / You are brave, or live / By discrete cowardice, together / With all soldiers, you love'.[67] Any army in action, then, is an army of lovers of a sort. Fear may be their mover, but what it arouses is love none the less.

ICHINOTANI

Beyond the partisan comradeship which exists between members of any one army, another form of erotic association is postulated, if not always enacted, by the poet of war: the love of foe for foe. When commanded both to 'Love thine enemy' and to shoot at him, men seem remarkably able (in retrospect, at least) to separate the individual foe – with whom they empathise, since he, too, is an unwilling pawn, acting under orders – from the representative of an alien nation or political system; and, therefore, to shoot the representative. If the individual happens to be a beautiful youth, as is so often the case, the inclination is to shoot him with the metaphorical pistol, or stab with the metaphorical bayonet, rather than with the actual. Usually, however, the outcome is that of the incident at Ichinotani: the individual is sacrificed to the need to kill the representative; and the actual weapon is used, after all.

We have seen how, in a sequel to the tale of the Japanese battle, Kumagai meets the ghost of Atsumori, whom he killed, whereupon the two are united in the love their first meeting conceived. This is the pattern followed by Wilfred Owen in one of the finest of his war lyrics, 'Strange Meeting'.[68] In Hell, Owen meets the man he bayonetted only yesterday, yet is recognised and approached by him as a friend. The dead German's speech and the poem both end with the line 'Let us sleep now. . .', which seems to have been a tentative afterthought on Owen's part. But this element is taken by Benjamin Britten as an emphatic and affirmative climax. Britten's *War Requiem*, opus 66, (1962) uses as its verbal text nine of Owen's poems, interspersed with the Latin of the Requiem Mass. Its final part, the 'Libera me', consists of 'Strange Meeting', sung by tenor and baritone, followed by the 'In Paradisum', by boys, soprano, and chorus. Through the latter part, the tenor and baritone sing, over and over again, the climactic 'Let us sleep now', as if the duet of amorous proposition were of more significance than sleep itself.

Sleep is always an equivocal image for death. The individual corpse, when merely sleeping, might dream, perchance; and a couple of corpses, sleeping, might wake up at any moment, to resume the love-making which exhausted them in the first place. One could lie down beside Rimbaud's 'Dormeur du val', and rouse his sleeping beauty with a kiss. Even where living soldiers are concerned, sleep is an effective escape from war and entry to the proper realm of love. In '1916 Seen from 1921', Edmund Blunden remembers an idyllic spot to which he and his 'friend of friends' used to go, to 'snatch long moments from the grudging wars' by crawling into the long grass and falling asleep together.[69] In *Miracle de la Rose*, Jean Genet describes two sleeping youths, in a brief passage which provides us with a convenient (if coincidental) gloss on Owen's vision of shared sleep: 'Ces deux coeurs dormants régnaient endormis et s'adoraient derrière le mur épais de leur sommeil. Ainsi s'aiment les guerriers morts qui s'entretuèrent.'[70]

Stephen Spender extends war's intimacy to cover the relationship, not only between opposed individuals, but also between opposed armies. Remembering his reactions to the Spanish Civil War, and in particular to the situation along the Madrid front, he writes: 'Suddenly the front seemed to me like a love relationship between the two sides, locked here in their opposite trenches, committed to one another unto death, unable to separate, and for a visitor to intervene in their deathly orgasm seemed a terrible frivolity.'[71] Transferred to verse, this insight informs his description of 'Two Armies'. While they sleep, 'a common suffering / Whitens the air with breath and makes both one / As though these enemies slept in each other's arms'.[72] In a more recent poem, Paul Muldoon likens the men who, at Christmas during the First World War, ventured into No-Man's-Land for a friendly celebration, to 'Friday night lovers' who, 'when it's over / Might get up from their mattresses / To congratulate each other / And exchange names and addresses'.[73]

However, it is not when armies are at rest that the image of the beloved enemy is at its most potent; but when individuals are pitted against one another in violent action. In D.H. Lawrence's 'Eloi, Eloi, Lama Sabachthani?' one soldier stabs another as if fucking him, and says, 'I, the lover, am consummate, / And he is the bride, I have sown him with the seed / And planted and fertilized him'[74] He is speaking of the seed of death – that same seed which, in Robert Duncan's 'Up Rising', takes a new and more deadly form, in the image of 'the all-American boy in the cockpit / loosing his flow of napalm'.[75] Death is a beautiful youth, acting out his given role, like the young man in the second of Dunstan Thompson's 'Songs of the Soldier', 'his sex a star'.[76]

When Whitman mourns the fact that 'my enemy is dead, a man as divine as myself is dead', and when he lightly kisses the dead man's face, he pays homage to the beauty of both the dead man himself and the concept which is the poem's title, 'Reconciliation'. This brings me to the final aspect of the loved enemy, and returns us to one of my original points: that it is preferable metaphorically to 'shoot' a beautiful youth than actually to gun him down. In this context, the enemy-as-lover has an immediate purpose, which is to persuade the reader that harmony is greater than enmity, love finer than war. The relative scarcity of this erotic theme in the literature of the Pacific half of the Second World War, of the Korean War and of the Vietnam War may be explained, I suspect, in terms of an unstated sexual racism, which magnanimously grants the Asian enemy the respect due a human being, and the right to life, but not the visual beauty required of a warrior-lover. I have found only one whole-hearted commitment to the sexiness of the Asian enemy, in an otherwise undistinguished poem by Konstantin Berlandt, 'Bring the Beautiful Boys Home', which ends with these lines: 'Beautiful Vietnamese man / Let's suck and fuck / Let's not kill each other any more / I love you brother / You're my buddy / We're gonna die tomorrow / I want to hold your cock and / make it feel good tonight / I want to put my cock in your body / and feel together with you / tonight.'[77]

Always approximate to this theme – that men should love rather than kill eachother – is another: that all men are better suited to love than to enmity, and that a soldier is a lover miscast. Referring to soldiers, in a poem called 'Autumn 1942', Roy Fuller wrote: 'Only events, with which they wrestle, can / Transfigure them or make them other than / Things to be loved or hated and soon dead'.[78] Adherents to our present theme might not see the need for the intervention of events. Whatever happens, they argue, the living soldier has been torn out of his natural context, which is peaceful and erotic; and, whatever happens, the dead soldier is a great loss, because he is a loss to love. To kill is to kill love. So, in Keith Douglas' 'How to Kill', a member of the damned professes amusement at seeing, in the killing of a man, 'the centre of love diffused / and the waves of love travel into vacancy'.[79] To conscript young men, according to Robert Duncan's 'The Soldiers', is to drive them from their 'beds of first love' to die for the sentiments of other men's political oratory.[80] The poetry is in the wastage: for nothing could be more pitiable than the hands of Herbert Read's soldiers: 'Hands wasted for love and poetry', which, instead of holding penis or pen, 'finger the hostile gunmetal'.[81] In a journal entry dated 22 June 1940, Keith Vaughan takes the sentiments of these poems to the explicit conclusion of the emotion their theme evokes. 'A soldier sits opposite you in the train', he writes. 'His mouth always open a little. Lips that were never meant to feel each other. His hands that you keep looking at – big and straight and generous. His body big and strong, harnessed over like a circus horse with brass and khaki. You felt you could love him? An impossible yearning to protect him – to put yourself between his clean body and the savage mechanism of destruction. Just to save this one fragment of the earth's springtime from being stamped out utterly.'[82]

But, when the observed youth is dead, that 'impossible yearning' turns to grief. Death emphasises the loss of love, if nothing else; and a common lament emerges. In 'Necrography', Yannis Ritsos calls the 'young and exuberant' faces of the dead 'more suited to beds of love' than to their places of rest on a beach. A shot man, in Robert Duncan's 'A Spring Memorandum: Fort Knox', attracts the remark, 'He might have been loved'. In the case of the boy in Stephen Spender's 'Ultima Ratio Regum', the elegiac remark is, 'He was a better target for a kiss'. Dylan Thomas parodies Spender with a poem in which the dead man's hands 'should have held in peace / A girl's two kind ones in a public park', and a gun is a 'cold threat to love'. In 'Vergissmeinnicht', Keith Douglas comments, on a German's rotting corpse, that 'here the lover and killer are mingled / who had one body and one heart. / And death who had the soldier singled / has done the lover mortal hurt'. While the soldier is trained to kill and expected to be killed, and therefore receives death as a necessary factor in his self-definition, the lover within the same man is denied and destroyed. Edward Thomas' poem, 'In Memoriam (Easter, 1915)', mourns the men who should be back from the war, picking flowers with their sweethearts. An 'Epitaph' by Edwin Muir gives some prominence to the fact that 'He was never truly loved nor truly a lover'. As extreme as its miraculous complement in Christian myth, Virgin Death is treated as the greatest tragedy to befall any man, and war's worst hurt.[83]

If the man who dies is one's own lover or comrade, grief is all the keener than for the loss of a beautiful but anonymous stranger. The extreme distress of Achilles when he learns of the death of Patroclus, and Roland's swoon when he sees Olivier dead, prefigure such poems as Robert Nichols' 'Fulfilment', in which the poet forgets both the woman he used to love and whatever grief he used to experience, in the intensity of his newer love for a comrade and newer grief at that comrade's death. The same poet's 'Plaint of Friendship by Death Broken' is in a similar vein: 'In him I had happiness. But he is dead.'[84] In 'Casualty', a later poem, Nichols wishes he could lie beneath and embrace his dead comrade, thereby warming the corpse back to life.[85] But a poem from the Vietnam War, by Basil T. Paquet, shows the futility of this hope, in its account of an attempt to revive a man with the so-called kiss of life. The poet says to the corpse: 'You are dead just as finally / As your mucosity dries on my lips / In this morning sun. / I have thumped and blown into your kind too often, / I grow tired of kissing the dead.'[86]

So, Ted Hughes' dead, who, in 'Griefs for Dead Soldiers', 'wait like brides / To surrender their limbs',[87] may find comfort, not in the living, but only in their fellow dead – as we saw in Owen's 'Strange Meeting'. A pietà is an enactment of division: that of the vertical figure from the horizontal, the quick from the inert. Only when the dead lie in eachother's arms is any lasting harmony achieved. Their implied 'Let us sleep now' is some consolation for the manner of their strange meeting.

* * *

I have deliberately not considered our century's wars separately. In the themes they bring to poetry, they prove to have more in common than people acknowledge. Here, however, we must defer to the possibility of difference. Paul Fussell sees in the poetry of the First World War a 'unique physical tenderness', coupled with a 'readiness to admire openly the bodily beauty of young men' and 'the unapologetic recognition that men may be in love with each other'. These elements, he suggests, are absent from the poetry of the Second World War, because the later poets had become self-conscious about such matters, associating them with the areas of 'abnormality' probed by the likes of Krafft-Ebing and Freud, whose texts had been partially assimilated into popular culture during the inter-war period.[88]

However, in its attitudes to horror as well as to beauty, the poetry of the First World War is more concerned with physical detail than that of the Second, as Mildred Davidson has mentioned.[89] One reason for this may be the static nature of the First World War, in which the individual soldier had only his own perspective on the hostilities: a few yards of mud and barbed wire. Intact or broken, perforce, the next man's flesh took up a large percentage of the view. Furthermore, the Second World War involved all generations and both sexes directly. So, able-bodied young men lost some of the attention. This is not to say, however – as Fussell seems to be suggesting – that the Second World War did not provide its share of comradely love poems. Of this, the various volumes of A.L. Rowse's poems are representative disproof.

We cannot overlook, either, the fact that the functions of the so-called war poets have changed, during a century in which the status quo has to some extent consisted of change. Siegfried Sassoon used his poetic abilities to present the jingoistic British public with a true and appropriately melodramatic picture of the horrors of the Western front. Why should anyone even begin to perform such a task, by sending poems home from Vietnam, when that war's iniquities had become already the commonplace fare of televised news bulletins? In fact, the poet of the Vietnam war generally sought to come to terms with the grey pictures which flickered endlessly in a corner of his bedroom. Given the public, exhibitionistic nature of the fighting, we need not expect the memorial function of the poetry of that war to operate quite as did that of the First and Second World Wars. When a nation flies its dead home as efficiently as the United States did from Vietnam, retrospective paper headstones are not needed to commemorate lost corpses; and when a man dies on film, one need not publicise his death in written stanzas months later.

Many individual poems from the earlier conflicts bear, as title or subtitle, the names or initials of a dead comrade, together with the dates of his birth and death, and, sometimes, the place of his death. After the end of the war in question volumes of poems and memoirs appear, with such inscriptions in the place of a dedication to lover or wife. For instance, David Jones' *In Parenthesis* (1937) is in memory of, among others, a lewis-gunner killed in action near Ypres, and Fussell's *The Great War and Modern Memory* (1975) is inscribed to the memory of a sergeant who was killed beside Fussell in France in 1945. In lieu of elegy, it seems, a gravestone will do. Given the twenty- and thirty-year gaps between the deaths concerned and the respective publication dates of Jones' and Fussell's tributes, there is no question of actual forgetfulness. But it seems important that commemoration should at least be seen to consolidate memory.

When two ancient Celtic armies met in battle, the poets of both sides would repair to a nearby hill, to discuss and assess the hostilities. This custom has fallen into disuse. Our poets are either thrown in with the warriors, or, just as often, left at home to regret myopia or flat feet. But, whatever their situation, they are no less the spectators of conflict – even when closely involved – than were the bards. Certain types of symbolic conflict often relate to their poets in a similar way, and it is to them, to sporting activities, that I now turn.

SPORTSMANSHIP

Since certain forms of sporting activity are, clearly, analogous to warfare, which in turn shares characteristics with sexual relations, we may expect to find a workable series of analogies between sport and sex. From Denis de Rougemont's *Passion and Society*, we can take a general statement and a corroborative example as a suitable beginning for a brief study of the subject. 'Sportive struggles always and everywhere contain a strong dramatic and an erotic element. In the medieval tournament these two elements had so much got the upper hand, that its character of a contest of force and courage had been almost obliterated by its romantic purport'.[90] The same has happened to some extent in the case of the modern wrestling bout.

In his study of *Greek Homosexuality*, K.J. Dover observes that experts in his field often misinterpret depictions of 'a typical pair of males engaged in intercrural copulation' as wrestling scenes.[91] In many cases, no doubt, the error is a deliberate bowdlerisation. But, if genuine, it can be excused: for many visual and verbal depictions of homosexual intercourse do, indeed, approximate those of wrestling bouts; and vice versa. Both involve physical proximity and strain, as well as a degree of nudity. The depiction of both usually focusses on youths in their physical prime, since both subjects are concerned with the beauty of the male body at its best. The exertions and intimacies of both make each a suitable metaphor for the other. Furthermore, the metaphoric resonance of each makes confusion with the other a constant factor in the interpretative process, fully understood and often exploited by the artist – sometimes, indeed, by the participants themselves. The interpretative 'error', therefore, can often be seen as a natural and desirable reaction to the ambiguous material it is said to distort.

The approximation of wrestling to sexual intercourse is most often expressed in the elementary simile, comparing wrestlers with lovers and lovers with wrestlers. A pet referential myth, in this context, since angels are beautiful men, is that of Jacob, who wrestled all night with the angel of God (Genesis 32.24–30). See, for instance, the eighth poem of Paul Goodman's *A Diary of Makapuu*, and Thom Gunn's 'Wrestling'. James Kirkup's 'All-In Wrestlers' mentions 'two great men battling like lovers'. Mutsuo Takahashi writes of 'Two slim wrestlers / entwined like boys making love', and of 'Wrestlers simulating love-making'. Watching the students on a wrestling team, he is moved to exclaim, 'Oh how they resemble those making love!' Takahashi uses the wrestler as the epitome of male fitness and beauty, as likely to take to homosexual intercourse as to his own sport, and as likely to excel. So, when he speaks of the 'male breasts, sexual as a wrestler's', he means that the body to which he refers is eminently suited to the wrestling ring, and, therefore, to a lover's bed.[92]

Wrestling is a 'safe' activity, in both life and art, bearing none of the weight of the taboo against homosexual intercourse. As such, wrestling can be used as a cover for sex. The one is, merely, an acceptable version of the other. There is a tradition, by which two supposedly heterosexual buddies may fight each other and in the heat of the contest, somehow, switch their athletic focus from limbs to groin. They may reach orgasm together, without in any way exchanging their roles of heterosexual buddies for those of homosexual lovers. After all, combat is combat. Wrestling is, therefore, the heterosexually acceptable form of homosexual foreplay. Semen can be showered off men's bellies afterwards, as if it were, merely, a wetter kind of sweat. For these reasons, fellatio and anal intercourse, those infallible signs of homosexual passion, rarely have a place in the gymnasia of heterosexual homosexuality. Clinch and hold take technical precedence. Intercrural and intercorporal convulsions, since they do not involve the entry of one man by the other, are permitted; as is mutual masturbation, by virtue of its use of that unquestionably virile weapon, the clenched fist. Kissing, of course, is against the rules.

One of best-known depictions of the American adolescent's way of wrestling comes at the start of Gore Vidal's *The City and the Pillar*. While staying in the country, Bob and Jim go down to the water hole and undress for a swim. Bob pauses to contemplate his own reflection in the water, then admires Jim's tan. In the water, they wrestle. Later, beside the camp fire, they wrestle again: 'Pushing and pulling, they fought for position; they were evenly matched, because Jim, though stronger, would not allow Bob to lose or win'. In the heat, they undress, and prepare to wrestle yet again; but this time, they make love, entering the conventions of Platonic discourse: 'Now they were complete, each becoming the other, as their bodies collided with a primal violence, like to like, metal to magnet, half to half and the whole restored'. Afterwards, they swim again, to wash away the semen and the sin; but embrace again, when they get back to the camp fire. The American boy's love of 'horseplay' excuses itself.[93]

From this type of sexual fun can come neither congratulatory odes, in the manner of Pindar, to celebrate outright victories, nor the weighty pretensions of the wrestling scene in Lawrence's *Women in Love*. Also alien to the modern tradition, if not unrelated, are the ritualistic clinches and throws with which the future lovers Enkidu and Gilgamesh introduce themselves to each other. Sexual wrestling must not, nor does it aspire to, ascend to the seriousness of decisive victory, which divides. Its essential power is in fun. When Francis Bacon turns one of Eadweard Muybridge's photographs of wrestling men into an image of apparent enmity, for worse or for better, he robs the subject of its weightless sexiness.

Like the barracks, the prison, and the boys' school, the fields and locker rooms of men's sport have acquired actual and literary status as suitable arenas for homo-erotic impulse and activity. Also, like members of the armed forces, sportsmen are required to wear certain types of clothing, which over the years have gained an erotic momentum of their own. That quintessentially sexy item of dress, the jock-strap, is its merely functional equivalent, the athletic support, only in the politest of society. The sporting scenario is relied on heavily by the pornography of male homosexuality, and by the sexual fantasies of men in general. Gore Vidal says, 'the only time when the heteros may openly enjoy what they secretly dream of' is when 'watching handsome young men playing body contact games'.[94]

Many men would have to agree with the suggestion that their sporting activities are at least partially motivated by erotic self-interest. The requirements of general fitness tend to duplicate those of sexual desirability. By jogging daily, or by regularly working out at the local gym, a man deliberately makes himself fitter and prettier, healthier and sexier. This concern may be casual, or, as in the case of the central characters in John Rechy's novels, obsessive; but the difference is merely quantitative, and both types of work-out have the same qualitative aims. Another reason for body-building and physical training has to do with traditional confusion about sexual role and the appearance of 'real' men. A strong, fast, muscular man is reckoned to be beyond accusations of homosexuality. He can kick sand in other men's faces. Even Rechy's homosexual heroes dread being identifiably homosexual, to other men on the make: for to be the stereotype – the mincing and limp-wristed faggot – would be to become undesirable to men like themselves, the men they most desire. As long as such men are 'virile' and associate only with other 'virile' men, they allow themselves a good deal of homosexual latitude, just so long as their fun does not speak its name.

One of the points Gore Vidal wanted to emphasise, in writing *The City and the Pillar*, was that homosexuality was not 'a form of mental disease, confined for the most part to interior decorators and ballet dancers', as it was then (and is still, to some extent) thought to be.[95] He therefore chose as his central character Jim Willard, 'a completely ordinary boy of the middle class'. Then, as if to underline the lack of causal connection between heterosexuality and conventional 'virility' – of which sporting ability was considered a reliable sign – he gave Willard an excellent backhand at tennis. Thus, the portrait of the acceptable homosexual man was completed. Vidal returned to this subject in a short story, 'The Zenner Trophy', about a youth who is thrown out of school for committing a homosexual offence. His transgression is particularly amazing to the members of staff who discuss it, because he was due to be awarded 'The Carl F. Zenner Award for clean sportsmanship, our highest honour'. Instead, the award goes to some lesser sport.[96] Other notable treatments of related themes include Francis King's *A Domestic Animal* and Patricia Nell Warren's *The Front Runner*, respectively concerned with soccer and track athletics.

A youth's first awareness of the beauty of sportsmen comes when he is still at school, where such influences as the 'colours' system cause the athletes among the senior boys to be set apart from their fellows, and to be valued more highly than the academics. From a junior's point of view, the top of the hierarchy always comprises the athletes, never the academics. Edward Carpenter describes the familiar consequence, recalling his own schooldays: 'I worshipped the very ground on which some, generally elder, boys stood; they were heroes for whom I would have done anything. I dreamed about them at night, absorbed them with my eyes in the day, watched them at cricket, loved to press against them unnoticed in a football melly, or even to get accidentally hurt by one of them at hockey, was glad if they just spoke to me or smiled; but never got a word farther with it all.'[97]

The narrator of Mishima's *Confessions of a Mask* watches with both sexual desire and burning envy, as an older youth, Omi, exercises on the horizontal bar in the school gym. The envy is for the strength in Omi's arms and shoulders, and the abundance of hair in his muscular armpits. The description is detailed and enthusiastic. It is not quite as if each of these thickets conceals a sexual orifice; but the implication they offer is, certainly, that Omi's genitals are as richly adorned as his armpits, and as 'muscular' (which is to say, well developed).[98] A similar display of gymastic skills and sexual potential, if less of hair, is given (in slow motion) by an older and watched by a younger boy, in Lindsay Anderson's film *If. . .* (In this case, the relationship between athlete and spectator is, eventually, consummated.)

But the essence of schoolboy eroticism is most divertingly caught in the game of cricket; and in the environment to which it belongs, the English public school. Unlike (say) footballers, cricketers are sexy only when still adolescent, and still subject to school rules. Cricket has a central atmospheric function, therefore, in such homo-erotically informed novels as Michael Campbell's *Lord Dismiss Us* and Simon Raven's *Fielding Gray*, as well as in many of Auden's early poems. In T.C. Worsley's autobiography, a chapter on his cricketing experiences at school is entitled 'Eros, Without Sex'. To him, the game was 'a kind of pagan religious rite' and the team for which he kept wicket had 'a kind of homo-erotic liaison binding it together'. As part of the atmosphere of a school term in which he was developing a romance with another boy, Simon Raven recalls 'long hours of cricket in the sun (oh, those white flannels and the faint, sweet smell of sweat)'. According to Cyril Connolly's memories of his own schooldays, boys were expected to have 'character', a virtue combining sporting ability with prettiness. It was boys of 'character' who, to the delight of their lesser fellows, punctuated the 'pagan' summer afternoons at Eton with the sounds of bat hitting ball. None of its connotations of Empire and imperial ruling class can interfere with the essentially pastoral quality of the game and its leisurely pace. Furthermore, no matter when a scene involving cricket is set, it will always seek to imitate the conditions of a match played before the outbreak of the First World War – in Brooke's Grantchester, perhaps, or Housman's Shropshire. The innocence of the young cricketer is marred only symbolically, and slightly, when gentle athleticism gets the knees of his whites stained with grass.[99]

A less likely success in this field of erotic imagery is tennis. Nijinsky's ballet, *Jeux*, which was first danced on 15 May 1913, to music by Debussy, involved two women and a man (Nijinsky himself) as tennis players. Nijinsky's diary reveals that this was a euphemistic representation of Diaghilev's often expressed fantasy of making love to two men at once. Paul Goodman's poem 'Lloyd (September 9, 1941)' describes how he was put off his game when his youthful opponent kept stroking himself in the groin. Goodman retaliated, by serving a direct hit on the area concerned; whereupon the game had to end, and an examination of the hurt to begin. Finally, Paul Muldoon's 'How to Play Championship Tennis' is a parable contrasting two types of homosexual relationship. The school caretaker arranges to give a pupil a tennis manual, but at the apparent cost of some kind of sexual encounter. Bookless, the boy escapes. As he does so, he catches sight of Joe and Cyril, the objects of much teasing by the other boys, lobbing a tennis ball to each other over the absent net – 'As if they had found some other level'. Playing

without net or manual, they manage a natural fluency of rela-
tionship, exempt from guilt and oblivious to insult.[100]

The image of the sportsman as a potential lover has its origins, of
course, in the institutionalised athleticism of ancient Greece; and,
therefore, allows the homosexual poet a respectable – because
'classical' – means of expressing admiration for male flesh. Just as
Pindar's odes were as much love poems to their subjects as hymns
praising athletic prowess, so modern poets can combine in one work
detached admiration with involved desire. Walter Pater's essay on
'The Age of Athletic Prizemen', from *Greek Studies* (1895), is a
statement as much of erotic interest in the subjects of statues like the
Discobolus as of aesthetic interest in the statues *qua* statues.
Housman's 'To an Athlete Dying Young' is a serious fictionalisation
of history, made palatable by its very real concern for the death of an
adolescent male; or a culpably sentimental pederastic ode, made
publishable by its historical seriousness.[101] George Santayana's
'Athletic Ode', also set in classical times, combines historical and
erotic interests in a similar fashion.[102] Whitman's 'The Runner',
although not explicitly in this tradition, was one of the least
controversial of his homo-erotic poems, since it admired muscles
which were as functional – because they belonged to an athlete – as
sexy.

In a few poems, the Uranians took what opportunity of erotic
subterfuge the sporting theme afforded. For instance, in *An
Appendix* (1929), Ralph Chubb describes a boxing bout between
two boys, with all the more enthusiasm because he is due to sleep
with the loser and his bruises. And Edward Cracroft Lefroy
addressed a sonnet to a young goal keeper, wishing he were poet
enough to transpose the boy's artless 'Sinew and breath and body'
into his art, which might then live. But the Uranians preferred to stick
to their favourite sporting arena, the pool or shore, where the naked
athleticism of swimmers inspired paintings and poems galore.[103]

Perhaps the most exuberant of the lovers of sportsmen is James
Kirkup, whose mind seems to fill with richly erotic puns at the first
thought of athleticism. In 'Sporting Man', a footballer 'dribbles' and
'shoots' from the loins, in order to conquer the goalie and earn a kiss
from each of his team-mates. (As it happens, two of them betray their
fear of appearing homosexual, by merely slapping the goal-scorer on
the back.) Playing 'Ice-hockey in Dalarna', men 'shoot wet stars into
the teeth of night', as though fellated, not only by their opponents,
but also by the entranced masses of their spectators. And in certain
'Football Action Photographs', rugby players appear to grapple
longingly with each other in 'a lusty pack', one of them every now
and then clutching by mistake 'Not what his safe hands intended'. All

of which goes to confirm that the sports field is pre-eminently the place 'where enemy is friend' and war is love.[104]

As finishing touch to this subject, I shall quote from Edward Dorn's 'Inauguration Poem 2', in which Dorn writes of the University of Alabama's football team, as follows:

they take the sperm of a universe they want to deny
into their open uptilted mouths every time they play, it drips
whether he knows it or not
across the white pearly acres of the quarterback's teeth,
that is the field he truly plays upon, there is where
those signals are called.[105]

The sportsmen evoke a sexual response in their spectators, in order to satisfy their own desires; but, like the resolutely 'heterosexual' man who regards his homosexual experience as mere 'horseplay', with no bearing on his actual sexual orientation, these sportsmen deny the erotic nature of their game, even to the extent of not tasting the semen in their mouths; that is, without acknowledging a large part of their own pleasure.

But what is the nature of the various sexual exchanges taking place when a match is in progress? The position of the spectators is relatively uncomplicated: they have the status of voyeurs, auto-erotically enjoying the activities of the men they are watching, from which their own activity is distinct. They enact a rather more restrained version of the scene in chapter six of Michael Moorcock's novel, *The Final Programme* (1965), in which the members of the audience of a wrestling match masturbate enthusiastically, as if watching a privately screened pornographic film. For their part, the players are providing the kind of spectacle which Roland Barthes saw in wrestling bouts, and they enjoy the exhibitionism of their role as much as their physical contact with one another. Their thrills are twofold, therefore. As for the nature of their physical activity, it is aggressive to the extent that a sadomasochistic scenario of slave and master is aggressive: the pain may almost be real, but the anger is not. The rules of the encounter exclude the possibility of death. This is controlled war, in which hurt is not final but victory is absolute.

COWBOYS AND SAILORS

One figure most erotically fills the roles of both sportsman and warrior: the American cowboy. His life is popularly represented as a sequence of dramatic duels and feats of horsemanship, with more than its share of both danger and fun. In the movies, from pornography to Saturday matinees, he seems the very essence of masculinity. Hard rider and crack shot, he couldn't but be good in bed. The paraphernalia of his profession – the leather chaps, battered boots, spurs, belt and holsters, even the pistols – are now, perhaps, to be found less often on the range than in the bedroom closet, ready for use. Men dressed only in stetsons and boots, posed against barn doors or hitching posts, commonly grace the pages of erotic magazines for gay men, where hints of violence and the sexual prowess of stallions are used to electrify the dullest physiques.

If the real cowboys could devise for eachother as exquisite a punishment as a 'chapping' – 'a laying on of leather after the manner of ancient disciplinarians, the offender's own pair of chaps sometimes the instrument'[106] – how much more imaginative could the cowboys of pretence, the urban outlaws who concentrate only on the sexual nature of their calling, turn out to be? Poets evoke both the real cowboy and his fake progeny, decorating the original with the sexier aspects of the myths which have grown up around him. Like Edward Dorn's 'Vaquero', he must be good-looking, with white wrists and blue eyes, and 'delicate' enough to be capable of loving. Like Vernon Scannell's 'The Cowboy of the Western World', he must deck those good looks in high-heeled boots, tight trousers, and a shirt of 'a temperate but sexy black'. Like Dorn's Gunslinger, he must have as few scruples about publicly unsheathing from those tight trousers his sexual weapon – to urinate, lengthily and ponderously, like the remarkable actor working to order in Warhol's *Lonesome Cowboys* – as about drawing his gun for the kill. Like Dennis Kelly's Gunslinger, modelled on Dorn's, he may choose to carve a notch in his penis for every man laid, as if in his pistol for each laid out. Like Jack Spicer's *Billy the Kid*, he may be loved by the poet. Like Thomas Meyer's version of Wild Bill Hickok, he may be actively and openly homosexual. Finally, like the 'good looking, clear-eyed boy', who is Michael Ondaatje's version of Billy the Kid, he may actually become, by a painful but glorious metamorphosis, the man-sized phallus which outshoots a mere man.[107]

On Spicer's version, Robert Peters makes the following remarks, as pertinent to other works as to Spicer's:

> Billy the Kid is to Jack Spicer what Adonis, Childe Harold, Alastor, and Werther were to the nineteenth century romantics. Prettify him, forget the fact that B. the Kid was an idiot, a moron, sadist, and incredibly naive; pretend that as symbol for the POET he stands against the bad guys of the outside world who think that poets are faggots or worse and who are out to git 'em; assume that

Billy's body is so pure that he never needs to bathe it – no jockey shorts beneath his tight, worn jeans.

In fact, Peters concludes, 'Billy is Spicer's invention'.[108]

In my chapter on Thom Gunn, the figure of the centaur will lead us to consider that arcane and energetic sexual mode, which passes through humiliation to the proper territories of Sade and Masoch, the *equus eroticus*: lamely, in English, the erotic horse. (Remember the passionate remark of Shakespeare's Cleopatra: 'Oh happy horse, to bear the weight of Antony!') According to Gerald and Caroline Greene, 'now that few people in our huge cities even see horses, let alone ride them for pleasure . . . fewer humans are being ridden . . . around bedrooms any more'.[109] The case seems unproven: for, although we do not see so many horses in the flesh, the screens of our televisions are constantly alive with old Westerns; and, as Parker Tyler showed in his famous essay on the subject, the erotic relation of man and mount in such films is by no means obscure.[110] The cowboy's role cannot be played without his two major props: pistol and steed. (In the bedroom, of course, penis and lover will do.) When Ondaatje's Billy the Kid speaks of 'neck sweat eating at my jeans', and of 'riding naked clothes and boots / and pistol in the air', the explicit reference to horsemanship shifts inevitably into *double entendre*.[111] Little, in fact, has changed since Theognis wrote verses comparing boys with horses.[112]

'The real kinship of the American cowboy', writes Douglas Branch, 'is with the men on that everlasting frontier, the sea.'[113] Both cowboy and sailor are wanderers, involved in strenuous physical labour, for most of the time absent from the company of women. Why sailors should have become more closely associated with homosexuality than other, similar groups is not clear. John Lehmann begins an explanation: 'Attractive young males, of course, herded together and living a purely physical life. . . Then they have freed themselves from the narrow confining limits of shore life, marriage and a family, the society of Mum and Dad, and job mates who have also gone in for the settled breeding game.' Then there is the matter of clothing. Quentin Crisp observes: 'Uniforms appeal to devotees of the fearless man of action. They also pander to the Cophetua complex so prevalent among homosexuals. When any of my friends mentioned that he had met a "divine" sailor he never meant an officer.' Lehmann continues: 'Uniform, yes, uniform also has something to do with it, particularly a sailor's uniform with open neck and bell-bottoms tight round the buttocks. Someone said uniforms were merely another form of nakedness.' Jean Genet says the main purpose of the French Navy is to decorate the coasts of France.[114]

Lehmann moves on from the question of appearance:

Sailors are adventure seekers. Homosexuals are adventure seekers, rejecting the rules that tie conventional society together. Freedom, yes, that's it, they are symbols of freedom, in spite of the fact that they're under close discipline. Perhaps, paradoxically, because of? Then, their closeness to death. The sea as an image of death. The sea as an image of boundless orgasm. All those stories of them being allowed to choose their boyfriends after a warship's been ninety days at sea.

Only in Pound's *Cantos* (II) can a captain claim to run 'a straight ship' when refusing to give 'a young boy loggy with vine-must' a lift. Anywhere else, the ship is an ideal place for male sexual activity and romance. From Melville's *Billy Budd* and *Moby-Dick* to more recent efforts, such as Leo Madigan's *Jackarandy* and William Golding's *Rites of Passage*, fiction, at least, has been convinced of this; and a number of memoirs, notably George Melly's *Rum, Bum and Concertina*, have provided corroborative evidence. Genet's Lieutenant Seblon sums the matter up, in a description of his own constantly pent-up state of desire while on board ship:

La navire dans ses flancs contient des brutes délicieuses, vêtues de blanc et d'azur. Qui choisir parmi ces mâles? A peine aurai-je lâché l'un que je voudrai l'autre. Seule me calme cette pensée qu'il n'existe qu'un marin: le marin. Et chaque individu que je vois n'est que la momentanée représentation – fragmentaire aussi, et réduite – du Marin. . . Chaque matelot qui passe sert à comparer le Marin. Tous les matelots m'apparaissent-ils vivants, présents, à la fois, tous, et aucun d'eux séparément ne serait le marin qu'ils composent et qui ne peut être que dans mon imagination, qui ne peut être qu'en moi et par moi. Cette idée m'apaise. Je possède le Marin.[115]

In 'Yet Another Ode for Sailors', F.D. Blanton makes a complementary, if more concise remark:

A sailor.
Any sailor.
All sailors.[116]

Likewise: a cowboy, any cowboy, all cowboys. As long as he has the appropriate clothing and small talk, any individual can fulfil the requirements of either role, thereby representing all its other players. Although, as Seblon says, the individual always falls short of the magnificent myth, at the height of sexual frenzy one's imagination can make up the discrepancy. The breath of cattle and swell of sea may be unnecessary (indeed, disquieting) embellishments.

3   CHILDLESS FATHERS

THE FUTURE TENSE

'Love', writes Ortega y Gasset, 'is complete when it culminates in a more or less clear desire to leave, as testimony of the union, a child in whom the perfections of the beloved are perpetuated and affirmed. . . The child is neither the father's nor the mother's; he [*sic*] is the personified union of the two and is a striving for perfection modelled after flesh and soul.'[1] It is my intention in this chapter to examine the ways in which this description of love's culmination applies to relationships between men.

Of course, Ortega's statement is an unexceptional example of heterosexual and male chauvinism, wholly in keeping with our general reluctance to attribute any but social and physiological capabilities to love. But if we extend his meaning to include male couples, we may find it still applies: for he is writing not about the actual production of children, but about the desire for them. Furthermore, if we refine his argument by eliminating its insistence on a child – if we accept that some object or symbol other than a child might serve the same purpose, of affirmation and perpetuation – it will easily accommodate the homosexual love affair. Finally, however, it may be that we can accept the statement as it stands, without qualification, in reference to unions both hetero- and homosexual: for myth and metaphor afford access to fecundity even in the midst of apparent barrenness.

The approximate course of this chapter will be as follows. If it is impossible for two homosexual men to produce children together, either may choose to propagate by routine, heterosexual means. But we know of a widespread belief in the possibility of male pregnancy, based on the supposedly magical properties of semen. Failing that, the homosexual man may turn to other (notably, artistic) forms of creativity, which perform many of the same functions as procreation's, thereby bypassing the heterosexual couple. However, love alone, seen as the creative principle, may suffice, as a more than adequate end in itself. . .

Our starting point, then, is impossibility. Reproduction, being dependent on woman, is beyond the immediate capabilities of the homosexual man. During periods of underpopulation, Onanistic withdrawal and Sodomistic intromission were anathamatised for their wrongful priority, of pleasure over productivity; and the notion was successfully put about that true sexual pleasure came only with reproductive intent. Whence, Ortega. To be heterosexual, therefore, is to have the opportunity, which only perverts and priests willingly relinquish, of marrying and starting a family; and to be homosexual, merely, to have lost that opportunity.

A routine version of the joys of parenthood is provided by Bertrand Russell, in his essay on the family in *The Conquest of Happiness* (1930). The production and care of children, he says, is 'psychologically capable of providing the greatest and most enduring happiness that life has to offer'. The reason for this is that 'To be happy in this world, especially when youth is past, it is necessary to feel oneself not merely an isolated individual whose day will soon be over, but part of the stream of life flowing on from the first germ to the remote and unknown future.' Ancestors and descendants stretch out on either side of the happy parent, like arms with which to touch the horizon. The parent develops an interest in, and exerts an influence on the future. On the other hand, any woman or man who, by inclination or force of circumstance, does without parenthood, is liable to regard existence in isolation as trivial and futile; and will become, according to Russell, dissatisfied, listless, and eventually 'desiccated'. We yearn for issue, and pine for lack of it. To leave descendants is to prolong one's life beyond that of one's own body, by an investment of identity in the heterosexual child and its children. Parenthood, like the Philosopher's Stone, secures what Russell calls 'the immortality of the germ-plasm'. For the childless, 'death ends all'. Of this, as we shall see, there is eminent disproof.[2]

When, in his study of *Love in Literature*, Wallace Fowlie writes about 'the homosexual who, of the sex act, knows only its aspect of death and never its meaning of birth', his readings of Arthur Rimbaud and Hart Crane collapse.[3] His point is derived from a common attitude to homosexuality, rather than from the poetry he seeks to elucidate. Furthermore, he considers this supposed knowledge of a deathly aspect of sex to be 'the darkest and most insoluble experience of man' – which, in the aftermath of Auschwitz, is clearly mere rhetoric. If what he claims of homosexual intercourse and what he implies of the poetry it inspires were true in any sense, we might find it surprising that there is no conspicuous sense of finality in homo-erotic poetry, still less any conspiracy of refusal to bear children. On the contrary: much of this material has a marked concern with racial, erotic, and artistic continuance. Indeed, a sense of future sometimes seems a more essential focus to homo-erotic than to hetero-erotic poetry: for, since lack of immediate physical issue is a root of the taboo against homosexual intercourse, the homosexual poet who seeks to assert the virtue of her or his love must project it forward in time, if not crudely to demonstrate its endurance 'until death us do part' and beyond, then at least to suggest that death is not final. The poetic meditations of Saint John of the Cross can be read as extreme examples of this tendency.

In *After Babel*, George Steiner writes: 'Through shared habits of articulate futurity the individual forgets, literally "overlooks", the certainty and absoluteness of his own extinction. Through his constant use of a tense-logic and time-scale beyond that of personal being, private man identifies, however abstractly, with the survival of his species'.[4] If so, projection can be done subtly, in recognition of the functions of future tense, without resort to polemic. The future is not merely bristles on a boy's cheek, or wrinkles on a man's – the symptoms of decay – but afterlife in heaven, love, or art. In Vergil's second eclogue, which inspired Milton's even more future-conscious *Lycidas*, Corydon warns Alexis, since flowers die and berries get eaten, not to rely on his beauty's outlasting present opportunities; and he offers the boy, as an alternative to solitary fading, partnership in a godly, artistic enterprise, learning to sing like Pan.

From the spilt blood of a beautiful youth stems the hyacinth; from the distress of his lovers, poetic lamentation. Bion's *Lament for Adonis* confronts the distressed Cytherea with this definition of the dead youth's immortality: 'There is time enough to come for your grief, / time to weep, time to sorrow, as year succeeds year'.[5] In the weeping is the continuance of life: for panegyric outlasts even the sexiest flesh. Paul Verlaine provides a commonplace Christian instance when, mourning the premature death of Lucien Létinois, he looks forward to 'l'instant si bon de revenir / A lui dans Vous, Jesus, après ma mort dernière'. García Lorca, by repeating inconsolably the hour at which Ignacio Sánchez Mejías died ('a las cinco de la tarde'), infects all future five o'clocks with past significance, thereby fixing as in amber the beauty of the dead man for posterity.

The distance time asserts is more than catalytic. It, too, is wrought into intimacy by the creative power of the artist, while retaining its perspectival character, thus fixing a spatial and temporal ambivalence of proximity and distance within the single work of art. If the artist mentions certain aspects of the past event as those he cannot remember, he comments not on the failure of memory – not, that is, on his relationship with the event – but on the selectivity of his method – on the work of art – since what he claims, truly or not, not to remember must be treated as what he has chosen to leave out. The oblivion of the forgotten, once a memory has been turned into a work of art, becomes that of the ignored. Elegiac poetry puts the blame on time, or gives time the credit, for the poet's expertise; and time is the plaything of only God. So, afterlives in heaven and in art are correlated by their joint kinship with time. This is the implication of Milton's 'fresh woods and pastures new' and of the closing lines of Tennyson's *In Memoriam*.

Of course, the commemoration of love and beauty need not be posthumous. It may be written, as were Shakespeare's sonnets, while the affair is still in progress; or when love, but not the beloved, has died. The love itself may be a memory suddenly recaptured, in a Proustian moment of lucidity, and recorded while fresh, lest it be lost again. The master of this form is Constantine Cavafy. He recalls a brief encounter, or even so insubstantial a sign of his own sexual orientation as a reaction to a face briefly glimpsed between the figures in a crowd, with an obsessive precision which not only fixes the past moment and the present mood, but also accommodates his intimation of artistic immortality, thereby casting as a significant future presence what might have remained an insignificant reaction in the past. Through the flux of memory and forgetfulness, the clockwork precision of the past begets the artistic precision of the future. So, in 'Their Beginning', although the described sexual encounter is both brief and clandestine, and although the two partners leave their secret rendezvous immediately, presumably in separate directions, the poet attributes potential to what has occurred. One of the lovers is an artist, and 'Tomorrow, the next day or years after will be written / The lines of strength that here had their beginning'.[6]

In a thematically similar poem, 'Cast', Yannis Ritsos outlines a man's remembrance of a particular summer, mentally associated with a glimpse he had then, of 'the bare, broad, sunburnt back of a young farmer'; and exactly pinpoints in time the sighting of this monumental image of proletarian wealth, at 2:00 p.m. The protagonist also remembers in detail the warmth, the smells, and the sounds of that moment, as if to prove the truth of his recall. But it is in its final line that the poem's shape emerges: 'Statues, of course, are made much later'.[7] Thus, as in the Cavafy poem, homo-erotic past event, however fleeting, is made substantial, future work of art, by combination of memory's selective discretion and the mind's interpretative skill.

Surely, Bertrand Russell's version of the childless man, rooted in a constant present until death, and nullified thereafter, is inaccurate. It is confined to a range of reference beyond which humanity moves with almost mundane ease. It confuses 'immortality of the germ-plasm' with immortality. It disregards religion's role in generating happiness. It disregards the acquired function of art, as access to immortality. It disregards the acquired powers of love. . . As simple a tool as the future tense does much of the job of Russell's child.

ADOPTIVE SONS

With gods as precedents, men seek to create, in order that they may become immortal. Accounting for the male's desire to harness creative energy in the absence of the female principle, Phyllis Chesler uses the concept of 'uterus-envy'. Our patriarchal myths of genesis, she says, have their origin in this condition; as has alchemy.[8] I would add, the work of male poets when not inspired by a loved woman or female muse. Indeed, it may be one of the prime functions of the arts in general, to placate male uterus-envy. The present chapter is on the symbolic elimination of the female principle, which ought not to be confused with the elimination of woman herself. The male, homosexual poet's unthought-of and unstated starting point is her absence from his bed. He does not seek to push her out (she was never there); but, rather, to adapt a creative system to the character and capabilities of his male lovers. Many of the sexist implications in what follows stem from sexual orientation itself – whose origins are not, and need not be understood – rather than from interpretations of it.

Life is insufficient reward for living. 'What is the charm of barren joy?' asks John Addington Symonds, in one of many poems on the love of boys, as if better reasons must be found for joy and love than love and joy themselves.[9] In a similar moment of doubt, John Gambrill Nicholson speaks of his own boyfriend, through the lips of Prudence personified, as follows:

His love is barren; surely it were wise
    In Love's broad field to sow more fruitful seed!
    What brood shall bear thy name and know thy need,
Or close in afterdays thy sightless eyes?[10]

The first solution to the homosexual man's lack of offspring is identical to that of the infertile heterosexual couple: adoption. I have neither the qualifications nor the wish, to speak of the quotidian side of this subject; but can discern and report, in literature, occasional links between paedophile and adoptive parental relationships. A man's separate desires for a lover and for a son may combine, in the choice of a boy as erotic focus. This transaction is both seduction and adoption, involving a pre-pubertal child; and the relationship it instigates may be so refined as to obviate the need for actual contact – with the exception of the visual – between its two partners. (Prurient nightmares of child-molestation are irrelevant.) Such are the ties between Aschenbach and Tadzio, in Thomas Mann's *Death in Venice* (1912). Verbal and tactile contacts are never made, although the former is once attempted. It is enough for Aschenbach to build a relationship, not with Tadzio himself, but with the sight of him: for the erotic experience is aesthetically based. The boy is, at once, the son the man never fathered, the male lover he never had, and the beauty he never created. It is with a father's kindness that he watches the boy resting on the beach. I shall examine other aspects of their relationship, later; but for the moment it is sufficient to note, as its fundamental cause, the boylessness of the man.

Adoption is not the prerogative of paedophile lovers alone. By 'adoption', of course, I do not refer to any formal, institutional contract, but to a relationship based loosely on the model of that between parent and child – based thereon by the older partner, in the manner of his reference to it. In the 37th sonnet, Shakespeare says he takes pleasure in the actions of his boyfriend

As a decrepit father takes delight
To see his active child do deeds of youth[.]

This mood has something in it of the archetypal Greek relationship, between man and youth, in which the man is responsible for the education of the youth, and the successes of the youth reflect glory onto the man. Theocritus's Heracles tutors Hylas, 'as any fond father teaches his son'.[11] To call oneself one's lover's father is akin to acceptance of responsibility for his education and, indeed, his adult character; and to accept that one day he will leave home and form new relationships. To call oneself one's lover's father is to confirm the possibility of having grandchildren by him.

When Verlaine fell in love with Lucien Létinois, he contrived a semi-parental relationship with him, at first, before revealing his intentions as a lover. That there was more to this tactic than mere expediency is suggested by the fact that in the volume *Amour* (1888), published in memory of Lucien (who had died of typhoid at the age of 23), he referred to theirs as an adoptive relationship, long after the need for circumspection had expired. 'Cette adoption de toi pour mon enfant', he writes to Lucien, was transacted by him in compensation for the loss of his own son, custody of whom he had lost to his wife, Mathilde, in April 1874. The first poem in the sequence, already quoted, is both prayer and lament, beginning with the words, which refer to Lucien, 'Mon fils est mort'.

Jean Cocteau 'was frequently to say that he longed for a son of his own, and to speak of his frustration in this regard as the reason for his continuing "adoption" – there was never a legal adoption – of young men.'[12] Christopher Isherwood 'often declared that he *felt* like a father to some of the boys with whom he had been involved. The fact that these relationships were also sexual was not incompatible with his outlook. Some of his strongest memories of his father were sexual, and he often had fantasies of an incestuous relationship with a mythical brother.'[13]

Perhaps because it does smack of incest, this motif occurs infrequently in the literature with which I am concerned. One final point is worth making, since it prepares us for some central questions we must consider: the adoptive relationship is no less strongly felt for being merely semantic – a matter of definition – the power of words being emotively greater than that of biological 'law'.

THE HETEROSEXUAL ALTERNATIVE

It would be unthinkable not to begin this section with Shakespeare. In the early sonnets, he treats reproduction as a simple, technical necessity: a preservative of beauty. (I am taking the poems literally, for the moment, and ignoring the possibility of ironic or parodic intent.) 'From fairest creatures we desire increase', not to increase the amount of beauty in the world, but to prevent its decrease. In this sense, Shakespeare sees reproduction as a purely defensive measure against ugliness, whose spread is characteristically likened to that of a weed. By this definition, sexual intercourse with reproductive intent betrays itself as an act as much of narcissism as homosexual intercourse is commonly supposed to be, insofar as it is intended as a means of producing a replica of the mirror image, whose considered beauty is thereby rendered proof against death. The beautiful must produce beautiful children, 'That thereby beauty's rose might never die' (sonnet 1).

But the deed to which Shakespeare incites his boyfriend is requested also as a proof of love – not for the mother of the proposed child, but for the poet himself. 'Make thee an other self for love of me' (sonnet 10). Such a child may be (as our quotation from Ortega had it) the 'testimony of the union, a child in whom the perfections of the beloved are perpetuated and affirmed'; but it will be testimony to the erotic relationship between its father and his male lover, rather than to the parental relationship of its father and his wife.

If a homosexual man wishes to have children, he may choose to marry. Whether or not this is an unjustifiable use of the woman concerned – a question which applies more to heterosexual men than to homosexual – is not the point at issue, here. On the other hand, if he eschews the sexual contact marriage would entail, he may take the option of artificial insemination – a less satisfactory alternative, since parenthood thus secured is at once curtailed by the father's more than merely sexual distance from the mother and what children she bears. Two poems examine these alternatives in detail: James Kirkup's 'To My Children Unknown, Produced by Artificial Insemination', and Allen Ginsberg's 'This Form of Life Needs Sex'.[14]

Shakespeare provided two means to immortality: poetry and parenthood. Kirkup looks at both claims, with explicit reference back to the sonnets. By taking on the role of the 'onlie begetter / Of these ensuing / Moppets', he becomes the Mr W.H. to whom the sonnets are dedicated and addressed, while the ensuing children become the sonnets themselves. But, because they were artificially begotten, Kirkup finds himself forced to accept them, merely, as the results on paper of a successful experiment, and has to disown them as people in order to carry out his obligations as a good donor, as opposed to parent.

Whereas the sonnets were produced out of Shakespeare's love for their begetter, these 'Moppets' have been bred at a distance, 'In a stark laboratory, / Sterile, / Beneath blazing lights, / Masked assistants all eyes'. They are the offspring of a sterile (loveless) disunion, fathered 'In the interests of science', and born, as far as the father is concerned, in oblivion. Kirkup likens this oblivion to outer space (his children may as well be on another planet and, indeed, of another race, despite the careful labelling of his Caucasian sperm samples). His ejaculation is a rocket trip away from Earth. The immortality he achieves is worthless. While he dies – having substituted, for Shakespeare's 'ever-living', 'ever-dying' – his off-spring are condemned by him to 'zoom on in that eternity', the darkness of lives lost to him, as if they were still spermatozoa.

The poem's point is that, despite the respectability of the poet's pseudo-heterosexual relationships, via a machine, with the women concerned, any relationship is validated only by love, not productivity, and invalidated by lack of it. So, 'Even before the nuptial night / Our divorce was final.' The experiment was a mistake.

Allen Ginsberg deals with an earlier stage in the process. Whereas Kirkup has undertaken the experiment and acknowledged its failure, Ginsberg is still trying to make the initial decision: 'I will have to accept women / if I want to continue the race'; 'Between me and oblivion an unknown / woman stands'; 'I'm fated to find me a maiden for / ignorant Fuckery'. He repeatedly rejects art, verbal and visual, as a means to self-perpetuation. The woman he seeks is 'Not the Muse but living meat-phantom', who possesses the genital organs 'that repelled me 1937 on'. He likens male homosexuality, as an inadequate 'answer to life', to a muscular statue seen and felt in a museum. Although he envied the statue its icy immortality, he knew 'You can fuck a statue but you can't / have children'. You can love a poem, but you can't have children by it.

The poet decides, therefore, to overcome sexual distaste, and apply himself to heterosexual intercourse, to 'bury my loins in the hang of pearplum / fat tissue / I had abhorred' – despite the embarrassment he knows he will feel, to be fucking clumsily, in ignorance again, for the first time since adolescence. None of his experience with men has equipped him to deal with this new sexual imperative. To date, he says (astonishingly), his sex life has been a misuse of his body: thighs at his brow, love pulsing through his ears, and, above all, the 'masterful Rape' of his buttocks, 'that were meant for a private shit'. Bearing in mind the usual relish with which he refers to sexual intercourse with men, and his undisguised disgust at the thought of female flesh, we cannot fail to read this part of his argument with scepticism. The mood will pass.

The homosexual man who wants to have children – whether with machine and woman or with woman alone – is automatically placed in an unnatural position, having temporarily to falsify his desires, in some cases by fantasy to deceive himself into believing that the machine or the woman is a man – just as he might transform his hand, when masturbating – in order to get ejaculation over and done with. When providing his sperm samples, Kirkup says, he was 'A kind of actor' in a public performance. Only the actor noticed the flaws in his performance, to which his audience of technicians was blind. His criteria for success were more demanding than theirs. All they wanted was the clinical fact of ejaculation; and they got it. If that is all there is to fatherhood, it has none of the 'continuous mystery' that Ginsberg seeks. Continuous mystery is eliminated by distance from the mother. What he might have written (after 'You can fuck a statue but you can't / have children') is that you can fuck a woman and have children by her, but she is 'no more answer to life' than the statue, since she is as distant as it from the actual objects of your desire. Like the statue, she is just something to fuck.

Ginsberg's explicit misogyny, rooted in physical revulsion, is atypical of homo-erotic poetry in general. The heterosexual alternative is less problematical than these two poems suggest, since homosexuality is synonymous with neither misogyny nor sexism. Kenneth Pitchford's collection of poems, *Color Photos of the Atrocities*, offers a convincing self-portrait of a politically radical gay man, whose conscientious struggle against sexism enables him and a woman friend to construct around their baby son relationships which, although not without their share of problems and doubts, give the lie to both Kirkup and Ginsberg.

DEFECATION AND CHILDBIRTH

The apotheosis of the anus as a male sexual organ, corresponding to the vagina in the female, gives rise to some mythic and literary correspondence between defecation and childbirth. Excrement is not consistently regarded as waste. Ulli Beier cites the Wapangwa tribal myth, of which Eugene Marais might have approved, of an earth originally consisting of the excrement of white ants.[15] In an Australian myth, 'Mingarope having retired upon a natural occasion was highly pleased with the red color of her excrement, which she began to mould into the form of a man, and tickling it, it showed signs of life and began to laugh.'[16]

In his essay 'On the Sexual Theories of Children' (1908), Freud writes that children are led by their ignorance of female physiology to formulate a theory of reproduction, in which 'The baby must be evacuated like a piece of excrement', through the anus. But no sense of degradation is attached to this association of faeces with humanity: for the children have not yet acquired their parents' sense of disgust in excretion. From this premise, of anal childbirth, the child makes a number of deductions; among them, that 'one eats some particular thing and gets a child from it' (the thing eaten being, in certain myths, the seed or semen, swallowed in the generative act of fellatio); and, that 'If babies are born through the anus, then a man can give birth just as well as a woman. It is therefore possible for a boy to imagine that he, too, has children of his own, without there being any need to accuse him on that account of having feminine inclinations. He is merely giving evidence in this of the anal eroticism which is still alive in him.'[17] In the essay 'On Transformations of Instinct as Exemplified in Anal Eroticism' (1917), Freud describes childhood fantasies in which 'penis and vagina were represented by the faecal stick and the rectum'. Likewise, child and vagina are linked with faeces and rectum: for the concepts of faeces, baby, and penis 'are ill-distinguished from one another and are easily interchangeable', since all three are solid bodies, and all three, 'by forcible entry or expulsion, stimulate a membranous passage'.[18] In *Ruling Passions*, Tom Driberg provides a relevant memory. At prep school, Driberg and a boyfriend, both ignorant of the facts of life, 'half-toyed with the fantasy that the pangs of constipation might mean that one of us was about to give birth'.[19]

Writers who are interested in the metaphoric resonance of anal intercourse, by making use of this potential, may make a connection between excrement and offspring. We can recognise the association of ideas which leads the narrator of Jack Kerouac's *Desolation Angels* to mention that, after sixty three days' fire-watching on Desolation Peak, he 'left a column of faeces about the height and size of a baby', and add, ambiguously, that 'that's where women excel men' (chapter 47). Similar reasoning prompts the cloacally obsessive Abel Tiffauges, in Michel Tournier's *Le Roi des aulnes*, proudly to note in his diary: 'La seule consolation de la matinée est d'ordre fécal. Je fais inopinément et sans la moindre bavure un étron superbe, si long qu'il faut qu'il s'incurve à ses extrémités pour tenir dans la cuvette. Je regarde attendri ce beau poupon dodu de limon vivant que je viens d'enfanter, et je reprends goût à la vie.'[20] This baby has an important edge on Kerouac's in that, unlike his, it is of living clay. In 'The Geography of the House', W.H. Auden refers to defecation as the 'ur-act of making'.[21]

An interesting variation on the concept of rectal childbirth is outlined in an essay called 'Negro Folklore of Male Pregnancy', by John Money and Geoffrey Hosta.[22] Interviewed by the authors, five black, homosexual men in their teens and twenties reported their knowledge, if not their experience, of 'blood babies', born *per rectum* to homosexual men some six weeks after they took the receptive part in anal intercourse. No internal organ is fertilised during conception: for it is the semen itself which develops into the amorphous foetus which is born. Delivery is said to occur during defecation; and the 'baby' is passed, along with faeces and blood, and disposed of down the lavatory. The authors remark that 'There is a possible experiential basis to the origin of belief in the folklore in some cases, namely, in blood passing per rectum following homosexual relations'. 'Psychodynamically,' their rather dull conclusion reads, 'the story of blood babies represents an envy of pregnancy'.

But, despite the productive nature of the intercourse involved, excrement remains inert and has no virtue, save as waste. Contrast the myth of Mingarope (quoted above) with that of the Kamschatkan god Kutka, apparently 'a great sodomite'. He is represented as 'falling in love with his own excrement and wooing it as his bride; he takes it home in his sleigh, puts it in his bed, and is only restored to a sense of his absurd position by the vile smell'.[23] The foetus is dead. In his lexicon of gay slang, Bruce Rodgers lists as one of many equivalents of 'to shit', the verb 'to abort'.[24] Excrement is the aborted foetus, once potential life, but now dead clay. What value it contains stems from the two facts: it contains the lover's semen, and it accumulates in and is passed from the rectum, which is a sexual organ.

It is this erotic potential, and not childbirth mythology, that characterises poetic references to excrement. In 'Their Imagination Safe', Michael Lally describes two male lovers, 'in each other's crevices creating seed from shit & loving it'.[25] In 'Journal Night Thoughts', Allen Ginsberg claims that he can 'create baby universes / in the mouth of the void – / Spurt them out of my mind forever / to fill the Unimaginable with its / separate being'.[26] He can fecundate the belly of his fellator. That the same poem ends with one of his more lyrical scenes of anal intercourse is evidence of his faith in the fact (belied only momentarily in the edginess of 'This Form of Life Needs Sex') that, although the rectum may in one sense be a void, it is not barren. Its, and the anus' excretory functions, like those of the penis, are secondary to their erotic role. In the magnificent final lines of Mutsuo Takahashi's 'Myself with a Motorcycle', food and excrement are used to draw attention, not to eating and shitting, but to mouth and anus as sexual organs: 'My god eats Kentucky fried chicken, drinks Coca-Cola, / and from the dawn-colored slit of his beautiful ass he ejects shit'.[27]

MALE PREGNANCY

According to Plutarch, Periander, the tyrant of Ambracia, was killed by his boyfriend for asking him whether, after all their love-making, he was not yet pregnant.[28] The question may have been tactless, but it was not a completely isolated whim. There are many myths of male pregnancy which grant the male a creative role in independence of the female. A fine example was collected from the Winnebago Indians of Nebraska by Paul Radin. 'In it a hero, a young tribal chief, is described as making himself a vulva and breasts, putting on women's clothes, marrying a boy from a neighbouring tribe, getting pregnant by him and giving birth one after the other to three fine children.'[29] In *L'Homme nu*, Lévi-Strauss lists a number of such myths. Several work on the following pattern: a mother throws, or gets ready to throw, her infant into a fire; but the baby is saved by a man, who hides it in his own body – in one of his knees, or under his testicles – goes home, and there, in the presence of a female member of his family, 'gives birth' to it, adopting it as his own child.[30]

As we saw in the case of the 'blood baby' folklore, the concept of pregnancy in the homosexual male can, and does, acquire relevance to everyday life; and is more complex than the mere linguistic joke, 'to abort', might suggest. False pregnancies appear from time to time in the psychological journals. See, for instance, James A. Knight's 'False Pregnancy in a Male'[31] and Gerald J. Aronson's 'Delusion of

Pregnancy in a Male Homosexual with Abdominal Cancer'.[32] In both essays, the case history is more interesting than the author's speculative conclusions. Aronson tells of a 60 year-old waiter, who when asked for the symptoms of his supposed pregnancy, replied: 'Well, I don't have any morning sickness, but I don't have my menstrual periods either. I guess I'm pregnant. I have a kind of fullness in the belly and I've begun to feel life.' However, on being told of the presence of a cyst in his abdomen, he dropped the delusion, with the comment: 'Well I thought I was pregnant – but it was kind of a crazy idea'. Knight's patient, a 33 year-old Catholic merchant seaman, announced to his physician: 'I think there is life in my abdomen. This may be a pregnancy.' Closely connected with his belief that with God all things are possible, the 'pregnancy' seemed to him a miraculous occurrence, designed by God as a means to produce a child resistant to atomic energy and radiation: a potential saviour of the human race. Asked about the delivery of the child, the patient replied, 'I suppose a cesarian section would be the only way'. Detailed exposition of his philosophy produced the following remarks: 'God creates from nothing, so if one believes in miracles, such a task would not be too difficult for Him. For I believe still in miracles of the spirit if not of the flesh. This is all tied up with my idea of seeing love prevail and not hate. I want my love to live, to be creative and not destructive.' He revealed that one of his friends on board ship had started planning to get married and have a child, and he wished that he himself could produce that child. The symptoms of pregnancy developed soon after – which says a good deal for the power of desire.

If we turn to literary manifestations of similar phenomena, we find – not least in the fact that poets are less sceptical than psychologists – considerable credence given to human creative potential. Delusion, of course, is still in evidence. In the twelfth of the *Cantos*, Ezra Pound has a fine, if long-winded joke, at the expense of another deluded seaman. The tale runs as follows: an alcoholic sailor is operated on in hospital. In the next ward, a poor prostitute bears a child, which the nurses bring to the sailor, telling him they cut it out of him. Years pass, and the reformed sailor dutifully gives his 'son' the best of up-bringings. But on his death bed, he decides to tell the boy the truth. 'You called me your father, and I ain't,' he says.

'I am not your fader but your moder,' quod he,
'Your fader was a rich merchant in Stambouli.'

His faith in the potential of nature redeems his ignorance: for, by accepting that mystery and the limited extent of human knowledge, together, make up the sum total of facts – the Universe itself – one can perceive the apparently contradictory nature of Creation as both orderly and apt. Unfortunately, Pound's patronage of the sailor denies the value of this revelation.

In Shakespeare, a man's stomach is his 'womb', stemming from a word for both, *wamb*, of German origin. So, in Auden's *The Sea and the Mirror* (based on *The Tempest*), Stephano addresses his belly as both bride and daughter. And in 'The Prince's Dog', Auden describes Narcissus, disconcertingly, as a fat man, whose paunch is his baby.[33] A poem by Dario Galicia, called 'J/J', reads in its entirety as follows:

> He keeps no diary;
> his body is the only record.
> He moves about awkwardly, lazily,
> for in his male stomach he carries a child.[34]

Again, here is the child as emblem and proof of love. It is a reminder of the emotions of which it is also the result. As such, it obviates the need for any clumsier device, such as a diary. This lover is himself the story of his love. What he carries within him is knowledge and sign of those of his lover's actions which were expressions of love; and was implanted in his belly, via anus or mouth, by the lover's penis, in the substance of the seed it emitted. It may be that the affair has ended, pregnancy being the development of a past action. In this case, the poem could be read as an indication that, although love itself may be short-lived, its effects are self-perpetuating, even beyond the deaths of the men concerned. Ortega's statement, with which I started this chapter, is wholly applicable, here. The child is the culmination of the love, belonging to neither lover nor beloved. Since we can presume the poem's voice to be that of the lover (in mechanical terms, the 'father' of the unborn child), the child exists as much in a part of him – carried, that is, in the poem itself – as in the beloved (the 'mother'). Out of the reproductive intent of their sexual union is born the symbol of affirmation and perpetuation. No matter which way one looks at the situation (Did the poem produce the child, we may ask; or the child, the poem?), its union of semen and male womb has denied its own apparent infertility.

An equivalent fecundity is achieved in some of Maureen Duffy's homo-erotic love lyrics.[35] Her 'Aria for Midsummer's Eve' depicts her female lover, convincingly 'pregnant with our high summer love'; and in a later piece, the two lovers 'make strong children / Of laughter' together. Nikolai Klyuev, sometime lover of Esenin, makes much poetic capital of the moment when, fully pregnant, he will deliver his testicles, as twins, to the thirsting earth, in keeping with his allegiance to a sect whose members, like Origen, practised self-castration as a means to perfection.[36]

In her *Revelations of Divine Love*, Mother Julian of Norwich describes Christ as our Mother, Brother, and Saviour. 'We owe our being to him,' she argues, 'and this is the essence of motherhood!'[37] Indeed so. What matters is the creative momentum. As we move on to consider the role of the artist, the concept of the male mother should become clearer. For the moment, however, I must concentrate on the source of the male's vision of the creative principle: his own semen.

SEMINAL FLUID

Osiris created all beings in an eternal, self-induced ejaculation which, contrary to the theories of the Victorian explorers, was the source of the Nile. Having masturbated Shiva, Agnee spilt some of the emitted semen while crossing the Ganges, thereby causing the birth of the misogynist war-god Kartikeh. When he ejaculated onto the ground while sleeping, Zeus unintentionally caused the birth of Agdistis. Allah created woman and man from a drop of his own semen, which coagulated into solid blood.[38]

Homosexual fellatio acquires early creative significance in the Egyptian myth of Seth and Horus, in which the former swallows some of the latter's semen (indirectly, on a lettuce leaf) and gives birth through his forehead to a golden disc, the moon. Lévi-Strauss relates the myth of Vison, who pisses in a stream, transforms his urine into a trout, and offers it to his hungry friend Renard. After eating it, Renard feels ill, and realises he is pregnant. He soon gives birth to a son.[39] And finally, who doubts that the mandrake grows spontaneously from semen spilt at the gallows-foot?

The move from myths to 'scientific' theories about the composition of seminal fluid is not far. Behind both, so consistently, lies the conviction that man is the creator and woman the bearer of children – as if, like a parasitic insect, the man lays his eggs in the woman so that, when hatched, his offspring can feed off her innards, before breaking out through her skin into life. Aristotle's *De generatione animalium* describes semen as a secretion of highly concentrated nutrient which, as an active agent working on passive matter within the female, is the principal creative force in all reproductive processes. In the *Eumenides* (657–9), Aeschylus has Apollo himself declare that only the father is a child's true parent; its mother is a nurse. Even when it was acknowledged that a woman is more than a repository, a mere furrow to the man's seed, her part in the reproductive process had to be rationalised by the invention of female semen, as by Lucretius.

Semen is the tangible element, the active force. A man's definition of his semen determines the value of his sexual acts. In the *Timaeus*, Plato attributes to it some of the qualities of the soul, since it is a distillation of our spinal marrow, one of the soul's repository substances. According to Burton's *The Anatomy of Melancholy*, the bones, gristle, ligaments, membranes, nerves, arteries, veins, skin, fibres, and fat of the human body may be termed its 'spermatical' elements, being all 'immediately begotten of the seed'. The alchemist Paracelsus sited semen in the brain. In *Purgatorio 25*, Dante's Statius defined the heart as its origin: for semen is a much purified form of blood which, instead of being passed around the bloodstream, is directed to the genitals for reproductive purposes. In *De rerum natura*, Lucretius had already established confusion with the blood-stream, by suggesting that the erection of the penis is caused by an accumulation of seed therein.

But it is in the idea of the Homunculus, beloved of Laurence Sterne, that the autonomy of semen is most exaggerated. This theory classifies the sperm as embryos in embryo, each ready to become a human being as soon as it has been deposited in the inactive womb. After Anton van Leeuwenhoek had legitimately identified and named the spermatozoa, a number of quacks claimed to have observed female and male versions. Some even saw pairs of them copulating.[40]

It is a relief to find the occasional dropped stitch in this great fabric of male self-importance. One gay voice, that of Ralph Chubb in his poem *A Fable of Love and War* (1922), dismisses the procreative imperative in an image which combines complete justification with the utmost simplicity:

Pollen's not *all* for fruitful cells:
Some on the pretty petals falls.[41]

PLATO AND GAY LOVE

It is difficult to find an important text on male homosexuality, at least among those published before 1969, which does not refer to Plato's dialogues. Karl Ulrichs (1825–95) coined the term for homosexual women and men, 'urning' ('Uranian', in English), because Pausanias says, in the *Symposium*, that homosexual love is of Uranian origins. Richard Burton's 'Terminal Essay' to *The Arabian Nights* (1885) uses the dialogues as historical sources, and disputes Aristophanes' version, in the *Symposium*, of the origin of the sexual orientations.[42] John Addington Symonds' essay 'A Problem in Modern Ethics' (1891) also refers to the Aristophanic myth, as having some bearing on Ulrichs' concept of the hermaphrodite. Later, Symonds points out the relevance of the *Symposium* to the themes of Whitman's poetry.[43] Edward Carpenter's essay on 'Homogenic Love' (1894) includes quotations from both the *Phaedrus* and the *Symposium*.[44]

It may seem by the way to mention, here, that Allen Ginsberg can trace his sexual descent from Whitman, via Carpenter, Gavin Arthur, and Neal Cassady. But it is in much the same way that, in 'The Portrait of Mr. W.H.', Oscar Wilde appears to be tracing his own intellectual descent from Plato. Having suggested that Shakespeare read Marsilio Ficino's translation of the *Symposium* (1492), Wilde follows the spreading of Plato's ideas, through Plotinus, Montaigne's essay on friendship, Giordano Bruno, Ben Jonson, and Richard Barnfield, to Winckelmann and beyond.[45] (The next step in the descent would be Walter Pater's essay on Winckelmann, published in 1867.[46]) In *De Profundis*, Wilde attaches some meaning to the fact that Christ may have spoken Greek; and comments: 'It is a delight to me to think that as far as his conversation was concerned, Charmides might have listened to him, and Socrates reasoned with him, and Plato understood him'.[47] The descent ends in the work and life of Wilde himself, influenced by the Greek and Christian traditions, of which Plato had become a common factor. One of Wilde's own volumes of poetry is called *Charmides*.[48] In a famous speech at his trial (1895), when called on to define the so-called 'love that dare not speak its name', Wilde called it an affection 'such as Plato made the very basis of his philosophy'.[49] Of one of his love letters, quoted in his disfavour, he later wrote: 'The letter is like a passage from one of Shakespeare's sonnets transposed to a minor key. It can be understood only by those who had [*sic*] read the *Symposium* of Plato, or caught the spirit of a certain grave mood made beautiful for us in Greek marbles.'[50]

In *Ioläus* (1906), Edward Carpenter quotes extensively from the speeches of Phaedrus, Pausanias, Aristophanes, and Socrates, in the *Symposium*; and from the *Phaedrus*.[51] In *The Intermediate Sex* (1916), he again quotes from both dialogues.[52] For his polemical study, *Corydon* (1917), André Gide took the title from Theocritus' and Vergil's cowherd, but the dialogue form from Plato; and subtitled it *Four Socratic Dialogues*.[53] Corydon himself recognises only Plato and Schopenhauer as worthwhile theorists of love. (On the other hand, Schopenhauer claimed to have 'no predecessors either to make use of or to refute', since he considered Plato's work on love to be 'confined to the sphere of myths, fables and jokes'.[54]) G. Lowes Dickinson's *After Two Thousand Years, a Dialogue between Plato and a Modern Young Man* (1930), as its subtitle says, includes Plato himself as one of the speakers; but it omits his powers of reasoning.[55] In the *Psychology of Sex* (1933), Havelock Ellis refers to Plato when dealing with non-physical homosexual relationships.[56]

Later, each study of homosexuality contains a brief 'famous names' section, as if to prove that if anything is more interesting than an oddity, it is a famous oddity; and Plato is one of the most famous. D.W. Cory's *The Homosexual in America* (1951) names him twice, lest we forget.[57] D.J. West's *Homosexuality* (1955) takes the worn path from the *Symposium* to the Theban Band.[58] Bryan Magee's *One in Twenty* (1966) says Plato 'made no bones' about his sexual activities with youths.[59] Finally, in Angelo d'Arcangelo's *The Homosexual Handbook* (1971), the philosopher crops up again, between Pope Paul II and Cole Porter.[60] It is significant that Dennis Altman's politically sophisticated *Homosexual: Oppression and Liberation* (1971) only quotes Plato's views on music.[61]

The apologist cites Plato for a number of reasons. The most fundamental of them is, of course, that Plato provides a philosophical system which invests value in erotic relationships between men. Secondly, he recognises the importance of the sexual element in such relationships and, although he sees it as a distraction, does not condemn it. Thirdly, he expresses the view that spiritual forms of creativity afford surer access to immortality than does mere reproduction; or, that to produce mortal children is less worthwhile than to produce immortal love poetry. It is not irrelevant to note, in this context, that of the above list of authors, Carpenter, Dickinson, Symonds, and Wilde wrote poetry; and Burton and Gide were both involved in the production of other forms of homo-erotic literature. Given the frequency with which Plato appears in the factual texts, we cannot be surprised to find him also in the fictional and poetic.

In Petronius' *Satyricon*, Encolpius, who is temporarily impotent, spends an involuntarily chaste night with a boy, Giton. When they get up in the morning, Giton thanks him, 'for loving me in such an honourable Platonic way. Alcibiades himself couldn't have been safer when he slept in his teacher's bed.'[62] For 'Platonic way', the original text has 'Socratica fide', referring to Alcibiades' account, in the *Symposium*, of a chaste night spent with Socrates. J.P. Sullivan, the translator of the *Satyricon*, comments, 'It is almost certainly this passage which is the origin of our concept of Platonic love'[63] – that is, of love with no carnal element.

Herein lies Plato's main role. He can be used to make homosexuality 'safe'. Because he was always regarded as a philosopher of some importance, but homosexual acts regarded as sins, it was necessary for Christian commentators to excuse his views on love as being concerned only with non-physical relationships – that is, with friendships. (Alternatively, he could be heterosexualised, as by Castiglione.) In fact, such relationships would be better named 'Plotinic' than 'Platonic'. However, any pro-homosexual lobby could put all this to its own advantage, by adopting 'friendship' and 'comradeship' as euphemisms for the erotic relationships with which they were actually concerned. In the speech at his trial, to which I have already referred, Oscar Wilde used the general misconception of Platonic relationships as non-physical – since in physicality alone lay what 'shame' the prosecution alleged, and what 'gross indecency' the law proscribed – to substitute for an uncomplicated sexual bout the respectability of friendship. In the same spirit, Carpenter's *Ioläus* was subtitled *An Anthology of Friendship*; as was Aleister Sutherland and Patrick Anderson's *Eros* (1961).[64] In Chicago in 1925, a group of homosexual men produced several issues of a magazine called *Friendship and Freedom*. In the Netherlands in 1945, a group started production of a magazine called *Vriendschap*.[65] Britain's main counselling agency for lesbians and gay men is called Friend. As often as not, today, a gay man in Britain will refer to his lover as his 'friend'. . . . This means, unfortunately, that the few texts which were genuinely on friendship are now liable to be interpreted as on sexual love, along with all the rest.

'To read Plato', says G. Lowes Dickinson, in his general introduction to *Plato and His Dialogues*, 'is to discuss our own problems without the exasperation caused when we are, as it were, embedded in them.'[66] That is to say, in our context, that without incriminating himself, a writer can speak of Socrates, when he means any man who loves boys; of Plato, when he means any homosexual philosopher or poet; of Charmides or Phaedrus, when he means any beautiful boy; and of friendship, when he means sex.

The implicit use and development of Plato's ideas on love between men take many forms, some of which I shall examine later; but I want to begin with explicit uses, which range from simple quotations from the dialogues to rather more ambitious schemes. Looking at a beautiful youth 'In a Town of Osroêne', Constantine Cavafy is reminded of Charmides. Although this is the simplest type of reference, it is not weightless. The youth has been injured in a drunken brawl and carried home. Thus far, he is an ordinary, modern tough, scarcely worthy of the distinction the poem confers on him. But the sight of his body in the moonlight, now that aggression and slurred speech have deserted it for the night, evokes not only an ancient, ideal world, but also an ideal love, based on beauty rather than on brute sexual strength.[67] In this sense, many modern references to Plato are steeped in the nostalgia, if not in the rural delights, of Pastoral: for, like the Pastoral world, the Platonic can only be glimpsed or imagined while the modern is at bay. However, to treat the dialogues as Pastoral is to accept a limited view of their quotidian level alone. Certainly, as history, theirs is a lost world; but they are not history books, and what they say must survive, as long as love and politics survive. When Christopher Isherwood and Charles Laughton 'worked together on a theatrical version of the dialogues of Plato, based on the life of Socrates', their project was doomed from the start.[68] Only when the costume drama aspect of the dialogues has been discarded, can their ideas be adapted to contemporary needs.

Plato has a revelatory effect on Clive Durham, in E.M. Forster's *Maurice*. The only text on homosexual relationships with which he was previously familiar was the apocalyptic myth of Sodom.

> Never could he forget his emotion at first reading the *Phaedrus*. He saw there his malady described exquisitely, calmly, as a passion which we can direct, like any other, towards good or bad. Here was no invitation to licence. He could not believe his good fortune at first – thought there must be some misunderstanding and that he and Plato were thinking of different things. Then he saw that the temperate pagan really did comprehend him, and, slipping past the Bible rather than opposing it, was offering a new guide for life.[69]

It is he, who subsequently advises Maurice to read the *Symposium*.

In Mary Renault's important novel *The Charioteer*, the three male protagonists are united by a copy of the *Phaedrus*. At the start of the novel, Ralph Lanyon gives the dialogue to Laurie Odell, who keeps and reads it for years, even carrying it with him at the evacuation of Dunkirk. At the end of the novel, Odell gives it to the third man, Andrew Raynes. The whole novel is structured around quotations from and references to the Plato text – in particular, from and to the passage likening profane and sacred love to two horses pulling a chariot, whose driver provides the novel's title. The *Symposium*, on the power of an army of lovers, is also quoted.

The middle section of Ian Young's 'David' offers us another view of the modern value of the dialogues.

> I remember reading *Lysis*,
> *The Symposium* the first time:
> the quickening joy I felt,
> a need to walk miles
> as if to some great event;
> and the next day, noticing, for the first time,
> the bright belly-muscles of a young swimmer,

warm torrents rushing down face and chest,
a graceful dive,
the strain of heading for land and the deep
sigh of making the shore —
almost a sleep.[70]

Plato's may not have been the first text he read on homosexuality, but it seems to have been the first affirmation; and there can be no questioning the depth of its effect on him. What mattered in the reading was not the archaic social context; but the radical devotion to male beauty, which still applies. The discovery of the texts confirmed Young's (or his protagonist's) already formed, if not affirmed or articulated, belief in the possibility of male love, generated by the appreciation of male beauty. The next day's vision of strength and grace is a homo-erotic commonplace, entirely suited to his espousal of the Platonic aesthetic.

So, Plato is still a formative influence on the lives of certain young, bookish, homosexual men. Not that he provides much insight into sexual matters. But, as an introduction to a world of male beauty, his dialogues may come as an interesting revelation to those youths who have not connected their own feelings with the seemier misinterpretations of the Sodom myth or the gossip of the Sunday newspapers. The fact that many young, homosexual women and men have never heard of homosexuality – or, if they have, associate it only with insulting stereotypes, between which and their own feelings there can be no link – leads us to another area in which Plato's ideas are still of direct relevance.

The Republic is based on Sparta. As such, it is Utopian only insofar as it deviates from its model. Sparta has a reputation for institutionalised homosexuality. The only indexed reference to homosexual love in Bertrand Russell's 800-paged *History of Western Philosophy* occurs, not in a chapter specifically on Plato, but in that on Sparta.[71] In his chapter on Pythagoras and Plato, in *Plato and Platonism*, Walter Pater is at his most eloquent when suggesting the valid relationship between the philosophy of music and the bodies of Spartan youths.[72] Pater then likens the unity of Plato's Republic to 'the consummate athlete whose body, with no superfluities, is the precise, the perfectly finished, instrument of his will'.[73]

The same comparison has been used in modern politics. In *The Greater Britain*, Oswald Mosley bases the ideal, corporate, Fascist Britain on the male body, in perfect physical condition. The moral pattern of this state would have to do with disciplined athleticism, explicitly based on that of Sparta (but tempered with the atmosphere of Merrie England).[74] Hitler's *Mein Kampf* moves from the premise that 'what has made the Greek ideal of beauty immortal is the wonderful union of a splendid physical beauty with nobility of mind and spirit', to the vision of a state in which 'those who have a beautiful physique should be brought into the foreground, so that they might encourage the development of a beautiful bodily form among the people in general'. The official view of Hitler's state was that the human ideal is to be found 'in a dareful personification of manly force and in women capable of bringing men into the world'.[75] As K.R. Popper has pointed out, all the principles of Spartan policy, except that of restricting the state's growth, correspond with those of modern totalitarianism.[76] Of course, no Fascist state could allow homosexuality, as such, to flourish (mainly because of a general association of male homosexuality with debilitating femininity). But anything can be given a new name. 'Comradeship' is a viable alternative; 'unity', another. Yukio Mishima tried to put comparable notions into practice, with his Spartan Samurai army, born of a characteristic fusion and confusion of Eastern and Western archaisms.

But Fascism does not have a monopoly on Platonic politics; still less, on a Spartan revival in other spheres. Dr Arnold's conception of the public school has its obvious correspondences with the ancient state, not least in its devotion to sports. (But Cardinal Newman's Oratory School came to a similar emphasis by a more circuitous and less physically exacting route, as implied by his and the school's motto, *Cor ad cor loquitur*.) After school, the world of sporting activity in general condones the embraces and locker-room sexual antics of male buddies, again, as long as their affection dares not speak its name. Appreciation of the male physique must have its base in the potential of muscles to do harm, as in those sports in which physical contact is *de rigueur*, or to perform supposedly non-erotic feats of speed, strength, and endurance. Mutual affection is also a necessary force in our armed and merchant marine services; but the law dictates that it be given some other name than 'homosexuality', lest it interfere with the discipline it helps to maintain. Finally, an important difference between ancient and modern versions of Sparta is that the modern unwittingly fosters homo-erotic ideals, by consistently segregating the sexes; which the ancient did not.

Perhaps the most influential passage in the *Symposium* is its least serious: the speech of Aristophanes, on the origins of sexual intercourse. Each of us, he says, is but a half of a single being, originally whole. Desire is the search for one's other half. Falling in love is recognising one's other half. Love, sexual and spiritual, is becoming whole again. At the height of sexual pleasure, lovers merge for an instant, united in the goal of their relationship. Hence, a tiresome obsession with simultaneity of orgasms, in both erotic literature and life. The idea that for every individual there is another, has its place in Romantic and romantic theories of love; and tends to lead to the opinion that lovers should be of identical background and class, if, at times, of opposite temperaments.

Frederick Rolfe's novel, *The Desire and Pursuit of the Whole*, is explicitly based on the Aristophanic myth, beginning and ending with references to it. When Crabbe, the narrator, and his emphatically boyish girlfriend embrace, 'Halves, which had found each other, were joined and dissolved in each other as one'.[77] A more subdued, modern version appears in the first section of Patrick White's *The Tree of Man*. After an awkward – and infertile – start to married life (in a place called Durilgai, which means 'fruitful'), Stan and Amy Parker eventually establish a common life, and are likened to two trees, growing from a single trunk. Only then, does Amy give birth to a child.[78]

The essence of adherence to the Aristophanic myth, then, lies in the belief that two human beings can unite in a single form, without superfluous appendages or thoughts. A common image is of lovers as two streams, uniting as a single river. Another is the sphere, from which, according to the myth, we are derived. The couple becomes autistic or self-sufficient, depending on one's point of view. Louie Crew and Rictor Norton cite a modern 'marriage manual', which contrasts the 'complete unit' of heterosexual intercourse, enacted face to face, with the 'incomplete fragment in a daisy chain' of (male) homosexual intercourse, front to back, evidently unaware that anal intercourse can be enacted face to face, and vaginal front to back.[79] In fact, since Aristophanes' original human beings, when running, 'turned rapidly over and over in a circle, like tumblers who perform a cartwheel', the most faithfully imitative act of sexual intercourse, homo- or heterosexual, would be mutual oral intercourse: like Trinculo and Caliban, 'Four legs and two voices: a most delicate monster!' (I am reminded, also, of Dante's daisy-chain of condemned sodomites who, in *Inferno* XVI, form a treadmill of flesh.)

Keeping Plato's influence in mind, I now return to the matter of love's productivity, in which the fullest significance of his thought will be felt. I shall examine art's role in satisfying Ortega's conditions for a satisfactory loving relationship. For reasons which should become clear, I begin with sculpture, move on to tattooing, and end on poetry itself.

SCULPTURE

If fatherhood is understood to mean creativity, we can invest in anything man-made the virtues of babyhood. If, however, reproduction is of value mainly because, by producing a likeness of oneself – a child, with the physical characteristics of its parents – it apes the creation of Adam by God, then any alternative mode of creation may be seen to share that apparently vital quality, of having to do with the re-creation of oneself. We must turn to the representational arts, and at first to the visual, to witness this mime of mimesis. Parenthood emerges as a form of self-portraiture; and vice versa. Had Narcissus been able to paint, he would never have become an object of scorn: for, between them, he and his model, the beloved image of himself, could auto-erotically have produced a child, an immortal likeness of themselves. We have no more reason to accuse Rembrandt of autism, for obsessively painting self-portraits (rather than because he was too poor to hire a model), than to attribute to a man with ten children the same fault. When Dürer painted himself as Christ, he usurped the position of the Father, as well as of the Son.

The urge to portray realistically – or even idealistically, since many parents try to make the ideal child – the human figure, as sculpture, scarecrow, humanoid robot, or whatever, has always led to the combined hope and dread that visibly perfect craftsmanship might, somehow, instil life into the created figure. Any number of examples of this theme can be unearthed, from Pygmalion, through Frankenstein, to Worzel Gummidge. It hangs upon the implicit notion that the only truly great artist is the one who can bypass sexual intercourse, yet still produce children; and can, subsequently, bypass incest, yet still make love to his child. Taken less than literally, the theme has some bearing on the way in which we interpret a painted human figure as a living, three-dimensional person; assume flesh tones on a bronze statue; and read life into a novel. The imaginative leap involved in transforming a work of art into the thing it represents is as much a reproductive act, in our present sense, as was the artist's original work.

If we look at contemporary reactions to the great classical sculptures, we find, again and again, outstanding works receiving the highest praise: they were so realistic that youths attempted to violate them sexually. According to Pliny, Allketas the Rhodian fell in love with Praxitiles' Eros, and left on it the traces of his lust. A certain Clysophus could not have his way with a statue in the temple of Samos, because the marble was too cold; so he fixed a chunk of raw meat to the appropriate part and, like Portnoy with the family meal, copulated therein.[80] Whatever the idealistic notions of the sculptors themselves, their works were frequently treated as pornographic aids to masturbation. As Yeats wrote, statues may have been, strictly, exercises in the application of the Pythagorean golden rule to human figures,

> But boys and girls, pale from the imagined love
> Of solitary beds, knew what they were,
> That passion could bring character enough,
> And pressed at midnight in some public place
> Live lips upon a plummet-measured face.[81]

If the classical statue is the ideal figure – in the prime of life, rarely pre-pubertal or old – it is also the sexiest; and must be reacted to accordingly.

Given this attitude to sculpture – that it has some kind of monopoly on human beauty, only rarely to be seen in the living figure – it is no wonder that one of the devices most often used in reaction to human beauty is the simile which takes us back from flesh to marble or bronze. J.R. Ackerley describes one of his boyfriends as having a body 'like the Ephebe of Kritios'. Watching a man shaving, Denton Welch reflects that 'he looked like a marble statue'. Mann's Tadzio has a face which recalls an Eros carved in marble, and his armpits are said to be as smooth as a statue's. Thom Gunn and a lover lie together, exhausted, 'Like wrestling statues'; and he later likens an orgy to the Laocoön.[82]

The derivative sculptural tradition of the Renaissance earns similar treatment. Harold Norse likens a boy to a Donatello, adding that he has the kind of 'sexual beauty found in museums / that he wouldn't think of entering'. Walter Griffin's poem 'Rough Trade' has a boy who looks like Michelangelo's David. In his 'Sex Poem', Robert Glück conceives of statues of himself and his lover, by Michelangelo and Rodin respectively.[83] These are, merely, random examples. An exhaustive list would be impossible to compile, since the convention of comparing beautiful human beings with beautiful statues is as old as the statues themselves; and the comparisons are more numerous than the statues, if not than the human beings.

It is when the simile becomes more than an aesthetic device, and is played out in actual metamorphosis, that its sexual meaning is made vividly explicit. In E.M. Forster's short story 'The Classical Annex', the living statue of a gladiator is lovingly entangled with the museum curator's adolescent son, when both are frozen by the power of the Sign of the Cross. The resulting piece has, later, to be exhibited under the euphemistic title 'The Wrestling Lesson'.[84]

Life becomes statuesque, worthy of the immortality which art, like nectar, bestows on beauty, under the conditions of sexual love, of which nudity is a reliable sign. At its most basic, this process of benign petrification (an appropriate tag for penile erection) is seen when an artist is inspired by the beauty of human flesh to make a lasting representation of it in inanimate materials, thereby breathing into the materials something of the life of the original figure. What life the statue possesses will endure beyond the decay and death of the model. When Gilgamesh needs to minimise the effect of the death of his lover, Enkidu, he has a statue made of him, in gold and lapis lazuli. I have already quoted from the Ritsos poem, in which the sight of a young farmer's naked back leads to the observation that 'Statues, of course, are made much later'. The same idea prompts Ian Young, in 'The Garden God', to say of a boy he is watching, 'He should be marble'. Not being a sculptor, he can only fix the boy's figure in a poem; but the effect is much the same.[85]

Implicit in all we have considered so far is the idea that a representation of life, somehow, both contains and preserves life. If so, just as life can become marble, there is no reason why marble should not spring to life. Apuleius, visiting Thessaly, the notorious home of sorcery and magic, is quite prepared to see the statues step from their pedestals.[86] No doubt this, rather than the possibility of theft, is why the Tyrians used to chain up their statues.[87] In Forster's story, before the curator's son could take on the qualities of sculpture, the statue of the gladiator had to come to life, in order to cast the necessary sexual spell. Life involves movement, if not in actual terms, at least in appearance. That is not to say that the most effective sculpture must depict the body in action, but, at least, that it should promote the illusions of heartbeat and breath. Even a carving of a dead warrior, or the figure of Christ in a Pietà, must look as if it has only just ceased to breathe. Even a sleeping figure must look as if it will get up, at the slightest hint of alarm clock or lark. The most restrained art historian must succumb to the illusion of movement in drapery or limbs, sculpted or painted, just as the literary critic must read character into verbal ciphers.

Allen Ginsberg announces to one of his journals that all the statues he has seen on his tour of Greece (in 1961) have 'buttocks / that do not shit'.[88] But such correctives to the aesthetic and erotic imagination are rare. Indeed, one of Ginsberg's own earlier remarks, dating from 1952, is far more in keeping with his general faith in the erotic potential of the extraordinary. It is a description of a dream. While at a party in his family's house, he sees a 'statue of Hermes & Eros – and statue moves, Hermes is lifting Eros' small boy's marble white behind from his loins in a single gesture upward & outward . . . Hermes had been fucking the child Eros.'[89] Here, it is worth remembering a statue described by Theocritus: through years of neglect, it has lost its legs and ears, 'but still has all it needs / to procreate'.[90]

A model is naked; but his statue is 'nude'. The model may be sexy; but his statue is 'erotic'. The model, by the very visibility of his penis, threatens an erection; but his statue's penis, although as hard as rock, is perpetually flaccid. In these false distinctions lies the respectability of the classical statue, as a body to be admired. (Let us ignore, here, as others have, the carvings of Priapus which consist of a monolith with a head and an erect penis.) Only in the context of 'high art' (or of sport) are men permitted to look at other men. Only a thigh of stone may be caressed – and even that, only when the custodian is looking the other way. A schoolboy may look at photographs of nude statues of men, but not at photographs of naked men. . . Yet, the imagination is effective enough to negotiate such minor obstacles. It can turn stone into flesh, and add a third dimension to a photograph, with ease. This is the quotidian moment for which our artists work: for, without it, all representational art, erotic or not, would perish for lack of purpose. The living statues of athletes (naked extras, posing as the Discobolus, and other classical sporting statues), with which Leni Riefenstahl begins her film of the Berlin Olympic Games, are neither their original models, long dead, nor the stone representations of them; but are the unfrozen forms we make of static images, their second metamorphosis enforced by their second artist. Manifestly representations of representations, human versions of stone versions of humans, they enact an acceptable, 'Hellenic' mime of the unacceptable fact that the modern Olympic Games might be acts of homage to physical beauty, if only the athletes could take part stark naked. The statue which moves is a testament not only to human beauty, but also to the sexual beauty of human life.

Returning to the questions of parenthood and self-portraiture, we now see that the sculpted offspring must be lover, as well as child. Furthermore, as is well established, that child, whether female or male, is an enduring impression of the parent. A poem by Yannis Ritsos, 'Face or Facade?', illuminates this context.[91] A sculptor claims to have carved a male figure, not with hammer and chisel, but 'with my bare fingers, with my bare eyes, / with my bare body, with my lips'. Plainly, he has caressed it into shape in an explicitly sexual form of artistic intercourse. The statue is its own second parent, the homosexual lover of the artist. However, 'I don't know', the artist complains, 'who is I and who's the statue.' Not that they are visually indistinguishable – the sculptor is ugly, his sculpture beautiful – but the statue has become its creator's disquieting *doppelganger*. It lives and moves. They walk about together, as lovers or Siamese twins, the artist's arm around the statue's waist. But doubts are raised about its independence. Could it live, let alone walk, without its creator's touch? Must he always be present, constantly creating life by touching it, lifting it, and loving it? He claims not. He claims it walks on its own. 'But who believes him?' demands the last sentence of the poem. The main question the poem proposes is whether the statue will die with the artist, or the artist live on with the statue. Although the last line, in a formal sense, leaves the matter open, the fact that the artist's character has been absorbed by the stone strongly suggests that his death will not be the end of his life. The artist alone need believe in the powers of art. It is of no consequence that nobody else believes him.

When the work of art is both lover and offspring, its subjects are the beauty and the mortality of flesh; and its purpose is preservative. In a child, the artist seeks to praise his own and his lover's flesh, and to preserve them both. He makes a statue, which could not more snugly fit Ortega's definition of love's desire for 'a child in whom the perfections of the beloved are perpetuated and affirmed', 'the personified union of the two', and 'a striving for perfection modelled after flesh and soul'. The artist turns beloved flesh to stone, and that to flesh again. The next step in my enquiry will lead us to an art which bypasses that central element, the stone: for it requires no metamorphosis to foster movement. Its medium is the living flesh itself.

TATTOOS

The frequency with which tattoos are mentioned in the literature of male homo-eroticism has to do with a number of discernible connections between male homosexual activity and the practice of tattooing. Both have been outlawed by the Church: tattooing, in Leviticus (19.28) and at a Council of Churches at Calcuth in Northumberland in 787. Both are legally available only to those who have reached an arbitrary age of consent: 18 years, in the case of tattooing in Britain, imposed by the Tattooing of Minors Act, 1969. Both can be responsible for the transmission of sexual disease: in 1877, for instance, a Philadelphian tattooist was tried for infecting with syphilis scores of men, having been in the habit of licking his needles to moisten the colouring agent. Both occur, in various forms, in initiation ceremonies. Both are considered to be predominant in groups of men forced to live closely together. Both are concerned with the beauty of flesh. In his study of tattooing, H. Ebenstein points out the erotic nature of his subject, with another parallel:

> The young man's first experience at the tattooist and with the sexual act resemble each other closely. Around both clings an aura

of having committed something 'dirty' and 'common'. Both are acts upon completion of which he considers himself to have attained manhood. Both combine a strange sensation of pain with unfathomed pleasure. Both are experiences which he may keep hidden from his parents but about which he brags with his companions.[92]

Furthermore, Ebenstein tells us of 'men for whom tattooing has become the sole source of sexual gratification'.[93] As decoration, message, or symbol, because carved in flesh, the significance of a tattoo inevitably has an erotic base.

Tattoos have moved beyond their merely decorative purpose, by having been applied to the flesh of particular types of men. In Genet's *Miracle de la Rose*, pirates are mentioned, so covered in frightful decorations that life in society has become impossible for them. The knowledge of the social unacceptability of the art leads the less heavily covered Americans, in Mishima's *Forbidden Colours* (whose title is not irrelevant), to conceal tattoos beneath the well-cut respectability of their suits. Linked with this aspect, is the conspiracy of manliness which unites the tattooed. Hence, the use of the tattoo in ceremonies of initiation into thug-hood. The tattooing ends the ceremony, as a final stamp of approval, with the implicit meaning that its bearer is an initiate, and therefore beyond society. A visual version of the enclosed group's argot, the mark's meaning is always of limited accessibility. One of Thom Gunn's leather boys, at his initiation into a group, was tattooed on his shoulders: 'The group's name on the left, The Knights, / And on the right the slogan Born to Lose'.[94] The slogan is similar to the 'Pas de Chance' with which the chest and personality of a sailor are adorned in Cocteau's *Le Livre blanc*, and may seem to contradict the aggressive spirit of the group's name; but these young men lose only their fight against bourgeois society, not the actual punch-ups they instigate. When, in 'El Rey de Harlem', Lorca refers to the sun as having been tattooed ('el tatuado sol'), he does so not only for visual effect, but also to attribute to it a particular type of aggressive virility, and to its heat on one's flesh a correspondingly erotic thrill.

The fullest and richest account of tattooing in a closed group of men occurs in Genet's *Miracle de la Rose*. Not confined to initiation, here, the infliction of skin markings is the very purpose and obsession of the group, the Order of Tattoos. Despite its lofty name, the group is not formal and, as far as ritual and administration might be involved, barely exists at all. No man can apply for membership. What members there are, merely share a particular boldness and the elaborate hierarchy of their tattoos. Superiority of strength is all that can assert the exclusivity of any single design. As usual, Genet's imagery is rarefied but revealing. Some men are devoured by drawings that portend future wounds; others, patterned like the interiors of sentry boxes, seem covered with the imaginatively obscene graffiti of bored and randy guardsmen; most are adorned with flowers. All partake of 'une chevalerie nouvelle', in which dispossessed thugs and pimps attain 'une sorte de noblesse d'empire'.[95]

The secret signs of tattoos take on practical, sexual significance if, and when, we can attribute to them the single meaning, 'homosexuality'. It has been supposed that gay men have themselves tattooed with special marks, for the purposes of mutual identification. As a caption to an illustration of 'The Skin Artists', Robert Giraud writes: 'The young man below proclaims his dedication to Greek love by means of a rose placed on his heart'.[96] The sailor who appears in the 'Eumaeus' episode of *Ulysses* has the number 16 tattooed on his chest; and, according to one book of notes, 'in European slang and numerology the number sixteen meant homosexuality'.[97] Ebenstein reports, without reference to evidence, that 'passive homosexuals find that obscene or humorous designs on their posteriors serve as expedient excitants to comparatively normal men in the forces or in other places where men are brought closely together'.[98] So, a man writes on his body, and we can read into his hieroglyphs aspects of his personality. In a poem called 'Tattooed', William Plomer describes just such a sequence of signs:

> The flower's pangs, the snake exploring,
> The skull, the violating knife,
> Are the active and the passive
> Aspects of his life[.]

They are both martial and (homo-) sexual.[99] This man has made of his body a complete picture of its sexual definition, suggesting (in the flower) the beauty and unease in his own vision of anal intercourse, and (in the snake and the knife) the aggressive, but no less beautiful, phallic aspect of his sexuality; but (in all three) the curious tension between contradictory symbols, which puts pride in receiving pleasure and explicit aesthetic intent in the attraction of a lover. His body tells prospective lovers, as they start to caress it, that they must not categorise him as one or other sexual type, 'passive' or 'active'; and must, therefore, reject any such categorisation of themselves.

The tattoo is self-evidently a work of art. In rare cases, its quality demands preservation. So, we hear of the wealthy New York collector, who arranged to become the owner of selected tattooed skins after the bearers' death.[100] In 'Damn the Culture Ministry',

James Kirkup describes a boyfriend of his, who wears 'the one garment / I could not divest him of', his intricate lacework of pictures: the goddess Kwannon, a carp on each buttock, and a butterfly on the tip of his penis, among others. But the boy is considered too exquisite and extraordinary for one man's love, and is bought on the nation's behalf by the Culture Ministry.[101]

Now, if the tattoo is a work of art – indeed, a 'Living Work of Art', as the tattooed woman, Carmen Sylvia, was billed – the tattooist is an artist, working on a specifically erotic genre. The best-known expression of this fact is Thom Gunn's 'Blackie, the Electric Rembrandt'.[102] The design involved is simple: ten stars, on the arm of a boy who has probably not been tattooed before; but the concentration on both faces is intense nonetheless. This tiny design may be the first in a series, ending only when the whole body is covered – just as one's first sexual activity, however mundane, is part of a much larger pattern of sexual events. When he goes into the shop, the boy's arm is 'virginal'. When he comes out, it is bandaged. Blackie's needle is paintbrush, knife, and penis to the boy's canvas, wound, and sexual orifice. So, Blackie's art contains birth and death, immortality and oblivion – all for a few shillings.

Rembrandt gives way to El Greco and others, in Ray Bradbury's collection of short stories, *The Illustrated Man* (1952). All night, the narrator watches the naked body of the Illustrated Man while, as breath moves the flesh, its tattooed pictures tell the eighteen stories in the book. In this case, what we have considered as a mainly visual art acquires certain literary faculties, beginning slowly to appoach the conditions of erotic poetry.

Of course, a tattoo may include words as well as pictures; but a subtler link can be established between skin pictures and speech. Writing of the ways in which his fellow convicts insult one another, Genet points out that each man tends to use a single abusive word or phrase more than others. His chosen insult takes on a consistent, emblematic role, which the author finds comparable with tattoos. The insult is as much an expression of the insulter's personality and rank, as are the markings on his flesh. This leaves us no cause for surprise, when we read the remark with which George Seferis prefaces his *Logbook II*: 'Sometimes it crosses my mind that the things I write here are nothing other than images that prisoners or sailors tattoo on their skin'.[103] The operative word is 'images'. Seferis articulates visual images, turning them into their poetic counterparts, just as tattooed images are themselves visual transformations, or articulations, of non-verbal emotions, such as sexual and martial desire. As literature, the markings state their bearers' personalities and styles of life. As erotic poetry, they state not only, symbolically, their bearers' desires, but also the very shape and texture of the flesh they advertise. In Nikos Kazantzakis' comparatively secularised continuation of the *Odyssey*, Odysseus himself is heavily tattooed:

> Dancing around his sunburnt loins, tattooed in blue,
> the twelve signs of the zodiac glowed like living beasts:
> the scorpion spread its claws, the lion leapt for prey,
> fishes in pairs sailed undulating round his belly,
> and the scales tipped in balance just above his navel.[104]

The zodiac has about it the cyclical nature of the hero's journeys, and a suggestion of the enormous time spans they cross. That its signs are tattooed, in similarly cyclical fashion, around his genitals, is an ironic addition to the author's criticisms of Odysseus' misogynistic philandery. It is as if Odysseus believes that the world revolves around his phallus.

If, finally, we return from tattoos to the act of tattooing – that is, from erotic literature to the sexual act itself – we discover the most immediate relevance of this art to our subject. The male tattooist, to highlight the beauty of his male customer's flesh, pricks it, evoking mixed sensations of pleasure and pain, and makes art of it. His is an act of homage to physical beauty, but far from passive admiration. In a long, erotic poem, Denton Welch describes the tattoos of dancing sailors as 'The permanent marks / Of ephemeral wooings'. Like the tooth-marks and scratches one sustains during sexual intercourse, the tattoo is, in many cases, a mark of love, imposed by a lover; or a love poem, written by a lover. On the hairy chest of 'The Tattooed Man', in a poem by Craig Raine, tattoos are like 'love letters lost in all the long grass'.[105] Next to the symbolical number 16, the sailor in *Ulysses* bears a self-portrait of his lover, Antonio (appropriately, 'a Greek'), doubtless executed as a ritual prelude to actual intercourse. In this way, the tattooist can adorn the body of the man he loves with the most potent signal of their love, his own portrait or a symbol of himself. The love poet may think of himself, scratching away with his pen, as performing much the same kind of service.

The poetic image of the tattoo, as well as being a pointer to a certain type of asocial toughness, has to do with visions of flesh as a medium appropriate to artistic intercourse; with the lover as an artist in flesh, and the artist as a lover; with the body as a work of art, and the work of art as a body; and with, in general, the direct relevance of artifice to flesh. If there is any literary work to which in particular this subject draws our attention, it must surely be Kafka's *In the Penal Colony*, where literature is scrawled directly, but not without style, on the body of the reader, who reacts at first with a scream, but at last with the silence of understanding and relief. Art is at its most immediate, when the body is its medium. The medium is, after all, the message.

THE BIRTH OF POETRY

It takes no great sophistication to understand that the tattooed image automatically falls short of its purpose. The tattoo may be a message or a work of art; but it is also, literally, the flesh it decorates. There is no distance between it and what it seeks to comment on. Both perish. Ultimately, the tattoo draws attention to itself. In recognition of this redundant concern, and in accordance with their tendency to progress beyond the simplifications of the concrete, poets exchange actual tattoos for the metaphor of the body itself as a work of literature.

Harold Norse finds that a hustler's body, 'like a poem', can be learnt by heart. Elsewhere, he refers to the male genitals as 'The Universal Poem between the legs'.[106] Charles Sayle questions the need for poetry, when the world is already in possession of a 'more perfect poem', the body of his beloved Jack.[107] Mutsuo Takahashi calls the testicles a 'book of wisdom', and the smegma on an unwashed penis, 'Adjective, adverb, and again, adverb that adorns the adverb / Blinding rhythms around true poetry'.[108]

Reverse the metaphor: when the body is a poem, the poem is a body. I am reminded of the long, visibly caesuraed line in Arabic love poetry, one of whose halves is known as the 'breast', and the other as the 'buttock'. In such a text, enjambement would be a sexual act. In 'So Long!' Walt Whitman addresses his reader as follows:

> Camerado, this is no book,
> Who touches this touches a man,
> (Is it night? are we here together alone?)
> It is I you hold and who holds you,
> I spring from the pages into your arms[.]

Leaves of Grass is his poetic version of the sculptural self-portrait, self and child. Its parts correspond with his. The reader of the 'Calamus' sequence, the genital part of the book, fellates Whitman. Every reader is his lover, whether mistress or comrade. A more explicit version of a literary physique is 'The Little Treatise of Anatomy', which forms the first half of James Kirkup's *The Body Servant* (1971). Here, each poem corresponds with a part of a hermaphroditic body, the reading of which is akin to a physical exploration.

If the body is literature, to generate more bodies one's literary activities must be sexual, and one's sexual activities must be literary. George Steiner's classifications of sexual intercourse as 'a profoundly semantic act', and of ejaculation as 'at once a physiological and a linguistic concept', coincide with the next necessary stage in my argument, insofar as they support an association of words with semen.[109] When Byron spoke of 'conjugating the verb to love in both Hellenic as well as Romaic' in reference to his bisexuality, and Steiner offered Oscar Wilde's bilingualism as an expression of his bisexuality, useful precedents were set.[110] In writing that the word 'balls' is a roundness in his mouth ('Le mot couilles est une rondeur dans ma bouche'[111]), Jean Genet referred not only to the loving way in which one speaks of his lover's balls, as if orally caressing them and the word which represents them, but also to the moment just after the lover's ejaculation into his mouth, when semen fills it as with the words of love. Pablo Neruda wrote a poem called 'Semen' which referred to itself (that is, to semen and to 'Semen') as a cry, thus enacting orgasm's simultaneous emissions of semen and of, if not a word, a meaningful groan.[112] As its title suggests, Aleister Crowley's *White Stains* contains the outcome of his ejaculations: pornographic poems as semen stains.[113] Paul Mariah has written 'A Poem to Swallow' by reading which, as fellators, we drink the poet's words.[114]

The words 'intercourse' and 'ejaculation' apply to both sex and speech. If 'Calamus' is Whitman's phallus, the words therein are its seed. If the testicles are Takahashi's 'book of wisdom', its words are the semen they contain. If, in the same poem, semen is the 'Love God's arrows that escape the mouth of a boy in love', his endearments are to his lover's ear as semen to sexual orifice; and his semen is to his lover's mouth as poetry to the ear.[115] If, further down the page, semen is 'The Word' itself, we need look no further to account for the Johannine formula, of the Word made flesh: for a causal relationship between seminal intromission and childbirth is well established . . . It is worth remembering, here, that old tag for oral intercourse: the 'lingua mala'. To put it simply, fellatio is thought of as bad language.

Now, if I say to my lover 'I love you', I do so not in order to convey to him, once and for all, the information in my words. While he might reasonably expect me to make such a statement as 'I love Mozart' only once, after which he will remember my stated preference as part of my character, he can as reasonably expect me to say 'I love you' as many times as it occurs to me to do so, in order to give pleasure both to him and to myself. After the first time I say so, he knows I love him, and what information the remark contains is

superfluous. From then on, my 'I love you' carries as little inform-
ation as my orgasm; and yet, is no less meaningful to us both.
'Orgasm', Roland Barthes writes, 'is not spoken, but it speaks and it
says: *I-love-you*'.[116] It has other messages, too. During a brief but
mutually agreed encounter between strangers, it is the sign of barter
compacted, like a handshake between satisfied merchants. During a
rape, it is the most refined expression of contempt, aimed at the
victim, but rebounding on the aggressor himself. Barthes says,
elsewhere, that there can be 'no distinction between the structure of
ejaculation and that of language'.[117]

The body is literature. Semen is words. We arrive, inevitably, at
what is really a figurative commonplace as old as the art it serves: the
poem is a baby. John Keats ends 'Sleep and Poetry' with the remark
that he leaves the poem 'as a father does his son'. It is in precisely this
simple, outspoken manner, that the theme recurs for centuries. In
some hands it gains enormous weight, as in those of Sylvia Plath,
who makes of several of her finest poems babies born dead. In
'Childless Woman', she expends all energy on making solipsistic
mirrors and 'Uttering nothing but blood' – the menstrual blood that
denies even pregnancy, let alone childbirth. In 'Thalidomide', mirror
image and poetic image (child and poem, one and the same) are
aborted, 'like dropped mercury'. In 'Stillborn', there have been
labour and birth, but of death. Dead poems lie inert, immortal only
through having been pickled in a jar.[118]

Few homosexual poets could afford such despair. When Maureen
Duffy takes up the theme, offspring lives. Her poems are 'Bastard
siblings I / Father on absence'; and 'Shoals of minnow rhymes', sent
'To spawn in your head'.[119] In a poem 'For My Brother', Paul
Goodman suggests that all artistic decisions, like most babies, are
made in bed, out of lust.[120] Having abandoned a play about the
Immaculate Conception, Jean Cocteau reused some of the material
already written, in a play about Orpheus and the birth of poems.[121]
The central character in Frederick Rolfe's *The Desire and Pursuit of
the Whole*, having finished writing a book, 'experienced sensations
very similar to those which follow parturition. He was relieved of a
weight, which he missed so much that he felt light-headed and feeble
and quite languid.'[122] These four disparate examples show, if not
singleness of intent in very dissimilar writers, a certain unity of effect.
But the resonance of this effect is best examined in the familiar and
detailed light of *Death in Venice*, to which I now return.

We have observed the statuesque qualities which the aesthete von
Aschenbach admires in Tadzio. He never sees the boy's beauty in
human terms. Tadzio is never as lovely as some remembered boy or
girl, but always as a sculpture of a mythological subject. Everything

about him, as if he were a muse, turns Aschenbach's thoughts to art. Even his voice, speaking a language the old man cannot understand, is heard as music. No merely human relationship between them can be established. If they met, what could either say of interest to the other? In fact, Aschenbach is not interested in the human Tadzio at all: for the boy has already been fathered, in sexual intercourse. Despite all the comparisons with art, he does not possess the gift of immortality. He is sickly and will, doubtless, die young. To Aschenbach, he represents a standard of beauty, to which art must aspire. The paternal feelings the boy arouses in Aschenbach take shape as the urge to create an artificial Tadzio, with all the qualities of the sculpture with which he is comparable. Aschenbach cannot father Tadzio. He must love him, so that from their union of shared paternity can be born a son, an immortal Tadzio of words. So, in the boy's presence on the beach, Aschenbach starts to write his last essay, as if sketching a portrait from life: 'This lad should be in a sense his model, his style should follow the lines of this figure that seemed to him divine; he would snatch up this beauty into the realms of the mind, as once the eagle bore the Trojan shepherd aloft.' As well as a reminder that by the act of writing the artist seeks to hoist his human material into immortality, this, the novel's only reference to Zeus and Ganymede, confirms the sexual nature of his inspiration. His co-operation with the boy is 'fruitful intercourse', 'between one body and one mind'; and after it has ended, Aschenbach suffers pangs of conscience, 'as it were after a debauch'.[123]

Plato is Mann's acknowledged source. In the *Symposium*, Socrates outlines Diotima's view of the nature of both poetry and love. Poetry, she says, means creation. Love's object is 'to procreate and bring forth in beauty'. So, love is a form of poetry, in its wider sense. By now, we have become used to the metaphor she adopts throughout her argument: that of pregnancy and childbirth. 'All men', she tells Socrates, 'are in a state of pregnancy, both spiritual and physical, and when they come to maturity they feel a natural desire to bring forth, but they can do so only in beauty and never in ugliness. There is something divine about the whole matter; in pregnancy and bringing to birth the mortal creature is endowed with a touch of immortality.' Later, Diotima distinguishes between heterosexual and homosexual lovers, as follows:

> Those whose creative instinct is physical have recourse to women, and show their love in this way, believing that by begetting children they can secure for themselves an immortal and blessed memory hereafter for ever; but there are some whose creative desire is of the soul, and who conceive spiritually, not physically,

the progeny which it is the nature of the soul to conceive and bring forth. If you ask what that progeny is, it is wisdom and virtue in general.

Insofar as it allows heterosexual relationships only physical issue, this distinction can be discarded. Let Dante and Beatrice stand as disproof. Also, the Greek legacy of respectable sexism cannot diminish the equivalent validity of homosexual relationships between women. However, Diotima's attribution of issue to love between men is our present concern. Given that he can conceive only in beauty, a man's first priority must be to find a physically or spiritually beautiful lover. Diotima continues:

> By intimate association with beauty embodied in his friend, and by keeping him always before his mind, he succeeds in bringing to birth the children of which he has been long in labour, and once they are born he shares their upbringing with his friend; the partnership between them will be far closer and the bond of affection far stronger than between ordinary parents, because the children that they share surpass human children by being immortal as well as more beautiful.[124]

An Aschenbach must meet his Tadzio early in his artistic career, and stay with him, if they are to produce more than one such child. In brief liaisons, however, the single love poem may suffice.

By accepting, in this sense, the babyhood of the work of art, we are close to seeing exactly why the Muses traditionally had to be female, given that the artists who invented them were male. The metaphor of sexual creativity having been taken in a near to literal sense, the relationship between Muse and artist had to be heterosexual, in order to be reproductive.[125] The poet Thamyris challenged the Muses, not merely by boasting that he could out-sing them, but by being, according to Apollodorus (I.3.3), the first mortal to make love to someone of his own sex. His acting on his homosexuality was as shocking a transgression as the boast, and it is no wonder that the Muses afflicted him with blindness, muteness, and amnesia, in return.

Shakespeare's love for his lover was so inspiring that he wrote to him, in sonnet 38:

> Be thou the tenth Muse, ten times more in worth
> Than those old nine which rimers invocate;
> And he that calls on thee, let him bring forth
> Eternal numbers to outlive long date.

See, also, sonnet 78. We have already noted the similar effect Tadzio has on Aschenbach.

Clearly, the tradition I have been examining must accommodate the possibility of a male muse. A Spartan man and his boyfriend were referred to as inspirer (*eispenēlas*) and hearer (*aïtas*), respectively. Their love involves a verbal and sexual dialogue, by which the elder educates (draws out) the younger, less as a teacher, in the modern sense, than as a kind of muse. The man's implications become the boy's inferences, so that it often seems as if the boy comes up with the wiser speeches. This is the form taken by most of Plato's dialogues. So, as well as representing one man's silent discussion with himself, the dialogue is also an enactment of love's creative processes and preaches what it practises. The same processes operate in adult relationships, hetero- or homosexual, beyond the rigid definition of the acceptable Greek love affair, between man and boy. Adult couples are the main focus of Ian Young's anthology of poems on male homo-erotic themes, aptly called *The Male Muse*.[126] With words and semen, the lover inspires whole volumes. (However, the opposite view must be acknowledged. In an interview in 1977, Thom Gunn said: 'I used to believe my muse was male; but I've come to realize that Graves is right, that the muse has to be female. The Goddess is a mother, not a wife or a lover. The feminine principle is the source and I think it dominates in male artists whether homo- or heterosexual.'[127] He discards the concept of the male mother.)

Interviewed for *Gay Sunshine*, Mutsuo Takahashi said, 'the homosexual's is a sex kicked out of the world's generative development, an alienated sex. So it has a strong desire to become connected once again with the world's generative development. When the desire becomes artistic impulse, the impulse may be fiercer, more to the point than the heterosexual's. At least, homosexuals are more keenly aware than heterosexuals that words are erotic beings.'[128] The last point is central to my argument. Words are as precious as the semen they represent, and are invested with equivalent magical properties. Exclusion from biological reproduction turned the search for, and knowledge of, alternative methods into potentially dangerous philosophical weapons. Such knowledge could not but subvert the teachings of the Church, and had to remain a secret, as closely guarded as that of the elixir of life, which in so many ways it resembled. Just as the wisdom of the alchemists had to be lapped in a coded complex of symbols, that of homosexual lovers, daring not speak its name, assumed an alias.

BEYOND GENERATION

E pluribus Unamuno. Everything we have seen in this chapter points to, and confirms, Miguel de Unamuno's version of humanity's hunger for immortality, outlined in *The Tragic Sense of Life* (1912). 'Everything', he says, 'endeavours to persist in its own being' – humanity, no less than any other. Indeed, our longing not to die 'is our actual essence'. Consequently, we cannot imagine ourselves not existing. Love is the thirst for eternity. He who loves seeks to perpetuate himself within his loved one. Our tragic need for immortality leads us to construct our religions, out of a combination of hope and the flexibility of our imagination. We must believe in a future, in order merely to exist, let alone persist. (His argument is of a consummate elegance, not apparent in my summary.)

If Unamuno is right, the shared purposes of religion and the arts can be identified with those of love. Artist, priest, and lover have a common goal, in the principle of creativity; which is a means of surviving death. Of creation, or birth, there are four types in human endeavour: biological birth, of a child; aesthetic birth, of a work of art; birth in love; and rebirth, after death. The first and third are equated, in a poem by William Cartwright (1611–43):

> There are two Births, the one when Light
>   First strikes the new awak'ned sense;
> The Other when two Souls unite;
>   And we must count our life from thence:
> When you lov'd me, and I lov'd you,
> Then both of us were born anew.

Two lovers, impregnated by their love, give birth to each other, irrespective of gender. In their intimacy, each learns the other, detail by detail, striving for total knowledge. Each detail learnt is a detail created, as it were, in the lover's mind, and transformed by love's new perspective.

There is a short story by Borges, 'The Circular Ruins', in which one man literally dreams up another, laboriously forming each organ in turn. The heart, with which he starts, is completed in a fortnight of nights. Within a year, he has reached the skeleton. He must even dream the man's hairs, one by one. Eventually, with the aid of a prayer, he dreams life into his creation, accustoms him to reality, and sends him out into the world. Clearly to do with literary creativity, the story is also a parable of love's concerns. When, true to the circularity of Borges' imagination, the dreamer understands that he, too, is dreamt, by a dreamer of his own, the story proposes a genealogy of thought, extending to infinity in the two directions of time. Infinity is the inconceivable point at which the autophagous snake Orobouros begins and ends; and where love's influence may fail. To introduce a point of origin, at which an undreamt God dreams of Adam, is to subject love to the possibility of its own failure. The undreamt is unloved.

Sexual fantasy takes the place of loving dream, of which it is a distillation, in William Burroughs' *The Wild Boys*. Isolated from the rest of humanity (so, from all women), the Wild Boys have developed their own distinctive method of self-perpetuation: the ultimate pornographic refinement, a fantasy which comes to life. Without touching his own erect penis, a boy moulds around it the object of his thoughts, pressing colour and air into a shapeless mass against his loins. From this, with his eyes, he sculpts a boy's figure, transparent still. Into the rectum of this embodiment of desire, he pumps semen, which solidifies the new-born flesh. Into its lungs, he breathes life. Thus, the thirst for immortality quenches itself in love. Father is lover, and loved one is son.

At this point, it is instructive to conjecture that our lives are limited only to the extent to which our perception of the world is limited. The baby's 'I am what I touch' or 'I am what I feel' becomes the child's spatially more ambitious 'I am what I see'. Then, when 'see' takes on its second meaning, the adult reaches his or her 'I am what I understand'. But the most refined stages, as well as the most perilous, are those of the mystic ('I am what I believe') and of the poet ('I am what I make') – perilous, insofar as they encroach on the qualities of godliness, and invite retribution on a Promethean scale. They extend the poet's range beyond quotidian impossibility, and render the more primitive conceptions of 'realism' irrelevant to his purpose. The chains of biological equivalence are broken wherever we find a myth of the Creation which does not involve the sexual union of a goddess with a god.

Finally, we come to the expendability of the creative theme. Poetry need not spell out the principles of creativity: for it is, itself, eloquent affirmation of them. The poetry of childbirth is always, at a certain level, about poetry. Furthermore, we may have to begin to ask whether all poetry is not, correspondingly, about childbirth. If a poem explicitly concerned with poetry is in some sense tautological, and if all other poems are implicitly concerned with poetry, then all poetry is in the same sense tautological. Poetic form draws attention to poetic form. The creative theme is present, whether stated or not. (All art seeks to justify its own existence.) The concern with creativity is fundamental to our understanding of the world, since we (or our ancestors) burdened Being with the theory of having been created, and continued Being with that of continued Creation. . . Having said this, I am inclined to add the qualification, which ought to be obvious, that there is no need to overvalue any one theme, to the extent of requiring its presence in all art. Many others demand attention. The explicit theme of creativity certainly has its place in erotic art; but it is one of many, and not a requirement of the genre.

My argument has revolved, now, to its starting point: for we have returned to the original fact, that homosexual intercourse does not produce children, and that the literature of homosexuality need not concern itself with them. Given the variety of alternatives we have considered, to concentrate on the theme of the child *qua* child would be irrelevant to the central subject: the sexual attraction of one person to another of her or his own gender, and the love which stems from it. Nor need the relationship in question be an artistic partnership, either between a major artist and a minor (as between Wilde and Douglas, Auden and Kallman, Ginsberg and Orlovsky) or on more equal terms (as between Auden and Isherwood, Britten and Pears). Actual collaboration is too literal a version of the creative relationship; as, indeed, is the metaphor of the poem as a child, conceived in the poet's bed. Rather, we must think in terms of contraceptive conception.

If homosexual intercourse, like contraceptive heterosexual intercourse, is sex without an ulterior motive – sex for its own sake and for love's – then I think we can speak of most erotic poetry in a similar way. The words 'I love you' have no more reproductive purpose than semen ejaculated into a lover's mouth. So, call swallowed semen sterile, if you like; but it is neither more nor less so than the love poem. I have consulted a number of travesties of actual reproduction in this chapter. But, as literal as it is, reproduction itself may be no more than a travesty of, or metaphor for, something more refined. The ejaculation of poetry and the writing of semen *signify* in a context beyond generation.

PART TWO

VARIATIONS

4 D.H. LAWRENCE

THE PHALLIC MALE

Because D.H. Lawrence used to be considered a finer novelist than poet, commentators on his work have tended to examine his use of their chosen themes in the fiction, not the poems. On the rare occasions when they consider his deep and obvious fascination with male homosexuality, they do so with reference to the bathing scene in *The White Peacock* and the wrestling scene in *Women in Love*. Less frequently, they also mention *The Prussian Officer*, the nursing episode in *Aaron's Rod*, and the initiation rites in *The Plumed Serpent*. Critical treatment of the homo-erotic elements in Lawrence's poetry barely exists, although such elements are equally important to, and no less thoroughly considered in the poetry.[1]

In his study of *Homosexuality and Literature*, Jeffrey Meyers convincingly introduces the significance of love between men in Lawrence's works, as follows: 'Though Lawrence is usually associated with the triumphant expression of heterosexual love, this love depends on male dominance and is seriously qualified by an ambivalent longing for homosexuality.'[2] Lawrence's main erotic preoccupation is with the possibility of love between a woman and a man; but when, in practice, this love looks doomed, he turns to the homosexual alternative, not necessarily as second best option, but as a less problematical version of the same thing. However, he never allows his men more than a brief physical flirtation (and some slightly less perfunctory kind of theoretical, cerebral encounter) with each other, before he marries or kills them off. He never manages to move beyond the problems inherent in each alternative. When distrust of women leads him to men, he is obstructed by his distrust of homosexual men. His most insistent, but necessarily self-contradictory, erotic grail is the passionate, physical union of two heterosexual men.

This sophisticated concept seems to have arisen from semantic misapprehension, to do with the problematical differences between substantive and adjectival uses of the word 'homosexual'. Lawrence's ideal men were actually bisexual, insofar as they accepted and developed their attraction to other men as well as to women; and they had to remain untainted by what Lawrence, less than rationally, saw as the destructive aspect of homosexuality. To love a member of one's own gender, if it really qualified as love at all, was to submit to the foul power of autism, to turn in on oneself. In some of the poems, egocentricity and homosexuality become signs of each other. So, the poem 'Ego-bound Women' announces that its subjects are 'often lesbian, perhaps always'. It then dismisses female homosexuality as the 'most appalling' of the passions, 'a frenzy of tortured possession / and a million frenzies of tortured jealousy' (p.475).[3] Similarly, in 'The Noble Englishman' (pp. 446–7), one of Lawrence's theorists on love asks, 'if a man is in love with himself, isn't that the meanest form of homosexuality?'

Furthermore, although in 'What Matters' (pp. 531–3) Lawrence claims that 'the sodomitical and lesbian stuff' constitutes a cheap thrill which easily exhausts itself, he also believed in homosexuality as a lastingly debilitating condition. He seems to have felt that once two men began a physical relationship, by performing homosexual acts (where 'homosexual' is adjectival, relating to a flexible span of time, dictated by the length of the relationship), both might at once turn into homosexuals (where 'homosexual' is a noun, denoting that relatively rare man who is permanently and only attracted to other men), thereby cutting themselves off from women, and compensating for their isolation by adopting a stereotypical brand of effeminacy or degeneracy. The theory is an elaborate edifice of false assumptions, invoking the illusory concept of what I shall call the 'otherwise-heterosexual': apart from their one-off relationships with eachother, the men concerned are *otherwise* mature and natural woman-penetrators and athletes. An artificial distinction is drawn between homosexuality and physical comradeship; that is to say, between the 'homosexual' (who is congenitally disordered) and the 'otherwise-heterosexual'. A permanent, regularly consummated, sexual relationship between two of the 'otherwise-heterosexual' would seem to be impossible.[4]

In fact, Lawrence's interest in penetratory heterosexual intercourse is limited. When he describes a woman's genitals in isolation, he tends to do so in terms of the ripe fig, succulent repository of the seed of life, demanding to be tasted in cunnilingus, that most gustatory of sexual acts. Furthermore, as he recognised, the fig is an ambivalent sexual symbol. In certain Oriental cultures, it signifies the male anus and is to be contrasted with the pomegranate-vagina: whoever is bisexual eats both.[5] Also, before a fig is opened, it may resemble the male genitals. In the poem 'Figs' (pp. 282–4), both conventions are acknowledged.

> The fig is a very secretive fruit.
> As you see it standing growing, you feel at once it is symbolic:
> And it seems male.
> But when you come to know it better, you agree with the Romans,
>   it is female.

The poem continues, with triumphant eloquence, by elaborating on the femaleness of the fruit. The initial note of doubt seems obliterated.

Meanwhile, Lawrence's version of the penis, as soon as it is erect, becomes the phallus, scattering seed as a god might, to fecundate the earth; or rearing its head as a serpent, to spit. It must come as it stands, in the open air. It must be masturbated, over the earth or the open vagina. It is to be seen, and described. The poem on a 'Virgin Youth' (pp. 38–40) shows the phallic god already present in a youth who has been startled by puberty into a fresh awareness of his own penis. Already, it is beyond his control. As yet, he is unable to direct its energy. When it is erect, he addresses it and defers to it, as if it were the kind of strong, apparently threatening young man he himself will eventually become:

> He stands, and I tremble before him.
> – Who then art thou? –
> He is wordless, but sultry and vast,
> And I can't deplore him.
> – Who art thou? What hast
> Thou to do with me, thou lustrous one, iconoclast? –

The same personified phallus stalks through the novels, man-sized, muscular and passionate. It is always to be contrasted with the flaccid penis of the impotent, as the lusty gamekeeper, Mellors, is to be contrasted with the cerebral and sedentary Clifford Chatterley. It is named (John Thomas) and spoken to. True, in its gentler state, dormant, or in the first, mobile stages of metamorphosis, the penis can be likened to a chick, to be warmed in cupped hands and caressed;[6] but, ideally, the healthy phallus should rarely detumesce. As it is, it sleeps only as the working man sleeps, from exhaustion; then works to earn its sleep. It never lazes and never thinks. Physical and asocial, it is the heroic male to whose style of life all of Lawrence's vital men aspire: the archetypal dictator. As the virgin youth's 'iconoclast', it should shatter more than his virginity. Upbringing and education have prepared him for a cerebral adulthood which, he now realises, is nothing but a dream of his teachers'. In reality, adulthood is more fleshly by far.

Lawrence compares the youth's phallus, firstly, with a man, then with a flame which flares into a column of fire; with a lighthouse, surrounded by a swell of pubic waves; with a pillar; and, finally, with an idol or god which must be worshipped in sacramental intercourse. The poem's irony is, of course, that with all this in his lap, the boy is still under the age of consent. He has to give his new master the following excuse for the solitary form his intercourse must take:

> Thou dark one, thou proud, curved beauty! I
> Would worship thee, letting my buttocks prance.
> But the hosts of men with one voice deny
> Me the chance.

Lawrence is keenly aware of the welling sexuality of children. Their enthusiasm and lack of guilt, he would wish on the adult. As in the poem 'The Best of School' (pp. 51–2), even their glances can be felt, like the touch of exploring fingers on one's flesh. From his desk at the front of a classroom, the poet watches his boys at work; and they, aware that he is watching them, look up occasionally, to meet his eyes. As 'pupils', the boys are aptly named: for all the force of youthful energy is invested in their glances. At first, their eyes peck at the teacher, like the beaks of 'birds that steal and flee', as if shyly filching guarded grain, which they 'taste delightedly'. But, as they get bolder, the image shifts to something more appropriately lingering. Now, like the tendrils of vines which cleave to a more substantial plant, the boys' glances 'reach out yearningly' and slowly rotate around the teacher as they begin to climb him.

> I feel them cling and cleave to me
> As vines going eagerly up; they twine
> My life with other lives, my time
> Is hidden in theirs, their thrills are mine.

This thrill has to do with the promise of actual contact, and with an actual ascent into the uninhibited, natural world, with which their glances have been compared. In the same context but another poem, 'Discipline' (p.926), Lawrence asks with all due rhetoric, 'And do I not seek to mate my grown, desirous soul / With the lusty souls of my boys?'

But what puberty grants a youth, as well as sexual direction, is inhibition. It severs the tendrils of his glance. Clearly, in 'The Wild Common' (pp. 33–4), the 'touchstone of caresses', the 'naked lad' over whose vital flesh the sun, the air, the waves and Lawrence's eyes move like lovers' hands, has not yet reached the debilitating phase of puberty, after which his inhibition will have to be fought against as a constant enemy. The boy is still a component of nature, made love to by the water which encloses as much of his body as it can. Together, he and his environment form 'All that is right, all that is good, all that is God'; and if the adult is to regain this condition – as he must – his relationship with the natural world is of central significance to his development.

Lawrence's interest in the honest vitality of plants leads him frequently to liken his ideals of human beauty and moral strength to the self-evident virtue of the flora. Indeed, some of his finest poems about plants become so heavily laden with elaborate personifications that their original subjects seem to have been justifiably put aside. This leaves the poet free to speak of human physique in its most natural conditions. In his meditation on 'Almond Blossom' (pp. 304–7), for instance, he compares the almond tree with 'a bridegroom bathing in dew, divested of cover, / Frail-naked, utterly uncovered' in a Sicilian January. The act of blossoming is suddenly a question of daring and manly strength, a victory over unnatural embarrassments, and the apostrophe which follows is as clearly addressed to the heroic young man on the verge of erotic victory as it is to the tree:

Oh, honey-bodied beautiful one
Come forth from iron,
Red your heart is.
Fragile-tender, fragile-tender life-body,
More fearless than iron all the time,
And so much prouder, so disdainful of reluctances.

The tree obviously serves as a standard of appearance and behaviour to which Lawrence's hypothetical future heroes will have to adhere. In 'The Rose of England' (pp. 534–5), there is another plant model, but of the failure of virility. The poet describes the evolution of wild roses into the overblown domestic variety whose stamens have been replaced by obsolete extra rows of petals. The vapid beauty of such blooms is a negation of the natural finery of maleness, and leads Lawrence to the inevitable human comparison:

So it is with Englishmen.
They are all double roses
and their true maleness is gone.

They have sacrificed their physical potential to an *idea* of beauty which happens to have emasculated them.

The kinds of young men who are least likely to be sidetracked by the decadent and inhibiting influences of convention and redundant patterns of thought are those who rely for their livelihood on physical, rather than cerebral exercise. Furthermore, because of the nature of their work, they are the most likely to be physically fit, and, as a consequence, physically beautiful. Lawrence's appreciation of male beauty has political implications if only because he often divides the beautiful from the beautyless along class lines. He tends to contrast the lean, muscular bodies of working men with the pale puppy-fat of the bourgeois. The active physiques of labourers are associated with all that is vital in nature. In the third part of 'Transformations' (p.73), Lawrence apostrophises them as the 'writhing forms of all beasts that sweat and that fight', but is careful to add to their energetic grappling with 'work or hate or passion' the gentleness of their repose, when they 'curl in sleep like kittens'. (Remember, we have already seen two such versions of the phallus: worker and chick.)

Lawrence's working heroes are embodied erections in whom all phallic power is invested. For instance, in the section of 'Guards' called 'Evolutions of Soldiers' (pp. 66–7), when a group of soldiers marches towards and past the poet, their apparent evolution is similar to that of a penis, through tumescence and detumescence. Perspective causes each man to seem to grow as he approaches with red tunic, black busby and 'dark threats'. He passes 'above us', in the classic position of sexual advantage. At 'ebb-time', when the group has just passed by, its phalluses remain erect for a glorious moment, before subsiding:

> But the blood has suspended its timbre, the heart from out of oblivion
> Knows but the retreat of the burning shoulders, the red-swift waves of the sweet
> Fire horizontal declining and ebbing, the twilit ebb of retreat.

A similar phallic cluster appears in 'For the Heroes are Dipped in Scarlet' (pp. 688–9). These are slim and bearded warriors with scarlet faces, and 'the loveliest is red all over, rippling vermilion / as he ripples upwards! / laughing in his black beard!' Conventionally, white is the most desirable colour for a boy's flesh and brown for a man's. (Sexual desire is, as well as the most sexist of motives, one of the most racist.) But Lawrence's manly hue is red: not the bilious pink of a sunburnt white-collar worker, but a deeper scarlet bordering on brown, which is the mark of a man whose flesh is used to the sun's glare. The courage to spend a large part of his life naked is one of the qualifications of the hero. Blood and sunlight cannot commingle through tweed.

The evidence for desire, then, is ample. Lawrence bases all of his ideal visions – political, aesthetic, and erotic – on the male body. And the male body is the symbol of its own sexual focus, the phallus. The vagina may be cornucopic, but only after it has been filled. Although Lawrence characteristically sees the female genitals as a ripe, bursting fruit, to be sucked dry, they are at their most succulent, when overflowing with semen from the withdrawn phallus. Man masturbates over woman's open vagina, from which cup he then drinks his own semen. Cunnilingus is Lawrence's oblique image of fellatio.

THE MALE BRIDE

Now, if the soldier is himself a phallic symbol, soldiership is liable to be of erotic consequence. The wartime memories of Lady Chatterley's lover have a familiar emphasis on comradeship. But more intimate still is the relationship with the enemy. In the long essay 'The Crown', Lawrence writes, of war, that 'The enemy is the bride, whose body we will reduce with rapture of agony and wounds. We are the bridegroom, engaged with him in the long, voluptuous embrace, the giving of agony'.[7] A detailed enactment of this notion occurs in 'Eloi Eloi, Lama Sabachthani?' (pp. 741–3), the protagonist of which finds himself facing a blue-eyed member of the enemy forces, who, instead of fighting back, is just

> Waiting. And I knew he wanted it.
> Like a bride, he took my bayonet, wanting it,
> Like a virgin the blade of my bayonet, wanting it
> And it sank to rest from me in him,
> And I, the lover, am consummate,
> And he is the bride, I have sown him with the seed
> And planted and fertilized him.

Tom Marshall believes that this poem 'expresses the agony of a soldier whose self-loathing has become so great that its only release and consummation is in murder. The enemy becomes the bride, "planted and fertilized" by the bayonet in a foul travesty of the cosmic marriage Lawrence believed in.'[8] But what we see here is (in Auden's phrase, detested by George Orwell) a 'necessary murder' by Lawrence's standards. Given the two premises, constant in his work, that the soldier or hero is of an essentially phallic nature, which can be fulfilled only in a phallic way, and that the erotic object or victim – here, the enemy soldier – is always to be engaged in sexual combat, never retreated from, then their bloody intercourse is inevitable. The moral compulsion not to kill would be a mere thinker's excuse for suppressing his own 'phallic consciousness', the focus of his manhood. The enemy's fatal wound is that fig-like orifice which must overflow with the manly foison of the aggressor, commingled with blood.

These images, of a vagina emitting semen and of a vagina carved in male flesh, coalesce in the figure of the male bride: the man made fertile by the phallus of another. In 'She Said as Well to Me' (pp. 254–6), the creation of man by God is envisaged as a sequence of muscle-shaped caresses which polished and hollowed out man's acquiescent flesh. A similar process occurs in 'Michael Angelo' (p. 69), where Lawrence addresses one of the artist's male nudes as follows:

> Who shook thy roundness in his finger's cup?
> Who sunk his hands in firmness down thy sides
> And drew the circle of his grasp, O man,
> Along thy limbs delighted as a bride's?

Here is the sculptor as God, forming Adam out of clay. He is also the father and the husband of the new man. The creative act involves the penetration of concavities by convexities, the shaping of each by the other. The creation is formed according to the shape of its creator. It is imprinted with the forms and marks of his flesh. In exactly the same way, two lovers shape each other. Then, once the body has been made in a sexual embrace, it is given life:

> Who, crouching, put his mouth down in a kiss
> And kissed thee to a passion of life, and left
> Life in thy mouth, and dim breath's hastening hiss?

The artist makes love to his creation as the lover creates his beloved. Art and love are governed in equal measure by the phallus. The 'bride' is the body, male or female, which is sculpted by the phallic thrust. Now, if you ram a phallus into wet clay, you form the cup of semen from which Lawrence's heroes long to drink: the vagina, made male. If the penises of two men are involved, two receptive orifices result. They may be mouths or anuses, or mere clenched hands, but are figuratively associated with the brimming vagina. Hence, the male bride. In certain poems, such as 'Love on the Farm' (pp. 42–3) and 'A Love-Passage' (pp. 870–1), Lawrence conventionally takes the role on himself, writing in the first person as a woman in love with and made love to by a man. In 'A Youth Mowing' (pp. 219–20), he is a girl made pregnant by a proud, young agricultural labourer. And in the fourth part of 'Two Wives' (pp. 156–7), he speaks as a wife who sculpted her young husband's manhood, moulding his lips with hers, drawing up his penis with her inventive fingers, and augmenting with knowledge his luxuriant pubic hairs. The poet's 'female' voice, here, has all the yearning creativity that it attributed to the hands of Michelangelo.

Why, then, given so heady an atmosphere of sexual affinity and activity between men, does Lawrence shy away from the idea of fellatio and anal intercourse between men? What are the reasons for his equivocal attitudes to homosexuality and homosexual intercourse? He has no objection to fellatio in disguise as cunnilingus: remember the vagina as a fruit-like and fruitful repository of seed, to be breached and emptied by the tongue. And he values anal intercourse, between man and woman at least, to the extent of making it a vital feature of *Lady Chatterley's Lover*. It has a specific purpose, in Connie Chatterley's case, of 'Burning out the shames, the deepest, oldest shames, in the most secret places'.[9] Furthermore, the anus is 'the source of the deepest life-force, the darkest, deepest, strangest life-source of the human body, at the back and base of the loins'.[10] This description occurs in *Women in Love*, as Ursula Brangwen hugs Rupert Birkin's loins, thereby discovering an important fact about the nature of his body. 'She had thought there was no source deeper than the phallic source. And now, behold, from the smitten rock of the man's body, from the strange marvellous flanks and thighs, deeper, further in mystery than the phallic source, came the floods of ineffable darkness and ineffable riches.' Out of context (Birkin fully clothed; Ursula about to pour them each a cup of tea), this reads like a coprophile rhapsody. Love and excrement are associated, also, in *Aaron's Rod*, where, in the nursing episode I have already mentioned, a lengthy and loving caress is executed by one man with the specified purpose of moving and opening the other's bowels.

There is no doubt that Lawrence himself believes in the 'ineffable riches' he mentions, and that his reluctance to commit himself to them has some cause other than distaste for excremental processes. In fact, as I have said, the problems he faced with regard to homosexual acts seem to have been primarily semantic. Heterosexuality and homosexuality alike are anathema to him, both being symptomatic of inhibition. Both are limitations on the phallus, which has to be free. His heroes may be bisexual, but they can never become 'sodomites': for that would imply a preference for one sexual mode at the expense of all others, and an acceptance of the penetratory impetus of a partner's phallus. To be entered was the sexual role of women; and, despite Lawrence's image of the male bride, he subscribed enough to the stereotypes of *machismo* to believe that a hero stabs. He may *be* stabbed only by a bayonet or knife.

Lawrence's statements on sodomy in the poems and letters are outspoken, if not always clear. In 'Bawdy Can Be Sane' (pp. 844–5), he writes, with primitive magnanimity (and stylistic negligence):

Even sodomy can be sane and wholesome
granted there is an exchange of genuine feeling.

But to become obsessed with it – presumably, to the extent of seeing oneself as exclusively homosexual – is pernicious, as is any obsessive concern. Thus, 'sodomy on the brain becomes a mission', which is not the purpose of sex. Another version of the same poem, 'What's Sane and What Isn't' (pp. 952–3), goes a little further. The premise is the same:

> Even, at the right times, sodomy can be sane and wholesome, granted there is proper give and take.[11]

(Remember, he means only occasional sodomy, 'at the right times'.) But he concludes: 'In fact, it may be that a little sodomy is necessary to human life'.

Is the whole, elaborate structure of his homo-erotic imagery, then, to be reduced to this, to 'a little sodomy'? Surely not. Surely, Lawrence could not condone any view which called for 'a little' sex as enough sex for a fulfilled life. That would smack of the disciplinary inhibition of the white-collar worker, for whom he had such searing contempt. The fact is that on this subject Lawrence was what he most feared being: inhibited and confused. In a letter to Henry Savage, dated 2 December 1913, an extremely ill-considered paragraph on homosexual relationships wanders from the proposition that 'nearly every man that approaches greatness tends to homosexuality' – which is less probable than possible, and remains unproven – to something about suicide. Finally, in exasperation but good humour, Lawrence writes, 'Again I don't know what I'm talking about' and leaps to the safer subject of the weather.[12]

POLITICS AND THE NEW MAN

Lawrence's confusion becomes even more apparent in the political poems, which are a tangle of semantic vagueness. The evident origin of his political dream, as of the free form he adopted for his verses, is the work of Walt Whitman, which he read with alternating enthusiasm and reservation. As W.H. Auden observed, whereas Whitman makes of himself a complex persona as American bard, containing multitudes, Lawrence uses verse as a means of expressing his most intimate emotions, and seeks always to avoid falsifying the self by expanding his voice beyond personal bounds.[13] He disapproved of Whitman's emotional megalomania. But 'adhesiveness' appealed to him, as manifested in Whitman's version of the ideal democracy. When Lawrence writes a poem on 'Future Relationships' (p. 611), therefore, a familiar pattern emerges:

> The world is moving, moving still, towards further democracy.
> But not a democracy of idea or ideal, nor of property, nor even of
>   the emotion of brotherhood.
> But a democracy of men, a democracy of touch.

However, his definition of democracy is characteristically unorth-
odox, as James G. Southworth explains: 'Lawrence believes that the
term "democracy" is generally misunderstood. Democracy is service,
but it is not to serve the common people. Democracy is the service of
the common people to life.'[14] De Tocqueville would have shuddered.
For a start, someone – Lawrence himself, or one of his leader-heroes
– has to decide how life is best served; and then the common people
must be coerced into its service. Finally, fidelity to the principle of life
must be continuously enforced. This is 'democratic' Fascism at its
simplest: enforced athleticism and the survival of the fittest.

With this in mind, we may find something sinister in the respect for
tenderness Lawrence shows in 'Signs of the Times' (p. 612):

> If you want to get a glimpse of future possibilities
> look at the young men under thirty.
> Those that are fresh and alive are the same in every country,
> a certain carelessness, a certain tenderness, a certain instinctive
>   contempt
> for old values and old people:
> a certain warlessness even moneylessness,
> a waiting for the proper touch, not for any word or deed.

But what of all the women; and the elderly men; and the young men
who are not 'fresh and alive' in Lawrence's sense? The problem with
erotic politics is that the vision of the ideal world or society often
comprises a hierarchy of relative physical beauty, based on the
political theorist's own sexual tastes. If 'instinctive contempt' is to be
the basis of a social system, that contempt must have an object, and
the object must be more or less anathematised.

So, there is one major flaw in Lawrence's physically-based
espousal of the workers' cause. It is evident in poems like 'Spiral
Flame' (pp. 439–40), in which the poet apostrophises young working
men in order to praise their erotic vitality:

> O pillars of flame by night, O my young men
> spinning and dancing like flamey fire-spouts in the dark ahead of
>   the multitude!
> O ruddy god in our veins, O fiery god in our genitals!
> O rippling hard fire of courage, O fusing of hot trust
> When the fire reaches us, O my young men!

This scorching, passionate heat of male strength, grace, and lust is
seen, in the stanza which follows, as the destroyer of a complacency
we must associate primarily with the interests of the bourgeoisie: the
dancing flame will burn the thick upholstery of armchairs containing
the upholstered corpses of the comfortable. But these throbbing

torches of erectile fire will effect their *uprising* (a word whose double meaning Lawrence always intends) in order to form a new elite 'in the dark ahead of the multitude'. *Some*, not all, of the vital class will rise up to lead the rest. In 'Democracy' (p. 526), Lawrence writes:

> I love the sun in any man
> when I see it between his brows
> clear, and fearless, even if tiny.

That is to say, he grants all men the potential of freshness and vitality. But the sun image has its origins in Aztec mythology and, fully developed, in the poem 'Sun-Men' (p. 525), leaves democracy far behind. I quote the poem in full:

> Men should group themselves into a new order
> of sun-men.
> Each one turning his breast straight to the sun of suns
> in the centre of all things,
> and from his own little inward sun
> nodding to the great one.
>
> And receiving from the great one
> his strength and his promptings,
> and refusing the pettifogging promptings of human weakness.
>
> And walking each in his own sun-glory
> with bright legs and uncringing buttocks.

The 'sun of suns' is the young god, Huitzilopochtli, who is served and nourished by the shedding of human blood, in the sexual form of sacrifice we witnessed in 'Eloi, Eloi, Lama Sabachthani?' He is instated by the plumed serpent, Quetzalcoatl, the guardian of wisdom and knowledge, and god of civilisation, whom we can associate with the artist. Huitzilopochtli is the fiery glans penis which, within the span of each day, rises, gives life to the earth and then sinks. Each morning he is ready to rise again, like the phoenix. And his anus is no longer required as a sexual organ: for the new god is, like the leader-hero, a penetrator never penetrated.

Now, if all men are to become sun-men, not only will a hierarchy of beauty have been established, but also a hierarchy of relative 'virility'. At the top is the phallic god, at liberty to move between the 'uncringing buttocks' of any and all of his worshippers. On the next level are the highest men, the closest to the phallic ideal, who may penetrate their subordinates but be penetrated only by the sun-god himself. At the lowest level, presumably, are men who (like women?) exist only to be penetrated, and who are denied any phallic power.

These are the 'sodomists' Lawrence most despises. They are as necessary to his state as slaves to Montezuma's; and it is their blood that will flow to slake the god's thirst. The phalluses of all above them will be the bayonets of political victors. The whole system assumes a collective neurosis, charged by a morbid fear of anal intercourse. We are reminded of the fake, strutting virility involved in the pseudo-religious movement described in *The Plumed Serpent*; and of the pseudo-political movement, based on love between men, described in *Kangaroo*.

What of women? Carried to its logical conclusion, such a system as I have outlined might result in a move to do away with them altogether – as in some of William Burroughs' comedies. Lawrence does not go so far. Are women, then, to be mere machines, to serve a dual masturbatory and reproductive purpose? Of course, this is far from Lawrence's intention. We have forced his ideas on male love to their unacceptable conclusion, and arrived at the apparent contradiction which must modify them. There is no questioning the fact that his art is primarily hetero-erotic in intention. And he repeatedly condemns the sexual manner which uses women's genitals as mere extensions of the masturbating hand. 'The ordinary Englishman of the educated class goes to a woman now to masterbate [*sic*] himself. Because he is not going for discovery or new connection or progression, but only to repeat upon himself a known reaction.'[15] Such men are heterosexual versions of the 'sodomist' – who has, then, no necessary connection with homosexuality or with anal intercourse, but is named for his attitude to sex (and is misnamed, therefore) – as we see in the poem 'The Noble Englishman' (pp. 446–7). The Englishman of the title is said to be like most of his fellow countrymen, because

> by instinct he's a sodomist
> but he's frightened to know it
> so he takes it out on women.

But, if he were to acknowledge his actual orientation (assuming that that is what it is, and the poet is not simply insulting homosexual men by laying on them the faults of heterosexual men), would Lawrence allow him more than 'a little sodomy'?

Auden may have been right about the source of Lawrence's confusion on these matters, when he wrote of him: 'The truth is that he detested nearly all human beings if he had to be in close contact with them; his ideas of what a human relationship, between man and man or man and woman, ought to be are pure daydreams because they are not based upon any experience of actual relationships which might be improved or corrected.'[16] It is certainly true that when a relationship appears to be failing Lawrence's characters tend to look, not for a solution, but for an alternative relationship in an alternative mode. As for his own homo-erotic experience, which may have led to the confusion, we know he said to Compton Mackenzie, 'I believe the nearest I've ever come to perfect love was with a young coal-miner when I was about sixteen'.[17] But his later attempt at a similar relationship, with the Cornish farmer William Henry Hocking, was by no means a lasting success. It is difficult to tell exactly how he envisaged the ideal relationship between men. He tried to explain, in 'Compari' (p. 499), but is rather more cryptic than revealing:

> I would like a few men to be at peace with.
> Not friends, necessarily, they talk so much.
> Nor yet comrades, for I don't belong to any cause.
> Nor yet 'brothers', it's so conceited.
> Nor pals, they're such a nuisance.
> But men to be at peace with.

Again, his problem (so, ours) is largely semantic. Does he mean lovers? He has evidently discarded his invented cause, of political cameraderie. He obviously seeks something much deeper than a chatty friendship. He certainly desires bodily contact, but not necessarily to the extent of 'a little sodomy'.

In 'Reach Over' (pp. 763–5), he says to a group of men who are as 'masculine as the sun':

> Reach over, then, reach over
> And let us embrace.

So, the desired physical contact is more than mere wrestling, even if it begins as such. Nor does Lawrence rule out kissing, as we see in an early version of 'Cypresses', published in *The Adelphi* in October 1923:

> Among the cypresses
> To sit with pure, slim, long-nosed,
> Evil-called, sensitive Etruscans, naked except for their boots;
> To be able to smile back at them
> And exchange the lost kiss
> And come to dark connection.[18]

This 'dark connection' is certainly physical, and certainly not combative. The men are certainly naked, and seem to want to emphasise the fact by keeping their boots on. Their 'connection' is certainly sexual contact of some kind. But it would be wrong to label it as involving any particular act, since that would imply a labelling on their part, also; whereas they are less likely to be setting out to complete a particular sexual act than to be embracing in whatever changing manner is called for by the spontaneous momentum of the embrace. Perhaps, at last, this is what is meant by 'a little sodomy'. Just as, between woman and man, many different attitudes and positions may be adopted in succession, so too, between two men, a number of different sexual events may take place within the duration of a single embrace. In that case, the penetratory imperative will have been disregarded, and the phallus cast again in its role as penis, one of a multitude of erogenous facts.

5 HART CRANE

The Bridge was published in 1930. Forty-five years passed, before any critic managed to explicate satisfactorily Hart Crane's observation, in 'The Tunnel,' that love had become 'A burnt match skating in a urinal'(p. 110).[1] Referring to this line, Robert K. Martin wrote, in 1975, 'The source of the metaphor ... is of course a sexual encounter in a subway men's room. Following the moment of "illicit" and covert sex in front of the urinal, all that remains is the burnt match, thrown into the bowl by one of the men, after its purpose has been served ("Got a match?").'[2] Quite. That it took a gay commentator to say so, is not insignificant. Although relatively few critics forget even to mention Crane's homosexuality,[3] most of those who refer to it do so in entirely negative terms, linking it with his alcoholism and other 'vices' as the ultimate causes of his suicide, yet refusing it significance enough to have any fruitful bearing on the poetry. Needless to say, had he been heterosexual, none of the commentators would have brought Crane's sexuality into the following contexts: 'he was an alchoholic and a homosexual';[4] 'Even toward the end, he never completely gave up the struggle against his two weaknesses, alcohol and homosexuality';[5] 'as his drinking became more furious, so did his homosexual liaisons, chiefly with sailors, become more squalid, more dangerous, and more hopeless';[6] 'uneducated, alcoholic, homosexual, paranoic, suicidal';[7] 'Sexual aberration and drunkenness were the pitfalls in which his spirit wrestled with a kind of desperation';[8] 'This vice, together with his alcoholism ... tended not only to weaken but to age him'; 'His homosexuality grew intense and his bouts of drunkenness multiplied'; 'His final leap from the "Orizaba" exceeded his homosexuality and his alcoholism not so much in intent as in degree'; 'The poet could ... descend for days into drunkenness and perversion';[9] 'his addiction to homosexuality and alcohol';[10] 'his exhibitionistic homosexuality, his alcoholism, his hysterical relations with friends and lovers and family, and finally his suicide at the age of thirty-three';[11] 'The increasing disorder of his personal life, dominated by alcoholism and homosexuality';[12] and 'He was certainly homosexual, however, and he became a chronic and extreme alcoholic. I should judge that he cultivated these weaknesses on principle'.[13]

John Unterecker writes that 'Hart had all of his reputations trailing in his wake: heavy drinker, homosexual, unpredictable spendthrift, extrovert, introvert'. But his comment that all these terms were 'accurate to aspects of his personality' yet 'false to the man' is incomprehensible.[14] Solomon Grunberg told Unterecker that 'Hart's drinking and his homosexuality were all tied up in each other'.[15] I do not mean to suggest otherwise. In much the same way, any heterosexual man's alcoholism would have intimate links – causal or not – with his sexuality. However, it is important not to write off Crane's homosexuality and alcoholism – if he was, indeed, alcoholic – as negative functions of each other. In its own right, Crane's love of alcohol and of the places in which it was served motivated much of his poetry, 'The Wine Menagerie' and 'Cutty Sark' in particular. Positive aspects of his homosexuality exerted a deeper effect on even more of his best work, and are inseparable from it. (But Herbert A. Leibowitz's belief that Crane's best poems are 'about himself', is atypical.[16])

The first of Crane's poems to be published (in September 1916) has as its title the number of the cell in which Oscar Wilde was held at Reading jail, 'C 33' (p. 125). Since, as Robert Martin says, 'the alienation of the artist and the persecution of the homosexual' are combined in the figure of Wilde, the cell itself is a symbol of interrelated philistinism and prejudice.[17] In this poem, as in 'Modern Craft', published two years later, Crane shows his keen awareness of the forbidden nature of homosexual love: 'My modern love were / Charred at a stake in younger times than ours' (p. 132).[18] But the white and gold within Wilde's cell can cause him, and us, to 'forget all blight'.

Crane is a connoisseur of the shades and connotations of white and gold. As several commentators have said,[19] he uses gold hair as a symbol of both physical and spiritual forms of beauty and love.[20] To gauge roughly the scope of his use of whiteness, one has only to list some of the things his poetry describes as being white: snow, hair, bed linen, a paraphrase, the wind, buildings, love's cheeks, cities, shadows, birds, surplices, a veil, a meteor, the Arctic, eyes, moonlight, a hostelry, love, wings, a flower, sea spray, milk, nights, swans, sand, and teeth. Related to this accumulation of detail are many references to objects of silver and pearl. Although Crane's allegiance to whiteness was established before his first reading of Melville's *Moby-Dick*, in 1922, after that date it developed, taking on much of the symbolic breadth outlined in the novel's 42nd chapter, on 'The Whiteness of the Whale'. At the height of his powers, Crane would invoke a whiteness which, while retaining its elementary connotation of purity,[21] had matured to epitomise the very crux of his concern: the apotheosis of sexual love.

White is the colour of semen. (Hence, in part, the erotic weight of Pierrot, and of sailors in summer, dressed entirely in white.) The 'white meteor' in 'The Dance' (p.74) and 'the meteorite's white arch' in 'Key West' (p. 171) are both images of ejaculation. The 'Southern Cross' is another stellar manifestation of the poet's non-reproductive, but not unproductive spermatozoa (p. 99). In 'To the Cloud Juggler', the line 'Your light lifts whiteness into virgin azure' shows both semen and the human soul, in a single flash of resurrection, fecundating the azure emptiness of death (p.159). The relationship between the gold of love and the white, or silver, of sexual fulfilment is comparable to the alchemical wedding of *sol* and *luna* (sun and moon), the central process in the transmutation of base metal into gold. A correct balance between the two must be sought, by conscientious lovers, if they are to receive the full rewards of their love.[22]

The early attempts at love are hesitant. In 'Episode of Hands' (p. 141), Crane describes, in the discreet third person, having attended to the wounded hand of a worker in his father's factory. A number of tensions is set up – between flesh and machine, worker and boss's son, blood and light, labour and leisure – to be resolved in the straightforward contact of one pair of hands with another. The poem works at a simpler narrative level than most of Crane's work, coming tonally close to Cavafy's version of a similar theme, 'The Bandaged Shoulder' (1919), in which the protagonist, having adjusted the dressing on a young man's wound, secretly presses his lips to a discarded fragment of bloody lint. But this fetish is twice removed from its object: from sexual orifice to wound, and thence to the wound's covering. Crane, being a less detached poet than the Greek, remains closer to the basic desire, by concentrating on the wound itself. As blood flows from the cut, through the mediating wheels of the machine, the heat and light of the sun flow in. The worker's embarrassment at Crane's attention to his welfare is not acute enough to prevent the small act of mercy which follows. The poet's hands, winding gauze around the wound, seem 'Like wings of butterflies / Flickering in sunlight over summer fields'. The denominator common to metaphor and surface narrative is the light which, as if liquid, both heals the wound and nourishes the fields. It isolates and proclaims the essential truth of the cut hand: that it is less a function of the machine it operates than of the landscape it calls to mind; and it has both under its control. By its intrusion into flesh, the machine wins less than the land, which is moral victor. This recognition of the union of the industrial worker and the land he serves is fundamental to Crane's vision of States united in more than government and name.[23] Sherman Paul comments that Crane 'may have used the poem as an oblique way of telling of his homosexual love. It dramatises homoerotic discovery, and makes it an occasion of the external world.'[24] Although 'Episode of Hands' seems the least oblique of all Crane's erotic poems, Paul's remark is pertinent to the works of this early period.

Even if we cannot state with R.W. Butterfield's confidence that 'The Moth that God Made Blind' (which dates from when Crane was 16) 'may be read as a poem written after a first homosexual relationship',[25] we can see in it the same sense of discovery, even of surprise, which informs 'Episode of Hands'. 'The Moth that God Made Blind' (pp. 122–4) ventures out of the lush oasis to which its fellows are confined, and finds itself 'pierroting over', around the 'fresh breasts of day', in a yellow desert landscape. It flies upwards, through 'a sea of white spray', until it reaches a point at which the sun 'shot out all white'. From here, for a moment, it is able to see 'what his whole race had shunned – / Great horizons and systems and shores all along / Which blue tides of cool moons were slow shaken and sunned.' This, barely articulated, is a prevision of that possibility of transmutation I have already mentioned: *sol* and *luna* in collusion, theirs the white crucible of sexual intercourse. (It is also a version of the ideal American geography, which Crane will later formalise, as the body of a woman.) In a final stanza, Crane associates himself with the moth, since his eyes, too, 'have hugged beauty'. As a result, he, too, has been left with secrets, and 'a tongue that cannot tell'. Despite the avowed privacy of the experience described, we are not meant to understand the moth's flight as a solitary act of folly, characteristic of the introverted. On the contrary, as in 'Episode of Hands', Crane is already seeking a verbal way to the wider question. The distanced view available only to the soaring moth – a view beyond the bounds of inherited constraint – is a primitive version of the view Crane takes of America in *The Bridge*, in full command of time and space, thus able to fill his voice with the materials of both history and geography at once.

One final poem from the early period seems to benefit from an explicitly sexual reading, if we do not insist on disallowing other interpretations. 'Postscript' (p.136) to a sexual encounter, this poem reflects the aching disillusionment of a period of detumescence, when the sexual organs of the two lovers are like fountains, which 'droop in waning light'. (Remember, we have already established the symbolic link between semen and light, in Crane's poems.) Feeling pain, which 'Glitters on the edges of wet ferns' in the region of his anus, the poet declares: 'I should not dare to let you in again'. In other words, he does dare, because of desire and in spite of pain. The 'sundered boughs / And broken branches, wistful and unmended' in the second stanza, are further images of detumescence, rendering the poet's imagined garden of physical love desolate and lifeless, promising no rebirth. Clearly, the depression of these thoughts has to do with the poet's physical pain, which will lessen in future encounters. But lack of pain is beyond the scope of this poem, which looks only into the immediate past. The mood of failure is blamed on the lover in a final line which says more about the poet's immaturity than about the lover's inconstancy. What seemed a postscript to the possibility of sexual love, in fact, barely introduces the subject.

WHITE BUILDINGS (1926)

White Buildings[26] necessarily attracts the attention of the reader who is interested in the verbal manifestations of Crane's homosexuality, because it is a more personal volume than *The Bridge*, and because it contains the 'Voyages' sequence of love poems. However, many of the other poems are significant in this respect, and I shall deal with them first.

John Logan's foreword to the 1972 edition of *White Buildings* dwells on the supposed bisexuality of Crane, and interprets the poems accordingly.[27] Three of the volume's opening poems – 'My Grandmother's Love Letters', 'Sunday Morning Apples', and 'Garden Abstract' – are cited as being relevant to what Logan calls 'bisexual balancing', which he explains as 'a problem of balancing the masculine and feminine elements' in oneself, 'in order to discover and develop one's own identity'. The conflict between these opposed elements 'is one which Crane felt painfully' (p. xxi). When Crane identifies momentarily with the grandmother whose old love letters he has found and read, he shows his concern with femininity and, therefore, 'with the homosexual aspect of his own bisexual feeling' (p.xxv).

'Garden Abstract' was originally written in the first person, but was changed to the female third when Crane noticed its phallic implications. The published version is an uneasy falsification of the original (which is to be found on page 76 of Brom Weber's *Hart*

Crane). However, in the poem's opposition of apple and sun, John Logan again locates 'bisexual balancing', and quite logically sees the mimicking of one element by the other as suggesting 'that the feminine is a metaphor for the masculine' (p.xxvii). I do not find Logan's premise – that Crane's proposals of marriage to women prove him bisexual – at all convincing, and I feel inclined to doubt his conclusions. In 'Garden Abstract', for instance, the image of the apple can as well be male as female, since to imagine testicles as fruit is a poetic commonplace. (Indeed, Crane's taking fright at the phallic connotation of the apple tree suggests a male, rather than a female aspect to its fruit.) However, Logan's ungrudging acknowledgement of the importance of Crane's attraction to men, rare as it is, outweighs the problematical insistence on his equal attraction to women.

R.W. Butterfield reports that the first draft of 'Garden Abstract' was 'blatantly homosexual in implication' and that this poem reflects Crane's 'discovery beyond doubt of his homosexuality'.[28] 'Stark Major' (p.10) seems to Butterfield to be 'a poem of self-solace, in which Crane convinces himself that it is not the homosexual alone who is doomed to loneliness and disillusion, but also the faithful husband and father'.[29] But his remark that 'Pastorale' (p.12) is 'a poem written after the early collapse of a homosexual love affair' is, as it stands, too gnomic to be of much value.[30] On 'North Labrador' (p.15), he is brief, but apposite: 'Crane's desperation must have been accentuated by the thought that his own homosexual love affairs, while beautiful to him, were also sterile'.[31] However, this was not always his opinion; far from it, indeed. The landscape of North Labrador is too icily white to sustain life of any significant kind. It seems lit by its own cold glow. Most of Crane's landscapes of love, as distinct from nocturnal cruising grounds in which lust alone operates, are sunlit.

More than any other of his poems, 'Possessions' (p.18) draws the attention of the commentators to the literary significance of Crane's homosexuality. After all, the crucial image of a monolithic 'fixed stone of lust' makes it difficult to pretend that the poem is not about sex. To Lewis, the poem's imagery is 'overtly homosexual'.[32] To Uroff, its images of torture 'are all sexual, in fact, phallic, and suggest the homoerotic nature of the poet's suffering'.[33] Butterfield sees this as 'a poem of homosexual anguish'.[34] More elaborately, Paul calls it 'a poem relating to the possession (madness) of wayward homoerotic desire, or lust'.[35] Spears comments that 'The situation would seem to be that the poet is embarking on a new (homosexual) affair, driven by his lust, and almost sure that this affair will turn out like all the others, but going on nevertheless with his tormented seeking.'[36]

Combs thoughtfully perceives here the 'self-degradation and self-pity' into which 'the deviant' can be forced by the hostility of social attitudes.[37] Only Robert Martin manages to shuffle off the supposedly objective heterosexual pose of the critics, by convincing us in his use of language that he has begun to understand the poem from Crane's point of view. It is about cruising, he says. In part of what follows, he reaches a conclusion similar to Combs'. 'Crane has written what is probably the first poem of the modern urban homosexual in search of sex, his hesitations the result of fear and self-oppression. He desires and yet he fears; he will go and yet he hesitates.'[38]

I cannot pretend to have fully understood this poem; but one or two observations on it seem called for. The phallic and totemic 'fixed stone of lust' is Crane's image of the insistence of his own desire: as it were, a demonic erection, forever demanding fresh blood. It is appeased only by sexual explicitness, both verbal and physical. Hence, the three dots of discreet self-censorship which follow each of Crane's two direct references to it. Lust requires him to say more than he may 'decently' say in a poetic context; but the reader must, therefore, be sure not to dismiss lightly the poem's unstated, parenthetical material. The absent speech of lust is at once explicit and inarticulate. One may cry out in ecstasy as one submits to a stranger's embrace, but may not use the sacred Word or words of love – which begin and end with 'love' itself. One need not know the other's name, or speak his language, to complete the necessary exchange of physical moves. A wink or smile to start with, and a sigh of completion, are sufficient.

From the first published version of the poem,[39] the poet cut the line, 'rounding behind to press and grind' (which came between the final version's lines 13 and 14), I presume, because rhythmically it merely acted out the previous line's musical image of a 'stabbing medley' of sex, thereby rendering itself redundant. It also belongs to the area of explicit pornographic description – of a position, and a renewal of pelvic thrusting – which is to be exiled to the rows of dots ending lines 9 and 17.

Among all its phallic images, 'Possessions' has one of Crane's most powerful: that of the 'smoked forking spires' which transfix him and on which he turns impotently, like a weather vane. The hellish furnaces of lust transform church spires into the Devil's horns, or his bifurcated penis. On the horns, the poet is tossed to death. On the two prongs of the penis, of course, he is stabbed to sexual death – stabbed, that is, in mouth and anus by the lusting men he meets on Bleecker Street – and he emits his 'Record of rage and partial appetites' onto the paper he writes on. The phrase 'partial appetites' refers to his lust for flesh, which at times burns stronger than his need for love, and which sends him out onto the streets at night to be fucked; or, on some occasions, to be beaten up, instead. R.W. Butterfield's reading of this poem becomes unacceptable when he writes that 'for the homosexual Crane coitus cannot be the sowing of a seed that will grow and bud but only the taking up of a stone'.[40] There is a very clear distinction in Crane's work between lustful and loving intercourse. In this poem, it is lust that interferes with growth. The sexual orientation might as well be heterosexual as homosexual, so long as intercourse involves only the phallus, or stone of lust. Anonymous encounters between cruising drunkards in dark corners of the city are forms of possession by a devil whose best plans are scotched by love.

'Lachrymae Christi' (pp. 19–20) seems to be derived from a similar quotidian context, in which a nocturnal townscape peopled with cruisers and prowlers is linked with the drinking of wine: in this case Lachrymae Christi, rich in the connotations of its name. The New Testament verse to which the name refers – 'Jesus wept' – has since become an oath, presumably much to be heard on the lips of the drinkers Crane was familiar with. The wine is white, and is linked in the poem with the moonlight which bathes the factories of the city area concerned. In its name, the wine (and, incidentally, the poem) is explicitly likened to the secretions of a man's body, his tears; which may duly be assumed to have, here, some covert reference to his semen: but semen emitted in sadness, rather than joy. The sexual image is of fellatio: for, like wine, the semen is drunk to excess in the moonlit streets, to intoxicating effect; and, like both wine and oath, it fills men's mouths to capacity.

'The Wine Menagerie' (pp. 23–4) is an outstanding poem on the consumption of alcohol, not least because its presiding genius is not Bacchus, but Orpheus. Erotic and poetic inspiration are as subjects too precious to be entrusted to the care of such a literary cliché as the god of wine. Butterfield classifies this, with 'Possessions', as 'a poem of homosexual anguish'; but, unlike 'Possessions', he says, 'it ends in a darkness without even a ray of hope'. He adds, with a flourish, 'Hope to the homosexual is a dream'.[41] In two footnotes, R.W.B. Lewis comments on this poem, and on the general critical relevance of Crane's sexual orientation, as follows. In the first: 'Such extreme male apprehension of female destructiveness [as Lewis finds in the poem] was no doubt – in Crane's individual case – rooted in a homosexual element, though for critical purposes I am not inclined to stress the fact'.[42] And, in the second: 'Abstracting a human impulse from various of Crane's poems, one can easily enough explain the impulse, as in a case history, by reference to homosexuality; but this would rarely deepen one's understanding of the poem itself. Such a method would yield particularly obvious results with "The Wine Menagerie" – a real-life sense of woman as lethal, as wanting in fact to cut one's head off, is patently homosexual in origin. But this is not what the *poem* is about.'[43] Glauco Cambon stumbles across the same 'particularly obvious results', and writes: 'Crane's devotion to art combines with his homosexual urge in portraying his male friend as the victim of an imperious woman (stanzas 3 and 5), endowed with cruel eyes ("mallets"), who ends up symbolically beheading the man, since in stanza 10 specific mention is made of Holophernes [*sic*] and John the Baptist.'[44]

The heads of John and Holofernes drift past the drunken poet, whispering to each other, as if in conspiracy to defy death. It is to the pagan origin of these biblical shadows that the manner of their passing refers. Crane is thinking of the poet Orpheus, torn to pieces by women for having recommended men to love boys, his severed head floats off, singing its way down river and out to sea, towards its resting place on the shores of Lesbos, citadel of female homo-sexuality and the lyre. The limbs of the god or sacred king are scattered, to enrich the earth: the myth is common. (Crane's source is *The Waste Land* and Eliot's footnotes to it. Contrary to Cambon, the inspiration of this passage seems to be literary fashion, not the id.) The poet's body dies, but the substance of his spirit transcends physique. The head will continue to sing, and be granted the gift of prophecy.

In the the third of the 'Voyages' poems, Crane will mention the 'transmemberment of song', referring to the rearrangement of parts which in physical intercourse leads lovers into new, spiritual form-ations. His reference to the dismemberment of Orpheus seems aimed at a similar notion, and may have some bearing on the dismembered syntax of this and other poems. Crane's poetry rivals some of Auden's in its obscurity; and Crane, like Auden, habitually fished in dictionaries for *mots* as arcane as *justes*. The result is a pattern of words which manage to look scattered, even though they are bound at a distance by the strictest of formal regimes. 'The Wine Menagerie' achieves its effects by pretending incoherence; by belying this, in the maintenance of its sequence of rhymes; and by allowing a frag-mented image of spiritual prowess to recohere, virtually, in spite of a tattered syntax. The poem is the spirit of Orpheus, shuffling off its bodily form.

Although the *dérèglement des sens* and *des sentences* – the dismemberment of the senses' tendency to 'reason' – are inherited from Rimbaud, perhaps together with an awareness of the alchemical meanings of white and gold, Crane's treatment of them is shaped by his persistent and increasingly successful efforts at Americanisation. Some of the early poems are no better than imitations of the *fin de siècle* masters. Later, however, the poet applies what he has learnt to a specifically American context, to distinctly American effect. 'At Melville's Tomb' (p.34) is exemplary. Butterfield complains of its obscurity, which is partially caused by 'the continual need for the homosexual to disguise the true nature of his passions in an esoteric symbolism'.[45] How curious, to have said so, here, rather than in reference to one of the love poems; but, on reflection, how apt! A monody, or elegy, on one of Crane's three American masters (Whitman and Poe being the others), the poem combines Melville's two spheres of activity, the sea and the book, to celebrate his lasting worth, not least in its proof of coincidence of spirit and physique. That this has a crucial bearing on Crane's erotic poetry, is obvious. That it is also relevant to his search for the soul of the body of America, is as important, although easier to overlook.

Sailors who once filled their rare moments of idleness with the rattle of dice now provide the same amusement for the idle sea. The rhythms of the game – shake and throw, shake and throw, eternally – used to inspire the novelist. Chance configurations of bones and shells dictated chapters, as a portent dictates actions to those who credit it. In death, the inspired becomes inspirer: for his bones join the others cast on the sea bed. Crane takes his place on the shore, inspired in turn. A rigidly ordered vortex of paradoxical images – the calm lashings of the waves, dead eyes that live, silent answers – are reconciled with eachother and themselves, like the impotent malice at the still point of the whirling pool.

Nothing falls apart; the centre holds. This vision of dynamic paralysis will be travestied later, in the line we began with: the image of love as a match-stick spinning on a stream of piss. But here it is of unequivocal value, not only on its own account, as an instrument of literary navigation, a 'coil' linking body and soul, life and art, sea and sky; but also as an introduction to the main concerns of the 'Voyages' poems, which follow.

'VOYAGES'

All but the first poem in the 'Voyages' sequence were influenced by Crane's love affair with Emil Opffer. Of this, we can be sure. But how significant is Opffer to us now, reading these poems so many years after their author's death? John Logan says, of 'Voyages', that 'Crane is *not* writing simply of homosexual love or of one person'.[46] Unterecker is at equal pains to make this point: 'Though the

"Voyages" set is a consequence of a love for a man, its subject matter is love itself. Crane would have been the first to be distressed if the poems were read simply as an account of a private love affair. He was writing poetry, not autobiography.'[47] Apart from the final sentence of the latter – which seems to overlook the possibility, not only of autobiographical poetry, but even of poetry shaped by personal experience – and despite the way in which both writers try to belittle the scope of homosexual love, by their insertion of the adverb 'simply,' these two views are apposite.

Samuel Hazo tries to make the same, or a similar point. The influence of the affair with Opffer, he says, is a matter 'best left to psychological disquisition'. Crane's experience is irrelevant to our reading of the poems, for the following reasons.

> There is nothing in the poems that explicitly betrays a perversion of the impulses of love, and there is no thematic reason that would lead a reader to relate the love imagery, where it does exist, to a source homosexual in nature. Consequently, a reasonable reader could find no compelling factors in the six parts of 'Voyages' that would suggest that he consider the impulses of love in any but a heterosexual sense, regardless of the relationship that may have prompted them and regardless of the person to whom they may have been directed.[48]

Ignorance, then, is to be an excuse for travesty. In this exhibition of heartfelt prejudice, by classifying a homosexual relationship as 'a perversion of the impulses of love', Hazo admits his willingness to ignore the poet's contrary view, and the poems' lessons on the nature and power of love in its widest sense. Furthermore – a matter of detail, but detail of some importance – to read 'Voyages' *simply* as a heterosexual love poem is to miss the point of its references to sailors.

Two comments are worth quoting, as correctives to the above. Lewis calls 'Voyages' both 'that rarity in American literature – genuine and personal love poetry' and 'the only truly moving and beautiful poetry of male homosexual love in English with which I am acquainted'. Lewis may not be widely read, but he explains his high opinion well. 'It is so because Crane has succeeded in making the passionate love of male for male representative of every kind of human passion: "the secret oar and petals of *all* love."'[49] Clinching the same argument, M.D. Uroff writes: 'That the inspiration of his love poetry was his own homosexual experience influenced obviously his choice of images . . . but in his power to transmute this experience into poetry, he speaks to all conditions of men'.[50] Just so, any worthy poet produces matters of general significance from those of particular experience.

The first poem (p.35), written before the start of the affair with Opffer, and once entitled 'Poster', precedes but prefigures love, in its open celebration of adolescent and pre-adolescent mutual and self-masturbatory activity. Sherman Paul counters Joseph Warren Beach's opinion that the poem is a warning against homosexual love, with the alternative, that 'it may also be read as a declaration of it'.[51] It may, indeed, be both. The children on the beach indulge in a guiltless and polymorphous form of sexual activity. It is close to play and is as shallow as the edge of the sea towards which it veers, but threatens, on the verge of young adulthood, to wander out of its depth. The poetic voice-over celebrates innocence of sexual activity but warns against precipitous entry into vacuous complexity: the self-deception of false love. Even the bright weather – the crash of waves on the sand, the flash of sunlight on the waves – proposes a storm: crash of thunder, flash of lightning.

One of the great virtues of Crane's poetry in particular, but of the poetry of homosexual men in general, is its insistence on the difficulty of love. Obviously, this theme arises out of the effort homosexual men must put into forming relationships which go against the social and political grain. Love is not an automatic entitlement to whoever finds a partner willing to attempt a lasting relationship. Love is not a civil right; but a comparatively rare capability, granted to those few souls who can balance the delights of shallowness with the dangers of depth. We must remember, when Crane writes of the dangers inherent in the attempt to love, that he was speaking as a homosexual man, and (then as now) that homosexual men were liable to be disowned by their families, dismissed by their bosses, condemned by their peers and priests, castrated or drugged or imprisoned by their doctors, or driven to suicide by the prurience of neighbours and press, for no other reason than their liability to attempt to love other men, rather than women. 'The bottom of the sea is cruel' indeed.

That the relationship with Opffer managed for some time to overcome all obstacles, including love's rarity, Crane, at least, was in no doubt. 'I have seen the Word made Flesh', he wrote to Waldo Frank, in a letter dated 21 April 1924.[52] The spiritual transubstantiation had happened, at last. The alchemical transmutation had happened, at last. There is a corresponding metamorphosis of language in the second section of 'Voyages', immediately more obscure than the first; and this obscurity lasts to the end of the sequence. As Leibowitz points out, Crane starts to mix the argot of sailors, and more formal marine technicalities, with the most intimate speech of lovers.[53] He thereby makes lovers of his sailors, and voyages of love. The poems are apparently inaccessible, like the whispered secrets of lovers, those 'wrapt inflections of our love' with which the second poem starts, all the more secret for pertaining to homosexual lovers who dare not publicise their joy.

This second poem (p.36) involves an elaborate scheme of associations between its three subjects: the sea, death, and sexual love. Crane's allegorical figure of the sea, although conventionally female, has as great an influence on the orgasms of the two male lovers, poet and addressee, as a light-emitting phallic moon has had on her vast, tidal belly, now pregnant. That her 'diapason knells / On scrolls of silver snowy sentences' is beyond paraphrase. The 'diapason' relates to the consonance of the highest and lowest points in an octave. Crane seems here, to be drawing a parallel between waves and sound waves. The sea's diapason spans the gap between the troughs and crests of her waves, in which most of her sounds and movements are concentrated. Each wave is associated with one toll of a knell. The slightest caress, the least movement of the voyagers' craft, includes an implied threat of death. The white script which appears as the visible sign of the knell is, at once, the foam cresting the waves in horizontal marks across the seascape; the lines of the poem; and love itself: the very whispers and ejaculations which fill the voyagers' throats.

The sea may be dangerous; but, at this point in the sequence, she tears apart everything except 'the pieties of lovers' hands'. These are sexual caresses, imaged as prayers. The articulate gesture of a hand, moulding itself to the changing shape of the flesh it strokes, affirms love and craves love's continuance. As long as the dialogue of hands is sustained, death – a final, debilitating orgasm – is, at once, approached and avoided. The movement of hands takes part in a prayer with which the poem ends, begging for love to be allowed to continue until death, the point at which 'spindrift' – a continuous driving of spray, captured in a gnomic description of vortex: spinning drift, spindled rift – promises access to a shared paradise.

The third poem (p.37) enacts a vertical sea voyage, from surface to bed; a ritual drowning, which is somehow confined to cupped hands. In a self-referential sense, this is also a journey of creativity, from the tendering of a theme (line 2) to the completion of the song. The first half is an over-exposed seascape, whose visual details fade into insignificance as the last image, of 'reliquary hands', appears. The second half moves indoors, as the features of a deeper seascape close in on it. Now, the details of location change rapidly, as in a dream; and, with them, the actions taking place within them also have to change. In quick succession, there are suggestions of a Baroque church, a ballroom, and, possibly, a stage. These interiors see worship turn to carnival, whose celebratory excesses turn at last to sexual intercourse – a song – to which death is the climax: as final as orgasm, which, of course, is not final at all. Those reliquary cupped hands have caught the relics of a sexual death: the lover's semen.

The movement from first to second half, exterior to interior, depicts the sinking of the lovers' craft into the enclosing pulsation of the sea. This is a sexual image, both of one man entering another and of men entering the female sea. The entry 'through black swollen gates', according to Leibowitz, 'refers both to the ship passing into the trough of the sea and Crane into his lover'.[54] More specifically, according to Robert Martin, the gates represent 'the anus of the lover'.[55] Therefore, beneath the theme of the vertical voyage, or sinking, lie the associated themes of heterosexual intercourse – the fecundation of the sea – and of male, homosexual intercourse. Considering the poem solely at the level of the latter, we find the following, selective scheme of verbal events: the tendering of a theme (love or a lover); the caressing of the lover; the lover's ejaculation into 'reliquary hands'; the entry into the lover's body; the rocking motions of intercouse, presided over by a version of Whitman's maternal, cradle-rocking sea; and the ejaculation of semen, as of the words of the song, into one flesh from the other. These are not, of course, the poem's only events, since others occur at the same time and in the same words. As Lewis comments, 'the erotic act of the lovers has become the model imitated by the universe at large'.[56] In other words, although anal intercourse takes place at only one of many levels, perhaps the most obscure, all other events depend on and are shaped by its progress.

The poem is held together by two governing principles – the long words with which it starts and finishes, 'consanguinity' and 'transmemberment', and by two pairs of hands. With these simple props, it acts out a metamorphosis, approaching the conditions in which the flesh of two lovers merges, over interlocking limbs, and becomes that one, spherical human being Aristophanes describes in Plato's *Symposium*: the original condition of humanity, the perpetual aim of love. Crane saw all relationships as journeys. Sex was a matter of crossing a gulf, on bridges made of flesh, or down tunnels through it. This poem covers a sexual act in that sense: the movement of two travellers towards and into each other, a process called 'transmemberment'. When the possibility of Flesh becoming Word arises, Crane calls this sexual unification the 'transmemberment of song', which is achieved only if the poem is a success.

The fourth poem (p.38) is obscure to the point of secrecy. Syntax and language have congealed, suggesting an interval of lassitude and detumescence. The poem contains none of its predecessor's dramatic events, although it refers to them all. While paired words in the third poem emphasised a coupling of exact equivalents – 'Light . . . with light', 'Star kissing star', 'wave on wave', 'dawn to dawn' – the fourth poem's pairs, after 'gulf on gulf' (line 3), begin to explore the creative properties of difference. Here, 'mortality' is coupled with 'immortally', 'fragrance' with 'irrefragibly', 'hour' with 'ours', 'region' with 'wreathe', 'port' with 'portion'. Two superficially similar lovers begin to learn about their differences, which will both consolidate and destroy their love. Eyes and lips explore and explain, 'making told' to each the other's secrets. Symbols of creative intercourse, the 'flowers and quills' (reproductive organs and pens) we can associate with anus and penis, must grow and die in their repetitive erotic cycle – 'the vortex of our grave', back in the second poem – before the poet is fully able to 'tell'. I associate these quills, as well as with Crane's pen and penis, with the 'white immutability' of albatross plumage: the ejaculated flash of white we find in so many of Crane's poems. The albatross is the symbol of a long sea voyage, and as such represents the relationship between the poem's two lovers. The bird used, also, to be thought to embody the soul of a dead sailor; whence, the ill fortune visited on Coleridge's ancient mariner. The 'white immutability' may, therefore, be taken as the spiritual element of the sexual relationship. Each sexual death involves ascension of a sexual soul, the gull.

Continued from the third poem is the theme of the word becoming flesh; the flesh, word. A phallic pen writes out the lovers' signature, individual mark of their passion; and 'bright insinuations' are passed between them. Although, in this post-coital poem, the goal of the voyage is Emil Opffer's blue eyes, rather than the sexual portals of anus and mouth, it is emphasised that the lovers' craft is still powered by their physical efforts, with the phallic 'secret oar' (associated with anal 'petals') of love. That is to say, the spiritual elements of love are dependent upon its physical base. Voyages cannot be made without the muscular efforts of sailors. The 'Spry cordage' of men's muscles (as mentioned in the first poem) and the 'oar' must be manipulated by skilled hands, for the voyage even to begin. This point, so important to the sequence, is repeated in the first stanza of the fifth poem (p.39), where 'clear rime' – that is, both rhyme and white frost – is associated with a 'merciless white blade' – the blade of the oar with which the previous poem ended, now becoming rather more dangerous, like that of a knife – thereby reasserting the importance of sexual love and love poem to each other; indeed, in the case of Crane's relationship with Opffer, their indivisibility.

We have now received three clear warnings of the ending of love's harmony: the explicit mention of the sea's cruelty, at the end of the first poem; the appearance of the albatross, in the fourth (such appearances being traditional omens of stormy weather); and the new mercilessness of the phallic oar. The cables of the lovers' craft hang, frayed, in frozen air. The cold moonlight of orgasm is losing its correspondences with lovers' speech and love poetry, as if newly deaf to them. Neither the ecstatic cry of one lover, nor the stabbing of the other's 'sword' – now, unequivocally, a weapon, not a means of propulsion – can undermine the suddenly felt 'tyranny of moonlight'. The speech of the loved one can now be quoted directly, in language accessible to all, as if the lovers no longer share such arcane bonds as obscure the poems of their love. Furthermore, what he is quoted as saying is that he has not quite reached understanding; their shared secrets were sometimes secrets, even, from themselves. A merchant ship, fraught with gold, ('the argosy of your bright hair') is endangered by piracy: new partners, perhaps. All the gold of earlier transmutations may soon, therefore, be lost to the poet-alchemist, along with the blond Emil Opffer himself.

All elements of the lovers and their love having undergone 'a sea-change / Into something rich and strange' (as Ariel puts it, in *The Tempest*), in the sixth poem (pp.40–1), their voyages come to an end. The night of the previous poem breaks into day, as silver moon is replaced by golden sun. The churning of the green sea around the bodies of the two men, now swimming together, is likened, firstly, to the 'beating leagues of monotone' emitted by a shell (at which point, we should recall the genital 'shells and sticks' of the first poem); and, secondly, to the passing of the 'kelson' (or keel) of the sun, through a trough of water, in apposition to 'the cape's wet stone' (inevitably, reminiscent of the 'fixed stone of lust', in 'Possessions'). All elements in the poem seem pressed together in a vast embrace: sea and sky; sea, sun, and stone; rivers, sky and harbour; the poet's blinded eyes and the forging 'prow' of either sun or lover. As a memorial to the 'seer' love temporarily made him, Crane begs his lover to cast onto the savage undulation of his flesh, as onto an unappeasable sea, some 'splintered garland' of wilting blooms. The blind seer, if taken from Greek myth, would be either the two-sexed Tiresias, compensated for his blindness with the gift of prophecy; or the first homosexual mortal, the poet Thamyris, blinded by the Muses for daring to compete with their poetic powers. (Influenced by *The Waste Land*, Crane probably only has Tiresias in mind.)

The voyages' end is formalised, now, with the reappearance of the allegorical female figure, a reclining goddess, whose articulate eyes make up for the decline in intimate communication between the two lovers. Despite their imminent parting, the two lovers are still bound by a 'fervid covenant', a 'white echo of the oar', audible souvenir of the verbal aspect of their orgasmic relationship. Belle Isle, the point at which the voyages end, is entwined in hair-like rainbows. The

'Word' is surrounded by the silent fronds of willows. With these two reminders of Opffer's golden hair, we are given a final evaluation of the 'Word' itself, that product of the sexual acts of the earlier poems. It is the unbetrayable and lasting mark of love. The ending of the affair cannot alter or lessen its significance: for it remains, here, on the page, as log or record of the finished voyages. As such, it is the permanent representation of love: a sequence of love poems.

THE BRIDGE (1930)

In *The Bridge*, Crane's public set-piece, his usual love themes are muted by his broader purpose. However, although the book's scheme is sometimes too formal to find favour with his most obviously lyrical talents, matters of personal relevance help to sustain his power. For instance, 'The Harbour Dawn' (pp.54–7) is clearly related to the affair with Opffer, which was partly conducted in Crane's apartment at Columbia Heights, Brooklyn, overlooking both harbour and bridge. The occasion of the poem is that quintessentially poetic time of day, the dawn, when in reality one is usually immersed in sleep, no matter how delightful one's partner, but when lyrical convention's lovers are woken by the songs of larks, to renew their lovemaking for a last time before its interruption by daylight business. Here, the larks are played by gulls and sirens. The predominant colours are the familiar white of feathers, steam, and flesh, and the lightening gold of sunlight and hair; both related to the elevating flash of orgasmic union.

This being the first part of the section entitled 'Powhatan's Daughter', we might reasonably expect a female influence in the poem. But, as in 'Voyages', its lovers are of sex unspecified. Crane's cryptic marginal commentary speaks of a merging of seed, but adds, perhaps playfully, ' – with whom?' It then asks, 'Who is the woman with us in the dawn?' We must, surely, associate her with the native American princess; and it is her influence that fulfils the promise of the section's title. The lovers in the Brooklyn bed may, therefore, be either man and woman or two men. To Sherman Paul, the poem speaks of 'love indeterminately hetero-homosexual';[57] and M.D. Uroff comments that Powhatan's daughter 'is called a woman but her seduction involves only hand-holding and kissing, and what Crane seems to be describing in this ... poem is a homosexual union'.[58]

The flurries and drifts of snow and clouds of steam outside muffle the harbour, softening its edges and giving rise to the image of the 'pillowed bay', by which the whole of the harbour landscape and its white emissions are implicated in the sexual events which are taking place in the poet's bedroom and bed. In the public world, feathers enable gulls to soar, and are imitated by snowflakes; while in the private world, a pillow's feathers buoy up the waking lovers. A chair is half covered with their clothes. Their pale flesh forms undulating drifts as they embrace each other. They are woken by sirens: literally, the claxons of shipping; and also, of course, exquisite voices to lure them from their nocturnal voyage onto the perils of daytime. But, for the time being, love's music and that of the dawn harmonise in a single air. The movement of bare arms joins in the song; the poet's tongue is moulded to the shape of his lover's throat; and the dawn light is drunk by opened eyes – all in a shuddering passage of italicised ejaculation, aptly punctuated with an exclamation mark.

That 'The window goes blond' at this point, directly after an explicit reference to the loved one's hair (and 'blond,' not 'blonde'), seems to me to sanction further association of what follows – description of the landscape in the window – with the bodies of the two lovers. The two one-eyed skyscrapers, their windows afire with reflected sunlight, their tops silhouetted against a sky animated with sun and gulls, require no further explication. The silently receding fog, the morning star, and the pearly, white berries of the so-called 'mistletoe of dreams' (with its ancient connotations of fertility and a festive kiss) all contribute to the same context: of the immediate aftermath of male orgasm or orgasms.

After a pair of insignificant references, to a man with 'a colt's eyes' and to youths 'with eyes like fjords', both in 'The River' (pp.62–9), Crane's erotic interests resurface with great vigour in 'The Dance'. I cannot improve on Leslie Fiedler's pithy version of what Crane is doing in this poem:

> What he yearns to celebrate is not the legendary Indian Princess at all . . . but the dusky Indian Prince whom he imagines his as well as her true lover. Indeed, Crane's name for that dusky Prince comes out of his own private mythological store, 'Maquokeeta' having been the actual middle name of a cabdriver boy friend; and it is to him, not to Pocahontas, that the poet chants the phallic song in which his verse – elsewhere flaccid and unconvincing – comes to life.[59]

In 'Indiana' (pp.76–9), a young man gives up tilling the soil to go to sea: he drops 'the scythe to grasp the oar'. His mother warns him against a quest for what may turn out to be false gold, and begs him to return home soon. True gold, she claims, is already within him, behind the 'engaging blue' of his eyes. The next poem, 'Cutty Sark' (pp.81–5), returns to the familiar themes of seafaring and drink. The speaker meets a tall man, whose green eyes fascinate him, and takes him to a local bar. Drunkenly, the man tells his story, to a repetitive background of sentimental music. At dawn, the speaker leads him to his ship, before walking home alone.

'Cape Hatteras' (pp.87–95) bears as its epigraph a line from Walt Whitman's 'Passage to India' (VIII): 'The seas all crossed, weathered the capes, the voyage done'. (Clearly, this doubles as epilogue to the previous poem and epigraph to this.) In Whitman's original, the line is followed by three more:

> Surrounded, copest, frontest God, yieldest, the aim attain'd,
> As fill'd with friendship, love complete, the Elder brother found,
> The Younger melts in fondness in his arms.

Crane elaborates on this for the climax of his poem, where, in 'living brotherhood', he and Whitman embrace, 'never to let go'.

Between the two descriptions of the one embrace, each written by one of the men involved, Crane, not at his most lucid, considers whether or not technology has really wrought radical change since Whitman's time. The unchanged constant seems to be true brotherhood, a vague notion, vaguely outlined. In fact, the relationship with Whitman seems no more impressive than that of any writer with an admired predecessor. There is a hint of eroticism in Crane's description of his reactions to first reading Whitman: 'White banks of moonlight came descending valleys', and 'Gold autumn . . . crowned the trembling hill!' But the poem's bombast and overgrowth of imagery (the former in pale imitation of Whitman himself) interfere with whatever contribution Crane had meant to make to his master's theories of democratic love. The personal note has been replaced by effortful myth-making.[60]

Three songs follow. In the second, 'National Winter Garden' (pp.100–1), Thomas A. Vogler reads the phrase 'cheapest echo of them all' as 'a reference to Crane's homosexuality', a point I do not understand.[61] In the third song, 'Virginia' (p.102), Sherman Paul sees in the mention of some crap-shooters 'an innocent homosexuality, or a sexuality not yet wholly differentiated'.[62]

As a modern equivalent to the classical descent into the underworld, 'The Tunnel' (pp.107–12) has been thoroughly and usefully explored by a number of Crane's commentators. I am half inclined to give it a rest. However, the burnt match goes on skating in its urinal, inadequately explained. It is 'a metaphor which realizes perfectly the final degradation of love, the quenching of its fires by the ineffable vulgarity of the modern spirit', according to R.W.B. Lewis.[63] It is an image of the modern American city's 'lack of liberty and love', a parodic 'degradation' of the Statue of Liberty, according to Richard P. Sugg.[64] It expresses the fact that 'in the modern world human love is felt only as lust', according to M.D. Uroff.[65] Of course, the general conclusions we must draw from the image may be these, or similar. But only by attending to the exact, quotidian details – as outlined by Robert K. Martin – can we relate the image to its detailed context. Crane is referring to a sexual encounter in a public lavatory. The reference is not isolated, because 'The Tunnel' is consistently scatological.

A sociological and avowedly voyeuristic study of *Tearoom Trade: Impersonal Sex in Public Places*, by Laud Humphreys, is the curious reader's best reference work on the kind of encounter Crane had in mind.[66] 'I find no indication', Humphreys writes, that the men who frequent public lavatories for sexual purposes 'seek homosexual contact as such; rather, they want a form of orgasm-producing action that is less lonely than masturbation and less involving than a love relationship' (p.115). Of the sample of men questioned, 54 per cent were married and living with their wives. In 63 per cent of these marriages, one or other or both of the partners was/were Roman Catholic. Of the emotions involved, the following remark is indicative: 'I have noted more than once that these men seem to acquire stronger sentimental attachments to the buildings in which they meet for sex than to the persons with whom they engage in it' (p.14). The attractive features of tearoom sex are said to be danger, availability, invisibility, impersonality, and variety.[67]

The reader who overlooks the burnt match's role in establishing a sexual encounter, and the scatological associations of the encounter's location, is liable to underestimate the sexual meaning, and miss altogether the faecal meaning, of the subway train's frenzied plunge into and emergence from the bowels of the earth. (This will subsequently undermine the reader's understanding of the triumphant cleanliness and whiteness of 'Atlantis', the book's next and final section.) An elementary pun on 'motion', early in the section, associates the train with excrement; and this correspondence is reinforced whenever the convulsive movements of the train are described. Meanwhile, several crude, venereal metaphors – a coin pressed into a slot; potatoes being dug in mud; the quivering train itself, which 'humps' its way through darkness – ensure that we connect movement (of the penis) into the rectum with movement (of faeces) from it. Furthermore, as the very idea of a sexual encounter at a urinal must remind us, the penis may emit either semen or urine. In a negligent sex life, the pleasure of orgasm may be no greater, and certainly no more meaningful, than the pleasure of releasing the contents of a full bladder. Indeed, the two emissions may be confused.

The distance between this version of intercourse and that of (say) the third poem in the 'Voyages' sequence is self-evident. Here, even white is devalued, by being linked with physical decay in advertisements for toothpaste (to fend off tooth decay) and dandruff remedies. The only approximation to gull feathers, here, is on the floors of train compartments, where old 'Newspapers wing, revolve and wing'. But all negative elements in the poem can be conceived of as having positive effects. There can be no rebirth without death; no purgation without excrement. Catharsis depends on filth. Only after enduring the humiliation of her occupation – the cleaning out of cuspidors, which is akin to being spat at – can the washerwoman fully appreciate returning home to her golden-haired children. Human waste highlights human creativity.

In the same relation to each other, as interdependent negative and positive factors, are lust and love. If a man could not inform all men he met that he was open to the possibility of a loving, sexual relationship with any one of them (that is, if he could not announce his homosexuality), and if he had no gay bar to frequent, where all clients announced by their presence the same possibility, then his only alternative would be to meet other homosexual men under the self-evident conditions of lust, and hope for a chance encounter with another seeker after love. In other words, the social oppression of homosexual men dictates that lust be a means of meeting – always in the secrecy of sordid locations at night – and that love, if it prosper at all, must grow out of the lustful circumstance imposed by the heterosexual empire. Unlike the conventional couple, whose relationship is expected to move from friendship to love to a wedding night of sexual climax, male couples have been forced to start with sex. Critics of the supposed brevity of homosexual relationships, and of the supposed promiscuity of homosexual men, should take into account their own detrimental influence on the balance between homosexual lust and love. I read the line about the burnt match as reflecting such external barriers to the progress of love.

The poem's scatological imagery seems to take part in an ironic reflection on the reduction of sexuality to sexual acts. The very concept of homo*sex*uality (emphasis on the *sex*: another imposition from outside the individual man-loving man), the law's detailed proscription of acts, and society's articulated sense of disgust at the thought of certain acts (anal intercourse in particular) have reduced pairs of lovers to the sum of their physical deeds. To think of a homosexual man, merely, as one who (say) presses his penis into the rectum of another is as asinine as to think of all human beings, merely, as bodies which eat and excrete. We are more than our physiques; we transcend our actions. The scatological vision of homosexual intercourse is an oppressive travesty with which critics of gay men deny them the capability of loving and the right to love. Crane uses this travesty with some force, before discarding it as he rises again to harbour level and the light of day.

Much of 'Atlantis' (pp.114–17), were it slightly less formal, would not seem out of place among the 'Voyages' poems. Its theme is announced in the epigraph, where Plato relates music to love. (Plato himself tells the story of Atlantis, in *Critias* and *Timaeus*.) In the first stanza, Crane embarks on a number of his favourite themes and makes of a radio mast's and a ship's elaborate rigging and, again, of Brooklyn Bridge, an Aeolian harp, whose harmonies can be associated with those of the voices of poetry. The proportions of both music and the human body being governed by the same ancient principle, the Golden Section, he is able to form a correspondence between this 'cordage' – reminding us of the 'spry cordage' in the first of the 'Voyages' – and the thews and sinews of a man's flesh. We cannot fail to recognise the erotic messages contained in the flashes and flickering of light, both natural and electric; and in the sounds of the vibrating wires. In a single phrase, 'gleaming staves', Crane has compressed his mass of interrelated material, dependent upon the following four meanings of 'stave': one of the strips of wood used in the construction of a ship's hull; a stick or rod; the five parallel lines and four spaces used in musical notation; and a stanza of a poem. To call the stave, in its manifestation as rod, a phallic symbol, seems indecently, but necessarily explicit. In this climactic poem, male sexuality soars above the problematical urinals of 'The Tunnel'.

The message of the opening songs, 'Make thy love sure', is borne upward, past the 'frosted capes' of moonlit 'twin monoliths', as phallic as one chooses to make them. They may be analogous to the 'fixed stone of lust' in 'Possessions'; but as stones, rather, of love. Above these, up a 'crystal-flooded aisle' between 'silver terraces', the words continue to rise into a white and stormy region of stars. The familiar image of 'seagulls stung with rime' takes on the submarine but no less orgasmic modification of 'glistening fins of light', as if Crane meant to fuse his two worlds, of sea and sky, by likening the transcendental messages of ejaculated semen to flying fish, which, having broken into open air, become gulls – lighter, perhaps, and more agile than the albatross – in order to continue to soar. The flight, the continuous beating of their wings on air, is described in the span of the phrase 'blade on tendon blade', which reinvokes the phallic oars of 'Voyages' and the complementary sinews of wrestling lovers. Where love, as opposed to lust, is concerned, ejaculation is never final. Lovers invoke semen, whose flight invokes lovers. Love and sex are similarly bound.

An additional word on whiteness is called for at this point. So far, I have concentrated on its positive aspects. In the chapter on 'The Whiteness of the Whale' in *Moby-Dick*, Melville acknowledges these, but goes on to speak of 'an elusive something in the innermost idea of this hue, which strikes more of panic to the soul than that redness which affrights in blood'. Among his examples of terrifying whiteness, he includes the plumage of the albatross, icebergs in the southern seas, and the surf which gathers over jagged rocks. Hart Crane's images of ejaculation seem to take this chilling aspect of whiteness into account. I have mentioned his belief in the difficulty of love; but he seems, also, to have understood the dangers of sex. Many of these are the dangers he faced when cruising by night: the vengeful fists of the self-hating, after orgasm; the cowardly fists of the queer-basher, before; the unmotivated fists of the drunkard. . . But one can conceive of other elements which might cause disquiet: the sheer force of ejaculation; loss of control; inarticulacy; and so on. The 'white seizure' in Crane's poetic system is as much embroiled in the struggles of a dying man as is any conventional literary description of orgasm. Death may lead to resurrection, but the struggle is no less in earnest for that.

'Atlantis' is the whitest of all Crane's poems; and nowhere else is his fusion of sound and light so complex and complete. But triumph, as an end to struggle, is always anticlimactic: Odysseus and Penelope reunited, Ithaca regained. The excitement of epic defeats its attempts at a satisfactory ending. The epigraph to 'Atlantis', justifiably, boasts 'harmony and system', the characteristics of 'To Brooklyn Bridge'. The imagery of the first poem repeats itself in the last. But in the last, it is, as it were, allegation backed with evidence. The proof of peace is lack of war; of harmony, lack of disharmony. The journey from Ithaca to Ithaca is needed as evidence that Ithaca is worth staying in. Until lost and regained, Paradise is unrecognisable as such.

In 'Voyages', a painful vortex of sexual pleasure drew lovers down into the profundity of love. In *The Bridge* they must pass the equivalent whirlpool of stale piss in 'The Tunnel', before descending to the heights of 'Atlantis'. The location of the final poem is familiar: a fusion of seascapes, both surface and submarine; and the bridge, uniting water, air, and earth. A ship seems to be 'hanging in the night', although its keel is as firmly planted in the sea as a plough in earth. The drowned city seems a constellation in the night sky. . . The role of love, here, is uncompromised: 'love strikes clear direction for the helm' of the voyagers' craft. If 'Cape Hatteras' failed to do justice to Whitman, the emergence of 'Atlantis' from 'The Tunnel' more than compensates for that shortcoming. Crane's final version of love in America, charged as it is with the personal force and imagery of

'Voyages', is no formal evocation of brotherhood or comradeship, no mere reassertion of the master's tenets, but an individual appeal for individual development, based on individual experience. It transcends the limitation of act. This point is 'pro-homosexual' (insofar as it is not anti-homosexual) and yet general enough for the squeamish critic to ignore. After all, what does it matter, which physical organ is doing what in which other, and on what sidewalk or bed the act is taking place, when the wave leaps or the star shoots?

LATE POEMS

Although the urban imagery of 'The Tunnel' takes the problematical balance between lust and love to some kind of extreme, Crane did not attribute such problems only to city life. They exist still in the later poems, so many of which are set in the relative isolation of Mexico and the Caribbean. In 'The Idiot' (p.163) and 'Lenses' (p.179), Crane refers to a boy who, although simple-minded and innocent, seems to have been in the habit of publicly fondling or exposing his penis. That Crane found him 'rendingly beautiful at times',[68] is not wholly irrelevant. What is the relationship between the boy's kite-flying serenity and his precocious sexuality? Were one to make love to so alluring a creature, what might be the damage (if any), either to him or to oneself? Would love, indeed, be possible with him? There is no point in seeking answers to such questions in the poems. Crane did not know. His terms of reference, lust and love, must suddenly have seemed inapplicable.

But he returned to them. In 'Moment Fugue' (p.173), using brief snatches of incomplete syntax and minimal punctuation, he depicts a syphilitic selling flowers. To whom but romantics should such emblems and tokens of love be sold? A victim of lust sells hyacinths, those symbols of beautiful youths, to lovers; and, although commerce intervenes ('dealing change for lilies'), it does not interfere. Both meanings of 'fugue', musical and psychological (a fugue is a temporary flight from rational consciousness, involving loss of memory), operate within the title, thereby enforcing the poem's leap from the quotidian to the abstract, and from act to sign. There are roses being sold, which, like the imitative genitalia of statues, refer to human sexuality but can take no part in it. As mere symbols of orifice, they are 'roses that no flesh can pass'. Hyacinths are at a similar distance from what they suggest. The physical past of the syphilitic debars him from any but symbolic intercourse; whence, his 'fugue' from memory into mime. Selling 'heaven perhaps' at the gates of hell (a subway news-stand), he has no message – no warning, no recommendation – but the theme of his forgotten past and the uncertain future of cut flowers.

Let Lewis provide us with a biographical introduction to another poem, 'Reply' (p.177). The year was 1930. 'One morning, after (as it seems) a night-long homosexual session, Crane hurried off a three-stanza poem conceived, as the title suggests, as a "Reply" to his still sleeping companion, and which oddly mingles the sense of shame and a poet's pride.'[69] The sleeper is evidently a man whose only means of expression – indeed, of intercourse – is sexual. He can 'read nothing except through appetite', a phrase which may have the literal meaning, that he does not read. Certainly, he is not an intellectual; and what Crane has to say to him can be expressed only in terms of physical act. It 'balks delivery through words'. The situation is not uncommon. After physical intercourse, the intellect of the poet consults the mute physique of his lover, to intellectual effect: a poem. So, not only is lust Crane's path to love; he sees that it is also an important route to poetry. Do the circumstances of this poem's composition, if Lewis' version is correct, not prove this? That the lover will never read the poem suggests, contrary to Lewis, that the 'reply' of the title is aimed not at the sleeping lover, but at some debate being conducted within Crane himself.

The poem contains two distinct images of physical intercourse. In the first, 'we join eyes' which, because unreading, are 'without sight', but still manage to forge a satisfactory 'conviviality'. In the second, 'swords' make 'wounds' in comprehending flesh, expressing therein a form of 'hate', which 'is but the vengeance of a long caress'. The two modes are not set up in opposition to each other. Each confirms the other's limitations. It is in the deceptive, aural similarity of 'fame' and 'shame', that Crane locates difference; and these two elements exist, not one in each lover respectively, but both in Crane. To that extent, the sleeper is no longer relevant to the debate. His blissful sleep will continue, regardless.

Equate 'shame' with physical acts; 'fame', with intellectual acts. This does *not* leave us with a simple poem, rejecting sex for poetry. As we have seen, Crane consistently argues for loving relationships based on physical union. His poetry depends on sex, as does his love. What I think he means is that, where love is absent (as here), the poet may compensate for what he sees as the limitations of unmediated lust, by reinforcing the creative impetus of his art. 'So sleep, dear brother, in my fame, my shame undone.' One cannot help feeling, in such a poem as this, the common regret of the intellectual, that he cannot be satisfied by a simpler, physical life. The naked lover is sleeping off the bliss of his lust without complication. But Crane sits nearby, obsessively worrying his way through the verbal repercussions of his pleasure: 'fame', 'shame'. . .

As we have seen, Crane's homosexuality and supposed alcoholism are linked by some commentators, not only with each other, but with his eventual suicide, as its causes. However, other perspectives are available. In fact, Crane committed suicide at the height of a *heterosexual* love affair. Whether or not the one had a causal bearing on the other is beyond my scope and interest.

Crane's affair with Peggy Baird during the final months of his life has been taken to call into question the fact of his homosexuality. Now, at least, he was homosexual no longer. He had always been, or had now become, bisexual. This is convenient: for it allows the commentator to interpret all of Crane's love poetry as though it were explicitly addressed to a woman. He is more or less, for the purposes of universality and good taste, safely heterosexual. . .

Such arguments do not reward consideration. Butterfield refers to Crane's last affair as 'his awakening from the nightmare of his homosexual past'.[70] Susan Jenkins Brown believes Crane 'exaggerated' his attraction to men.[71] John Logan is confident that 'Crane was bisexual', merely because he 'twice asked women to marry him, first Lorna Dietz and then Peggy Baird Cowley'.[72] Even Peggy Baird herself, in her careful account of the affair, remarks that Crane only '*thought* of himself as a homosexual'.[73]

Certainly, he seems to have been both shocked and delighted at his mastery of the mechanics of heterosexual intercourse. 'Boys – I did it!' was his announcement, after the successful first night with Baird. She commented, later: 'It was embarrassing to him to find himself so suddenly changed, after living his adult life . . . in the firm conviction that he was a homosexual and could be nothing else'.[74] Indeed, Crane himself remarked buoyantly to a guest: 'I'm very happy because I have discovered that I am not a homosexual!'[75] This narrative of redemptive undeviation is not to be taken, gullibly, at face value: for the poet's moods were alternating rapidly, throughout this period. In a restaurant, talking to Lesley Simpson about Peggy Baird, Crane burst out with: 'She thinks she can reform me, does she? I'll show her! Why, God damn her, I'd rather sleep with a man any day than with her!'[76] The relationship with Baird was not monogamous on Crane's part, since he was receiving the sexual favours of local Indian youths during the same period.[77] On the last night of his life, he was attacked and robbed while visiting – no doubt, for sexual purposes – the crew's quarters of the ship on which he was voyaging with Baird to the United States and marriage.

One magnificent poem, 'The Broken Tower' (pp.193–4),

commemorates this troubled period, seeming, therefore, to excuse my concern with these biographical details. Robert Combs provides the following comments, on the final love affair's relevance to the poem. 'The woman referred to in stanza seven is probably Peggy [Baird] Cowley, who was, it is thought, the first woman Crane loved. And it is possible to read these last stanzas as a celebration of the sense of rightness and wholeness Crane may have felt as he was able to reconcile his personal sexual experience with one of the strongest "generalized appearances" of our society, heterosexual love.'[78] While, as we have seen, there is no lack of 'rightness and wholeness' in such homo-erotic celebrations as the 'Voyages' sequence, Combs' point about society is well made. Crane needed to be no longer beaten up or robbed for proposing sexual intercourse. He needed his sexuality to be accepted as a part of love. Society allowed these exemptions and privileges – for so they were treated – to married (heterosexual) couples alone.

'The Broken Tower' is a detailed and honest, retrospective examination of Crane's love life, encompassing sexual acts both with men and with a woman, and attachments both lasting and brief. The poem was written during a period of Mexican festivities, when the church bells seemed to be ringing without pause. Crane hears them, alternately, as a joyous peal and as a knell ('Antiphonal carillons' as he puts it). As in the third section of 'Voyages', the poem's movements are vertical, befitting the nature of the tower. Already, in the first stanza, the poet has 'dropped down' and gone up again, from the pit of a grave to the crucifix atop a cathedral tower, thereby enacting the processes of death, burial, and resurrection. The tower itself being, as most commentators have agreed, an intended phallic symbol, these processes take on their sexual connotations of detumescence and retumescence. The second stanza, then, is of masturbatory significance, ending in the by now familiar orgasmic image of silver stars, emitted into sunlight as golden as honey.

The music of the bells has a similar function to that of the singing in 'Voyages' and the humming of the Aeolian harp in 'To Brooklyn Bridge': all three have to do with the lasting, spiritual outcome of temporary, physical processes; and all three are connected with the image of the ascent of spirit in a white flash of semen. The tower emitting the antiphonal music of bells is, therefore, associated with Crane's own ejaculating penis. When he comments, in the third stanza, that 'the bells break down their tower', he refers to the loss of erection attendant upon emission. Calling himself the 'sexton slave' to his 'long-scattered score / Of broken intervals', he turns from the subject of masturbation to that of intercourse with another person: the burial of his musical score in a lover's flesh.

At this point, he declares the barrenness of his briefer affairs. 'Oval' in their potential productivity, rather than their shape, his ejaculatory 'encyclicals' are not disseminated. Instead, they collect in an oral and rectal 'impasse', where their voices are slain. Despite the 'reveilles' sounded from other towers – 'Pagodas' and 'campaniles', representing the penises of anonymous sexual partners (often foreign sailors; hence, the foreign towers) – his spermatozoa do not wake up. They lie dead, 'prostrate on the plain', like the Theban Band at Chaeronea. As Crane explains in the fifth stanza, most of the encounters he is referring to resulted from 'desperate' choices, and lasted 'not for long': minutes, one would guess, rather than days. He encountered at the urinals of 'The Tunnel' just this kind of love: no less 'visionary' for its location; but of little worth, in that the voice of its song, together with the semen emitted, was lost, as if hurled into the wind. He poured out his 'word', he writes, without relating it to the sun, that transmuting 'monarch of the air'. The phallic sun emits a 'crystal Word' only into men who conduct hopeful love affairs, rather than desperate fumblings for relief in dark, public places.

The last four stanzas of 'The Broken Tower' are concerned, almost exclusively, with sexual potency: the maintenance of erection. As we know from the biographical accounts, Crane was relieved to find himself capable of the mechanics of making love to (meaning, specifically, penetrating and sustaining his penetration of) his new mistress. Whether he could continue to do so seems, on the evidence of the poem before us, to have caused him some anxiety. When he asks if blood can 'hold such a lofty tower', he means the blood which fills the erectile *corpus cavernosum* of the penis. Or can it, indeed, be 'she' (Peggy Baird), who excites him enough to stir the 'latent power' of his latent heterosexuality? He is so conscious of possible failure in this respect, that he begins to feel and hear every stroke of the blood in his veins, tolling like an Angelus bell, in remembrance of the Annunciation and – more significantly, in this context – the Incarnation. This insistent throbbing of the poet's blood 'builds, within, a tower that is not stone', the erection required for tonight's performance. In the phrase 'matrix of the heart', Crane seems to rely on an archaic meaning of 'matrix': the womb. The 'eye' referred to in the same line is the vagina, which 'shrines the quiet lake' – a stretch of water noticeably unlike Crane's favoured, stormy seascapes of masculinity – and which 'swells a tower'. The orgasmic shower with which the poem ends confirms that the tower is no longer the ruin claimed by the title.

6 W.H. AUDEN

UNAUTHORISED BIOGRAPHY

There is more than ample evidence that W.H. Auden's private and public lives were not separate and cannot be separated. Richard Ellmann has said, 'As befitted a lyric poet, Auden's sexual life was the center of his verse.' Auden himself, in a letter dating from April 1931, gave John Pudney this literary advice: 'Never write from your head, write from your cock'.[1]

Humphrey Carpenter's biography of Auden provides numerous examples of erotic works which arose from distinctly homo-erotic occasions.[2] And many other poems not mentioned by Carpenter had similar origins. Even some of the best-known pieces contain once-private, crude jokes with which the interpreter ought now to be acquainted. For instance, the 'Letter to a Wound' (*The Orators*) was inspired by the after-effects of an operation Auden underwent in 1930, for a rectal fissure; and 'The Novelist' refers to a bout of V.D. suffered by Christopher Isherwood. Other, blatantly homo-erotic works were written for Auden's own and his friends' amusement, and were never intended for publication. The most famous of these, 'The Platonic Blow' or 'A Day for a Lay', was published under Auden's name but without his permission.[3]

But Auden raised a substantial barrier to our understanding of the relationship between his life and work, by arguing that 'he had written his published love poems to be read without reference to the sex of the person addressed'. This was the reason he gave for not allowing a poem of his to be republished in an anthology of gay verse.[4] He would systematically cover up the origins of his poems, by referring to a lover as the genderless 'you', and by adding misleading dedications and facetious titles to what began as love poems. As one understandably exasperated, gay commentator said: 'Auden . . . was unhappy about his homosexuality. In his own circle, he played the role of outrageous queen, but in public, he took the view that the sex of his beloved objects was a matter of indifference so far as poetry was concerned (an opinion which, so far as I know, has never been expressed by a heterosexual poet).[5] Furthermore, Auden requested that after his death all letters from him should be destroyed, 'to make a biography impossible'. In any case, even if a biographical account were to be written about a particularly interesting artist, it would throw 'no light whatsoever upon the artist's work'.[6]

However, Auden's views on the biographies of artists were ambivalent, if not contradictory. He seems to have allowed himself the intrusive curiosity that he frowned on in other critics. Since he believed there was a great symbolic difference between oral and anal intercourse, and since he imagined all gay men preferred one of these acts to the other, he was particularly interested in finding out what other homosexual artists liked to do in bed.[7] His own critical method involves telling us that A.E. Housman was 'an anal passive', or that J.R. Ackerley, being neither oral nor anal, enjoyed the Princeton rub.[8] Of course, two can play at this. Auden was oral: he liked sucking cocks.

Unfortunately, where sexuality is concerned, the critics have not found it difficult to act within the spirit of the ban on biographical revelation. Auden's reluctance to write openly about his homosexuality resulted in a corresponding reluctance, on the part of his commentators, to grant his sexual orientation any but the most limited relevance to his work. In a curious way, the 'discretion' (for which, read 'ambiguity' or 'obscurity') of the poems was accepted as a gag on any attempt to understand the experiences which were their source and often, indeed, their subjects. Critical perception of the poems has largely failed to reach what turns out to be a rich strain of interest in the nature of homosexual love and, thus, managed to distort Auden's view of sexuality, and of love in general.[9] *The Penguin Book of Homosexual Verse* does both Auden and itself a disservice by including only one of his poems, the trivial 'Uncle Henry'. And even Ian Young, who rarely seems reluctant to include an item in his bibliography *The Male Homosexual in Literature*, grants Auden only five entries: *About the House*, *Academic Graffiti*, the *Avant Garde* edition of 'A Day for a Lay', *The Orators*, and *Thank You, Fog*. An asterisk, denoting any work 'in which homosexuality is a major aspect' or which is 'otherwise of particular relevance', is awarded only to 'A Day for a Lay'. One might almost be persuaded it was someone else, not the elusive Auden, who wrote *Look, Stranger!* (1936) and *Another Time* (1940).

François Duchêne writes that Auden's 'secretiveness about his private life is ostentatious, one might almost say exhibitionist'.[10] Conversely, the clear diction and imagery, the transparency of the individual line, make for deceptively simple poems which turn out to be maddeningly obscure. Clive James places Auden's homosexuality at the core of this early style. His fluent concern with *things*, and his formidable 'capacity to elevate facts from the prosaic to the poetic', might have led a heterosexual poet at once to the heart of his erotic themes, without any need for dissimulation. However, with sexual acts between men as crimes, and homo-erotic poetry as admissible evidence of them,

> The need to find an expression for his homosexuality was the first technical obstacle to check the torrential course of Auden's unprecedented facility. A born master of directness was obliged straightaway to find a language for indirection, thus becoming immediately involved with the drama that was to continue for the rest of his life – a drama in which the living presence of technique is the antagonist.[11]

If this is so – and I can find no reason to doubt it – one response to the ambiguous 'you' of the love poems may be to reject the customary excuse for it (that is universalises the poem, by flexibly referring to either a female or a male lover, according to the inclination of the reader), and to read it, instead, as a flaw, perpetrated not by the poet, but by external pressure on him. Edouard Roditi has answered objections to the reticence of such poets as Auden, Spender, and himself, by pointing out that their omission of lovers' genders from their poetry 'should distinguish it clearly from the love poetry of most heterosexual poets, who rarely leave the reader in doubt about the sex of their Celia, Clelia, Delia, Dark Rosaleen or Lalage'.[12] If this is the understanding on which such poems were written – if the reader was meant to infer that the 'you' meant 'he' – the universalising factor ceases to function. And from that moment, the unvaried 'you' has all the look of a mark of censorship: the black smudge which, far from obliterating what it covers, actually draws attention to it.

Ambiguity is of no great value in itself. It is a result, rather than a goal. William Empson (whose *Seven Types of Ambiguity* came out in 1930, two years before *The Orators*) is inclined to condone 'trying not to be ambiguous', for the sake of clarity, and he implies that ambiguity is a critic's thing, rather than a poet's. The diversity is in interpretation; and is apprehended, not made. With reference to the famous lyric 'Lay your sleeping head, my love', we see that the poet cannot write to a lover of indeterminate sex – a 'he or she', referred to as such – without turning his passion into an abstract conceit: 'Let the winds of dawn that blow / Softly round *his or her* dreaming head. . .' (There is the 'universal' poem, in all its barrenness.) The poet can only omit to specify sex, while still thinking of a particular person, of a particular sex: in the case of Auden's lovers, male. Auden is nothing, if not a poet of the particular; and it is plain, here, that he has a certain man in mind (Isherwood, in fact).[13]

Auden clearly accepted the undifferentiated 'you' as a viable mode of address. It depends on the view, which is now a liberal commonplace, that there is no essential difference, behavioral or qualitative or whatever, between a homo- and a heterosexual love affair. Love is not affected by the minutiae of its physical expression. What matters is not the 'he' or the 'she,' but the moral impetus of the love.

The problem is, of course, that this does not tally with Auden's own views on sexual orientation. Homosexuality was a psychologically disordered or a sinful condition, and so was heterosexuality (if in a different way), all of humanity being disordered or sinful; but homosexuality always seemed *more so*. Auden consistently refers to gay men in such negative terms as pouf (EA, p.101), pansy (p.152), pathic (pp.102, 123), bugger (pp.42, 71, 105), and queer (p.198). Such references are as often flippant as not. Unlike Isherwood, Auden never completely outgrew the sniggery vicar-and-choirboy version of gay relationships. Nor did he ever renounce the belief that homosexuality is a 'weakness' (EA, pp.33, 86, 237; CP, p.370) or a 'crooked' deviation from the 'straight' logic of heterosexuality (EA, pp.118, 154, 243, 244).

However, although he used some of the oppressor's tools, Auden never condoned the oppression, which had a profound effect on the content of his poems. The briefest glance at the 1930 *Poems*, at *Look, Stranger!*, and at *The Orators*, will reveal an atmosphere of suspicion, and of political and social subterfuge. Auden refers again and again to leaders, heroes, fighters, borders, locked and unlocked doors, raids, betrayals, bombs, interrogation, physical and moral torture, sentries, traitors, enemies, spies, conquerors, bribery, tricks, and so on – all in a recognisable English context of schools and villages, factories and playing fields, which in some of the verse of his contemporaries seems reassuringly domestic. Auden never sought to reassure. When he thought of social pressures on individual liberties, he came up with an image of 'Sentries against inner and outer', which neatly fuses both oppression and self-oppression. Illicit loves seemed to exist behind a door which was locked on both sides. The hunted transgressor would adopt a disguise, with which, involuntarily implicated in his own hounding, he falsified himself. His chin has 'hairs to hide its weakness in' (EA, p.33). All along the frontier between 'inner and outer', armed men lie locked in stalemate; and only the occasional spy gets through.

The Great War is the vehicle to Auden's metaphor of the confrontation between private and public lives.

THE ORATORS (1932)

Of those few critics who do mention themes of homosexuality in Auden's work, most cite *The Orators* (EA, pp.59–110). Most of these references are brief and unhelpful.[14] However, although he does not once mention *The Orators* by name, much of Clive James' valuable essay on the homosexual nature of the poetry (see above) is derived from it.

In public school and Fascist state alike, hero-worship is *de rigueur*. (It is useful to remember that Auden felt he had a particular insight into Fascism, by having been through the public school system: 'The best reason I have for opposing Fascism is that at school I lived in a Fascist state' (EA, p.325).) The hero is associated with the discipline exerted by the political system, be he prefect or officer, but is more or less exempt from it himself. He flies above it, sportsman or warrior, and in either case beautiful. At this early point in his career, Auden is so fascinated by authoritarianism that his sense of guilt at being homosexual seems politically inspired. His resistance to Fascism will interfere with his desire for some of its erotic side-effects. (Later, of course, his guilt will be religiously inspired.) The ambivalence of *The Orators* arises out of the young Auden's need to have the best of both worlds. It is not clear whether Stephen Spender, the book's dedicatee, is referring to the homosexual man (in general) or to the Airman, when he writes that 'His chief danger is his remarkable irresponsibility which leads him to indulge in Fascist day-dreams of fantastic and murderous practical jokes'.[15] The book itself is just such a joke, fantastic while not murderous. For what it lacks in murderousness it compensates in descriptions of cruelty. The 'Address for a Prize Day' is an incitement to betrayal, packed with fools' (and Fascists') logic. It urges the schoolboys to harry the sinners in their midst, who are divided into Dante's three Purgatorial types: those guilty of, respectively, excessive love, defective love, and perverted love. The speaker's definitions of these types are vague. It seems certain that they include all the boys who have been ordered to do away with them.

The Orators is full of boys. Actually, many are men; but they are all treated as ex-boys: for they are the Old Boys of the school, and their common memories are of boyhood. In the 'Letter to Lord Byron' (1936), Auden quotes his own 'first remark at school', addressed to the matron, as 'I like to see the various types of boys'

(CP, p.95). In *The Orators*, he lists them. In the 'Statement' which precedes the 'Letter to a Wound', as Duchêne observes, 'the encyclopaedist of beautiful boys overcomes the poet'.[16] This is the only time in his career when he does so.

The names on the school roll-call are the terms of endearment by which he who reads them out may praise and make love to them all in one linguistic act. The list is also, of course, a school's Roll of Honour, commemorating lost Old Boys ('One is arrested for indecent exposure') and their more heroic contemporaries, the dead ('One slips on crag, is buried by guides'), lest we forget. The whole book must be read in the company of these men-boys: for theirs is its only world. It is when one of them is singled out for detailed treatment that the full homo-erotic significance of the book becomes apparent.

The 'Journal of an Airman' is a sustained portrayal of oddness. The Airman is an individual, and nothing but. If he works as a cog in the State machine, he does so on his own terms. He is allowed this freedom – the air – in return for a convincing performance as the beautiful young hero, less Rupert Brooke than Lawrence of Arabia. As any interesting private document should, the journal portrays the gap between actor and act. All the self-assertion and cockiness of the hero are here – in his lunatic geometry – but so, too, is the anxious guilt-ridden private man: epileptic, homosexual, and a kleptomaniac.

At various times, it has been rumoured that Julius Caesar, Cromwell, Peter the Great, Napoleon, and Hitler were epileptic. Theirs is the 'sacred disease' of Hippocrates. Its victims, in their fits, were said to be either in a religious trance, communicating with God, or possessed by the Devil. It is sometimes hard not to associate the vast influence of the merely human conqueror with a more aptly powerful devil or god. In his military and heroic role, the Airman's epilepsy seems a bridge between public function – as a manifestation of the State's link with God, or, from the other side, the enemy's allegiance to the Devil – and private unrest.

But his kleptomania is problematical. John Fuller says the Airman is 'probably a kelptomaniac, though his remarks about this frequently suggest masturbation.'[17] This is because of the involvement, in both, of the hands; the solitary nature of both; and the sense of guilt both cause. Kleptomania is a compulsion not necessarily to possess – Saint Augustine confessed that, as a youth, he used to steal, but only things of which he already had enough – but to take possession. Prometheus could be called a kleptomaniac, if the theft of fire (the challenge to the gods) were more important to him than its possession (power itself). Masturbatory fantasy is, in a similar sense, appropriation for its own sake, in that the sum of all fantasies contains the sum of all sexually desirable people (or types) – a sum like that of the earlier Statement's list of ex-boys – without in any way impinging on, or seeking to possess them. The *Malleus Maleficarum* (1486) speaks of witches who 'sometimes collect male organs in great numbers, as many as twenty or thirty members together, and put them in a bird's nest, or shut them up in a box, where they move themselves like living members, and eat oats and corn, as has been seen by many, and is a matter of common report.' Here is precisely that combination of fetishism and the magpie instinct which compels the masturbator. Norman O. Brown has shown how the custom of bride-seizure in ancient Greece, being an appropriation of goods, may lead to an association of love with trickery and theft. If we take the link between sex and theft a little further, we can give credence to the 'scientific' myth of a necessary connection between kleptomania and homosexuality. That Auden takes such correspondences at least half seriously, is our reason for not discarding them.[18]

The Airman is not entirely alone. His late Uncle Henry, although fourteen years dead, is a constant presence; as is the Airman's lover, referred to only as 'E'. Also mentioned several times is an Uncle Sam. There may be some connection between the relationship of the Airman and Uncle Henry, and that of Isherwood and his Uncle Henry. Both pairs forge a close link on the basis of their shared homosexuality, and communicate by the two means, of dinners together and letters.[19] It is possible that Uncle Sam is also homosexual. He arranges for two 'boy fishermen' to give an exhibition of Japanese wrestling in the lounge after tea; and the Airman writes: 'Uncle Sam, is he one too? He has the same backward-bending thumb that I have. I wonder' (EA, p.79). The absurd physiological clue could as well refer to kinship or to shared kleptomania.

The third companion, 'E', is, like his name (and, indeed, his gender[20]), the least substantial. He appears in the Airman's dream, tied to a railway track as punishment for an unspecified act of sabotage (EA, p.85). He lives in a house called 'The Hollies', where the Airman visits him for a farewell supper. Photographs of, and letters from him are destroyed by the Airman, two days before his final flight. That is the extent of their described relationship; but, of course, more can be inferred. It is only after their parting that the Airman can record the last item in his Journal, with reference to sexuality and kleptomania: 'hands in perfect order' (EA, p.94).

George T. Wright says Auden was 'Incurably the psychologist'.[21] This very neatly packages his early mode. Despite critical characterisation of him as a 'pylon' poet, whose world was industrial Britain, his actual landscape was that of the brain; and his allegiance was to the brain, not to Britain. His industrial landscapes are expressions of human sophistication. As Spender wrote, in reference to *The Orators*, 'It is important to realize that this particular airman is not only an airman with an aeroplane, but he is a psychological airman as well'.[22] The aeroplane has a role as an aspect of the mind. Hence, the sabotage of which 'E' is accused in the Airman's dream: he has tinkered with the Airman's mind. Fuller believes 'the aeroplane becomes associated with homosexuality, and flying seems an unnatural activity'.[23] As such, it apparently requires professional scrutiny.

The Airman is a patient, jotting down his thoughts to show an analyst. But the matter is complicated by Southworth's pioneering essay, which has Auden himself as the patient: incurably the psychologist, seeking cure from the psychologist within himself, who cannot cure, being himself one of the symptoms of unease. Southworth writes:

> With an honesty akin to that of Gide's *Si le grain ne meurt*, Mr Auden has recorded the history of his attempt at reaching a satisfactory emotional adjustment. I say attempt because his latest work [up to April 1938, when this essay was first published] would indicate that he has not yet succeeded. Aware of the anomalous position of the Urning in modern society he has sought by his frankness of utterance to rid himself of any guilt or inferiority.

At odds with anything else on Auden, this essay makes extraordinary claims; but its premise, that Auden is his own case study, is important. It is hard to credit Auden with having appreciably altered the situation of homosexual men or women in Britain or America for the better. What Southworth says later (that Auden 'makes an impassioned plea for tolerance toward the Urning whose position in society is anomalous even though he is the product of that society') is, simply, not true. But the other statement, that Auden's 'frankness' was meant as a self-examination, which might rid him of his sense of guilt, is more acceptable. He occupies his own analyst's couch, and makes notes on his own replies.[24]

THE CRITICS' CHOICE

In reference to Auden's view of love, and of homosexual love in particular, it is instructive to examine those shorter poems to which the critics have referred with this aspect in mind. The curious thing about these poems is that few are mentioned in more than one place: where one critic discerns homo-erotic themes, the others seem not to.

Of all the commentators, Southworth and James are the most perceptive in this area, insofar as they cite more poems than the others; but their selections coincide on one poem only, 'Through the Looking Glass'. A second important point is that, of those individual poems dealt with, none appears later in the 1976 *Collected Poems*, which stretches over 673 pages, than 'In Sickness and in Health' (1940) on page 247 – apart from *The Age of Anxiety*. It is as if the critics thought Auden had ceased to be interested in his homosexuality, or inspired by it, after he came under the influence of his Kierkegaardian angel.

John Fuller sees the first piece (I, a-h) in the 1928 *Poems* as 'a kind of farewell to the homoerotic romanticism of school', quoting in evidence Auden's sketch of 'dazzling cities of the plain where lust / Threatened a sinister rod' (f).[25] The first section, then, resounds with a poignancy of nostalgic reflection, as it invokes the drawing of stumps at the end of a cricket match, and the languid disappearance of the 'last boy', his blazer half on, into the woods (a). Fuller's point is valid, but incomplete. Although Auden does bid farewell to one brand of homo-eroticism here, in the second poem (EA, pp.439–40) he greets another, formulated as a dream:

> Last night, sucked giddy down
> The funnel of my dream,
> I saw myself within
> A buried engine-room.
> Dynamos, boilers, lay
> In tickling silence, I
> Gripping an oily rail,
> Talked feverishly to one
> Who puckered mouth and brow
> In ecstasy of pain,
> 'I know, I know, I know'
> And reached his hand for mine.

Here, as in Crane's 'Episode of Hands', is the need of the bourgeois, homosexual poet to make physical and, if possible, spiritual contact with a working man, a need which is the basis of Auden's early politics. In Auden's dream, even the workplace is involved in the sensual experience of union. There is no polished chrome here, below deck, but an oily rail to be gripped, and a silence which itself is tangible: but touching, not touched. No doubt, Auden was aware of the anal nature of funnel, burial, 'tickling silence', and oil; not to mention the painful ecstasy of penetration. But a wet dream is not sexual intercourse. This early in his career, his poems show a marked gap between desire and actuality.

The next piece but one, 'Because sap fell away' (EA, p.441), is an uncharacteristic expedition into fetishism, inspired by Auden's love for Gabriel Carritt, and set in the varsity/public-school arena of 'the lower changing-room', where, after a football match, the exhausted players sit 'In close ungenerous intimacy', recalling details of the lost game. In a silent mood of failure, they, or some of them,

> Open a random locker, sniff with distaste
> At a mouldy passion.

The next line, 'Love, is this love, that notable forked-one' (re-used in *The Orators*), confirms the erotic nature of their deed, the 'forked-one' being the man who has worn the clothing in the locker. Distaste concerns the staleness, not the passion. But, as intermediary, the cloth is as unsatisfying, although as evocative, as the earlier poet's dream. Any intermediary between erotic subject and object must fail to carry out its task – unless it is intermediate in name alone, and has itself become the object. The poem ends with an intermediate consummation, which is no consummation at all:

> Brought in now,
> Love lies at surgical extremity;
> Gauze pressed over the mouth, a breathed surrender.

By the criteria of the later works, love, here, is a misnomer for desire, kept distant from its ultimate object. The action of kissing the cloth is sterile, if not sterilised; clinical, if not clean. What motivates the poem is the very real and immediate force of male beauty, remembered or imagined. The mediating fetish gives focus to the fantasy, a centre to the dream. Beauty rubs off on what makes contact with it: on the inanimate fabric which frames it, on the eye which beholds it, the nose which smells it, and on the mind which, even in beauty's temporary absence, can conjure it up out of thin air. Beauty is nothing in itself without the power thus to move beyond itself, exerting everywhere its influence, at once soothing and arousing. There may be no such thing as beauty unperceived; but, as far as Eros is concerned, a beautiful man is better perceived by eye (to start with) than by effort of thought alone.

Southworth's examination of the next period in Auden's career is as sketchy as Fuller's, of the first; but a good deal more suggestive. He argues that many pieces in the 1930 *Poems* and in *Look, Stranger!* (1936) 'reveal with amazing candour episodes in the love-life of an Urning'. The reverberation of this statement is more significant than the timidity that follows it: for Southworth now, merely, states the obvious – for instance, that 'From the very first coming down' is about 'the end to a love after a year had passed', a fact which applies, whether or not the described relationship is homosexual – without going into the deeper implications of the homosexual aspect, without explaining how he concludes that one poem is on such a relationship but another not, and without fully examining what difference the sex of the loved one makes to the love poem in question. (This does not diminish the importance of what he does say.)[26] In fact, in 'From the very first coming down' (EA, p.25; CP, p.39), we notice not only the ended love, but also the urge to 'a different love' – differing, presumably, from that which has ended and from those dictated by social morality – and reference to a god

> That never was more reticent,
> Always afraid to say more than it meant.

If, as I imagine, we can identify this 'god' with lover and poem, the 'it' reveals reticence on the poet's part, too. In that case, the poet's distance from his love is not merely spatial, and is as much grounded in the individual mind – that which writes the poem – as in the physically divided couple.

Southworth calls the poem 'It's no use raising a shout' (EA, p.42) 'a variation on a similar situation'; but the loving *cul de sac* here described has none of the earlier piece's pointers to distance and difference. It just repeats the familiar bewilderment of intimate estrangement, common to both hetero- and homosexual relationships:

> Here am I, here are you:
> But what does it mean? What are we going to do?

The more suggestive song, 'What's in your mind, my dove, my coney' (EA, p.56; CP, p.59), leads Southworth to conclude 'That the beloved might not be too honourable'. This is not sufficient: for here, again, we meet confusion between the 'making of love' and 'the plans of a thief', the motif of the caressing hand as hunter and pickpocket, and the following sexual invitation, to a male lover:

> Rise with the wind, my great big serpent;
> Silence the birds and darken the air;
> Change me with terror, alive in a moment;
> Strike for the heart and have me here.

These are commonplaces of erotic literature; but it is precisely because they are so familiar that they may not be ignored. The point is not that the loved one 'might not be too honourable', but that the affair itself bears the stigmata of insincerity, for which both partners are responsible, and of which both are aware. Only its sexual element is intact.

Of the poem Southworth mentions next, 'Before this loved one' (EA, p.31; CP, p.44), we now know more than he did, or more than he said he did. His comment is that the poem 'reveals that there had been other relationships before the present one'. Isherwood fills out the picture: the poem was written 'largely to please' the young novelist, and dealt specifically with the boyfriend he calls 'Bubi' (Berthold Szczesny) in *Christopher and his Kind*. To some extent, the 'Before' is Auden himself, whose sexual relationship with Isherwood had preceded and would succeed this. The frontiers mentioned are those which exist between people, as between peoples: between Auden, Isherwood, and Szczesny, as well as between Isherwood's London and Szczesny's Berlin; and flesh is as much a divided landscape as Europe itself.

> Touching is shaking hands
> On mortgaged lands[.]

Landed wealth is an accumulation of past encounters. Only an uncultivated landscape can hope to transcend ownership. Such a place is the domain of 'Through the Looking-Glass' (EA, p.144; CP, p.107).

Southworth claims that this poem's theme, 'stressing the awareness of one person of another, would be impossible in a heterosexual relationship. It possesses genuine passion. The poet realizes that any attempt on his part to forward the matter brings failure'. Here, landscape is both familiar and distant. The portrait of the loved one can be wooded or stony, but is essentially English to start with: 'You are a valley or a river bend'. It is peopled, curiously, by a domestic assortment of the poet's relatives. Even in *The Age of Anxiety*, much of the landscape of 'The Seven Stages', barring its deserts, is recognisably English. So Auden's pronounced sense of lost ways is made especially distressing, by the apparent familiarity and domesticity of the scene. How disconcerting, to need a map, to find one's way round one's own home town; how depressing, not to know well the body of one's lover. But in 'Through the Looking-Glass', the poet makes his own landscapes of the lover's face: for here, it is in his own mind that he is the lost wanderer. It is not love that gets him lost, but thinking of it, and writing. He loses those childhood landmarks, those points of reference for which the lost voyager searches a blank horizon, and is left on open sea. His map, the portrait of the loved one, has no relevance to his present position; but is no less of a comfort, for that. Yet hope remains.

> Lost if I steer. Gale of desire may blow
> Sailor and ship past the illusive reef,
> And I yet land to celebrate with you
> Birth of a natural order and of love[.]

So pastoral England gives way to a coral island, beyond the ownership of earth and flesh. This paradise is to be reached only if the ship is left to the unconscious devices of desire. 'Lost if I steer'.

But it is in the nature of the apparently safe place, whether it be coral island or locked room, to invite a siege. Southworth's point, that this poem's self-evidently 'genuine passion' is not available to hetero-erotic poetry, could only have been validated by further explanation. Where I do think 'Through the Looking-Glass' declares its homo-erotic concern is in its sceptical attitude to safety in love. 'All lust', here, is 'at once informed on and suppressed'. And even verbal secrets, such as those of the poem itself, are seen through: for 'Language of moderation cannot hide'.

A slightly earlier poem, written in August 1930, confronts some of the same themes. If, as Clive James says, 'the idea of the homosexual's enforced exile is strongly present, although never explicit', in the first stanza of 'The Wanderer' (EA, p.55; CP, p.62); and if the second stanza's mention 'Of new men making another love', is a reference to homosexual intercourse, as Edward Mendelson suggests; then it is not unreasonable to interpret the third and final stanza as a plea for the safety of an unnamed, homosexual man, under siege in his own home. The mentioned dangers seem lifted from a combination of the Bible and adventure fiction: 'hostile capture', 'sudden tiger's leap', 'thunderbolt', and 'gradual ruin'. But this man is no adventurer, to whom 'tiger's leap' might be an amusing challenge. He is ordinary. Were he heterosexual, he would not merit a poem. As he is, his main wish seems to be to be left in peace.[27]

Another poem cited by James shows how *opinion* takes over a homosexual affair as public property. In 'Dear, though the night is gone' (EA, p.161; CP, p.117), the room in which two lovers spend the night may be a mere double bedroom, but it is thought of as a cavernous dormitory full of strangers, which in turn is compared with a railway station.

> We kissed and I was glad
> At everything you did,
> Indifferent to those
> Who sat with hostile eyes
> In pairs on every bed,
> Arms round each other's necks,
> Inert and vaguely sad.

Despite the claim of indifference, the lovers are obviously all too aware of the opinions which cluster around them like an audience. Indeed, their private caresses become involuntarily exhibitionistic, their love a performance, because of the insatiable curiosity of the watchers. Heterosexuality, self-appointed policeman and spy, is here the voyeur, unable to take its eyes off the view from which it pretends detachment, 'with hostile eyes'. The watchers are formally divided (as if by convention, by marriage) into couples, and formally wed by an inert caress: a limp arm around a neck. They do not move, except vicariously, in the envious sadness of their stares, which pass slowly over the lovers' flesh . But the seed of separation has been sown. Some secret 'guilt' or 'doubt' has interfered with the loved one's commitment to the affair. In fact, it seems, he goes over to the other side. His confession of 'another love' (rather than just another lover) suggests that even he, one of the participants in the night's performance, was himself a watcher; and that what seemed to be sexual intercourse was, in fact, a most vicious form of double-crossing.

Naturally, the figure of the impostor is common in poetry which isolates pretence as one of the prominent features of false love. To expose the impostor is one of the duties Auden adopts as moralist. We see him in action in the early version of 'Consider this and in our time. . .' (EA, pp.46–7), where, as Frederick Buell says, a Financier is 'partly exposed as a decadent and exploitative homosexual'. And in 'The Questioner Who Sits So Sly' (EA, p.35; CP, p.47), according to Fuller, Death 'is personified as hypochondriac, eccentric, and possibly homosexual'. As such, he is trebly the impostor: for aping the illnesses of his intended victims, while he is actually healthier than ever; for behaving oddly, as if to persuade people that he is not the most common aspect of life; and, worst of all, for pretending to be able to make love.[28]

In a world where real allegiances are so hard to perceive, even the earth itself fosters doubt. In 'The chimneys are smoking' (EA, pp.116–18), an apparent unity of lovers with natural landscape is sundered by uncertainty:

> Last week we embraced on the dunes and thought they were
> pleased;
> Now lakes and holes in the mountains remind us of error,
> Strolling in the valley we are uncertain of the trees:
> > Their shadow falls upon us;
> > Are they spies on the human heart
> > Motionless, tense in the hope
> > Of catching us out?

At first, the slopes of the dunes seemed to respond as flesh under flesh, like a third lover. But dunes are equivocal representatives of human beings: their curves, only lightly grassed, could be female or male. When he considers the more hyperborean landscape of mountains and lakes, forest and caves, the poet is reminded of the offending double-maleness of the embraces on the dunes, and begins to doubt the collaboration of landscape in his joy. Those trees, reminders of the hirsute, become potential spies at once, 'For our hour of unity makes us aware of two worlds'.

Samuel Hynes does not probe far into this poem, when he says it 'deals with a relationship that may be either revolutionary or homosexual, or possibly both'. Southworth, as usual, goes further. He says the poem 'makes an indirect plea for the day when the homosexual will be recognized by society, so that he . . . need feel no shame'. There is certainly an affirmation of homosexuality:

> And since our desire cannot take that route which is straightest,
> Let us choose the crooked, so implicating these acres,

and thereby beating the spying flora at their own game. (Edward Mendelson has shown how Auden used straightness and crookedness to mean hetero- and homosexuality, respectively.) The poem is a late dismissal of the myth of a cure for homosexuality, and a recommendation of self-acceptance: 'For our joy abounding is, though it hide underground', both 'quick' (in the sense of living) and 'real'. To escape the landscape-spy, we go 'underground'; which is the loving penetration of the landscape-lover. The frontier between danger and safety is still not at all clear.[29]

Southworth is not helpful on two other poems he cites. According to him, 'Where do they come from' (EA, p.243; CP, p.201) and 'Not as that dream Napoleon' (CP, p.203) both seem to be of a 'homosexual character'.[30] The semblance is not explained. In 'Where do they come from,' 'when the blond boy / bites eagerly into the shining / apple', like a male Eve miming oral intercourse, a huge weight of 'shocking fury' and hatred falls on the poem. Beneath it, 'we' lovers, jointly characterised as a bride conceiving in the arms of a 'hairy and clumsy bridegroom', struggle to bring forth, within 'a love / we have never outgrown'. At the same time, an interfering 'they', whose origins are obscure, and 'whom we so much dread', endanger not only our relationships with 'the melting friend' (an unpleasant fusion, this image, of a man who 'melts' into one's arms, and one who is literally burnt or blasted to death), but even our water supply and our flowers. (Actually, these last victims, 'aqueduct' and 'flower,' may also have sexual relevance, if we take them as referring to the subsidiary excretory and reproductive functions of genitalia; in which case, 'they' are in a distinctly castratory mood.) They direct their 'hate' at us; they resent us as 'outcasts'; 'on us they work / out their despair'; and they wear 'our weeping' as if it were a badge of merit. I see no great problem in interpreting who 'we' and 'they' may be.

If 'Not as that dream Napoleon' is, indeed, as Southworth says, a poem of a 'homo-sexual character', that character must assert itself somewhere in the third stanza's disdain for mere *tolerance*, and implicit demand for the response of *acceptance*. Entering a foreign country, Auden says, one may be received with all the formal niceties: the civilised conversation of ambassadors, the respect of bankers, the passionless kisses of rich women at cocktail parties, and free access to mountains and shops. 'But politeness and freedom are never enough, / Not for a life'. In terms of heterosexual reactions to homosexual relationships, the poem may be suggesting that tolerance is granted only to those relationships which most resemble the monogamous formalities of marriage ('a bed that only looks like marriage'), and that for two homosexual men to imitate marriage in order to court tolerance would be to travesty the actual shape of their love; a shape which should only accept acceptance.

On Tristan and Isolde and Don Juan, the models of lover mentioned in 'In Sickness and in Health' (CP, pp.247–9), Fuller comments: 'Both types in this poem suggest the homosexual predicament'.[31] So, let us suppose that Auden has taken heterosexual archetypes to illustrate homosexual particulars: he writes a poem to Chester Kallman, and gives it a title from the marriage vows. Fuller describes the illustrated predicaments as homosexual, because Tristan and Isolde are said to be 'great friends' who 'Make passion out of passion's obstacles'; and Don Juan is a compulsive cottager:

Trapped in their vile affections, he must find
Angels to keep him chaste; a helpless, blind,
Unhappy spook, he haunts the urinals,
Existing solely by their miracles.

The first point of this hetero-homosexual transposition is, of course, to demonstrate the essential similarity between the sorrows and triumphs of the two sexual orientations. Do not imprison the man who persistently engages in sexual encounters in public places, if you continue to regard Don Juan as an admirable and amusing rakehell; and do not persecute homosexual lovers, if you continue to regard Tristan and Isolde's example as evidence of the nobility of human love.

Auden himself is not uncritical of his models; nor is he uncritical of the homosexual lovers they represent here. Tristan and Isolde make the mistake of allowing irrelevant, external pressures to stand in the way of their love, thereby 'postponing their delight' until the intervention of death. On the other hand, Don Juan, whom Auden calls 'their opposite', seems to be concentrating too obsessively on the objects of his desire, and ignoring what obstacles Tristan and Isolde encountered. The chastity his sexual angels confer on him consists of an avoidance of death: myriad sexual events which do nothing but prove him to be alive. Auden always deplored the use of love and sex for such irrelevant purposes. Love should never be a means, but an end. The use of the phallus as a lesser version of the sword, a means to power, leads to a situation in which 'Eros is politically adored', and which Auden firmly rejects. Lover and lover must love point blank; not at a distance, through imposed or self-imposed connotations.

The final example in my collection of critical references to homosexuality in relation to Auden's poems comes from an essay by Cyril Connolly:[32] 'I always felt that the influence of Shakespeare's sonnets . . . was extremely stimulating in the younger poet seeking to revive a convention in which it was possible to celebrate homosexual love'. Whence, according to Connolly, five sonnets which appeared in *New Verse* in 1933: 'Turn not towards me lest I turn to you', 'At the far end of the enormous room', 'The latest ferrule now has tapped the curb', 'Love had him fast, but though he fought for breath', and 'I see it often since you've been away' (EA, pp.146, 147, 147, 150, 423–4). These poems were part of a sequence Auden sent to Isherwood in 1934, and contain at least one serious erotic joke: in 'Love had him fast', Auden addresses the lover's spermatozoa.[33] Connolly's point seems valid, and deserves a leisurely, analytical proof. But, here, we can pause only briefly, to regret Auden's failure to learn from Shakespeare the use of the gendered third person when appropriate. Without it, these sonnets read as the exercises of a poet who is faking love in order to write love poems; and that, I imagine, is the last impression Auden wanted to create. He never saw love as a poetic conceit.

THE AGE OF ANXIETY (1948)

After *The Orators*, *The Age of Anxiety* is the most obvious of Auden's book-length works to cite in reference to homosexuality. Yet, several studies of the book make no mention of this side of its sexual content.[34]

Southworth says, of the unrest of the four characters in *The Age of Anxiety*, that 'we could call it loneliness'.[35] Whether or not it is the whole trouble, loneliness is certainly one of the roots of their problems. The two types of sexual force, desire and desirability, are represented here, with the young naval officer, Emble, exemplifying the latter almost alone, despite the presence of Rosetta, who will later shoulder the desires of all four. The ultimate quest of the work is of the two older men for the younger, with Rosetta as the means to conquest. She is the buyer: she acquires the goods, which her customers (and not she) will possess. Emble's profession is emblematic of his desirability, placing him among the young, the active, and the close to death.[36] We know from the start that he is 'fully conscious of the attraction of his uniform to both sexes', and is 'slightly contemptuous' when he catches the glance of an admirer, but 'slightly piqued' when he does not. So, his narcissism places him among the four, as he searches for the type of lover of which he is himself the best visible example.

The common purpose of the four enables Auden to divide the aspects of the searching mind between them, and makes Edward Callan's formulation of their characteristics entirely credible. He writes that 'The chance encounter . . . becomes, as psychological allegory, a manifestation of Jung's concept of the disintegration of the psyche into four differentiated functions: Thought (Malin), Feeling (Rosetta), Intuition (Quant), and Sensation (Emble)'.[37] Auden is most at home, therefore, in the verses he attributes to Malin; and least, perhaps, to those he attributes to Rosetta. He is pre-eminently a thinker, even when he feels. Any conflict between thought and feeling is his most exacting and most stimulating theme.

So, to Clive James's point (on how Auden's involuntary discretion about his homosexuality forced abstraction into the concreteness of his style) we can add another. The distance between homosexuality and opinions of it – that is, between one's erotic inclination towards members of one's own gender, and one's own, or other people's inherited opinions on the moral value of such an inclination – is one of the bases of the intellectual detachment of Auden's lyrics from their objects. Homosexuality is entirely non-verbal, an emotional matter. Opinions of it are entirely verbal; yet they seek to usurp its place. The opinion is posited as a replacement for what it is an opinion of: the word 'homosexuality', for those unspoken emotions. After all, only by verbalising the non-verbal, by giving it a name, and so on, can one argue it, *speak* it out of existence.

Think of an adolescent boy who falls in love with a girl. Enough said. (Only the emotion matters.) Now, think of a boy who falls in love with another boy. At first, his emotion is undifferentiated. It surges through his veins like a physical transcription of 'I love him', without words. But, as soon as he realises, or someone tells him, that this love makes him 'homosexual', the gigantic and irrelevant burden of other people's opinions drops on him. In a sense, when his private love takes a form one can call 'homosexuality', the boy and his lover become public property. One is expected to have an opinion (preferably hostile) about this perfect stranger. As a result, he himself must construct an intellectual response to, an *opinion* of, his emotions. He must try to live within and beyond them at once.

Taboo is reflected in the sense of guilt which interferes with personal intimacy. Ultimately, this interference has external causes, even if its principal impetus comes internally, from the intellect. In *The Age of Anxiety*, Malin is the character least likely to accept readily the impulsive motives of Emble and Rosetta; but even he, alone with Emble, cycling towards the genital garden, lapses into doubt. He says:

> As we cycle through a serious land
> For hens and horses, my hunger for a live
> Person to father impassions my sense
> Of this boy's beauty in battle with time.
>
> These old-world hamlets and haphazard lanes
> Are perilous places; how plausible here
> All arcadian cults of carnal perfection,
> How intoxicating the platonic myth.

Significantly, his urge to paternity bypasses motherhood. He desires a close relationship with the young man alone, and rationalises his desire as a parental motive, if only because he is, indeed, old enough to be Emble's father; but the moment is cast in erotic terms. His sense of Emble's beauty is imbued with passion by his hunger for issue; and, although he perceives the danger in their mutual approach to the 'hermetic gardens' of the genitalia, his intellect allows itself common ground with emotion, by reflection on religious and philosophical history, where they touch on the senses. His invocation of 'carnal perfection' is a rationalisation of the more immediate 'boy's beauty'; and Plato tempers his 'hunger'. The landscape of sexual perception is alien to him, precisely because it is an 'old-world' contrast to his safer environment, the New York of the bars, and a 'haphazard' deviation from New York's orderly and rational grid of intersecting avenues and streets. Needless to say, however, Emble's reaction to the shared journey is a polite but formal barrier to intimacy – 'Pleasant my companion but I pine for another' – and, more to the point, the recognition, as if desire were a commodity to be weighed on scales, that no loving transaction can be compacted between them: 'Unequal our happiness: his is greater'.

To this situation, Malin has two responses, equal in length: one entirely intellectual, the other personal and acute. In the former –

> To know nature is not enough for the ego;
> The aim of its eros is to create a soul,
> The start of its magic is stolen flesh.

– he inters in Platonism his sudden desire for Emble, referring to the body, in keeping with the emblematic nature of their journey, as 'nature'; to himself as 'the ego'; to sexual desire as 'its eros'; and to the products of love as 'a soul'. But in these terms he reaches the same conclusion, of 'stolen flesh' and the guilt of the thief, as that to which the kleptomaniac Airman's jottings led. His second reaction –

> Girlishly glad that my glance is not chaste,
> He wants me to want what he would refuse:
> For sons have this desire for a slave also.

– has, at least, the virtue of percipience, dealing directly with Emble's vanity. The young man will withhold the prize to which they all aspire, perhaps even from himself. His flirtatiousness arouses what it must destroy, aiming to make love out of acquaintance, and labour out of love; to attract and to repel. That Malin is not predominantly homosexual, makes his a far more important conquest to Emble than Quant might be.

All four meet again at the 'hermetic gardens', and find the charm of the place disturbing: 'It seems an accusation. They become uneasy and unwell'. In terms of landscape, they are unused to the natural beauty of the garden, being all city dwellers. In terms of the body, they are unused to the intimacy, sensitivity, and physicality of the genital zone. Malin immediately develops a psychosomatic but explicitly sexual ache: 'Reproached by the doves, / My groin groans'. Rosetta's head, Quant's knees, and Emble's teeth are also affected. Rosetta, as Feeling, is attacked in the zone of the intellect; Quant, as a man of inaction, in his legs: Malin, as a thinker, in his groin. (The transference or displacement of ache from active to inactive organs is another of the poem's many signs of dislocation: absence has more effect than presence.) But Emble's two sides are both affected; for the teeth are at once the jewels of his winning smile and the blades of his cruelty, situated in his mouth, both orifice *dentatus* and organ of speech.

Throughout the book, events are watched and commented on by Quant, the only one of the four who is exclusively homosexual.[38] His personality is indistinct, perhaps because he is aware of the need to blend in with his background: 'The safest place / Is the more or less middling: the mean average / Is not noticed' (CP, p.383). At his distance from the others, he sees a cruel world reminiscent of that of *The Orators*. The war leaves castrated corpses floating at the edge of the sea (CP, p.350). Even childhood consists of secret meetings and initiations concealed by billboards (CP p.357). The indiscreet will always be spied on: 'Unknown to him, binoculars follow / The leaping lad' (CP, p.363). The dangers of adulthood are even greater: 'Ingenious George reached his journey's end / Killed by a cop in a comfort station' (CP, p.370).

Quant's extensive but purposeless reading of mythology has left him with a keen sense of individual isolation. He makes a flat joke about forming a discussion group, 'the Ganymede Club / For homesick young angels' (CP, p.356). But he is ominously serious when he reflects on the slaying of Orpheus for having 'sinned against kind'. In Quant's version of the myth, the severed head floats off downstream, singing to an audience of 'deaf Nature' (CP, p.365). His sense of alienation from the natural world leaves him with no illusions about love. It is he, therefore, who teaches Emble the fundamental lesson about the worth of human beauty: it is 'market-made'. It exists not for its own sake, but for that of the plain or the ugly. The beautiful man is 'a commodity / Whose value varies, a vendor who has / To obey his buyer' (CP, p.364). He is beautiful only insofar as he is desired.

THE PRICE OF LONELINESS

A brief allegory, written in 1963 or 1964 (CP, p.554), reads as follows:

> Loneliness waited
> For Reality
> To come through the glory hole.

In gay slang, a 'glory hole' is a hole drilled for sexual purposes in a partition between public lavatory cubicles.[39] The suggestive obscenity of this poem and its two male figures, of Loneliness and Reality, touches on more than fellatio, enacted through the hole. Future movement, set in the verb 'to come', is meant both spatially and sexually. Reality is a phallus. When it comes, it will come. The expected event will be both beginning and end: intromission and emission. But it is the role of Loneliness to continue to wait. It is not just the irony of casting the poem in haiku form that gives it its resonance; for much stems from the fact that the allegorical figure of Loneliness must always be lonely – just as Justice is never unjust – even when giving Reality a blow job.

Aloneness, apartness, and loneliness are, in Auden, the natural conditions of humanity. The major outline of this view is *The Age of Anxiety*. But most of his poems bear its mark, in the form of Auden's notorious detachment. The tone of his poetry is a demonstration of what he seeks to prove; as was his refusal to release information about his private life. The individual is unapproachable. He is unapproachable because of his psychological condition; and, because he is unapproachable, he increases the apartness of other individuals, thereby aggravating their psychological conditions. It is the natural fate of human beings, by seeking proximity to their fellows, to emphasise their distance from them. The attempt to love is invariably harder than it might have seemed in the popular arts, and is only rarely a success. There can be as little baring of breasts in human intercourse as there is in Auden's love poems; or, if one individual actually manages to probe another, what he finds there will be as confusing as the fragmentary Journal of the Airman, and not half as well composed. What happens, Auden seems to think, is that the lonely individual, in revolt against his condition, tries to forge an intimate bond with another individual – a possibility which our culture treasures as one of the most worthwhile, and yet as one of the most readily available – but he discovers, to his horror, that love's ease is a myth: for, even when seeking to love and be loved, the human being resists intimacy, in the belief (like that which attributes to the camera the demonic power to rob one of his soul) that to be known is to be kidnapped. Again, we meet the spectre of the kleptomaniac. Because of him, the individual sets up around himself impenetrable barriers against what he would most welcome.

So, throughout the *Collected Poems*, we find individuals subject to contrary forces within themselves: of extroversion towards the possibility of love, and of introversion against the likelihood of theft. At times, though, extroversion approximates its opposite, notably when directed at the love, not of other men, but of God; and it is in this fusion of the two contrary forces that an ideal situation (Auden's great compromise) is reached. The man at prayer is enclosed, but not alone. In human relationship, on the other hand, enclosure ensures natural solitude, except in cases of detached sexual encounters. This does not mean Auden's muse is misanthropic. The poet's diagnoses of conditions not readily conducive to loving, erotic or agapeic, would not have been made in the first place, had he not scrutinised humanity's ailing psychological state with the characteristic interest and care which clearly betray his love of people. If he points out our defects, as they seem to him, he does so with concern and, indeed, with hope of improvement ('cure'), not cynically. His identification with our condition, which he recognises as his own, removes the

possibility of cynicism; and it is in this sense that we can acknow-
ledge him as one of the least detached of poets. He approves of our
patchy solutions to our problems, and celebrates them in light verse
which, while affirming their value, leaves no illusion that they are
anything but temporary measures.

'Minnelied', the third of three posthumously published poems (CP,
pp.561–2), begins with the statement that,

> When one is lonely (and You,
> My Dearest, know why,
> as I know why it must be),
> steps can be taken, even
> a call-boy can help.

Sex, then, can alleviate loneliness, if not end it. The image of the
body as a commodity to be bought, bartered, or stolen is at its
sharpest when Auden makes commerce of human relations. Here is a
fragment written between 1929 and 1931:

> I'm beginning to lose patience
> With my personal relations:
> They are not deep,
> And they are not cheap.
>   (EA, p.51; CP, p.56)

This remark, doubtless, has its origin in the economic dependence of
the working-class boy, often unemployed, on his middle-class lover.
It was Auden who, in March 1929, introduced Isherwood to a Berlin
bar called The Cosy Corner, to which unemployed, working-class
youths used to come to be picked up by middle-class homosexual
men and turn sex into money, by mutual consent. Low charges
obviated depth. And not just in Berlin. 'Brussels in Winter' is
available to any tourist, since 'fifty francs will earn the stranger right /
To warm the heartless city in his arms' (EA, p.236). The body is real
estate, but bought in a shady deal: for ownership is illusory, lasting
only as long as the night. With dawn comes the repossession order.
One can hire the body, but not buy the heart. When, in 'Sentries
against inner and outer', Auden likens the face to a fortress, the
loving glance to a siege, and the tongue's entry in a kiss, to the
breaching of walls, he outlines just what effort, he considers, love
requires: the effort expended in conquest, and, conversely, absorbed
in subjugation or death (EA, p.33).

Barter becomes big business in the hands of the man we can call
the capitalist lover: he who has more (of flesh or companionship)
than he needs for survival, yet wants more than he has. In his case,
exchange turns into the acquisition of capital for its own sake,

without significant reinvestment, and thereby aligns itself sym-
bolically with kleptomania. In effect, he takes from his 'loved' one
all he desires, giving little or nothing but his attention in return. In a
fragment dating from 1963 or 1964, a pair or group of such men
indulge in sexual reminiscences, which remind us of nothing if not
of commerce:

> Cigars. Scotch.
> They recalled (inexactly)
> How many, how big, how much.
>
> (CP, p.554)

Quantity is their quality. They recall sexual partners in terms of
number, genital size, and fee. In much the same way, they may
remember this conversation: how many glasses of scotch, how big
the cigars, how much the bill, rather than how convivial the
company. That their computations are inexact is further evidence of
their detachment from the boys who, even as mere items on an
expanding sexual list, are liable to be forgotten. Sexual partners are
collected like unwanted objects, stolen for the sake of the theft.
That they were paid for, is inconsequential, when the buyer could
afford to pay more than he did.

No commerce but the dishonest results in gain: barter must
involve commodities exactly equal in value, or one side's gain will
be the other's loss. What Auden insists is that such equality – even
if desired, by two parties of absolute integrity – is unattainable; and
his poetry is the acutely sensitive balance which detects the
discrepancy in a given erotic transaction. In a sexual context, he
measures the differences between the bodies of the two lovers (as
many when the two are of the same sex as when they are female
and male); and in terms of love, he contrasts the schemes and
routine deceptions of their minds. That is not to say that his
scrutiny always produces results: for, in some relationships, erotic
barter seems to be conducted with such meticulous grace as renders
discrepancy imperceptible. But Auden bases his examinations of
love on doubt, assuming that what is imperceptible nevertheless
exists. While not detracting from the high value he attributes to
love, his scepticism affirms the difficulty of love's path and the
distance of its goal. His own persona willingly engages in
commerce, openly aware that in any exchange of goods he may
swindle or be swindled; but hopeful, at least, that there will be one
honest trader in the market place, from whom to buy true love with
true love.

The 1949 poem 'Secrets' (CP, p.472) offers a possible definition
of 'precisely what we mean by love'. To love, the theory goes, is 'To

share a secret'. The secret need not be profound, as Auden goes on to explain:

> The joke, which we seldom see, is on us;
> For only true hearts know how little it matters
> What the secret is they keep:
> An old, a new, a blue, a borrowed something,
> Anything will do for children
> Made in God's image and therefore
> Not like the others, not like our dear dumb friends
> Who, poor things, have nothing to hide,
> Not, thank God, like our Father either
> From whom no secrets are hid.

Unlike animals, we have things to hide; and, unlike God, we have things hidden from us. This makes us eminently – indeed, uniquely – suited to love. By sharing secrets with his beloved, the lover approaches the conditions of animals and God at once: for lovers who hide nothing from each other are like the animals, in being completely open; and like God, each in knowing all about the other. But Auden's scepticism allows only approximate resemblances in these respects. After all, even if the lover hides nothing from, and sees all of his beloved, his honesty and insight operate only where the beloved is concerned. Besides, who needs complete openness? Token secrets, like the trivial bits and pieces worn or carried by a bride, are quite enough, to give a relationship its necessary air of conspiracy. 'Anything', it seems, 'will do'. To find great passion, lovers need not violate religious vows in secrecy, nor be members of opposed factions, nor, behind locked doors, be breaking the law. Love requires no specialised qualification or equipment.

The theory is, then, that love is available to all. That may be so; but, in practice, one's acquisitive instincts may get in the way – as did those of the cigar smokers already considered. Groddeck associated constipation with miserliness. Auden evidently thought of the hoarding instinct, as manifested in all his kleptomaniacs, as being symptomatic of a certain type of anal fixation, which reduces the world to a store of exploitable bodies and articles. The hoarding of faeces and money, and the collection of sexual conquests, are closely linked symptoms of a world view which leaves nothing beyond possible use: the capital which is hoarded in case of use, but allowed to waste when found useless. As a condition, this, the capitalist's disease, becomes most debilitating, when the excuse of possible future exploitation is forgotten, and things are hoarded for no reason other than the urge to hoard. Thus, to pay a different boy every night, in order to take pleasure from his flesh, is a purely capitalistic sexual mode; whereas, to do so merely in order to add to a list of past conquests, is kleptomanic. The transition from one stage to the other is no Ovidian metamorphosis, but a simple over-stepping of the bounds of detachment; and, as such, a constant danger.

In 'Glad', a poem dated March 1965 but published posthumously (CP, p.561), Auden describes the development of a literally commercial relationship into one bordering on love. The subject is the bisexual Hugerl, 'for a decade now / My bed-visitor', whose path crossed Auden's,

> At a moment when
> You were in need of money
> And I wanted sex.

The first phase of the relationship is implemented by coincidence: the two traders meet, by chance, in the market place. In an elementary transaction, one hires the other's flesh. The bargain is struck without haggling, and each party is satisfied with his side of it (stanza 5). In the second phase, because the first was satisfactory, their exchange becomes habitual. In the third, with mutual respect and wary trust, each examines the other's character and commercial methods, covertly hoping that a lapse in the other's security will lead to his own slight gain: more sex for less money, or vice versa. Here, Auden's financial metaphor comes into operation. The commodities they have to offer – basically, flesh and an interest in cars, on the one hand; money and an interest in literature, on the other – are irreconcilable, but exactly equivalent (stanza 3). Neither can gain, but by the other's loss. So, the honesty of the two traders is given its first real test.

In the fourth phase, the less honest trader, Hugerl, for the first and last time, takes his chance to swindle Auden. He steals from him, to supplement the fee he already receives. He steals from others, too, and is imprisoned (stanza 4). These thefts must be separated in the reader's mind from those which operate within the metaphor – the appropriation of one person by another, for love's purposes, as exemplified by the theft of Ganymede by Zeus. Hugerl's thefts are of actual goods. The bearing they have on his relationship with Auden is indirect; but no less significant, for that. From them, both men learn that personal relationships, like trade, are subject to all the temptations of gain; and must, like trade, be conducted openly, so that the necessary dishonesty of the parties concerned can be monitored, before it destroys empathy altogether. I speak of 'necessary dishonesty', because Auden's view of the essential frailties of human nature is clear. Isherwood quotes his having said that, while he agreed that homosexual acts were sinful, he fully intended to go on sinning.[40] In other words, as I interpret him, he acknowledged the guilty or sinful nature of human deeds, but was unashamed to be a part of them, sinfulness being, after all, a necessary condition of humanity. But he obviously wanted to conduct his relationships as responsibly and generously as possible: to sin, if he must, as venially as he could. The dishonest component of the human character had to be identified, and either nurtured or opposed.

The reading of Auden's poems has barely begun. The general reluctance to respond to the 'private' elements in his personal lyrics may have aggravated his sense of detachment from them; which in turn enabled him to sever all links between his own history and theirs. As public property, personal lyrics seem to have lost their sentimental value to him. Hence, his willingness to tamper with the originals, by addition or cutting, by arbitrary dedication, by a retrospective and cavalier choice of titles; and his apparently vengeful eagerness to excise popular lines from later editions, or to leave out of his selections some of those whole pieces which had proved most popular. Although he had lost the private poems, he seemed determined to retain some control over the public poems they had become. Detached already from what they said, how could he be anything but as detached from whatever whimsical alterations he chose to make? I know of no other body of verse which seems so palpably to have been stolen from its author; but which, piecemeal, he stole back.

The truest poetry is the most feigning. Auden used this statement, in inverted commas, as the title of a poem (CP, p.470) in which fellow poets are given handy advice on how, in the event of sudden political change, to turn a love song into a laudatory ode to the 'new pot-bellied Generalissimo'. The first thing to do, of course, is to 'Re-sex the pronouns'. With a few other details altered, the ode will go on to win a pension or a prize for its author; and only the initiated, only

> True hearts, clear heads will hear the note of glory
> And put inverted commas round the story,

wondering who the lover they discern really was. In this way, the moral witness of resistance is visible even behind the most apparently hypocritical mask of the immoral witness. Although not always characterised by a 'note of glory', Auden's testimony to his own sexual orientation was visible all the time, to the perceptive, behind his expedient homage to what Isherwood referred to as the heterosexual dictatorship. Like it or not, we must put inverted commas around all his works on love – unless we *wish* to be seduced into all kinds of false readings.

7 ALLEN GINSBERG

INDISCRETION

The argument that one's homosexuality is entirely her or his own affair, a private matter to be lapped in secrecy, cannot honestly be upheld. Sexual orientation has as much to do with social life and politics – if only because a homosexual person is well advised to choose approving friends, and not to vote for disapproving parties – as with internal emotion and the gymnastics of the boudoir. Supposedly private emotions, particularly those of writers, yearn for the freedom of release. So, a literature of homosexuality will seek to be affirmative (or confessional, at least), within the bounds of expediency. Clearly, where homosexual desires and acts are punishable by death, homo-erotic literature will tend to be metaphorical and oblique, whereas, in freer circumstances, it will tend to be descriptive and direct. Coming out is no mere fashion, but in several respects a personal, social, and political necessity. Of course, anyone who comes out, no matter how quietly, is accused of 'flaunting' her or his homosexuality, as if wedding rings, joint mortgages, maternity dresses, prams, and children were not also, and in equal measure, affirmations or 'flauntings' of another sexual orientation.

I offer this preamble, not as an incidental pronouncement on the facts of life in general, but as having direct and central relevance to the reception of Allen Ginsberg's poems. Despite the programmatic use of his homosexuality, sometimes disguised as bisexuality on the model of Walt Whitman, as both subject matter in itself and a spring-board to wider political questions, a number of critical essays on him manage somehow to run their course without reference to it.[1] Others mention it only reluctantly, and by indirect means.[2] But, of those that deal with it directly, most classify what they call his indiscretion as no more than an instrument with which to shock the bourgeoisie, perversely and without good reason. Leslie Fiedler, proving for once more exemplary than idiosyncratic, calls Ginsberg 'a deliberately shocking, bourgeois-baiting celebrator of a kind of sexuality which the most enlightened post-Freudian man-of-the-world finds it difficult to condone'.[3] Paul O'Neil writes of 'Ginsberg's public and repeated boasts that he is a homosexual'.[4] Both opinions can be found, similarly phrased, wherever Ginsberg's books are reviewed. Both miss the point.

It is never properly acknowledged that Ginsberg is working in a gay tradition. Three of the poets he refers to most often, and with most reverence, are Whitman, Rimbaud, and Crane. All three were homosexual or bisexual, and he refers to all three in erotic contexts.[5] His verse is impregnated with their memory. In his relationship with all three, he maintains his awareness of and affinity with the homo-erotic bases of modern poetry. His less frequent references to Lorca, who also refers back to Whitman, serve a similar purpose. (His other masters are, of course, Blake, Louis Ginsberg, and William Carlos Williams.)

If we start, as the commentators had to, with 'Howl', we actually encounter what hindsight reveals as reticence where homosexuality is concerned, despite the fact that the San Francisco police department and the U.S. customs found in the poem enough material to warrant a prosecution for obscenity.[6] What references there are are fixed at arm's length, in the third person plural, wherein they incriminate the author only by the implication of his enthusiasm. That they are in the vernacular, makes no more of them than what they say: that members of his generation – and he does not specify percentages – found anal intercourse with motorcyclists pleasurable, fellated and were fellated by sailors, indulged in indiscriminate sexual activity in parks and Turkish baths, lost their lovers, and promiscuously formed sexual bonds with women. In the light of Kinsey's revelations of 1948, these (of 1956) are unexceptional. Given the terms on which the poem presents itself – terms of Whitman-like candour and inclusiveness, and of social disaffection – the sexual passage is in tonal, formal, and ideological keeping with the others, neither more nor less emphatic than they. The manner of the whole poem dictates the manner of its parts. If its sexual content is hysterical – an arguably appropriate epithet – its hysteria does not stand out in any way from that of the other pages. The pitch of 'Howl' is uniform.

By investing aesthetic value in spontaneity, just as by tailoring length of line to the requirements of breath, Ginsberg establishes an intimate co-operation between poet (body and all) and poem. To excise sexuality from the page would be akin to self-mutilation, and nothing could be further from his purpose. The over-publicised occasion, on which he removed his clothes at a poetry reading, proved more a manifesto than a stunt: for his work has involved a systematic rejection of subterfuge and disguise – if not always of pretence – and a refusal of discretion, as if the poem were a body, to be presented either clothed or naked, in part or as a whole. Ginsberg has sought, with varying degrees of success, to leave nothing out. He includes his homosexuality as he includes all observations and opinions. To accuse him of boasting about his sexual orientation seems, merely, an over-reaction to the fact that he mentions it at all. The naked body does not boast genitals: it simply has them. The emphasis is the viewer's.

Ginsberg himself locates the outrageousness of 'Howl' more exactly than I have. In the interview he gave *Gay Sunshine*, he suggested that what gave most offence in the sexual passage was the line, 'who let themselves be fucked in the ass by saintly motorcylists, and screamed with joy'. Not the buggery, but the joy. The line's ending is a deliberate contradiction of his straight readers' expectations, that a buggered man should scream with pain. This and the line about sailors (a reference to Hart Crane) are affirmations of 'the basic reality of homosexual joy', and as such contravene an unwritten literary rule, that homosexuality is a fit subject for literature only as a vehicle for pathos, debasement, and pain.[7] In the same interview, Ginsberg says:

> The use of sex as a banner to *épater le bourgeois*, to shock, show resentment or to challenge, is not sufficiently interesting to maintain for more than ten minutes; it's not enough to sustain a program that will carry love through to the deathbed or help out Indochina. Or even get laid, finally. You have to have something more. You have to relate to people and their problems, too.

Hence, the concern to transcend stereotype. If the poet proposes to take sexuality as one of his subjects – as he must, to some extent, if he is to deal with people – he must move beyond the barriers of public prejudice, or accept defeat.

The truly autobiographical Ginsberg does not appear until the 1961 volume *Kaddish*, whose title poem (CP, pp.209–24) contradicts general critical opinion, by being at once the most personal and one of the least sexually outspoken of all his long poems, despite the volume's dedication to his lover, Peter Orlovsky. Unlike those in 'Howl', the reference in this poem to homosexuality is entirely personal. It begins as a memory of being in love with his high-school hero, and of wanting to declare himself to him. Thus far, it is a routine memory, similar examples of which are liberally scattered through American and English literature and is not, for that reason, particularly indiscreet. Just one line takes the matter further, by extending homosexuality into adulthood: 'Later a mortal avalanche, whole mountains of homosexuality, Matterhorns of cock, Grand Canyons of asshole – weight on my melancholy head' (CP, p.214). The line's verbal extravagance lays it open to accusations of boasting, but is justified by the poet, again in the *Gay Sunshine* interview (p.103), as follows:

> When I was a sensitive, little kid, hiding, not able to touch anyone or speak my feelings out, little did I realize the enormous weight of love and numbers of lovers, the enormity of the scene I'd enter into, in which I finally wound up a public spokesman for homosexuality at one point. . . Taking off my clothes in public and getting myself listed in *Who's Who* as being married to Peter.

Here is the common phenomenon, of the homosexual youth who at first believes himself the only one, or one of only a few, of his kind. The extravagance of the line we are concerned with is in keeping not only with the tone of the whole poem, but also with its implicit indictment (and note that 'implicit' is a word the poet's critics rarely use, being out of step with the view they have formed of him) of a society which allows and encourages such subtle emotional tortures. One's adolescent discovery of how many people are homosexual is, indeed, sudden and extravagant – and might have merited more than the one line it receives here, had Ginsberg not been a poet (again, contrary to his critics) of some economy, as aware that the requirements of poetic form are constrictive as that those of spontaneity are expansive. His attempts to balance the two sets of requirements are what give even his longest poems their tension. As in Whitman, the broad sweep of the poem does not invalidate the compression of the individual line.

It is necessary, then, to accept that Ginsberg's programme includes his sexuality to the extent to which his sexuality has a bearing on his life, either literally, insofar as he writes down his thoughts as they occur to him and refrains from extensive correction and alteration (like Lawrence); or metaphorically, insofar as the concept of spontaneous poetry is more important in what it stands for, than in that each poem should actually be spontaneously composed. We must also accept that he highlights his sexuality by verbal and tonal means no more than he highlights, say, his politics or his family history. If I seem to be defeating my own argument by concentrating, here, only on the sexual side of his subject matter, thereby placing on it the emphasis which, I claim, he does not place on it himself, let me admit and declare the narrowness of my concern; and offer the excuse that this aspect of Allen Ginsberg's poetry has not yet been adequately considered.

THE SEXUALITY OF POLITICS

Just as Whitman's ideals of spiritual and physical comradeship shaped his idea of a truly democratic America, so Ginsberg's attitudes to sex inform his political dialectic. Only with love, he believes, can the 'lost America of love' be re-established (CP, p.136). In 'Howl', he speaks of young men 'investigating the FBI in beards and shorts with big pacifist eyes sexy in their dark skin passing out incomprehensible leaflets'. The strength of their activism lies in their eyes, rather than their leaflets. Recognising this, the police arrest them not for political subversion, but for their 'wild cooking pederasty and intoxication' (CP, p.127). The police maintain the sexual, as well as the political status quo, in their consistent and aggressive opposition to love. Law always interferes with the expression of love. In 'I Am a Victim of Telephone', Ginsberg complains of being called away from love-making by someone who needs to be bailed out of jail (CP, p.344). Wherever he travels, he finds 'boys and girls in jail for their bodies poems and bitter thoughts' (CP, p.553). The policemen of Texas are described as 'cock-detesting' (CP, p.388). Only when in retreat does Ginsberg allow himself the pleasure of identification with Catullus, who 'sucked cock in the country / far from the Emperor's police' (CP, p.545).

If police activity is one of the most visible signs of the loveless state of the USA, then the ideal vision of a changed nation must include some change in the role of the police. Again, Ginsberg sees such a change in sexual terms. In 'Angkor Wat', he expresses the hope 'to get next time befucked by / a Cambodian sweet policeman', meaning 'fuck' in a literal sense, involving pleasure, rather than a metaphorical, implying defeat (CP, p.316). Elsewhere, he provides the following, partially definitive couplet, on the age of love: 'O Love, my mouth against / a black policeman's breast' (CP, p.338). Blacks will make love with whites, men with men, and policemen with poets. Until then, alas, phallic aggression rules.

The authorities in the United States are either totally sexless – like George Washington and Minerva, the 'goddess of money' (CP, p.186) – or obsessed with sexual dominance, and governed by their lust. The 'phallus spire' of Paterson City Hall is no image of comradely love, uniting a peaceful nation (CP, p.216). The Establishment is too involved in its institutional 'whoredom' to notice the complaints and prophecies of its poets (CP, p.169).

When he turns his sexual metaphor to the individuals who have power in the States, Ginsberg is no less critical. Eisenhower is 'heartless' (CP, p.277). J. Edgar Hoover is both a voyeur (CP, p.535) and a 'sexual blackmailer' (CP, p.551). The U.S. Postmaster, who intercepts erotic materials in the mail, is a 'first class sexfiend', depriving people of their right to joy (CP, p.278). Henry Kissinger is portrayed as the most unappetising sadist, 'bare assed & big buttocked with a whip, in leather boots' (CP, p.631). One of the most striking of these images is of the effect a demonstration has on the Vice President:

> The teargas drifted up to the Vice
>   President naked in the bathroom
> – naked on the toilet taking a shit weeping
>
> > (CP, p.507).

The crocodile tears, artificially induced by gas intended for the subversives outside, are not half as surprising as the fact that the Vice President actually has to take a shit. This means he has, at least, some loving potential: for he has an anus, as well as a miniaturised version of Paterson City Hall's spire. When, in 'Wichita Vortex Sutra', Ginsberg asks, 'How big is the prick of the President?' he implies two possible answers: one, that in accordance with the phallic nature of his power, the President has the biggest prick in the world, a kind of atom bomb, forever on the verge of being detonated; and the other, that in an ideal world we would know the literal answer, but not care: for we would have seen him naked and human, but would not have made any connection between penis size and the capacity for love (CP, p.395).

However, we must not overlook the value invested in the image of Che Guevara's allegedly big penis, which, together with Fidel Castro's pink balls, is mentioned in the first poem of *Planet News* (CP, p.265). Leslie Fiedler referred to Kennedy as 'our first sexually viable president in a century'.[8] But, as Ginsberg's 'Elegy Che Guevara' makes clear, even Kennedy cannot compare with Che:

> More sexy [Che's] neck than sad aging necks of Johnson
>   De Gaulle, Kosygin,
>   or the bullet pierced neck of John Kennedy
>
> > (CP, p.484).

More loving his politics, therefore, than theirs. Not that the poet is uncritical of left-wing regimes. They receive the same treatment as any. In Cuba itself, he makes love with 'teenage boys afraid of the red police' (CP, p.348). And, as 'Kral Majales' (King of May), he is arrested in and expelled from Prague, 'for losing my notebooks of unusual sex politics dream opinions' (CP, p.353). Capitalism and Communism are repressed and oppressive, alike.[9]

The relevance of Ginsberg's homosexuality to these, as to other themes in his poetry, cannot be overestimated. The widespread illegality even of consensual homosexual acts between male adults is a vivid and literal example of one of the poet's central subjects: the political control of the individual. To homosexual men, the state is an intrusive and uncaring force, undermining love for no practical purpose. It is a voyeur who interrupts the performance he most desires to watch. It employs, literally and metaphorically, *agents provocateurs*, to initiate the sexual events they then disrupt.[10] It imprisons lovers, having judged them criminal, in order to subject them to electric shock programmes – crude tortures, euphemised as 'electro-convulsive therapy' – meaning to cure them of their ability to love. It forbids youths the physical expression of their desires. So on. The pretence that Ginsberg's specifically homosexual perspective on politics and culture has no significant bearing on how we should react to his poetry, is critically inept. His homo-erotically concerned opposition to the war in Vietnam can only confirm this.

One of the more popular slogans of the sixties was 'Make love, not war'. It reflected the coincidence of an attempt at a sexual revolution in the Occident, and the Vietnam War in the Orient. These two sequences of events were married by their incompatibility. How could stereotypical versions of aggressive virility be removed, when thousands of young, American men were being trained to conform to stereotype? How, on the other hand, could an efficient army be built up, when homosexual men – barred by law from joining the forces – were refusing to pretend to be heterosexual; and when, in some quarters, human relationships were being given precedence over national pride?

In his record of one of the great anti-war demonstrations, *The Armies of the Night*, Norman Mailer shows how closely sexuality and politics had become linked during this period. One demonstrator said, before the march, 'We're going to try to stick it up the government's ass ... right into the sphincter of the Pentagon'. Another stated objective was to 'try to kidnap LBJ and wrestle him to the ground and take his pants off', as if to answer Ginsberg's question about presidential penis size. Although neither of these two aims was achieved, sexual weapons were, indeed, used during the demonstration. Confronting rows of silent, motionless soldiers, some young women 'unbuttoned their blouses, gave a real hint of cleavage, smiled in the soldier's eye, gave a devil laugh, then a bitch belly laugh at the impotence of the man's position in a uniform, helpless to reach out and take her'.[11] To some, it seemed as if the young people of America really were living through the plot of *Hair*, the musical in which the demands of the war interfere with a generation's sexual rites and rights.

In *Out Now!*, his account of the anti-war movement, Fred Halstead makes an important point about the Gay Liberation Movement's presence at demonstrations against American involvement in Vietnam. He says, 'The gay rights movement was just beginning to assert itself in a dramatic public way. It still wasn't easy in most places for gays to demonstrate by themselves. But on anti-war demonstrations during this period, and especially on the April 24 [1971] marches in Washington and San Francisco, they could come out in full force without fear of harassment and show themselves to be a significant part of the population.'[12] A movement committed to peace and love would have been ill advised to turn on those in its midst who demanded the loosening of oppressive sexual constraints. Therefore, given the mood of the time, confronting war with love, it was possible for a speaker to cover demands for peace and gay liberation in a single sentence, such as John Kerry's denouncement of a 'government more worried by the legality of where we sleep than by the legality of where we drop bombs'.[13] Considering various poets who wrote in opposition to the war, James F. Mersmann says: 'All freedoms have been in demand, but for many protestors sexual freedom has been one of the stronger obsessions. It is understandable, then, that these poets should frequently compare the obscenity of war with the sex-related "obscenities" that the establishment fears, and come to see war as the inevitable expression of the establishment's repressed and perverted sexuality.'[14]

Allen Ginsberg's opposition to the war took such forms. According to his analysis, the United States had submitted to the influence of a 'war-creating Whore of Babylon', by involving themselves ignobly in the affairs of south-east Asia (CP, p.170). In 'Wichita Vortex Sutra' (CP, pp.404–5), he provides the image of

> boys with sexual bellies aroused
>   chilled in the heart by the mailman
> with a letter from an aging white haired General
>   Director of selection for service in
>   Deathwar[.]

On one occasion, he gave such boys the following advice on how to dodge the draft: 'Make it inconvenient for them to take you, tell them you love them, tell them you slept with *me*'.[15] To make love with Ginsberg, or with any other man, made any man ineligible to fight the Viet Cong. Ginsberg's belief that 'only boys' flesh singing / can show the warless way' (CP, p.452) was meant to show the way to an immediate, practical means of draft evasion, as well as to state in broader terms his sexual philosophy. When, in the same poem (CP, p.432), he wills two soldiers on a train to give up their conversation on Cambodia, and to fuck him instead, he maintains a similar balance between the practical suggestion on how to get thrown out of the forces for engaging in homosexual activity, and faith in an ideal world, where men would go rather to bed than to war.

Ginsberg resolves to substitute for the 'loveless bombs' of the armed forces (CP, p.142) 'lovely / bombs' of his own devising (CP, p.236). One of them is a line in 'Wichita Vortex Sutra': 'I here declare the end of the War!' (CP, p.407). Fred Halstead's comment on this declaration – or, at least, on a version of it made in November 1966 – is his only mention of Ginsberg in his long account of the anti-war movement, and displays a representative bewilderment at Ginsberg's tactics. He interprets the declaration as a deliberate means of ignoring or forgetting the real issues at stake. Ginsberg's remarks 'made me angry at the time because what we all needed in those days was some inspiration to hold on and reach out, not advice on how to put the problem out of mind. There was already too much of that in a variety of forms.'[16] Needless to say, Ginsberg never advocated the closing of minds to the war. He did seem to believe that individuals could collectively will a withdrawal from Vietnam, by refusing to give the war support of any kind. On that understanding, any individual could make a personal declaration of peace, thereby dissociating her or his mind and body from the carnage. By January 1967, Ginsberg had adopted a slightly different position, declaring, 'I hope we lose this war' (CP, p.478).

THE POLITICS OF SEXUALITY

Whilst he classifies and describes the sexuality of politics, clarifying links between areas previously considered incompatible (the personal and the political), Ginsberg also pays attention to the complementary matter of the politics of sexuality. Given that political conditions reflect sexual attitudes, we may conclude that positive political change must be accompanied by sexual revolution. The Cuban revolution turns out to be extending pre-revolutionary Catholic moral control and the rules of Hispanic *machismo*, having taken place within rigid assumptions of masculine and feminine role, the virility of violence, and the heroism of the proletarian male. One form of oppression replaced by another, albeit more egalitarian than the first. Ginsberg's hopes for America involve far less crude mechanisms of change and progress. In order to overcome the 'lackloves of Capitals & Congresses / who make sadistic noises / on the radio', one must create love for them, thereby softening the violent edge in their voices. 'Who Be Kind To' ends with the optimistic remark,

>　That a new kind of man has come to his bliss
>　　to end the cold war he has borne
>　　against his own kind flesh
>　　since the days of the snake.
>
>　　　　　　　　　　　　　(CP, p.362).

The effort Ginsberg has continuously put into becoming such a new man is visible and instructive.

The first requirement of a society seeking to attain Whitman's democratic ideal is a collective awareness of individual sexual conditions and desires. When Ginsberg writes of the 'assholes basic to Modern Democracy' (CP, p.279), he states the crux of his belief in the interdependence of sexual and political freedom, and in the virtual synonymity of repression and oppression. The constipation of the presidents of banks and nations alike is intimately linked to their obsession with that useless commodity, gold. The hoarding of lucre and faeces negates all the pleasurable functions of the anus. In fact, as Ginsberg writes in 'Chicago to Salt Lake by Air', prosperity comes with an accumulation not of gold, but of orgasms. Furthermore, in the Capitalist system, 'It's a gold crisis! not enuf orgasms to go round' (CP, p.491). The way to a solution of this problem is suggested in the poem 'Kiss Ass' (CP, p.493), which reads as follows:

>　Kissass is the Part of Peace
>　America will have to Kissass Mother Earth
>　Whites have to Kissass Blacks, for Peace and Pleasure,
>　Only Pathway to Peace, Kissass.

The image is of anilingus, not, of course, as a pleasurable humiliation or a form of homage to a superior – as it is, for instance, in 'Please Master' – but as the most intimate means of expressing love and of giving and taking pleasure. It is, emphatically, an erotic act between equals. As a symbol, it covers most of the areas of Ginsberg's sexual and political concern. The anus is a levelling agent, since (theoretically) every one of us has one, whether we are female or male, white or black, homosexual or heterosexual, rich or poor, president or dissident. The anus is the focus of the heterosexual repression which fuels male homosexual oppression, and must be set free to set free. The relationship between inanimates such as America and the Earth should be like that between two lovers, each gently tongueing the other's anus. America's relationship with other nations should be of the same type, devoid of the pride and distrust which characterise it now. This is, indeed, a true kiss of peace.

I have mentioned Ginsberg's visible effort to practise what he preaches, by becoming a new kind of man. This effort becomes most apparent whenever he writes in detail about women's bodies, a subject which arises frequently, when he worries about his childlessness. The image he projects of woman's body is based on memories of his mother, Naomi, who is so vividly present throughout 'Kaddish'. He remembers her in her hospitals and asylums, places where the social intercourse of family life is reduced to a condition of (often) naked physical presence and howled recriminations. In one terrible scene, Naomi vomits, shits, and pisses, all at once: 'convulsions and red vomit coming out of her mouth – diarrhea water exploding from her behind – on all fours in front of the toilet – urine running between her legs – left retching on the tile floor smeared with her black feces' (CP, p.218). Her body seems to eject a limitless amount of waste from every orifice, as if calculating to shock, if not to disgust. On another occasion, she draws up her dress in her son's presence, exposing a 'big slash of hair, scars of operations, pancreas, belly wounds, abortions, appendix, stitching of incisions pulling down in the fat like hideous thick zippers – ragged long lips between her legs – What, even, smell of asshole?' His reaction to these tattered remnants of flesh is important: 'I was cold – later revolted a little, not much – seemed perhaps a good idea to try – know the Monster of the Beginning Womb – Perhaps – that way' (CP, p.219). Despite the power of his imagery and diction, and the extremity of his mother's condition, Ginsberg's reaction is oddly muted. After a while, he is 'a little' revolted. What has captured his imagination – woman's body (albeit in the worst state of disintegration) and the mechanics of sexual reproduction – prevents outright disgust, by fascinating him. I am reminded of the image, in 'Magic Psalm', of a 'Softmouth Vagina that enters my brain from above' (CP, p.255) – the revolutionised female principle, having acquired the hitherto only phallic capacity to penetrate, gently presses its way into the poet's mind, where concentration on his theme becomes a cerebral but productive form of intercourse. The 'vaginal' brain gives birth to the following considerations.

'He inserts his penis into her vagina.' Formal sex education begins and, customarily, ends with this classically inadequate sentence; or with some variation on it. The young Allen Ginsberg regarded it as 'a weird explanation!' (CP, p.346). But his instinctive distaste for any purely mechanical version of sexual intercourse – in this case, the insertion of one organ into another, for a reproductive purpose – has to be overcome, later, when he decides that he must impregnate a woman, in order to father a child. Uncharacteristically, therefore, in such poems as 'This Form of Life Needs Sex', he dwells on the need to carry out a particular, narrowly-defined act – insertion and emission – regardless of his and his partner's probable lack of feeling for each other. She is reduced to functioning as the receptacle for his sperm. He is reduced to functioning as sperm source. Their intercourse would be 'ignorant Fuckery', rather than love-making (CP, p.284). The intervention of one of his gurus settled the matter. His advice was firm: 'Give up desire for children'.[17] The temporary obsession with offspring was false to his sexuality, to his respect for women, and to his aesthetics; and was, as far as one can tell, discarded as falsehood.

In a number of poems, Ginsberg emulates the sexual egalitarianism of Whitman, by celebrating a female, as well as a male subject. Like Whitman, he, too, sometimes fails to convince. When he writes that 'it's too long that I've sat up in bed / without anyone to touch on the knee, man / or woman I don't care what anymore', he speaks out of exasperation, rather than any real desire to make love to either woman or man (CP, p.183). The urgent need for love may lead him into a woman's arms, but only – on this occasion, at least – as a last resort. A similar imbalance of desire is evident in the following declaration: 'I delight in a woman's belly, youth stretching his breasts and thighs to sex, the cock sprung inward / gassing its seed in the lips of Yin' (CP, p.259). The reference to woman is formal and unenthusiastic, expressive merely of a static idea of desirable women, a theory. On the other hand, the reference to the boy quickly covers several erogenous zones, which move under the poet's words as if, literally, under his tongue, stretching out in the ecstasy which leads to the mention and emission of seed. The reference to the woman is brief, exact, and minimal; that to the boy is leisurely, exploratory, and metaphoric. There is no comparison. Even though the poet's duty is done, his personality remains clear and unembarrassed. The object of the duty is defeated.

Perhaps the most successful of the poems of bisexual celebration is the famous 'Love Poem on Theme by Whitman' (CP, p.115). Here, as Ginsberg imagines lying between bride and groom, and making love to both, he avoids his own and Whitman's frequent error, of alternating references to man and woman, which beg to be contrasted (as above). Here, he mixes references to the two genders into a polymorphous whole, into which defining characteristics only occasionally intrude.[18] The result is an admirable expression of that human condition to which neither of the limiting epithets 'homosexual' and 'heterosexual' applies. The emphasis is on shared physical detail, such as shoulders, breasts, buttocks, lips, hands, and bellies – apart from one reference to a 'cock in the darkness driven tormented and attacking', but even this could be either the poet's or the groom's. An orifice is left uncategorised as a 'hole'. At the climax, when 'white come' flows 'in the swirling sheets', the three seem to merge even into their surroundings, as well as into eachother. However, this was an early, Utopian piece, somewhat undermined by the later poems of distaste for female flesh. In order to come any closer to the distant ideal, which has remained unchanged since the writing of 'Love Poem on Theme by Whitman', Ginsberg had first to pass through the matter of the sexism of sexual orientation. The love poem establishes a goal, but the poems of distaste were calculated to show how far he still was from it.

The next stage in the development of his sexual politics came with the slow acceptance of and growth into his own middle age. Even at the early age of 33, he let out the frustrated whine, 'my hair's falling out I've got a belly I'm sick of sex' (1959: CP, p.229). Later, he admits to being 'rueful of the bald front of my skull and the gray sign of time in my beard' (1965: CP, p.352). He begs a sexual master to 'put your rough hands on my bald hairy skull' (1968: CP, p.494). He combs his 'gray glistening beard' (1969: CP, p. 536). He complains, 'I'll never get laid again' (1973: CP, p.596). Finally, he sings the 'Sickness Blues', augmenting his 'don't want to fuck no more' with the new theme, 'can't get it up no more' (1975: CP, p.639). Remember, on the other hand, that he is still writing his habitually lusty verses, such as 'Sweet Boy, Gimme Yr Ass' (1974: CP, p.613) and 'Come All Ye Brave Boys' (1975: CP, p.637). In the *Gay Sunshine* interview (1972), he says: 'I find, as I'm growing older, no less flutterings of delightful desire in my belly and abdomen. But also I'm becoming more tolerant of other resolutions between people besides sex' (p.101). This is crucial to the direction his latest poetry seems to be taking.

Later in the interview (p.102), Ginsberg describes his relationship with a young Australian. Theirs was that kind of 'platonic friendship in which people sleep together naked, caressing each other, but [if they are men] don't come, saving their seed for yogic or other reasons'. In other words, they practised a form of *carezza*, as recommended by Whitman and Carpenter. With the Australian, Ginsberg says, 'I was feeling another kind of very subtle, ethereal orgasm that seemed to occupy the upper portions of the body rather than the genital area'. In this way, 'You can get real close with people that you love who wouldn't otherwise want to sleep with you sexually'. *Carezza* allows the formation of a physical, erotic relationship between, for example, two 'heterosexual' men; or a 'homosexual' woman and man; or a youth and an old-age pensioner. It may lead to a 'full' sexual relationship, or not. If not, no matter: for *carezza* is sufficient expression of desire. It fails, not conventionally, with absence of erection, but with lack of love. The criteria by which great lovers are assessed are no longer the size and potency of his penis or the shapeliness of her breasts and bottom; but their capacity for love, regardless of artificial divisions set up between races, ages, and genders. The last two poems of *Mind Breaths*, 'I Lay Love on my Knee' and 'Love Replied', state the case for *carezza* in the simplest terms. The beloved youth Love asks Ginsberg to concentrate less ardently on genital caresses: for 'I myself am not queer / Tho I hold your heart dear'. He invites kisses on his heart, 'my public part', rather than his penis; yet still offers the poet 'All the love I can give' (CP, p.685).

Because of his insistence on providing an individual perspective on his subjects, Ginsberg's sexual politics have never been the most sophisticated. He always allows – indeed, expects – his prejudices to interfere with his principles, in order to show as honestly as possible the distance between the real and the ideal. He refuses to hide his sexism, lest he be allowed to forget it and the need to eradicate it. He seeks not only to provide an ideal system of sexual politics, but to show how the individual must wrestle with her or his own life, in order to satisfy the best systems proposed by the better theorists. His current preoccupation with the pairing of old man and youth arises out of his undiminished desire to make love with young men. It is not necessarily proposed as the solution to any general problem, but as one aspect of the continuation of his own personality.

THE PHALLUS AND BEYOND

In one of the most impressive of his love poems, 'Journal Night Thoughts', Ginsberg produces the image of a man 'born with genitals all over / his body' (CP, p.269). This male equivalent of Diana of Ephesus, the multi-breasted Earth-Mother-Goddess, stands for all of the positive qualities the poet sees in phallic sexuality: the distinct, but conjoined powers of phallus and seed. In order to examine these, we must first consider 'Please Master', the poem which most explicitly and enthusiastically celebrates the physical power of the male body and of its phallus in particular (CP, pp.494–5).

The repeated phrase, 'please master', carries several meanings, occasionally all at once. It is the subservient introduction to a request (Please, master, may I. . .) or an imperative (Give the master pleasure, or Please master me). When it works as an imperative, it is the subservient partner's means of controlling (that is, of mastering) the master's means of controlling him. The slave-as-master orders the master-as-slave to carry out the actions which will supplement the multiplicity of their roles. One is the verbal, the other the physical master of their bout.

Furthermore, most elements of the poem, like the poet's 'bald hairy skull', are amalgams of opposites. Fellatio is both verbal and mute, since the 'dumb' penis fills the throat of the fellator as the sound of his voice, which goes on speaking. The penis itself is both gentle and rough. It is 'delicate', but has the hot 'barrel' of a fired pistol. It is both hard metal and pliant flesh. The hands of the master both caress the poet, stroking his neck, and crucify him on a frame of tables and chairs. The poet himself, bent over the table, is being crucified and loved at once. His position is that of a child, being or about to be beaten, as well as that of a poet, poring over the book he is writing.

As the master's 'vehicle', the poet thinks of himself as a mere object, to be manipulated by the master for purely selfish ends, an automobile to take him where he wants to go. But 'drive me thy vehicle' also means Drive your vehicle (penis) for me, where the penis is the speedy and dangerous, but pleasure-giving machine, which in its past is known to have frequented the appropriate urban areas of Denver and Brooklyn and the car lots of Paris. To drive this car is to experience the quickening rhythm of sexual intercourse, the throbbing 'thrill-plunge & pull-back-bounce & push down' of the excited penis, and the danger of impending catastrophe: the sudden crash, bloodshed, and a scream. Again, we are faced with the problem of deciding which of the two partners is in the driving seat, and which the passenger. (The motoring image reappears in a later poem, when the poet addresses all 'heroic half naked young studs / That drive automobiles through vaginal blood' (CP, p.637).)

Since 'Please Master' is the poem's title, we can read the poet's sexual requests as being addressed to the poem itself, calling on it by name. The poem speaks to itself. It is its own masturbatory fantasy, its own resulting orgasm, and its own master and slave. It exists only as the fantasy of sexual intercourse between itself and itself. The reader's involvement is lessened by the nagging suspicion that the poet's claimed involvement is counterfeit, because he must have been taking notes throughout the session he describes. He must have touched lips to the lover's thigh, then swiftly jotted down that it was 'hard muscle hairless'; kissed the anus, then noted that it was rosy (and for how long did he ponder on the association of anus and opening bloom?); sucked the penis, then noticed its similarity to a gun; felt it thrust in his rectum, and written a brief history of the master's cosmopolitan sex life; sensed the orgasm, then scribbled a quick memo to the effect that he loves the man who is inside him. Perhaps he merely loves him in gratitude, for providing the material for another publishable poem.

In the first fourteen lines of the poem, the master is immobile and passive, like a statue, and it is here that his physique is most fully explored by the 'I', the slave. In these lines, we move swiftly from cheek to feet to belly, thighs, ankles, thighs, stomach, buttocks, pubic hair, anus, and balls. . . But when the master breaks into action, paradoxically, his physique seems limited to the monstrous penis ('your thick shaft', 'your prick-heart', 'your dumb hardness', 'your delicate flesh-hot prick barrel veined', 'your shaft', 'your cock head', 'it', 'your droor thing', 'the prick trunk', 'your sword', 'the tip', 'your self', and 'your selfsame sweet heat-rood') and to those few other parts of the body which, by forcing the slave's body into a fuckable position and lubricating his anus, directly serve the penis's needs. These are, primarily, the arms and hands ('your rough hands', 'strong thumbed', 'grab', 'your hand's rough stroke', 'your palm', 'your thumb stroke', 'your elbows', 'your arms', 'your fingers', and 'your palms'). In addition, his thighs push the penis, and his mouth provides spit with which to lubricate it. Even his eyes, the only other part of him explicitly involved in the action ('please look into my eyes', 'stare in my eye', the slave begs him), contribute only to the elaborate menace of his genital power. They glare, without blinking. Surely, they stare, not into the slave's eyes, but at the plunging penis.

There are two slaves here, then; two physiques, serving one master: the master's penis. Remember, the slave refers to it as 'your self', as though the rest of his body were that of a third person, a mediator, obediently guiding the master's penis into the slave, and submissive to the point of humiliating absence from the action. In the throat of the slave, the word 'love' is a meaningful scream of delight, whose meaning is not 'love'.

However, two slaves serve a master (the penis), who is in turn enslaved to a fourth element in the poem. Being, above all, a celebration of 'passivity' (that is, of being penetrated), 'Please Master' has as its true focus the arse of the speaker ('my ass', 'my backside', 'my hole', 'hairmouth', 'my wrinkled self-hole', 'my behind', 'my rear', 'my asshalfs', 'the bottom', 'my ass', 'my belly', 'my asshole', 'a wet asshole', and 'soft drip-flesh'). The poem's apparently single-minded obsession with the master's phallus turns out to be illusory. There are more references to the slave's arse. (Not to mention his mouth and throat.)

The phallus-as-firearm is, as it were, spiked by its need for a wound, a 'hole'. It cannot act alone. (What stud could survive the ignominy of having as his phallus-master's only slave that other weapon, his clenched fist?) As a 'self' in isolation, it is impotent. So when, in 'Come All Ye Brave Boys', Ginsberg addresses all the supposedly heterosexual youths sunning themselves on upper Broadway, with the intention of teaching them 'a new tenderness' and 'new joys', he is careful not to repeat the welcoming servility of 'Please Master'. In effect, he offers them all a way out of their phallic impasse: firstly, by calling on them to 'Turn over spread your strong legs like a lass' so as to be 'jived up the ass;'[19] and secondly, by inviting them to join him in a session of embraces which will involve not just their phallic 'automobiles', but arms, heads, shoulders, brows, bellies, necks, anuses, penises, lips, tongues, armpits, breasts, and legs (CP, p.637). He dares them to taste for the first time the pleasures, not only of his, but of their own flesh. If they take his advice, these boys, who are now just 'tight assed & strong cocked young fools', will have the opportunity of becoming complete creatures, their wayward parts unified by joy. Ginsberg (or his poem) will introduce them to themselves.

The phallus may be isolated, as a fetish; but its allure need not be merely solipsistic, self-referential. The male Diana of Ephesus, 'born with genitals all over / his body', would bristle with erections when aroused, like a mirror-image of Saint Sebastian: a body clad in gentle arrows, all pointing outwards. Like Diana's, his physique will give suck at any point. In effect, this image is an expression of the ordinary body, any part of which has potential as an erogenous zone, no less productive of pleasure than the genital zone itself. To sleep with a man who has allowed himself to develop this full physical potential is, therefore, equivalent to sleeping with a whole crowd of phallocentric studs. The multi-penised man, paradoxically, invites one to partake of erotic pleasures beyond the dominance of the phallus: he attacks our obsession with the groin. After fucking and ejaculation, there is intercourse.

8 THOM GUNN

LIMITATION

Critical analysis of the erotic elements in Gunn's poems has followed a recognisable course. As we have come to expect, many commentators say nothing about the poet's homosexuality.[1] Some go further and assert heterosexuality, by referring to the loved ones in the poems as female.[2] Even *Gay News*' reviewer of the 1979 *Selected Poems* writes that 'Those seeking homo-erotic poetry . . . must look elsewhere'.[3] Since most writers, particularly those reviewing Gunn's first three volumes, concentrated on the apparently violent aspect of his subjects, and on his conception of men's *will*, one might have expected them to begin to analyse the erotic vision to which these themes adhere.

Of fourteen explicit references to the will, in twelve poems, none appears in a collection later than 1961, when *My Sad Captains* came out. Of the fourteen, one is in *Fighting Terms*, eleven are in *The Sense of Movement*, and two in *My Sad Captains*. The four main later volumes, *Touch*, *Moly*, *Jack Straw's Castle*, and *The Passages of Joy*, contain none apiece.[4] The first function of these fourteen references is literal, of course; but in most cases Gunn seems, also, to be telling the old but serious joke, familiar to readers of Shakespeare's sonnets, in which 'will' has at least two meanings, of which the second is 'phallus'. One will is the visible manifestation of the other: the phallus, of the interior force of manhood. (Women will find the joke unpleasant in most of its implications.)

The phallus as 'will' is high technology in comparison with the mere penis. As an instrument of control, it is associated with any number of inorganic symbols of authority (sword, sceptre, baton, truncheon, swagger-stick, cosh, thyrsus, wand, crucifix, totem pole, dildo. . .) before finally alluding to itself, as penis. Similarly, the will-powered man is uniformed as a type (cowboy, biker, fireman, soldier, quarter-back, sailor, cop. . .) long before he reveals himself, or is exposed, as a mere individual. Even naked, he is clad in iron, tattooed and tense, forever on his guard. You could make love with him all night long without ever getting to *feel* him or getting him to feel.

In Gunn's early poems, therefore, sex is characteristically described in martial terms, as an element in human beings' constant struggle to gain control of their relationships. To seduce is to surround and lay siege to an enemy territory. Sex is attack and victory. The stratagems of love operate, not in a shared private place of contemplative joy, but in a public arena where thought is subordinated to the instinctive lunges and side-steps of attack and defence.

While action supercedes thought in Gunn's work, the actions he values are, in general, thoughtfully conceived. Abstract thought – 'mere thought' – does not interest him. Nor does the kind of thought which, for its own sake, feeds pointlessly on action. ('Description and analysis degrade, / Limit, delay...' (FT, p.36).) In much of the second collection, *The Sense of Movement*, Gunn took an aggressive line according to which, to be tyrannised by the desire for rest, comfort, security, familiarity, sufficiency, and inaction, is to be little better than dead. The most extreme statement of this position was the controversial poem 'Lines for a Book' (SM, p.30), which Gunn later repudiated as being 'fascistic and foolish'.[5] Here, the violent man is seen as the epitome, not of death, but of life and action: 'I think of those exclusive by their action, / For whom mere thought could be no satisfaction'. The liberal Stephen Spender is made to look a sissie next to Alexander the Great. Furthermore, in an image of the castrated statues of athletes, 'gelded so they cannot hurt / The pale curators and the families / By calling up disturbing images', Gunn seems to nominate sexual intercourse as the epitome of living action; impotence, as that of death. The dirt under which some of these athletes are lying is both the obvious soil of a deep grave or future archaeological site, and the other kind of 'dirt' heaped on the memory of their beautiful bodies: visual and verbal pornographies created by and for sexual intellectuals, in two, safe dimensions.

Perhaps more disquieting than the poem itself is the later retraction, since 'Lines from a Book' is only a more outspoken version of themes which arise in many other poems from the same period. What once seemed an ironic overstatement of some of the poet's favourite themes is now revealed as being, embarrassingly, in earnest.

The reference to Alexander is one of a series in which Gunn pays homage to the virile power of historical figures like Achilles and Patroclus, John of Gaunt, Mark Antony, and Coriolanus. But most of his interest is invested in contemporary men: nameless bikers and

national servicemen, greasers and Teds, presided over by the spirits
of James Dean and Elvis Presley. What all have in common is the
freedom they have given themselves to make choices about their
lives, and the 'limits' or 'limitations' these choices impose on them.
This can be partly explained by Gunn's account of the 'theory of
pose' which, as a student at Cambridge, he derived from readings of
Stendhal and Yeats:

> The theory of pose was this: everyone plays a part, whether he
> knows it or not, so he might as well deliberately design a part, or a
> series of parts, for himself. Only a psychopath or a very good actor
> is in danger of *becoming* his part, however, so one who is neither is
> left in an interesting place somewhere in between the starting point
> – the bare undefined and undirected self, if he ever existed – and
> the chosen part. This is a place rich in tensions between the
> achieved and the unachieved.[6]

Gunn's men are often to be found in this 'interesting place', where
they are both at large and confined, jailer and jailed, tamer and
hawk, master and slave. They embody an idea of self-control – in the
sense of the attempt to control one's own destiny – which demands
that one man be both controller and controlled unto himself. It is no
wonder that one of Gunn's repeated themes is the *doppelganger* or
double.[7]

Of all his audiences, the posing tough guy is himself the most
appreciative, but at the same time the most critical: he adores his
own performance, but is not convinced by it. He knows that, despite
his real physical prowess, his exaggerated pose of self-confidence and
inner strength is a sham. Since his doubts survive each sexual bout he
initiates and each fight he picks, the show of strength must go on.
The butch poseur is the perpetual victim of his own ambition, a penis
which is forever erect but never ejaculates. His personality *consists of*
his frustrated satyriasis.

In the second of the two 'Modes of Pleasure' poems (MSC, p. 24),
Lust itself is personified as such a man, who 'marks time / Dark in his
doubtful uniform / Preparing once more for the test'. Each sexual
encounter is an exam, for which Lust feels distinctly ill-prepared. The
excessively 'male' male is as scared of himself as are the less
aggressive men he threatens. *Machismo* is a cover for uncertainty.
Look at the lost soldier in 'Captain in Time of Peace' (FT, p.34),
whose habits of violence leave him, when peace arrives, so ashamed
of his inability to adapt to inaction, that he has to offer this apology:

> So please forgive
> All my inadequacy: I was fit

> For peaceful living once, and was not born
> A clumsy brute in uniform.

The fitness for peaceful living is confined to childhood, before virility can be called into question.

A man becomes a soldier to defend not so much his nation as himself. His enemies are those whom his pose of virility does not impress. He fights in order to impress them; seeks to impress them in order to assure *himself* that the pose is impressive. Ultimately, of course, he is his own enemy. In failing to impress, he needs even further to exaggerate the pose; but by doing so, he lessens its plausibility and heightens his own insecurity. His uniform becomes more and more an empty shape, muscular and forbidding, but life-like only to those who play-act to the same extent.

The kind of definition these men require is as exact and limiting as a prison cell, affording its captive as few alternatives as possible: bed, floor, or stool. In 'In the Tank' (T, p.52), Gunn shows how a cell safely reduces the amount of intellectual activity required of its occupant to a minimum of eye movements and the simple registration of the results: the listing of a few insignificant but essential objects: bowl, towel, bed, soap, lavatory. The non-intellectual metaphysics of the convict provide a comfortingly uncomplicated universal vision. Night begins at nine sharp, and the empty order of creation is forever within range of sight. Mystery is banished. 'And then he knew exactly where he sat'. He is at the centre of a series of Chinese boxes, each as orderly and safe as the next. Even the need to escape has been eliminated.

> The jail contained a tank, the tank contained
> A box, a mere suspension, at the centre,
> Where there was nothing left to understand,
> And where he must re-enter and re-enter.

The compulsion to move inwards, to curl up in total, foetus-like wisdom, satisfies him fully. He imagines himself at liberty, free to confine himself at will.

Gunn takes things even further when he makes Jack Straw 'the man on the rack', 'the man who puts the man on the rack', and 'the man who watches the man who puts the man on the rack': fantasy, pornographer, and masturbator, all in one (JSC, p.52). Man, the object of his own desire, convinces himself that his masturbation – with or without a partner – is directed outwards. He makes love to his own erection, thinking he is thinking of someone else. Call this autism or self-sufficiency; the effect is much the same. Either way, the consequent satisfaction with and reliance on *self* precludes real contact with *other*.

The tough guy's strutting figure is a pose of sexual potency – his advertisement for his correspondingly massive, powerful, and enduring erection – and so Gunn's men (like Lawrence's) are sometimes characterised, in accordance with their obsession, as phalluses, embodiments of the *will*. The man is a personification of his own sexual desire (erection); and his actions are symbolic representations of *its*. One man's whole body pulses with tenderness, 'Like an erection'; and at the onset of desire another not only gets, but also becomes an erection, 'as if his body had / rolled back its own foreskin' (JSC, pp.43,55). On the other hand, the detumescent old

> Inch down into their loosened flesh, each fold
> Being sensible of the gravity
> Which tugs
> And longs to bring it down
> And break its hold.
>   (T, p.58)

Impotent and weak, they are no competition for the virility of young men.

A muscular frame conveys two messages, in two directions: to its possessor and to anyone he confronts. The messages are, respectively, concerned with violence and sexuality; and each can be either a threat or a promise. But, in the end, they merge ('I shall do you violence with these muscles') and are both threat and promise at once ('It may hurt but you will enjoy it'). It is important to remember, also, how the man looks: swaggering, leather-jacketed, he stands with his feet apart, thumbs hooked heavily in the top of his jeans, torso tapering down from apparently massive shoulders to slender waist and hips. He is studiously casual but as tense as twisted rope. The focus is his crotch, tight-clad, padded if need be. The threat is inevitably sexual.

In 'Lofty at the Palais de Danse' (FT, p.14), a soldier refers to his prick as 'another muscle' (in addition to those of his two arms), and his seduction of a woman is pared down to its essentials: she feels his arms, gauging his strength, and is then taken outside to feel his prick. She says 'yes' to each arm; a third 'yes' will be voiced as the prick punches its way into her. His penis is, therefore, less a delicate and sensitive instrument of mutual pleasure than a muscle, a part of the soldier's armoury, just another aspect of his physical power. As such, it is a *symbol* of his masculinity. His erection, objectified as mailed fist or dagger or gun, is the tautological phallic symbol of itself.

In 'Black Jackets' (MSC, p.29), Gunn describes a crowd of leather boys in a gay bar, huddled together in their scratched, black jackets, 'Concocting selves for their impervious kit'. They are relaxing, having harmless fun in their weekend clothes. During the week, they do such mundane jobs as driving delivery vans. The leather of their jackets is 'taut across the shoulders grown to it'. The bulky, apparent muscularity of the leather makes these men appear twice the size they were. Twice as strong, twice as potent. They cluster in a gang, so as to assure themselves of their own most appreciative audience, themselves. Of course, their other motive for togetherness is sexual. Here in the bar and (with any luck) later in bed, van drivers become heroes.

I do not mean to have suggested that all of these youths are inadequate, sadistic wife- or boyfriend-beaters. They are not. They are simply interested in themselves and eachother as exemplars of the butch, the manly. Only those who are convinced by their own most outrageous poses, only the psychopaths, become dangerous. The fact that the rest, the majority, 'strap in doubt' when they put on their leather gear (SM, p.11) indicates that their posing has a built-in safety-feature and sign of real strength: self-doubt. Once that distance between actor and act is confidently established – that is, once the man accepts, with graceful irony, that he enjoys his act even if he does not really measure up to it – he is free to think up all kinds of playful scenarios for the thuggish brute he is not. A few who have established this dynamic self-confidence in their self-doubt become involved in actual sadomasochistic games, which take the implications of the tough-guy fiction to their logical conclusion.

FALSE VIOLENCE

Consider the instruments – or\'toys' as they are often affectionately called – with which the body of the masochist is circumscribed: the manacles which hold his ankles in position, far apart; the leather straps which cradle his torso, and with which he may be hoisted from the ground; the cuffs which hold his wrists together, beyond his head or behind his back; the weighted clip on each nipple; the studded collar and leash; the buckled gag whose leather tab fills his mouth to keep his tongue still; the hood, or mask, over eyes and ears; the rack, or pillory; the dildo, enema, or plug in his anus; the bullwhip, curling round his buttocks; the tight ring around the base of his genitals, imprisoning blood in his penis; the weighted straps which stretch the scrotum and separate his balls; the catheter. . . All this, the high technology and high glamour of bedroom Grand Guignol, although apparently threatening, apparently pain-inducing, actually removes the possibility of violence. Like armour, it comes between the aggressor and his victim, thereby limiting both the former's actions and the latter's reactions. It *represents* sadomasochism; it *stands for* the giving and receiving pain; in fact, it *replaces* violence.

One writer on the practical aspects of sadomasochistic relationships between men restates one of the Marquis de Sade's fundamental principles that 'each action should be deliberate, not accidental or carelessly executed. Nothing should be done in real anger or fear even though anger or fear may be part of the dialogue.' He continues that 'perhaps the easiest way to determine what separates sadomasochism from acts of brutality is to ask whether the relationship is being established by consent or by force'.[8] Even if the power and pain are genuine, the violence, because carried out with caring intent, is a sham. Both parties are aware that, should the submissive partner, reaching the limits of endurance, make a certain pre-arranged sign, the bout will end, as if it were a children's game. What is required, as by all representational art, is a willing suspension of disbelief — here, on the part of the two partners. To progress beyond the viable post of naivety — belief in each other's gestures and script — is to eliminate sexual rapport.

Like his jacket and jeans, the instruments of sexual violence conform to the masochist's physique. They are the concave and convex images of his convexity and concavity. Even when stacked in the closet, they continue to narrate their pornographic fiction. When his victim is away, the sadist can consult their narrative to edifying effect. The cold touch of a chain and the sweaty stench of leather combine to replace the body they might otherwise adorn. The solitary sadist may even put on his victim's chains, thereby himself enacting the masochist's part, by carrying out his own orders. At times, toys may effectively eliminate the need for the sexual contact they symbolise. Slave and master may correspond with each other at a distance, via their paraphernalia.

In 'The Beaters', Gunn again makes the point that the leather uniform, the muscles, and all other gadgets and signs sadomasochists use on one another 'are emblems to recall identity' (SM, p.36). This poem gives us the most detailed and intimate view of the actor-lovers who recite threats and deal out on request their delightful thrusts and blows. They are 'careful, choosing limitation', so as to be best able to identify and define themselves. And they break out of loneliness, that chosen prison cell, only for the sake of a 'perfect counterpart' — another aspect of the self, a double, or a twin; or a jailer who will swap places with his prisoner; or, simply, a male lover with whom to alternate sexual and martial roles. This mirror image of the beater must be one who will accept as the sweetest pleasure the humiliations to which he will be subjected, the restraints which will be forced upon him, and the sharp blows he will receive. He must play with the utmost appearance of conviction his role of 'toiling toward despair'. As for the beaters themselves, 'Through violent parables their special care / Is strictly to explore that finitude' of imposed and accepted limitation.

Where violence is a parable, strength is a narrative skill. The parable is of an enclosed, universal cell, wholly devoid of enigma, in which two similar beings strive at the same time to impress, to love, and to enter each other. In order to reach that core, the inner cell, each must discipline his counterpart as a jailer might his prisoner, so that the restraints on the prisoner ever intensify the fact of his imprisonment; so that, as a result, the prisoner becomes more a prisoner, the jailer more a jailer and, therefore, apparently more free. Thus, their ritual of pain and pleasure, abhorrence and desire,

> Both limits and implies their liberty.
> Ambiguous liberty! it is the air
> Between the raised arm and the fallen thud.

Ultimately, it is a complex compromise between all the extremes with which we have been concerned: the union which comes about between tumescence and detumescence, adolescence and death.

In the later, more sophisticated poem 'The Menace' (PJ, pp.36–41), Gunn returns to the idea of playing in this way with 'the dull idea of the male / strenuous in his limitations'. Whereas the earlier poem was openly meant to shock – and lived up to this intention – 'The Menace' is at once more relaxed and playful, and more genuinely serious. It centres on a quotation from Gregory Bateson, about dogs at play: 'The playful nip denotes the bite, but it does not denote what would be denoted by the bite'. Clearly, we must extrapolate from this the obvious (but all too conveniently over-looked) fact, that the kinds of sexual act Gunn is talking about may denote torture, but not what torture would denote.

Gunn postulates a syntax of control to complement his own unerring control of syntax. He describes men who

> frame fantasies like the beginnings
> of sentences, form opening clauses,
> seeking a plausible conjunction
> that a sentence can turn on
> to compound the daydream.

I would suggest that the 'but' in Bateson's sentence is just such a 'plausible conjunction': the 'but' that spans the distance between aggressive (actual) bite and affectionate (apparent) bite. The human, sexual sentence begins with 'opening clauses' of pure fantasy, hinges on the 'but' of mutual consent, and culminates in a subsidiary main clause of action. It is the copula that makes a sentence copulative. Thus:

He is not a real soldier
but a soldier
inducted by himself
into an army of fantasy
and he greets another.

Each action or item of dress denotes sex; *but* connotes violence, domination, humiliation, service, and so on. The former depends on the latter. In 'Jack Straw's Castle,' Jack's dream depends on 'A real Charles Manson', *but* is a dream nonetheless (JSC, pp.48–56).

Now, some critics have objected to Gunn's preoccupation with the violent male. Alan Bold, for instance, has complained strongly of 'Gunn's apparent inability to apprehend the true nature of violence'.[9] He continues: 'The concentration camps were full of people like "The Beaters" and it is surely an abrogation of human concern to state that such people, too, can "do their own thing" simply because it fits into his version of an existentialist view of things. Gunn does not necessarily admire the Beaters, but he rather naively gives them the benefit of the doubt.'[10] This reading of the poem, assuming as it does a lack of complicity between the two subjects, is a travesty. It seems to me to trivialise concentration camps; and to commit its own sin, of failing to apprehend the nature of the violence in question. We should, rather, think in terms of a masquerade of violent non-violence, in which the choice of aggressive action is dictated by mutual concern. Ekbert Faas comes close to the point in an essay on Ted Hughes: 'If one were to answer that exam question: Who are the poets of violence? you wouldn't get very far if you began with Thom Gunn . . . and not merely because his subject is far more surely gentleness.'[11] And John Press says Gunn is 'not greatly perplexed or fascinated by the problem of violence in the universe', but concentrates on order and control.[12]

TRANSITION

With regard to the question of form, several metaphors will do. The poem is stretched on a metrical rack; it is trodden under feet; it lies in bondage; it is subjected to the poet's disciplinary will (pun intended). . . One could go on. From Robert K. Martin's premise, that 'Gunn's poetry is marked by a concern with style, conceived as definition of self', it may be possible to deduce a sadomasochistic relationship between form and content.[13] In the early poems, at least, form is the master of content, whipping it into shape; and yet, the master often *is* the content, the subject. They imprison each other, he imprisons himself. Colin Falck sees Gunn's metres as 'a formal equivalent of the protective gear of his motorcylists'.[14] Alan Bold feels that the 'temperamental reason for Gunn's use of Metaphysical matter in a traditional manner is surely that he wished to be completely in control of the poems he was creating. It would be ludicrous to pose as the poet of discipline and control in verse that fell apart at the edges.' Bold goes on to envisage a 'future definitive edition' of *The Sense of Movement*, 'tightly bound in leather, with a buckle for a clasp, so that readers can appreciate in full its fetishistic character'.[15]

My Sad Captains is well known as the volume in which Gunn changed course. Its sixteen metrical poems are followed by thirteen in syllabics. As Gunn himself said, 'From now on, a bit more flexibility'. It is interesting to note that he associated the decision with having become 'more humane'.[16] Robert Martin believes that Gunn's personal and (later) public acknowledgement of his homosexuality had a hand in the change; and 'one can argue that the poetic form was altered to suit a new sense of himself'.[17] (There is also the move to America, and the increasing influence of American poetic traditions, to be taken into account. Martin tends to take the early poems at face value, as if Gunn were an American, without giving him credit for some very English flights of irony. The very idea of the Metaphysical, homosexual biker is Gunn's best serious joke; and I see it as a distinctive mark of an English poet.)

After metrical regularity, intellectual conceits (on 'unintellectual' themes), and remorseless end rhymes, the enjambments of 'My Sad Captains' and 'Touch' seem like the utmost freedom. Eventually, in such poems as 'The Geysers' (JSC, pp.21–7), completed syntax gives way to unpunctuated fragments of phrase. 'The Geysers' is as polymorphous as the sexual scenes it portrays. Gunn no longer needs to prove his poetical dexterity; his literary muscle, as it were. He has provided himself with choice. Just as one man may be, at different times, active, passive (or both), sadistic, masochistic (or both), detached, romantic (or both), promiscuous, monogamous (or both), and heterosexual, homosexual (or both), thereby imposing limitation on his physique during individual encounters, but living his life in general as an experiment in physical metamorphosis; so, too, the poet may choose to adopt all the poetic modes at his disposal. The technical variety of *Jack Straw's Castle* is not a demonstration of formal pyrotechnics for their own sake (which one often feels to be the case in Auden's *Collected Poems*, for example); but a deliberate expression of breadth of life, of personal life-style. This seems even more true of *The Passages of Joy*. Like a lover, the poem may come to one naked or clothed; and, if clothed, in any of a number of costumes. Like lovers, individual poems act on us in individual ways.

The transition from control to release is enacted not only in Gunn's prosodic development, but also in many of the individual poems, as their theme. Gunn has the habit of seeing love and sex, for better or worse, as metamorphic forces. Hence, 'The Allegory of the Wolf Boy' (SM, p.35). Gunn has said that this poem is about himself, 'leading a straight life and being gay'.[18] Its evocation of a boy's 'sad duplicity' in relation to conventional afternoons of tea and tennis, and his wild discomfort after dusk, combine in a pathetic portrayal of teenage loneliness and yearning. The fur of puberty and wolfishness is the sudden outward sign of his reluctant return to nature. Yet, even as he drops on all fours in the moonlight, he is branded as a 'clean exception to the natural laws'. The 'sad duplicity', therefore, is as much nature's as his. The blood on his paws is a mere foretaste of the moral violence to which the very existence of his sexual instincts is bound to subject him.

According to Burton's *Anatomy of Melancholy*, Gerardus de Solo classifies lycanthropy (or *lupinam insaniam*, the wolf madness) as an 'amorous' condition. And Boccaccio shows that a dream of an attack by a wolf can be as much a manifestation of loving concern as a murderous wish-fulfilment (*Decameron* IX, 7). In *L'Histoire de la magie* (1860), Eliphas Levi puts forward the view that lycanthropy splits, rather than metamorphoses, the subject, who sleeps in his own bed and *dreams* of being a wolf, while at the same time his astral body wanders the countryside in search of meat. The intellect desires, but the animal in us actually goes out and hunts. The intellect of the Wolf Boy hangs back, concocting dreams, while, in its solitude, his animal body tries to act them out. Detachment feeds on involvement's deeds.

'The Allegory of the Wolf Boy' is about adolescence and sexual awareness; about the potential harshness of the landscapes of ecstasy and the means by which an explorer of such places can survive their harshness, in order to go on to discover their more placid regions. We need only consult Ovid and William Burroughs to see how central to eroticism is the idea of total or partial metamorphosis. A dead boy, planted in a fertile grave, becomes a flower: for the male is a husk, repository of the human seed. Each total change is both birth and death: birth of the flower, death of the boy; but continuation of the essence of the latter within the new shape of the former. Sex, too, is both birth and death: consummation and parting. Orgasm, for as long as it lasts but no longer, makes us morally equal to the beasts of the field, by robbing us temporarily of the intellectual capacities which are supposed to make us special. (Only the narrators of pornographic stories manage somehow to maintain, simultaneously, both seminal and narrative flows.) We cry out, wordlessly, like the howling youth. Semen is the life flowing out of the ailing phallus; the intellect, out of the man. By undergoing metamorphosis during intercourse, a man finds his relationship with his natural environment – the body of his lover – changed: for he now becomes a part of its natural cycle, where before, as thinking man, he had imposed his own patterns, his own artificial behaviour, on it. Only at orgasm, therefore, is the beloved body truly entered. It follows that one of the goals of a loving, sexual relationship might be to shuffle off the alien skin of intellectual inhibition well *before* the orgasm itself.

Moly is Gunn's main book of transformations. Its single-minded concern with what he calls 'Rites of Passage' makes it seem likely that this will prove to be the most unified and purposeful of his books. (It also happens to be the most relaxed.) From its epigraph onwards, the book circles, in thoughtful fascination, around the episodes in the *Odyssey* when Circe's sorcery turned men into swine and Odysseus sought the protection of the magical plant Moly. Gunn's modern equivalent of the plant is LSD.

Like 'The Allegory of the Wolf Boy', 'Rites of Passage' itself (M, p.13) deals with the actual moments of a metamorphosis, at once of human into animal and of child into adulthood. 'Moly' lingers on the condition of animality, here referred to as a 'Nightmare of beasthood' (M, p.14). 'From the Wave' makes of a fleet of surfers strange, composite creatures, 'Half wave, half men' (M, p.26). In 'The Rooftop', a man speaks of watching a park emerge into the dawn, watching so closely that he starts 'Becoming what I see' (M, p.33). The 'Street Song' of a drug pusher promises that he can gain you entry 'Into whichever self you choose' (M, p.38). In 'The Messenger', a man concentrating on a flower seems to be 'turning angel' (M, p.47).

The book's main account of transformation is in the five ambiguous 'centaur poems' collectively entitled 'Tom-Dobbin' (M, pp.28–32). The image of the centaur is appropriate to the context of sadomasochistic play-acting: for it is conveniently close to the sport of literally treating one's sexual partner as a horse, the *equus eroticus*. We note that, when Shakespeare speaks of horsemanship, he sometimes means sexual prowess. Riding the partner is both prelude to and metaphor of – rather than substitute for – entering him, and of doing so when in at least nominal control of his movements.[19] While it is not *about* a sadomasochistic relationship, 'Tom-Dobbin' does seem to me to illustrate aspects of the exertion of control in sexual intercourse, and of the relationship between intellect and instinct in the type of game-playing sexual activity with which we have been concerned. In its first section, we read of light as 'luminous seed', passing from Tom to Dobbin and back, 'crossing / in an instant / passage between the two / seamless / imperceptible transition' at a point of contact between them, where 'there is the one / and at once it is also the other'. This is where metamorphosis is sparked off, where Tom and Dobbin enter and become each other. (Remember, as the Indians of the New World demonstrated when the Conquistadors arrived, without prior knowledge it is difficult to see that an ordinary horse and rider are, indeed, separate beasts.)

The second poem works as two parts: the first being to emphasise the separateness of the centaur's two aspects; and the second, to reaffirm the oneness they achieve in sexual intercourse. In the first, the man watches the stallion copulating with a mare. Tom is a detached voyeur, the disinterested (if not uninterested) intelligence, smiling 'with pleasure' as he watches the muscular rearing of Dobbin's enormous body. For a few moments, their relationship is like that between a man who is fucking for the sake of it, and his penis, objectified as a mere instrument with which to carry out the act: a tool. Then, in the second half, he ejaculates:

> In coming Tom and Dobbin join to one –
> Only a moment, just as it is done:
> A shock of whiteness, shooting like a star,
> In which all colours of the spectrum are.

At orgasm, intellectual detachment falters, and the voyeur becomes one with his tool. The two halves of the centaur unite, but stallion and mare do not. Even now, she is no more than a part of the landscape. It is as if the two halves of the male figure were making love together, alone.

All demarcations are confused as the third poem starts. The 'he' is either or both of 'them'. The 'them' is Tom and Dobbin, or Dobbin and the mare, or all three. The character of the bout has changed. The female – if she is still present at all – is a part of the composite beast. Otherwise, she has been refined out of existence by the sophistication of Tom and Dobbin's union: she was supernumerary to their perfected means to joy. Either way, this orgy is a far more complicated affair than the previous poem's lunging act. Even to the extent of unifying its participants with their environment (when the landscape becomes 'extensions of self') as well as with one another, this love-making actually seems to be *making love*.

The fourth poem is parenthetical insofar as, by describing a platypus giving birth, it is distinct from the man-horse-centaur of the rest of the sequence. It takes us into a new dimension of the sequence's theme, by paralleling gestation and delivery with intercourse and ejaculation. Like the centaur, the pregnant duck-billed platypus is a composite creature, as wonderful as any mythological invention. As well as being an amphibious bird-mammal, she is herself an egg, from which her son is 'Hatched into separation', and newly a mother, whose 'brown fur oozes milk for the young one'. But it is the 'visible' relation between her and her son that is most revealing: 'If you could see through darkness you could see / One breaking outline that includes the two'. This image has an obvious affinity with Plato's, of the original human condition as rounded, two-faced, eight-limbed creatures with two sexual organs. Love is the desire and pursuit, and to a lesser or greater extent the achievement, of this prelapsarian whole. Pregnancy is a good imitation, but one which must 'break'.

By the fifth poem, the platypus-madonna is an influential memory. The lovers have dropped their centaur fantasy the Tom-Dobbin masque of separate identities, which was their elaborate foreplay — and are making love, their bodies naked, their movements fluid, as if buoyed up by the brimming waters of a womb. Each is the foetus, not of the other, but of their shared flesh. Each is subordinated to the relationship between them both. Indistinguishable from each other, 'they' are now a singular 'we', the first-person voice of 'one flesh'.

Contrary to the lycanthropic conventions, which generally give rise to the nightmare of the werewolf, to become an animal in Gunn's books often involves becoming more human, more humane. It is a means of release from pose, an emancipation of the poseur. Gunn's respect for domestic pets leads to some of his most humane poetry, and two of his most convincing portrayals of domestic warmth concern a pair of men in bed, with the household pet on top of them: see 'Touch' (T, p.26) and 'New York' (PJ, p.17). Animals and children play in Gunn's world as innocently as though the world knew how to accommodate their innocence. His apparent belief that their polymorphous perversity can be *relearnt* by conscientious adults, is the most conspicuous sign of the poet's optimism.

This relearning is one of the themes of 'Three' (M, p.23), in which Gunn describes a family of two parents and a small son, all naked on a Pacific beach. In his account of the genesis of the poem, his short essay 'Writing a Poem', Gunn relates how his temporary preoccupation with the question, 'In what sense might you say that innocence can be repossessed', was brought to fruition by the encounter with the naked family.[20] The parents, although fully relaxed, still bear the scars of self-consciousness: notably, white patches left by the clothing they have now discarded. 'Only their son / Is brown all over.' Absorbed in the playfulness of his existence, the little boy swims 'as dogs swim' and yells his enthusiastic 'Hi there hi there' to the passing poet, as though anything and anyone in the world were his to enjoy. The two parents, 'who had to learn their nakedness', seem as utterly changed as if they had undergone one of Gunn's more radical metamorphoses. They have cast off the pallor of their nakedness, and now glory in their apotheosis as human beings.

RELEASE

Clearly, there are degrees of nakedness, as there are of love. In 'An Amorous Debate' (JSC, pp.57–8), when Fleshly has unzipped the Leather Kid's leather and stripped him of it, she finds him still clothed. As she says,

> You
> are still encased in your
> defense. You have
> a hard cock but there is
> something like the
> obduracy of leather
> still in your countenance
> and your skin, it is like
> a hide under hide[.]

But her touch eventually has the desired effect, and she manages to cast off the tense cuirass of his physique:

> a tremor passed
> through his body, the sheen
> fell from him, he
> became wholly sensitive
> as if his whole body had
> rolled back its own foreskin.

Of course, if we read the poem as having ironic reference to hindsight, we can see that there may be even more layers to discard. Remember the armoured phalluses of the earlier poems: erection is not the answer.

Already, in *Touch*, Gunn was showing concern about the obduracy of skin. In 'Pierce Street', he spoke of soldiers

> Bodied within
>   the limits of their station
> As, also, I am bodied in my skin,

as if flesh itself were regimentation (T, p.54). In the beginning of
'Touch' itself, he spoke of his own skin's 'superficially / malleable,
dead / rubbery texture' (T, p.26). The male body seems swaddled in a
wet-suit of neurosis which needs to be unzipped. The problem is, of
course, that men are *scared* of lowering their defences. The intimacy
of self-exposure may, they feel, wipe out their identities as
individuals. Anyone who is at all familiar with Gunn's poetry must
have noticed his preoccupation with the elusiveness of identity
during sexual intercourse. Remember the question which Tom and
Dobbin asked of each other in the last of their poems: 'Which is me,
which him?'

In 'The Feel of Hands', the body of the speaker is caressed by
prowling hands, which both arouse and terrify him. He comments,
'It strikes me that / I do not know whose hands they are'. They may
even be his own (MSC, p.42). The protagonist of 'Touch' gets into
bed beside his lover, who is already asleep. The lover's warmth
slowly envelops them both. Then, says the speaker,

> You turn and
> hold me tightly, do
> you know who
> I am or am I
> your mother or
> the nearest human being to
> hold on to in a
> dreamed pogrom[?]
>   (T, p.27)

In the bath-house section of 'The Geysers', the bather loses focus on
his surroundings and on his naked companions of both sexes:

> it is hazy suddenly
>   it is strange
> labouring through uneasy change
> whether toward ecstasy or panic
>   wish I knew
> no longer know for certain who is who[.]
>   (JSC, p. 24).

The participants in 'Saturnalia' have, in stripping, 'thrown off /
the variegated stuffs that / distinguished us one from / one' (JSC, p.43).
In 'An Amorous Debate', the Leather Kid so badly misjudges identity
that he 'moved his head to suck at / the nearest flesh to / his mouth
which turned out / to be his own arm' (JSC, p.58).

The blurring of edges may be feared when you are solitary; but by
the time you are in love and the body with which you merge is that of

the man you love, the effect of such fusion is liable to be positive. By loving, you make love safe. Love eases and erases unnecessary fears, and the obsession with a distinct self is shown to be both selfish and self-defeating. (I can only assume it is from the expression of such fears that Robert Martin draws his unsubstantiated conclusion: 'Gunn clearly feels guilt and unhappiness about his homosexuality, and these feelings pervade his poetry'.[21]) In general, Gunn sees the loss of self as a *release* from self, by means of which one can live up to the demands of each moment in a condition of limitless adaptability.

Adaptation is a watchword of the poet Gunn has become. But the relatively new flexibility does not allow for intellectual flabbiness: he is still meticulously conscious of himself. Despite lapses, he is not usually a self-indulgent poet. In a letter to Alan Bold, he said, 'I am not "confessional" by nature, and I think too much biography is going to distort a poem rather than otherwise'.[22] And he said to Tony Sarver, 'I like Eliot's remark that art is the escape from personality. I am tired of poets, straight or gay, who use it as a gymnasium for the ego.'[23] In 'Expression' (PJ, p.21), he complains about the poetry of his juniors, as follows:

> Mother doesn't understand,
> and they hate Daddy, the noted alcoholic.
> They write with black irony
> of breakdown, mental institution,
> and suicide attempt, of which the experience
> does not always seem first-hand.
> It is very poetic poetry.

He goes on to admire the Madonna and Child in an Italian altar piece, their 'two pairs of matching eyes / void of expression'. We have seen the detachment of these eyes before. Art has the eyes of the stud on the street corner, menacing potential lovers. And we have seen 'escape from personality' before, in boots and jeans, jacket and helmet, sunglasses and pose. Not for Gunn, the spontaneity of a Ginsberg. Gunn's own version of the spontaneous is the most carefully constructed 'free' verse one could hope to find, and is manifestly unfree. Like the verse of the master, William Carlos Williams (who believed that *vers libre* was a contradiction in terms), its finest effect is the illusion of liberty.

The poems are still evolving, of course, and in a manner directly related to their author's sexual orientation. When Tony Sarver asked him, after the publication of *Jack Straw's Castle*, if the Gay Movement had helped him as a writer, Gunn replied:

> Yes, very much I think. In my early books I was in the closet. I was

discreet in an Audenish way. If a poem referred to a lover, I always used 'you'. I figured it didn't matter, it didn't affect the poetry. But it did. Later I came out, and Ian Young included me in his *Male Muse* anthology, so that I'd officially gone public. Now, I wouldn't have expected that to make so much difference as it did. In the title poem of *Jack Straw's Castle* I end up in bed with a man, and I wrote this quite naturally, without a second thought. Ten years ago, I doubt if the incident would have appeared in the poem. It wouldn't have occurred to me to end it in that way.[24]

A volume as humane and mature as *The Passages of Joy* would be inconceivable without the limited social and political advances which homosexual women and men have made in the past twenty years. Let it serve as representative disproof of the belief that homosexual liberation will damage the literature of homosexuality. Self-censorship (the past mode, in which metaphor was extensively used as a means of concealment, a mask) is not the same as self-exploration (where metaphor is used to reveal). Mask and costume are not sufficient to themselves. If that were the case, they might as well be exhibited empty, like suits of armour in a museum. Dressing must imply undressing. The apparel should proclaim the man.

* * *

In the fifth book of *Paradise Lost*, when a nervous Adam is preparing to welcome the archangel Raphael to Eden, Milton takes care to emphasise the aptness of Adam's nakedness to so splendid an occasion. He writes:

> Mean while our primitive great sire, to meet
> His god-like guest, walks forth, without more train
> Accompany'd than with his own complete
> Perfections: in himself was all his state,
> More solemn than the tedious pomp that waits
> On princes, when their rich retinue long
> Of horses led, and grooms besmear'd with gold,
> Dazzles the crowd, and sets them all agape.
>
> (V.350–7)

A man's flesh is its own finest attire: armour and regalia unto itself. It contains all the elements of courtly splendour – the elegance, the wealth, the dynastic symbolism, the controlled animal power of saddled horses, all the brilliance of those gilded grooms – but with an extra characteristic of its own: simplicity. Alone, it is enough to dazzle the most sophisticated crowd. Ever mindful of spiritual protocol, Milton is exact in his choice of this most *correct* of nudities. How but thus could one dress to greet an emissary from God, the Designer?

· Before the Fall, Adam's body was fetish enough for the most arcane of Eve's tastes. It spoke for itself. But banishment from Eden enforced a sequence of erotic similes: Adam's genitals were tacitly compared with the fig, by being hidden in its leaves; his penis with the serpent, also hidden in leaves; and his balls with the fruit of knowledge and guilt. At the first moment of shame, the body was suddenly clad in associations, and thereby made distant from itself. Sufficient splendour became (over–)abundant complexity. More- over, humanity's new, comparative approach to the world had the effect of eroticising nature. The discarded leaf or buckskin, still hot with Adam's sweat, had gathered connotations of human sexuality; not a leaf but the nettle's was safe from being sewn into breeches and taken off at bedtime; and Adam had to delve the earth itself as well as Eve's physique.

This inheritance has reached us undiminished – enriched, in fact – by time. We have imposed layers of meaning on our bodies, to turn them into fictions, pornographic travesties of ourselves. Thom Gunn, having once dressed his versions of men in the most restricting of sexual uniforms, seems since to have been trying to undress them. Poems like 'Three' and 'The Geysers' have been instrumental in this attempt. But Gunn knows that the process will involve more than a mere casting off of clothes. When man has stepped out of his uniform, he must submit to a flaying of the mind.

At the centre of his occasionally unconscious polemic on the theme of masculinity stands the poet himself. Unless we read Gunn's collections with his personality in view, T.S. Eliot notwithstanding, many of the poems will seem desiccated and theoretical. It is what he hides at the outset of his career and what he reveals as the years pass, that gives the *oeuvre* its solid thematic unity. In the psychological striptease he has been performing for over thirty years – slowly but with diminishing reluctance, yet always avoiding the tendency to become 'confessional' – his writing has displayed an extreme self- consciousness in both senses: the negative embarrassment which prompts the personality to draw down its shutters and hide, and, later, the positive self-scrutiny which results in a relaxed mood of confidence and ease.

I therefore take Gunn as a model of the contemporary gay poet in transition. As one who has progressed from pre-Wolfenden Cam- bridge to post-'Liberation' San Francisco, he has built a career in parallel with modern gay history. His leisurely growth into openness is an affront to the sensibilities of those who believe that homosexuality, if it must exist, should be neither seen nor heard. Objecting to the openness is a question not, as some would claim, of aesthetic judgement, but of aversion to homosexuality itself. The explicit literature of homosexuality is problematical only to the extent that homosexuality itself is a problem. If we *require* homosexual men to behave like lunatics, sinners, and criminals, we must exclude their behaviour from the limits we set to sanity, virtue, and legality. Similarly, if we *require* our homosexual writers to employ the elaborate fabrications of neurosis and guilt, we must censor them or, better still, demand that they censor themselves. Otherwise, we should welcome their emergence into lucidity.

NOTES

Introduction

1. Robert K. Martin, *The Homosexual Tradition in American Poetry* (Austin, Texas, 1979) p. xviii.
2. George Steiner, *On Difficulty, and Other Essays* (Oxford, 1978) pp. 95–136.
3. Jeffrey Meyers, *Homosexuality and Literature, 1890–1930* (London, 1977), p.3.
4. Bonnie Zimmerman, 'Lesbian Feminist Criticism', in Gayle Greene & Coppélia Kahn, eds., *Making a Difference: Feminist Literary Criticism* (London, 1985) p. 185.

Chapter 1: The Male Body

1. Margaret Walters, *The Nude Male* (London, 1978) p.13.
2. See, for instance, Petronius, *Satyricon* 86–7; and Tony Duvert, *Journal d'un innocent* (Paris, 1976) p.152: 'Ses érections elles-mêmes ont une fixité photographique. Solides et impassibles, elles sont lentes à provoquer par les moyens habituels, mais, une fois en place, elles s'y tiennent et rien ne les décourage.... Quand il a joui et me décule, il part se laver, se repeigner, chercher à boire, et reapparaît la queue aussi raide qu'avant; il la promène devant lui, inutile, magnifique, comme ces aigrettes, ces bosses, ces cornes décoratives qu'ont certains animaux. Son foutre lâché, il a le temps de mettre la table et de cuire une omelette avant que sa bite se soit assoupie.'
3. Marquis de Sade, *The 120 Days of Sodom, and Other Writings* (N.Y., 1966) pp.229–30, 259–60. *The Complete Marquis de Sade* (L.A., 1966) pp.180–3.
4. Picano in Winston Leyland, ed., *Orgasms of Light* (San Francisco, 1977), p.181. Elmslie in Leyland, p.71.
5. Winston Leyland, ed., *Angels of the Lyre* (San Francisco, 1975) p.84.
6. Harold Norse, *Carnivorous Saint* (San Francisco, 1977) pp.168–9.
7. Paul Goodman, *Collected Poems* (N.Y., 1973) pp.280–1.
8. Young in Leyland, *Angels of the Lyre*, p.236.
9. Norse, p.194.
10. Lacey in Ian Young, ed., *The Male Muse: A Gay Anthology* (Trumansburg, N.Y., 1973) pp.64–5. E.A. Lacey, *Path of Snow* (Scarborough, Ontario, 1974), p.90. Ian Young, *Double Exposure* (Trumansburg, N.Y., 1974) p.33.
11. Rolfe: Brian Reade, ed., *Sexual Heretics* (London, 1970) p.420. John Giorno, *Balling Buddha* (N.Y., 1970) p.28. Kelly in *Gay Sunshine* 35 (Winter 1978) p.28. Galicia in *Gay Sunshine* 31 (Winter 1977) p.18.
12. Goodman, pp.293–4. Farinella in Leyland, *Orgasms of Light*, p.77. Young, *Double Exposure*, p.9.
13. Lacey, p.78. Norse. p.92.
14. Allen Ginsberg, *Airplane Dreams* (San Francisco, 1969) pp.31–2.
15. Norse, pp.171, 124–31.
16. Norse, p.232. Young, *Double Exposure*, p.36. Mitchell in Young, *The Male Muse*, p.78.
17. Lacey, p.74. Cox in Leyland, *Orgasms of Light*, p.56.
18. Dennis Cooper, *Idols* (N.Y., 1979) p.53. Norse, p.105.

19. Allen Ginsberg, *Indian Journals* (San Francisco, 1970) p.175. Wieners: Leyland, *Angels of the Lyre*, pp.214–15. Lacey in Leyland, *Orgasms of Light*, pp.120–1. Norse, p.217.
20. Curtis in *Gay Sunshine* 36/37 (Spring/Summer 1978) p.26. *The Collected Books of Jack Spicer* (L.A., 1973) pp.149–67. Inman in Leyland, *Orgasms of Light*, pp.103–4. Norse, pp.106–7.
21. Norse, pp.214, 215.
22. Norse, pp.33, 35–7.
23. Lacey, pp.56–58, 75–76.
24. The law-makers might do well to read Roger Peyrefitte's *L'Enfant Amour* (Paris, 1969), which reminds us that Theseus was 16 when he set out to kill the Minotaur. Alexander fought at Chaeronea at 16. Nero was engaged at 13, wore the adult toga at 14, and became emperor at 17. Marcus Aurelius was prefect at 16. Tutankhamun ruled from 9 to 18; Ptolemy, from 13 to 15. Jesus discoursed with the doctors at 12. And when Mahomet was raised to Paradise to see the face of God, 'Dieu lui apparut avec le visage d'un jeune garçon de quinze ans.'
25. *Poems by C.P. Cavafy* (London, 1951). 20 year-olds appear in 'The Next Table', 'Kimon Son of Learchos', 'Lovely Flowers and White', and 'According to the Magic Prescriptions'; 23 year-olds in 'He Came to Read', 'The Illness of Kleitos', 'A Young Artist in Words in his Twenty-fourth Year', 'Picture of a Youth Twenty-three Years Old', 'Kimon Son of Learchos', and 'According to the Magic Prescriptions'; 23 to 24 year-olds in 'Twenty-three to Twenty-four'; 24 year-olds in 'Before Time Should Change Them', and 'The Twenty-fifth Year of his Life'; a 24 or 25 year-old in 'The Funeral of Sarpedon'; 25 year-olds in 'The Grave of Eurion', 'In the Street', and 'Days of 1908'; 26 year-olds in none; a 27 year-old in 'Aimilianos Monaê, Alexandrian'; 28 year-olds in 'The Tomb of Ignatios' and 'At the Harbour'; and 29 year-olds in 'For Ammones, who Died Aged 29 in 610', 'Days of 1901', and 'He was Asking about the Quality'.
26. Williams in Leyland, *Angels of the Lyre*, pp.224–6. W.H. Auden, 'A Day for a Lay,' *Avant Garde* 11 (March 1970) pp.46–7. Norse, pp.44–5.
27. For comparative purposes, there follow the ages of some beloved boys/men, chosen at random from dramatic and fictional works on homo-erotic themes: Edward Albee, *Zoo Story*: Jerry was 15 when he had a 16 year-old lover. Richard Amory, *Frost*: Frost is 28. Sherwood Anderson, 'The Man who Became a Woman': the narrator is 19, while his beloved Tom Means is 24. George Andrzeyevski, *The Gates of Paradise*: Jacques de Cloyes is 15. James Barr, *Quatrefoil*: Phillip Froelich is 23 but looks 18. Giorgio Bassani, *Gli occhiali d'oro*: Eraldo is not yet 20. Edwin Emmanuel Bradford, *Boris Orloff*: the narrator is 14 and 16 at the times of his romances with two younger boys. William Burroughs, *The Wild Boys*: Audrey is 16; Mark is 18 when he initiates 15 year-old John; and the Frisco Kid is 23. Maurice Capitanchik, *Friends and Lovers*: Joseph is 16 when he first makes love with Ted. Truman Capote, 'A Diamond Guitar': Tico Feo is 18. Capote, *Other Voices, Other Rooms*: Joel is 13 when his voice breaks in the middle of the word vir-gin. Alfred Chester, 'In Praise of Vespasian': Joaquin is 18 when he first makes love with another man. Jean Cocteau, *Le Livre blanc*: Alfred is 19. Mart Crowley, *The Boys in the Band*: the Cowboy is 22. Will Allen Dromgoole, *The Island of Beautiful Things*: the boy is a very soppy 6. Tony Duvert, *Récidive*: the boy is 15. Jean Genet, *Haute Surveillance*: Maurice, Yeux–Verts, and Lefranc are 17, 22, and 23. Genet, *Notre-Dame des Fleurs*: Mignon is 20. Genet, *Pompes Funèbres*: Jean was 16 when Genet met him and 20 when he died; Erik was 18 when fucked by the Executioner. Genet, *Querelle de Brest*: Querelle is 25. Penelope Gilliatt, *Sunday Bloody Sunday*: Bob Elkin is 25. Ernest Hemingway, 'A Simple Inquiry'; Pinin is 19. James Leo Herlihy, *Midnight Cowboy*: Joe Buck is 27 when he first goes to New York. Herlihy, 'Miguel': Miguel is 18. Andrew Holleran, *Dancer from the Dance*: Malone is a surprising 38 (but the same age as Lady Chatterley's lover). John Hopkins, *Find Your Way Home*: Julian Weston is 23. Francis King, *A Domestic Animal*: Antonio is in his thirties. D.H. Lawrence, 'The Prussian Officer': the

orderly is about 22. Robin Maugham, *The Wrong People*: Riffi thinks he is 14. Herman Melville, *Billy Budd*: Billy is 21. Yukio Mishima, *Forbidden Colours*: Minoru is 17, Yuichi is 22. Henri de Montherlant, *La Ville dont le Prince est un enfant*: André is 16, Serge is 14. George Moor, *The Pole and Whistle*: John is 25, Frank is 28. Iris Murdoch, *An Accidental Man*: Ralph Odmore is under 18. Murdoch, *The Bell*: Toby is 18. Murdoch, *Henry and Cato*: Beautiful Joe is 17. Murdoch, *The Sacred and Profane Love Machine*: David Gavender is 16, going on 17. Roger Peyrefitte, *Les Amitiés Particulières*: Georges is 14, Alexandre is 12. Peyrefitte, *L'Exilé de Capri*: Loulou is 14 or 15, Nino is 15. Barbara Pym, *The Sweet Dove Died*: James is 24. Simon Raven, *The Feathers of Death*: Malcolm Harley is 18. Raven, *Fielding Gray*: Christopher and Fielding are both 17 at the time of their affair. John Rechy, *Bodies and Souls*: Billy and Stud are both 18. Umberto Saba, *Ernesto*: Ernesto is 16. Mario Soldati, *La Confessione*: Clemente is 14. Angus Stewart, *Sandel*: David meets Tony when the latter is 13. Gore Vidal, 'The Zenner Trophy': Flynn is 18. Patricia Nell Warren, *The Front Runner*: Billy Sive is 22 when the narrator meets him. Oscar Wilde (?) and others, *Teleny*: Teleny is 24. Tennessee Williams, 'One Arm': Oliver is 20. Angus Wilson, 'Et Dona Ferentes': Sven is 18. Donald Windham, *Two People*: Marcello is 17. Graeme Woolaston, *Stranger than Love*: Rick is 19.

28. Raymond Radiguet, *Collected Poems: Cheeks on Fire* (London, 1976) p.48. Thomas Mann, *Death in Venice, Tristan, Tonio Kroger* (Harmondsworth, 1955) p.58. Cavafy, p.82. *Artist* recommendation in: Timothy d'Arch Smith, *Love in Earnest* (London, 1970) p.182. Saale in Reade, *Sexual Heretics*, p.228.

29. Pausanias tried in vain to perpetuate a heterosexual version, in which Narcissus gazed at his reflection to remind himself of his dead twin sister, with whom he was in love. In *Britannia's Pastorals*, William Browne of Tavistock further homosexualised the myth with the claim that Narcissus fell in love, not with himself, but with the exquisite swain Doridon (I.ii, 411–14).

30. James Kirkup, *A Correct Compassion* (London, 1952) pp. 55–6.

31. Tony Duvert, *Récidive* (Paris 1976), p.73 (He gets undressed. He tries to embrace himself in the mirror. It doesn't work. There's no use grabbing what can't be held, and, besides, it's his own physique. The game of standing in for what you most desire is complex and repugnant when you're not in love with yourself. Lips leave a greasy wet smudge on the mirror).

32. Philip Roth, *Portnoy's Complaint* (London, 1971) p. 18. Susan Sontag, *The Benefactor* (London, 1964) ch. 14. Norse, p.64.

33. Kinsey, Pomeroy, and Martin, *Sexual Behavior in the Human Male* (Philadelphia, 1948), p.510. Tom Driberg, *Ruling Passions* (London, 1977) p.66. Francis Steegmuller, *Cocteau: A Biograhy* (London, 1970) p.426.

34. Elmslie in Leyland, *Orgasms of Light*, p.71. Norse, pp.42, 168–9.

35. John Allegro, *Lost Gods* (London, 1977) p.109.

36. Jean Cocteau, *Le Livre blanc* (Paris, 1970) p.75 (On one occasion, a Narcissus who fancied himself came up to the mirror, glued his mouth to it and took his affair with himself to its conclusion. As invisible as a Greek god, I pressed my lips to his and followed his movements. He never suspected that instead of just reflecting him the mirror was active: it was alive and had loved him).

37. *The Collected Poems of A.E. Housman* (London, 1960), p.23. Mutsuo Takahashi, *Poems of a Penisist* (Chicago, 1975) p.19. Federico García Lorca, *Selected Poetry* (Harmondsworth, 1960) p.29.

38. There is an alternative version of the myth, in which Eos abducts Ganymede to Olympus. Zeus robs her of him, to use him as his own cup-bearer. Since this account does not concern our poets, it need not concern us.

39. John Boswell, *Christianity, Social Tolerance, and Homosexuality: Gay People in Western Europe from the Beginning of the Christian Era to the Fourteenth Century* (Chicago, 1980) p.253.

40. J.R. Ackerley, *My Father and Myself*

(London, 1968) p.139. Michael David-
son, *The World, the Flesh and Myself*
(London, 1962) p. 82. John Lehmann,
In the Purely Pagan Sense (London,
1976) p.112. Keith Vaughan, *Journal
and Drawings 1939–1965* (London,
1966) p.164.

41. D'Arch Smith, *Love in Earnest*, p.149.
42. Shaykh Nafzawi, *The Glory of the Per-
fumed Garden* (London, 1978) pp.40,
57.
43. A.R. Nykl, *Hispano-Arabic Poetry and
its Relations with the Old Provencal
Troubadours* (Baltimore, 1946)
pp.309, 238–9.
44. Takahashi, p.90.
45. Jean Genet, *Oeuvres Complètes* II
(Paris, 1951) p.366 (I seemed to be
underneath him already, with him
already fucking me, bearing down on
me with all his weight and holding me
to him as the eagle held Ganymede –
just as he would finally do on the fourth
night we spent together when, better
prepared, I let him delve right into me
and his huge bulk swooped down (a
whole sky collapsing on my back),
talons digging into my shoulders, teeth
into the nape of my neck).
46. D'Arch Smith, p.93.
47. D'Arch Smith, p.142.
48. William Plomer, *Collected Poems*
(London, 1973) p.210. Eggeling in
Leyland, *Orgasms of Light*, p.66.
Williams in Young, *The Male Muse*,
p.106. Leo Madigan, *Jackarandy*
(London, 1972). Dirk Vanden, *All is
Well* (London, 1972) p.198.
49. W.H. Auden, *Collected Poems*
(London, 1976) pp.152–3.
50. Goodman, pp. 249–50.
51. William Bell, *Mountains Beneath the
Horizon* (London, 1950) pp. 43–6.
52. Giles and Phineas Fletcher, *Poetical
Works* I (Cambridge, 1970) p. 78. *The
Poetical Works of William Drummond
of Hawthornden* (London, 1856),
p.170, lines 31–42. J.W. von Goethe,
Poetical Works (London, 1903) pp.
209–10. For detailed treatment of
visual versions of the myth, see James
M. Saslow, *Ganymede in the Renaiss-
ance* (New Haven, 1986).
53. Jacques Damase, ed., *Saint Sébastien
dans l'histoire de l'art depuis le XV°
siècle* (Paris, 1979) p.xxiv (The beauty
of nudity, youth, the apparent might of
soldiers, special friendships, symbolic

arrows, pain, bleeding wounds, the
savour of death in heroic bliss).
54. Summers in d'Arch Smith, p.121.
Frederick Rolfe, *Collected Poems*
(London, 1974) p.57. Frederick Rolfe,
The Desire and Pursuit of the Whole
(London, 1934) p.156.
55. Yukio Mishima, *Confessions of a Mask*
(Norfolk, Connecticut, 1958) pp.39,
44. Pablo Neruda, *Twenty Love Poems
and a Song of Despair* (London, 1969).
56. Aitken in *Gay Sunshine* 35 (Winter
1978) p.23. James Merrill, *The Coun-
try of a Thousand Years of Peace, and
Other Poems* (N.Y., 1970) pp.23–4.
57. Herbert Marcuse, *Eros and Civiliz-
ation* (London, 1969) p.139.
58. Norman O. Brown, *Love's Body*
(N.Y., 1966) p.184. The Yeats is from
'Crazy Jane Talks with the Bishop'.
59. Robert Duncan, *Bending the Bow*
(London, 1971) pp.63–5.
60. To quote one of Michel Tournier's gay
characters: 'The hetero riff-raff imag-
ines that penetration is necessary, some
play with orifices in imitation of their
own mating. Poor fools! For us, all
things are possible, none obligatory.
Your loves are clamped within the
reproductive process, ours are open to
all innovations, all inventions, all dis-
coveries.' *Gemini* (London, 1981)
p.178.
61. Thom Gunn, *Fighting Terms* (London,
1962) p.35. Gavin Dillard, *rosie emis-
sions* (Scarborough, Ontario, 1975)
pp.7, 16, 22.
62. D.H. Lawrence, *Lady Chatterley's
Lover* (Harmondsworth, 1960) p.229.
Norse, pp.55, 71. Chadwick in *Gay
Sunshine* 40/41 (Summer/Fall 1979)
p.35.
63. *The Kama Sutra of Vatsyayana*
(London, 1963) pp.191–2.
64. Irving Buchen, ed., *The Perverse Imagi-
nation* (N.Y., 1970) p.216.
65. Norse, p.209. Lacey in Young, *The
Male Muse*, p.64. Giorno, p.140.
66. Cocteau, p.62 (this fabulous little
marine plant – dead, crumpled, stran-
ded on moss – which becomes smooth,
fills out, stands up straight, and scatters
its sap the moment it regains the
element of love).
67. Takahashi, pp.9, 10, 73. James Kirkup,
White Shadows, Black Shadows
(London, 1970) p.30.
68. Pisanus Fraxi, *Bibliography of*

Prohibited Books III (N.Y., 1962) pp.107–12. Norse, p.182. Lacey, pp.44, 53.

69. Dylan Thomas, *Collected Poems 1934–1952* (London, 1966), p.21. Ian Young, *Common-or-Garden Gods* (Scarborough, Ontario, 1976) p.38. Lacey in Leyland, *Orgasms of Light*, p.120. Jean Genet, *Oeuvres Complètes* III, p.227 (the infected penis oozing like an Easter candle encrusted with five grains of incense).

70. Takahashi p.90. Jackson in Young, *The Male Muse*, p. 53. Patrick White makes a similar association of semen and moonlight, in chapter 5 of *The Vivisector* (an instance of exhibitionistic masturbation in the white glare of the moon), and in *Riders in the Chariot*, while Mrs Godbold waits for her husband at Mrs Khalil's brothel ('the moonlight lay in sticky pools').

71. Robert Graves, *Collected Poems 1975* (London, 1975) p.506.

72. Reade, *Sexual Heretics*, p.173: Sir Richard Burton's terminal essay to *The Arabian Nights*, citing Plutarch on the customs of the Nilotes.

73. Nuwas in *Gay Sunshine* 32 (Spring 1977) p.5. Yafar in *Gay Sunshine* 29/30 (Summer/Fall 1976) p.18. Bruce Rodgers, *The Queen's Vernacular: A Gay Lexicon* (London, 1972) p.172.

74. Nilkolai Klyuev, *Poems* (Ann Arbor, Michigan, 1977) p.18. Sylvia Plath, *Winter Trees* (London, 1975) p.16. Miller in *Mouth of the Dragon* 1 (May 1974) p.19.

75. Paul Mariah, *Personae Non Gratae* (San Lorenzo, Cal., 1971) p.16. Rodgers, p.32.

76. Günter Grass, *The Flounder* (London, 1978) p.204.

77. Malcolm Barber, *The Trial of the Templars* (Cambridge, 1978) p. 178 ff.

78. Mario Mieli, *Homosexuality and Liberation: Elements of a Gay Critique* (London, 1980) p.145.

79. Arthur Rimbaud, *Oeuvres* (Paris, 1960) p.328. Cooper, p.38. Genet, *Oeuvres Complètes* III, p.161.

80. Leonard Cohen, *Beautiful Losers* (London, 1972) p.71. Farinella in Young, *The Male Muse*, p.32. Larry Kramer, *Faggots* (London, 1980) p.33.

81. Brown, *Love's Body*, ch.7.

82. Goethe, pp.309–11.

83. Whitman, 'Song of Myself' 6. Tak-

ahashi, pp.48, 76. Genet, *Oeuvres Complètes* III, p.263. Takahashi, p.10. Ginsberg, *Indian Journals*, p.190. Stephen Spender, *Collected Poems* (London, 1955) p.46.

84. Lacey, p.36. Christopher Isherwood, *Christopher and his Kind* (London, 1977) p.39.

85. Elytis in *Four Greek Poets* (Harmondsworth, 1966) p.85. Klyuev, p.35.

86. Genet in James Kirkup, *Refusal to Conform* (London, 1963) pp.117–20. Shurin in Leyland, *Orgasms of Light*, p.214. Edward Lucie–Smith, *The Well-Wishers* (London, 1974) p.45.

87. Ernst and Johanna Lehner, *Folklore and Symbolism of Flowers, Plants and Trees* (N.Y., 1960).

88. William Burroughs, *The Wild Boys* (London, 1973) pp.40–2. Another instance of tree-violation occurs in chapter 5 of Michael Tournier's Freudianisation of the Robinson Crusoe story, *Vendredi ou les limbes du Pacifique* (Paris, 1967). Crusoe is discouraged from continuing with this practice, when a spider in the hollow of a tree mimics a venereal disease, by biting the tip of his penis.

89. Roy Campbell, *Collected Poems* I (London, 1949) p.91.

90. Norse, p.91. Steven Marcus, *The Other Victorians* (N.Y., 1974) ch.7.

91. Robert Duncan, *The Years as Catches* (Berkeley, Cal., 1966). Geoffrey Hill, *Tenebrae* (London, 1978).

92. Rolle in Brian Stone, ed., *Medieval English Verse* (Harmondsworth, 1964) p.57. *The Poems of St John of the Cross* (London, 1951) p.29.

93. Adolphe Napoléon Didron, *Christian Iconography* I (N.Y., 1965) p.339.

94   Wayland Young, *Studies in Exclusion I: Eros Denied* (London, 1965) p.167. The proximity of divine and human love prompts Reade to comment: 'It is not difficult . . . to understand the transition from the repressed homosexuality of certain Tractarians to the emphasis on Christ, not the Virgin Mary, in the poems of Newman and Faber after both men had been converted to the Roman faith.' (*Sexual Heretics*, p.4). The bond with Christ is often seen in remarkably physical terms. For instance, Saint Catherine of Siena claimed Christ's foreskin as her engagement ring – Leo Steinberg, 'The Sexuality of Christ in

95. *The Poems of Digby Mackworth Dolben* (London, 1911) pp. 47–51.
96. Didron, pp. 259–60.
97. Walters, *The Nude Male*, pp.72–3, 82, 84.
98. Tennessee Williams, *Memoirs* (London, 1976) p.47.
99. John Logan, *Ghosts of the Heart* (Chicago, 1960) pp.54–5.
100. The image of the heart as glans is clearest in Deuteronomy 30.6, where Moses promises that God will circumcise the hearts of the people, so that they can love Him better.
101. Steinberg, pp.1, 8, 17, 58. In his postscript to Steinberg's essay, John W. O'Malley cites Francesco Cardulo's sermon to the papal court (*c.* 1495), proving Christ's humanity by reference to His penis, which 'is fondled, taken in the hand, receives a wound, feels pain' (p.202).
102. Pisanus Fraxi I, pp.198–236.
103. Peter Webb, *The Erotic Arts* (London, 1983) p.182, plate 137.
104. John Allegro, *The Sacred Mushroom and the Cross: A Study of the Nature and Origins of Christianity within the Fertility Cults of the Ancient Near East* (London, 1973). Norse, p.208. See also John Michell, *To Represent Our Saviour as 'that great cock' (Kirkup-Gay News) is not Blasphemy but Eternal and Christian Orthodoxy* (London, 1977); and Georgia Pešek-Marouš, *The Bull: A Religious and Secular History of Phallus Worship and Male Homosexuality* (Rolling Hills, Cal., 1984). The latter is imaginative and occasionally illuminating, but is marred by vicious homophobia and anachronistic puns.
105. Brown, *Love's Body*, pp.167–8.
106. John G. Bourke, *Scatologic Rites of All Nations* (Washington, 1891) p.220. I begin to see why Saint Teresa of Avila stated a preference for large hosts – Miguel de Unamuno, *The Tragic Sense of Life* (London, 1962) p.80.
107. Oscar Wilde, *De Profundis, and Other Writings* (Harmondsworth, 1973) p.175. Antler in *Gay Sunshine* 40/41 (Summer/Fall 1979) p.36. Inman in *Gay Sunshine* 32 (Spring 1977) p.25.
108. Lawrence Durrell, *Collected Poems* (London, 1960) p. 65. Robert Duncan, *The Opening of the Field* (London, 1969) p. 28.
109. Boswell, pp.225–6.
110. Philip Henderson, *Christopher Marlowe* (Brighton, 1974) pp.60, 63. *The Complete Marquis de Sade* I, pp.105–6. Stevenson, Wright in d'Arch Smith, pp.175, 142. *The Collected Poems of Frank O'Hara* (N.Y., 1972) p.47.
111. *Gay Sunshine* 40/41 (Summer/Fall 1979) p.5.
112. Frank Kermode, *The Genesis of Secrecy* (Cambridge, Mass., 1979) pp.73, 58.
113. Dolben, p.2. Aleister Crowley, *White Stains* (London, 1973) pp.105–8. Duncan, *Bending the Bow*, pp.24–5.
114. *Gay News* fell victim to Mary Whitehouse's search for a guineapig on which to test Britain's ancient blasphemy laws. For details, see Michael Tracey and David Morrison, *Whitehouse* (London, 1979). For an account of the trial, see Nicholas Walter, *Blasphemy in Britain: The Practice and Punishment of Blasphemy, and the Trial of Gay News* (London, 1977).
115. Gustave Flaubert, *Three Tales* (Harmondsworth, 1961): 'The Legend of St Julian Hospitator'.
116. Takahashi, pp.16–17.
117. Robert Graves, *The Greek Myths* II (Harmondsworth, 1960) pp.84–206.
118. Winston Leyland, ed., *The Gay Sunshine Interviews* I (San Francisco, 1978) p.267.
119. Norse, p.31.
120. James Kirkup, *The Prodigal Son* (London, 1959) p.26.

Chapter 2: Men of War

1. Georges Bataille, *L'Erotisme* (Paris, 1957) p.23.
2. Aleister Crowley, *White Stains* (London, 1973) pp.57, 67. E.A. Lacey, *Path of Snow* (Scarborough, Ontario, 1974) p.83. Eric Partridge, *Shakespeare's Bawdy* (London, 1968) p.23. Allen Edwardes and R.E.L. Masters, *The Cradle of Erotica* (N.Y., 1962) p.46.
3. Paul Goodman, *Collected Poems* (N.Y., 1973) p.129. Robert Duncan, *Bending the Bow* (London, 1971).

Harold Norse, *Carnivorous Saint* (San Francisco, 1977) p.41.

4. Gavin Dillard, *rosie emissions* (Seattle, 1975) unpaginated. Mutsuo Takahashi, *Poems of a Penisist* (Chicago, 1975) p.79. Norse, p.63. *The Collected Poems of Frank O'Hara* (N.Y., 1972) p.169. Norse, p.132. Allen Ginsberg, *Collected Poems 1947–1980* (Harmondsworth, 1985) p.146. See also Bruce Rodgers, *The Queen's Vernacular* (London, 1972), entries under 'Bullets' and 'Holster'.

5. *The Collected Poems of Wilfred Owen* (London, 1967) pp.39–40.

6. Norse, p.18.

7. Owen, p.43.

8. Susan Brownmiller, *Against Our Will: Men, Women and Rape* (London, 1975) ch.3.

9. Denis de Rougemont, *Passion and Society* (London, 1940) p.274. André Gide, *Corydon* (London, 1952) p.109.

10. Marcel Proust, *Time Regained* (London, 1970) pp.65, 137, 166, 145.

11. Francis Steegmuller, *Cocteau: A Biography* (London, 1970) p.153.

12. Norse, pp.9, 27.

13. Paul Fussell, *The Great War and Modern Memory* (London, 1975) p.270.

14. John Lehmann, *In the Purely Pagan Sense* (London, 1976) pp.128, 130.

15. Keith Vaughan, *Journal and Drawings 1939–1965* (London, 1966) p.84.

16. Quentin Crisp, *The Naked Civil Servant* (London, 1968) pp. 156–7.

17. John Lehmann, *I Am My Brother* (London, 1960) p.186.

18. Martin Green, *Children of the Sun* (N.Y., 1976) p.320.

19. Green, pp.59–60.

20. Tennessee Williams, *Memoirs* (London, 1976) p.78.

21. Jonathan Fryer, *Isherwood* (London, 1977) p.218.

22. T.E. Lawrence, *Seven Pillars of Wisdom* (London, 1935). Eric Hiscock, *The Bells of Hell Go Ting-a Ling-a Ling* (London, 1977). Dan Billany and David Dowie, *The Cage* (London, 1949).

23. Of these, three with typically violent (and anti-homosexual) endings were filmed in the sixties: *Billy Budd* (1962), *Reflections in a Golden Eye* (1967), and *The Sergeant* (1968). See Jack Babuscio, 'Military Masks,' *Gay News*

86, p.18. Other modern fiction relevant to our theme includes Robert Musil's tale of adolescent sadomasochism in a military academy, *Der Junge Törless* (1906); Calder Willingham's *End as a Man* (1947), set in an American military academy; John Horne Burns' *The Gallery* (1947), on the Allied occupation of Naples, best read in tandem with Curzio Malaparte's *La pelle* (1949); James Barr's *Quatrefoil* (1950), on an affair between two US naval officers; Walter Baxter's *Look Down in Mercy* (London, 1951), given a happier ending for its American readers in 1952; Genet's *Pompes funèbres* (1953); Mary Renault's classic account of the Second World War, *The Charioteer* (1953); Lonnie Coleman's 'The Theban Warriors,' in *Ship's Company* (1955); Mary Renault's venture back to the wars between Sparta and Athens, *The Last of the Wine* (1956); Brian Aldiss' *A Soldier Erect* (1971); Susan Hill's *Strange Meeting* (1971), set in the First World War, and aptly taking its title from the poem by Wilfred Owen; and Lucian K. Truscott IV's *Dress Gray* (1979), on another American military academy.

24. H. Montgomery Hyde, *The Other Love* (London, 1970) ch. 6, part 7. Sodomy and bestiality cases in England and Wales increased from 134 in 1938 to 670 in 1952. Attempts to commit 'unnatural offences' increased from 822 to 3,087. Cases of 'gross indecency' between men rose from 320 to 1,686.

25. Robert Duncan, *Derivations* (London, 1968) p.22.

26. This remark caused Peter Orlovsky to be discharged from the military, according to Allen Ginsberg's cover note to Orlovsky's *Clean Asshole Poems & Smiling Vegetable Songs* (San Francisco, 1978).

27. De Rougemont, pp.274–5.

28. 'Y', *The Autobiography of an Englishman* (London, 1976) pp.76–7.

29. Alun Lewis, *Selected Poetry and Prose* (London, 1966) pp. 74, 78.

30. Lewis, p.123.

31. Owen, p.59.

32. Owen, pp. 67–8.

33. Richard Trudgett, *Lost Soldier, Lost Town, and Other Poems* (London, 1945) p.12.

34. Keith Douglas, *Complete Poems* (Oxford, 1978) p.99.
35. Fryer, p.69.
36. Lehmann, *I Am My Brother*, p.193.
37. Roy Fuller, *Collected Poems 1936–1961* (London, 1962) p.42.
38. Robert Nichols, *Aurelia, and Other Poems* (London, 1920) pp. 75–80.
39. Fussell, pp.275–6.
40. Robert Graves, *Good-bye to All That* (London, 1929) p.342.
41. A hetero-erotic approximation to this tragedy occurs in Torquato Tasso's *Gerusalemme Liberata*, canto XII, sections 64–7, where Tancredi fights and kills an armoured figure, which, once the mortal blow has been struck, turns out to be his beloved Clorinda.
42. Donald Keene, ed., *Anthology of Japanese Literature to the Nineteenth Century* (Harmondsworth, 1968) pp.171–3 (*The Death of Atsumori*) and 275–81 (*Atsumori*).
43. Kenneth Clark, *The Nude* (London, 1956) p.191.
44. Fussell, pp.299–309.
45. Curzio Malaparte, *Kaputt* (N.Y., 1946) p.321.
46. On the Uranians' interest in this theme, see Timothy d'Arch Smith, *Love in Earnest* (London, 1970) pp.169–72.
47. Steegmuller, p.142. Jean Cocteau, *Le Cap de Bonne-Espérance* (Paris, 1967) pp. 180–2.
48. *Poems from the Desert: Verses by Members of the Eighth Army* (London, 1944) pp. 38–9.
49. Brian Reade, ed., *Sexual Heretics* (London, 1970) pp.279–80.
50. Reade, p.5.
51. Jeffrey Weeks, *Coming Out: Homosexual Politics in Britain, from the Nineteenth Century to the Present* (London, 1977) p.118.
52. See Michael Mason's report on the march in *Gay News* 171, p.15.
53. Lige Clarke and Jack Nichols, *Roommates Can't Always be Lovers* (N.Y., 1974) p.119.
54. Allen Ginsberg, *Collected Poems 1947–1980* (Harmondsworth, 1985) p.240.
55. Owen, pp.112–13, 111, 41.
56. Rupert Brooke, *1914, and Other Poems* (London, 1916) p.13.
57. George Macbeth, *In the Hours Waiting for the Blood to Come* (London, 1975) pp. 49–50.
58. Duncan, *Derivations*, p.20.
59. Andrew Sinclair, *Guevara* (London, 1970) pp.88, 93.
60. Ginsberg, p.484.
61. Lawrence, p.308.
62. Edmund Blunden, *Poems of Many Years* (London, 1957) p. 136.
63. 'Look Down Fair Moon.' Salvatore Farinella refers back to Whitman's poem in 'New Moon' – Winston Leyland, ed., *Orgasms of Light* (San Francisco, 1977) p.76.
64. Giuseppe Ungaretti, *Selected Poems* (Harmondsworth, 1971) pp.28, 76. There is a precedent for the latter poem in Italian literature: Ariosto's story of Cloridano and Medoro, in cantos XVIII and XIX of *Orlando Furioso*.
65. Douglas, p.96. John Berryman, *Selected Poems 1938–1968* (London, 1972) pp.14–15. *The Collected Poems of Roy Campbell* I (London, 1949) p.157.
66. David Jones, *In Parenthesis* (London, 1963) p.42.
67. Dunstan Thompson, *Lament for the Sleepwalker* (N.Y., 1947) p.15.
68. Owen, pp.35–6. The main thematic difference between Susan Hill's *Strange Meeting* and its namesake is that the novel is about a relationship between two Englishmen.
69. Blunden, pp.82–3.
70. Jean Genet, *Oeuvres Complètes* II (Paris, 1951) p.321 (These two sleeping hearts ruled while they slept and adored each other behind the thick wall of their slumber. Dead warriors who have killed each other love like this).
71. Stephen Spender, *World Within World* (Berkeley, Cal., 1966) p.223.
72. Stephen Spender, *Collected Poems 1928–1953* (London, 1955) p.98.
73. Paul Muldoon, *Why Brownlee Left* (London, 1980) p.26.
74. *The Complete Poems of D.H. Lawrence* (London, 1964) p.742.
75. Duncan, *Bending the Bow*, p.81.
76. Thompson, p.8.
77. Len Richmond and Gary Noguera, eds., *The Gay Liberation Book* (San Francisco, 1973) p.149.
78. Fuller, p.77.
79. Douglas, p.112.
80. Duncan, *Bending the Bow*, pp.114–15.
81. Herbert Read, *A World Within a War* (London, 1944) p.24.
82. Vaughan, p.26.

83. Yannis Ritsos, *Selected Poems* (Harmondsworth, 1974) p.100. Robert Duncan, *The First Decade* (London, 1968) p.10. Spender, p.99. Dylan Thomas and John Davenport, *The Death of the King's Canary* (London, 1976) ch.1. Douglas, p.111. Edward Thomas, *Collected Poems* (London, 1965) p.45. Edwin Muir, *Collected Poems 1921–1958* (London 1960) p.153.

84. Robert Nichols, *Ardours and Endurances* (London, 1917) pp.44, 51–4.

85. Nichols, *Aurelia*, pp.75–6.

86. Larry Rottmann, Jan Barry, and Basil T. Paquet, eds., *Winning Hearts and Minds: War Poems by Vietnam Veterans* (N.Y., 1972) p.22.

87. Ted Hughes, *The Hawk in the Rain* (London, 1957) p.53.

88. Fussell, pp.279–80.

89. Mildred Davidson, *The Poetry is in the Pity* (London, 1972) p.20.

90. De Rougemont, p.254.

91. K.J. Dover, *Greek Homosexuality* (London, 1978) p.4, n.5.

92. Goodman, pp.243–4. Thom Gunn, *Jack Straw's Castle* (London, 1976) pp. 40–1. James Kirkup, *The Prodigal Son* (London, 1964) p.27. Takahashi in Harry and Lynn Guest and Kajima Shozo, eds., *Post-War Japanese Poetry* (Harmondsworth, 1972) p.155. Takahashi, *Poems of a Penisist*, pp.95, 77, 8.

93. Gore Vidal, *The City and the Pillar* (London, 1965) ch.2.

94. Winston Leyland, ed., *The Gay Sunshine Interviews* I (San Francisco, 1978) p.298. Wiley Lee Umphlett's *The Sporting Myth and the American Experience* is marred by neglecting these aspects of the subject (London, 1975).

95. Vidal, afterword to *The City and the Pillar*, 1965.

96. Gore Vidal, *A Thirsty Evil* (London, 1956).

97. Edward Carpenter, *My Days and Dreams* (London, 1916) p.29.

98. Yukio Mishima, *Confessions of a Mask* (Norfolk, Connecticut, 1958) p.78.

99. T.C. Worsley, *Flannelled Fool* (London, 1967) pp.84, 86. Simon Raven, *The English Gentleman* (London, 1961) p.115. Cyril Connolly, *Enemies of Promise* (London, 1973) pp.175, 192.

100. Goodman, p.262. Paul Muldoon, *Mules* (London, 1977) p.19. See also Christopher Isherwood, *A Single Man* (London, 1964) pp.42–3.

101. *The Collected Poems of A.E. Housman* (London, 1960) pp.25–6.

102. *Poems of George Santayana* (N.Y., 1970), pp.112–15.

103. D'Arch Smith, pp. 228, 72–3.

104. James Kirkup, *Refusal to Conform* (London, 1963) p.63. *The Prodigal Son*, p.32. *The Descent into the Cave* (London, 1957) pp.33–4.

105. Edward Dorn, *The Collected Poems 1956–1974* (Bolinas, Cal., 1975) p.102.

106. Douglas Branch, *The Cowboy and his Interpreters* (N.Y., 1961) p.31.

107. Dorn, p.4. Vernon Scannell, *The Loving Game* (London, 1975) p.38. Edward Dorn, *Gunslinger 1 & 2* (London, 1970), p.8. Dennis Kelly, 'Gunslinger', *Gay Sunshine* 36/37 (Spring/Summer 1978) p.11. Jack Spicer, *Collected Books* (L.A., 1975) pp.79–83. Thomas Meyer, *The Bang Book* (N.Y., 1971). Michael Ondaatje, *The Collected Works of Billy the Kid* (Toronto, 1970) pp.77–8.

108. Robert Peters, 'The House that Jack Built has an Atwater Kent in the Living Room, or Jack Spicer's Romanticism Didn't Come Easy,' *Manroot* 10 ('The Jack Spicer Issue') (Late Fall 1974/Winter 1975) pp.181, 182. Peters exaggerates. The romanticised Billy the Kid is an established convention. Kent Ladd Steckmesser writes: 'There are two Billy the Kids in legend. The first is a tough little thug, a coward, a thief, and a cold-blooded murderer. The second is a romantic and sentimental hero, the brave and likable leader of an outnumbered band fighting for justice.' – *The Western Hero in History and Legend* (Norman, Oklahoma, 1965) p.57. Around the second version, Aaron Copland created a ballet, in 1938; and Arthur Penn filmed *The Left-Handed Gun*, in 1958, starring Paul Newman as the Kid.

109 Gerald and Caroline Green, *S–M: The Last Taboo* (N.Y., 1974) p.182.

110. Parker Tyler, 'The Horse: Totem Animal of Male Power – an Essay in the Straight-Camp Style,' *Sex Psyche Etcetera in the Film* (Harmondsworth, 1972) pp.29–38.

111. Ondaatje. pp.11, 14.
112. Theognis, *Elegies* 1249–52, 1267–70. C.L. Sonnichsen writes that, 'Without getting deeply involved in the gay community, a fair proportion of recent Western novelists have experimented with what might be called unorthodox sex as public tolerance has grown and authors have probed deeper into the Formerly Forbidden.' – *From Hopalong to Hud: Thoughts on Western Fiction* (College Station, Texas, 1978) p.166. Sonnichsen comments: 'In the golden years of the western such an idea would have provoked raucous laughter. Hopalong Cassidy a member of the gay community? Ridiculous! Impossible! These are new times, however.' (p.23)
113. Branch, p.164.
114. Lehmann, *In the Purely Pagan Sense*, p.117. Crisp, p.96. Genet, *Oeuvres Complètes* III, p.319.
115. Genet, pp.262–3 (The ship's flanks are alive with delicious brutes dressed in white and blue. Who can choose between them? I could barely turn away from one before wanting another. The only thought that calms me is that there is but one sailor: *the* sailor. Each one I see is just a temporary impression – incomplete and scaled down – of The Sailor . . . Each sailor that goes by is a mere replica of The Sailor. Even if every sailor appeared before me at once, every living one of them, no individual would be the sailor they collectively embody. He exists only in my imagination; he can only exist in me and thanks to me. This idea soothes me: I *own* The Sailor).
116. Leyland, *Orgasms of Light*, p.31.

Chapter 3: Childless Fathers

1. Jose Ortega y Gasset, *On Love . . . Aspects of a Single Theme* (London, 1967) pp.33–4.
2. Bertrand Russell, *The Conquest of Happiness* (London, 1930) pp.186–207.
3. Wallace Fowlie, *Love in Literature* (Bloomington, Indiana, 1965) p.134.
4. George Steiner, *After Babel* (London, 1975) p.160.
5. Anthony Holden, ed., *Greek Pastoral Poetry* (Harmondsworth, 1974) p.170.

6. *Poems by C.P. Cavafy* (London, 1951) p.124.
7. Yannis Ritsos, *Selected Poems* (Harmondsworth, 1974) p.47.
8. Phyllis Chesler, *About Men* (London, 1978) part I. Erich Fromm's interpretation of the Red Riding-Hood story gives central significance to uterus envy, in that the wolf 'attempted to play the role of a pregnant woman, having living things in his belly' by devouring Red Riding-Hood and her grandmother – *The Forgotten Language* (N.Y., 1957) p.241.
9. Timothy d'Arch Smith, *Love in Earnest* (London, 1970) p.73.
10. D'Arch Smith, p.167.
11. Holden, p.92.
12. Francis Steegmuller, *Cocteau: A Biography* (London, 1970) p.420.
13. Jonathan Fryer, *Isherwood* (London, 1977) p.264.
14. James Kirkup, *White Shadows, Black Shadows* (London, 1970) pp.32–4. Allen Ginsberg, *Collected Poems 1947–1980* (Harmondsworth, 1985) pp.284–6.
15. Ulli Beier, *The Origin of Life and Death* (London, 1966) pp.42–6.
16. John G. Bourke, *Scatologic Rites of All Nations* (Washington, 1891) p.269.
17. Sigmund Freud, *On Sexuality: Three Essays on the Theory of Sexuality, and Other Works* (Harmondsworth, 1977) pp.187–204.
18. Freud, pp.293–302.
19. Tom Driberg, *Ruling Passions* (London, 1977) p.13.
20. Michel Tournier, *Le Roi des aulnes* (Paris, 1970) p.98 (The morning's only consolation is of a faecal nature. I unexpectedly and faultlessly lay a superb turd, so long that it has to curve at each end to fit into the bowl. Fondly gazing at this lovely, plump baby of living mud which I've just given birth to, I regain my zest for life).
21. W.H. Auden, *Collected Poems* (London, 1976) p.527.
22. *Journal of Sex Research* 4, 1 (1968), pp.34–50.
23. Bourke, p.267.
24. Bruce Rodgers, *The Queen's Vernacular* (London, 1972). The same conjunction occurs in the German language.
25. Winston Leyland, ed., *Angels of the Lyre* (San Francisco, 1975) pp.123–4.

26. Ginsberg, p.270.
27. Mutsuo Takahashi, *A Bunch of Keys* (Trumansburg, N.Y., 1984) p.95.
28. *Plutarch's Moralia* IX (London, 1969) 768.
29. Raymond de Becker, *The Other Face of Love* (London, 1967) ch.1, part 1.
30. Claude Lévi-Strauss, *L'Homme nu* (Paris, 1971).
31. *Psychosomatic Medicine* 22, 4 (1960), pp.260–6.
32. *Bulletin of the Meninger Clinic* 16, 5 (1952), pp.159–66.
33. W.H. Auden, *The Dyer's Hand* (London, 1963) p.196.
34. *Gay Sunshine* 31 (Winter 1977) p.18.
35. Maureen Duffy, *The Venus Touch* (London, 1971).
36. Nikolai Klyuev, *Poems* (Ann Arbor, Michigan, 1977) pp.14–15.
37. Julian of Norwich, *Revelations of Divine Love* (Harmondsworth, 1966) p.167.
38. The Furies, Giants, and Nymphs were born from drops of blood which fell to earth when Uranus was castrated by his son. Bearing in mind that the semen and blood co-exist in myth, and that this particular blood is from the genitals of Uranus, we can safely imagine an alternative version in which, without the violent interference of the son, Uranus merely ejaculates onto the ground, and the Furies, Giants, and Nymphs are born from his semen.
39. Lévi-Strauss, p.339. The displacement of semen by urine is common – and accurate, since the male's urine contains spermatozoa.
40. Vern L. Bullough, *Sexual Variance in Society and History* (N.Y., 1976) p.12 ff.
41. D'Arch Smith, p.224.
42. Brian Reade, ed., *Sexual Heretics* (London, 1970) pp.158–93.
43. Reade, pp.248–85.
44. Reade, pp.324–47.
45. Reade, pp.388–391.
46. Reade, pp. 76–104.
47. Oscar Wilde, *De Profundis, and Other Writings* (Harmondsworth, 1973) p.174.
48. Oscar Wilde, *Charmides, and Other Poems* (London, 1913). *Complete Works of Oscar Wilde: Poems* (N.Y., 1909) pp.117–52.
49. H. Montgomery Hyde, *The Trials of Oscar Wilde* (London, 1948) p.236.
50. Wilde, *De Profundis*, p.120.
51. Edward Carpenter, *Ioläus: An Anthology of Friendship* (London, 1906).
52. Edward Carpenter, *The Intermediate Sex* (London, 1916).
53. André Gide, *Corydon* (London, 1952).
54. Arthur Schopenhauer, 'The Metaphysics of the Love of the Sexes', *The Will to Live* (N.Y., 1967) p.71.
55. G. Lowes Dickinson, *After Two Thousand Years* (London, 1930).
56. Havelock Ellis, *Psychology of Sex* (London, 1933) ch.5.
57. D.W. Cory, *The Homosexual in America* (N.Y., 1951) ch.15.
58. D.J. West, *Homosexuality* (London, 1955) ch.1.
59. Brian Magee, *One in Twenty* (London, 1966) ch.4.
60. Angelo d'Arcangelo, *The Homosexual Handbook* (London, 1971) p.273.
61. Dennis Altman, *Homosexual: Oppression and Liberation* (London, 1974) p.167.
62. Petronius, *The Satyricon* (Harmondsworth, 1965) p.146.
63. Petronius, p.201.
64. Aleister Sutherland and Patrick Anderson, eds., *Eros: An Anthology of Friendship* (London, 1961).
65. Bullough, pp.664–5.
66. G. Lowes Dickinson, *Plato and his Dialogues* (London, 1931) p.14.
67. Cavafy, p.80.
68. Fryer, p.257.
69. E.M. Forster, *Maurice* (London, 1971) pp.61–2.
70. Ian Young, *Common-or-Garden Gods* (Scarborough, Ontario, 1976) p.49.
71. Bertrand Russell, *History of Western Philosophy* (London, 1979) p.120.
72. Walter Pater, *Plato and Platonism* (London, 1893) ch.3.
73. Pater, p.255.
74. Oswald Mosley, *The Greater Britain* (London, 1932).
75. Adolf Hitler, *Mein Kampf* (London, 1939) pp.342–5.
76. K.R. Popper, *The Open Society and its Enemies* I (London, 1962) p.182.
77. Frederick Rolfe, *The Desire and Pursuit of the Whole* (London, 1934) p.298.
78. Patrick White, *The Tree of Man* (London, 1956) ch.7.
79. Louie Crew and Rictor Norton, 'The

Homophobic Imagination', *College English* 36, 3 (Nov.1974) p. 275.

80. Benjamin Tarnowsky, *Anthropological, Legal and Medical Studies on Pederasty in Europe* (N. Hollywood, Cal., 1967) pp.81–2.

81. W.B. Yeats, 'The Statues', *Collected Poems* (London, 1950) p.375.

82. J.R. Ackerley, *My Father and Myself* (London, 1968) p.126. Denton Welch, *Maiden Voyage* (London, 1968) ch.20. Thomas Mann, *Death in Venice, Tristan, Tonio Kroger* (Harmondsworth, 1955) pp.35, 50. Thom Gunn, *Jack Straw's Castle* (London, 1976) pp.13, 43.

83. Harold Norse *Carnivorous Saint* (San Francisco, 1977) p.85. Griffin in Ian Young, ed., *The Male Muse* (Trumansburg, N.Y., 1973) p.45. Gluck in Leyland, *Angels of the Lyre*, p.102.

84. E.M. Forster, *The Life to Come, and Other Stories* (London, 1972).

85. Young, *Common-or-Garden Gods*, p.46.

86. Apuleius, *The Golden Ass* (Harmondsworth, 1950) p.41.

87. *Diodorus of Sicily* VIII (London, 1970) xvii.41.

88. Allen Ginsberg, *Journals, Early Fifties Early Sixties* (N.Y., 1977) p.224.

89. Ginsberg, p.7.

90. Holden, p.157.

91. Ritsos, p.113.

92. H. Ebenstein, *Pierced Hearts and True Love* (London, 1953) p.73. George Burchett, himself a tattooist of repute, confirms that 'tattoos have been and still are closely connected with sex life' – *Memoirs of a Tattooist* (London, 1960) p.69. However, Burchett is concerned to defend the virtue of his profession, as the following remarks testify: 'Naturally, I am angry if it is suggested, and it has been, that tattooing is associated with abnormality' (pp.20–1). 'Of course, I have had some obscene requests from customers, who really needed skilful attention by a medical practitioner I have not hesitated to tell them so' (p.21). 'There is sex in [tattooing], thank goodness, but it is clean sex. Sometimes it is called love' (p.21). During the war, Burchett received many requests for marks 'on parts of the body which I normally refuse to tattoo', from members of the

Free French forces of de Gaulle (p.71). Under the circumstances, it seems, he relaxed his rules.

93. Ebenstein, p.75.

94. Thom Gunn, 'Black Jackets', *My Sad Captains* (London, 1961) p.30.

95. Jean Genet, *Oeuvres Complètes* III (Paris, 1951) pp.292–4.

96. *The Best of Olympia* (London, 1966) pp.70–5. See also Keith Howe, 'Designs on You', *Gay News* 139, p.21: 'It was believed at one time that homosexuals had special marks (on the cheeks, the eyelids or the web of the thumb and index finger) to identify themselves to each other.'

97. Don Gifford with Robert J. Seidman, *Notes for Joyce: An Annotation of James Joyce's* Ulysses (N.Y., 1974) p.445. I am unable to verify this suggestion.

98. Ebenstein, p.77.

99. William Plomer, *Collected Poems* (London, 1973) pp.211–12.

100. Ebenstein, p.31. See also Roald Dahl's short story 'Skin', in which an old man is divested of the skin of his back by an art dealer, anxious to profit from the masterpiece thereon – *Someone Like You* (N.Y., 1954) pp.127–49.

101. Kirkup, pp.25–6.

102. Gunn, p.40.

103. George Seferis, *Collected Poems 1924–1955* (London, 1969) p.267.

104. Nikos Kazantzakis, *The Odyssey: A Modern Sequel* (London, 1959) pp.18–19, lines 679–683.

105. Denton Welch, *Dumb Instrument* (London, 1976) pp.44–6. Craig Raine, *The Onion, Memory* (Oxford, 1980) p.7.

106. Norse, pp.35, 12.

107. D'Arch Smith, p.79.

108. Mutsuo Takahashi, *Poems of a Penisist* (Chicago, 1975) pp.83, 86.

109. Steiner, *After Babel*, pp.38, 39.

110. George Steiner, *Extraterritorial* (London, 1972) p.5.

111. Jean Genet, *Journal du voleur* (Paris, 1949) pp.261–2.

112. Pablo Neruda, *New Poems (1968–1970)* (N.Y., 1972) p.10.

113. Aleister Crowley, *White Stains* (London, 1973).

114. Paul Mariah, *This Light Will Spread: Selected Poems 1960–1975* (San Francisco, 1978) p.103.

115. Takahashi, *Poems of a Penisist*, p.90.

116. Roland Barthes, *A Lover's Discourse* (N.Y., 1978) p.149.
117. Roland Barthes, *Sade/Fourier/Loyola* (N.Y., 1976) p.129.
118. Sylvia Plath, *Winter Trees* (London, 1971) pp.16, 31–2. *Crossing the Water* (London, 1971) p.35.
119. Duffy, pp.46, 52.
120. Paul Goodman, *Collected Poems* (N.Y., 1973) pp.312–14.
121. Steegmuller, p.349.
122. Rolfe, p.154.
123. Mann, p.53.
124. Plato, *The Symposium* (Harmondsworth, 1951) pp.87, 86, 90, 91.
125. Exceptions exist, in the cases of artists who needed more than the Muses' help. In *Paradiso* I, Dante calls on Apollo's help as inspirer.
126. See note 83, above. Just as aptly, Young's follow-up anthology was called *Son of the Male Muse* (Trumansburg, N.Y., 1983).
127. W.I. Scobie, 'Gunn in America: A Conversation in San Francisco,' *London Magazine* 17, 6 (Dec. 1977) p.15.
128. *Gay Sunshine* 31 (Winter 1977) p.3.

Chapter 4: D.H. Lawrence

1. For instance, the following texts are useful, but consider only the novels: Margaret Bolsterli, 'Studies in Context: The Homosexual Ambience of Twentieth Century Culture', *D.H. Lawrence Review* 6 (1973) pp.71–85; Carol Dix, 'Homosexuality', *D.H. Lawrence and Women* (London, 1980) pp.93–107; Jeffrey Meyers, 'D.H. Lawrence and Homosexuality', *D.H. Lawrence: Novelist, Poet, Prophet*, ed. Stephen Spender (London, 1973) pp.135–46; Kate Millett, *Sexual Politics* (N.Y., 1969) ch.5.
2. Jeffrey Meyers, *Homosexuality and Literature, 1890–1930* (London, 1977) p.161.
3. *The Complete Poems of D.H. Lawrence* (London, 1964). All references are to this edition unless otherwise stated. Hereafter, page numbers appear in parentheses in my text.
4. If Emile Delavenay's convincing thesis is correct, and Lawrence was, indeed, closely acquainted with the works of Edward Carpenter, we must reluctantly conclude that he was muddled by them. See Emile Delavenay, *D.H. Lawrence and Edward Carpenter: A Study in Edwardian Transition* (London, 1971).
5. Allen Edwardes, *The Jewel in the Lotus* (London, 1965) pp.226–7.
6. *Lady Chatterley's Lover* (Harmondsworth, 1961) p.124: straight after the episode in which Connie cuddles one of Mellors' chicks, his stirring penis is likened to a live bird.
7. *Phoenix II* (London, 1968) p.400.
8. Tom Marshall, *The Psychic Mariner: A Reading of the Poems of D.H. Lawrence* (London, 1970) p.101.
9. *Lady Chatterley's Lover*, p.259.
10. *Women in Love* (London, 1921) p.331.
11. Sanity and wholesomeness are Lawrence's highest form of compliment. Mellors is sane and wholesome (*Lady Chatterley's Lover*, p.116); but, ultimately, we can trace these two adjectives back to the sanctity of the author's mother, since Gertrude Morel is also described as being sane and wholesome, in chapter 7 of *Sons and Lovers*.
12. *The Collected Letters of D.H. Lawrence* (London, 1962) pp.251–2.
13. W.H. Auden, *The Dyer's Hand* (London, 1963) pp. 287–8.
14. James G. Southworth, *Sowing the Spring* (Oxford, 1940) p.70.
15. *Collected Letters*, p.319.
16. Auden, p.288.
17. Meyers, 'D.H. Lawrence and Homosexuality', p.139.
18. Marshall, p.128; quoted in a footnote. Marshall comments: 'This is open to obvious misunderstanding. Such a passage is probably best understood as the symbolic expression of an internal process by which Lawrence accepts and releases the qualities of his father which were driven underground in his youth.' Granted that to do so is 'obvious', I have chosen to 'misunderstand'.

Chapter 5: Hart Crane

1. *The Complete Poems and Selected Letters and Prose of Hart Crane* (London, 1968). All parenthetical page references to Crane's poems are from this edition.
2. Robert K. Martin, 'Crane's *The Bridge*, The Tunnel, 58–60', *The Explicator* 34, 2 (Oct. 1975), section 16.
3. Among critical works containing no

reference to Crane's homosexuality are the following: R.P. Blackmur, 'New Thresholds, New Anatomies: Notes on a Text of Hart Crane', *Language as Gesture* (Westport, Connecticut, 1977) pp.301–16. Waldo Frank, 'Foreword', *The Complete Poems of Hart Crane* (1958) pp.xi–xvi, reprinted in Brom Weber's 1968 edition, pp.269–73. David Bulwer Lutyens, 'Hart Crane (1899–1932): Order Wrested from Chaos', *The Creative Encounter* (London, 1960) pp. 98–127. Sister M. Bernetta Quinn, 'Eliot and Crane: Protean Techniques', *The Metaphoric Tradition in Modern Poetry* (N.Y., 1972) pp.130–67. Roger Ramsey, 'A Poetics for *The Bridge*', *Twentieth Century Literature* 26, 3 (Fall 1980) pp.278–93. Richard P. Sugg, *Hart Crane's* The Bridge (Alabama, 1976). Allen Tate, 'Introduction' (1926), Crane's *White Buildings* (N.Y., 1972) pp.ix–xvi. Hyatt Howe Waggoner, 'Hart Crane: Beyond all Sesames of Science', *The Heel of Elochim* (Norman, Oklahoma 1950) pp. 155–92.

4. A. Alvarez, 'The Lyric of Hart Crane', in Guy Owen, *Modern American Poetry* (DeLand, Florida, 1972) pp.173–84; p.174.

5. Susan Jenkins Brown, *Robber Rocks: Letters and Memories of Hart Crane, 1923–1932* (Middletown, Connecticut, 1969) p.14.

6. R.W. Butterfield, *The Broken Arc: A Study of Hart Crane* (Edinburgh, 1969) p.232.

7. L.S. Dembo, *Hart Crane's Sanskrit Charge: A Study of* The Bridge (Ithaca, N.Y., 1960) p.133.

8. Wallace Fowlie, *Love in Literature* (Bloomington, Indiana, 1965) p.129.

9. Samuel Hazo, *Hart Crane: An Introduction and Interpretation* (N.Y., 1963) pp.8, 13, 15. 133.

10. Vincent Quinn, *Hart Crane* (N.Y., 1963) p.20.

11. M.L. Rosenthal, 'Hart Crane', *The Modern Poets* (N.Y., 1960) pp.168–82; p.178.

12. Monroe K. Spears, 'Hart Crane', in Allen Tate, *Six American Poets from Emily Dickinson to the Present* (Minneapolis, 1966) pp.195–232; p.201.

13. Yvor Winters, *On Modern Poets* (Cleveland, Ohio, 1959) p.131.

14. John Unterecker, *Voyager: A Life of Hart Crane* (London, 1970) p.735.

15. Unterecker, p.566.

16. Herbert A. Leibowitz, *Hart Crane: An Introduction to the Poetry* (N.Y., 1968) p.80.

17. Robert K. Martin, *The Homosexual Tradition in American Poetry* (Austin, Texas, 1979) p.117.

18. Martin, p.120.

19. See, for instance, Hazo, p.30, and R.W.B. Lewis, *The Poetry of Hart Crane: A Critical Study* (Princeton, N.J., 1967) p.39.

20. See, for instance, 'Praise for an Urn' (p.8), 'For the Marriage of Faustus and Helen' (p.33), 'Virginia' (p.102), and 'The Tunnel' (p.111).

21. Leibowitz (p.111) writes: 'In a peculiar way Crane was an idealist of the senses, and the fact of his homosexuality may have caused him to return so often to the word "white," since it probably connoted a holy desire unvitiated by guilt or mortification.' Certainly, this is one of its connotations. But the Crane of 'Voyages' believed such whiteness could be achieved in a homosexual love affair.

22. In the early poem 'October-November' (p.126), published in late 1916, sunlight gilds silver and the moon turns to gold. But this is an experiment in atmospheric effect, and seems to have no real bearing on Crane's poetic pursuit of love.

23. Martin (p.139) places this poem in the tradition of Whitman's 'Calamus', 'as a strong statement of social and political unity founded on sexual bonds'.

24. Sherman Paul, *Hart's Bridge* (Urbana, Illinois, 1972) p.41.

25. Butterfield, p.10, n.42.

26. Hart Crane, *White Buildings* (N.Y., 1926).

27. Hart Crane, *White Buildings* (N.Y., 1972) pp.xvii–xxxiii.

28. Butterfield, p.30.

29. Butterfield, p.69.

30. Butterfield, p.38, n.40.

31. Butterfield, p.21, n.60.

32. Lewis, p.134.

33. M.D. Uroff, *Hart Crane: The Patterns of his Poetry* (Urbana, Illinois, 1974) p.29.

34. Butterfield, p.112.

35. Paul, p.110.

36. Spears, p.214.

37. Robert Combs, *Vision of the Voyage: Hart Crane and the Psychology of Romanticism* (Memphis, 1978) p.68.

38. Martin, p.128.

39. *Little Review* 10 (Spring 1924) p.19.
40. Butterfield, pp.79–80.
41. Butterfield, p.112.
42. Lewis, p.196, n.7.
43. Lewis, p.339, n.6.
44. Glauco Cambon, *The Inclusive Flame* (Bloomington, Indiana, 1965) p.174.
45. Butterfield, p.114.
46. Logan, p.xxxi, his emphasis.
47. Unterecker, p.378.
48. Hazo, p.56.
49. Lewis, p.168, his emphasis.
50. Uroff, p.113.
51. Paul, p.142.
52. *The Letters of Hart Crane, 1916–1932* (Berkeley and L.A., 1965) p.181.
53. Leibowitz, p.84.
54. Leibowitz, p.99.
55. Martin, p.133. Robert Boyers, who has ideological objections to Martin's book, thinks this interpretation does 'terrible things' to Crane's poem – 'The Ideology of the Steam-Bath', *Times Literary Supplement* 30 May 1980, p.604.
56. Lewis, p.162.
57. Paul, p.16.
58. Uroff, p.81.
59. Leslie A. Fiedler, *The Return of the Vanishing American* (London, 1972) p.88.
60. 'Doubtless, one of the troubles with the "Cape Hatteras" section . . . is the falsification by Crane (probably even to himself) of his relation to the image of Whitman. The homosexual sensibility which they shared is ignored in favour of Whitman's legendary representativeness as an "American"' – Leslie A. Fiedler, *An End to Innocence* (N.Y., 1972) p.169.
61. Thomas A. Vogler, *Preludes to Vision: The Epic Adventure in Blake, Wordsworth, Keats, and Hart Crane* (Berkeley, Cal., 1971) p.180.
62. Paul, p.250.
63. Lewis, p.355.
64. Sugg, p.101.
65. Uroff, p.213.
66. Laud Humphreys, *Tearoom Trade: Impersonal Sex in Public Places* (Chicago, 1975).
67. Other poems worth consulting on erotic activity in public lavatories include the following: W.H. Auden, 'Loneliness waited', *Collected Poems* (London, 1976) p.554. William Barber, 'Explanation', in Ian Young, ed., *The Male Muse* (Trumansburg, N.Y., 1973) p.12. Dennis Cooper, 'Two Guys', *Idols*

(N.Y., 1979) pp.35–6. David Eberly, 'Poem', and Steve Jonas, 'Poem', in Winston Leyland, ed., *Angels of the Lyre* (San Francisco, 1975) pp.56, 114. Harold Norse, 'Masturbation' and 'Vespasian Ballet', *Carnivorous Saint* (San Francisco, 1977) pp.29, 111. Mutsuo Takahashi, 'Winter: 1955' and 'Ode', *Poems of a Penisist* (Chicago, 1975) pp.21, 47–97. Takahashi, 'Myself with a Glory Hole' and 'Ode', *A Bunch of Keys* (Trumansburg, N.Y., 1984) pp. 96, 28–73.
68. Unterecker, p.452.
69. Lewis, p.390.
70. Butterfield, p.239.
71. Brown, p.14.
72. Logan, p.xix.
73. Baird's 'The Last Days of Hart Crane' is printed in Susan Jenkins Brown's *Robber Rocks*, pp. 147–73. The quoted remark is on p.147, my emphasis.
74. Unterecker, p.716.
75. Unterecker, p.739.
76. Unterecker, p.736.
77. Unterecker, pp.739–40.
78. Combs, p.176.

Chapter 6: W.H. Auden

1. Richard Ellmann, 'Getting to Know You', *New York Review of Books* 27, 16 (23 Oct. 1980), p.35. Auden to Pudney: Humphrey Carpenter, *W.H. Auden: A Biography* (London, 1981) p.118.
2. 'Because sap fell away' refers to Auden's unrequited passion for Gabriel Carritt, whom he met at Oxford in 1927 (Carpenter, p.76). The unpublished 'Quique Amavit' is a declaration of love for another fellow-undergraduate, William McElwee (p.68), whose initials appear on a version of 'From the very first coming down' (p.76, n). In 1929, a German boyfriend, Otto Küsel, inspired both 'Upon this line between adventure' and 'Sentries against inner and outer' (p.103). The second of the six Odes in *The Orators* is addressed to Gabriel Carritt (p.128). An affair with an unnamed man produced 'That night when joy began' and 'For what as easy' (p.131), and a later poem refers to the end of the affair (p.137). Various sonnets from the summer of 1933 coincide with another affair with an unnamed youth (p.157). 'Underneath

the abject willow' contains sexual advice for Benjamin Britten, with whom 'Night covers up the rigid land' is also concerned (p.188). The relationship with Chester Kallman influenced most of Auden's writing at the time, but the following in particular: 'Perhaps I always knew what they were saying' and 'Not as that dream Napoleon', both written within a month of meeting Kallman (p.262); 'In Sickness and in Health', whose dedication to Maurice and Gwen Mendelbaum post-dates it (p.263, n); 'While explosives blow to dust', ostensibly for the wedding of Elizabeth Mann in 1939 (p.263); 'Time will say nothing but I told you so' and 'Leap Before You Look', both dating from just after Auden's conversion (p.300); 'Though determined Nature can', arising out of a crisis caused by Kallman's affair with an English serviceman (p.311) and some of Joseph's thoughts in 'The Temptation of St. Joseph' (*For the Time Being*), from the same difficult period (p.313); 'Many Happy Returns', despite its dedication to the then 7 year old John Rettger (p.321); 'Prospero to Ariel' (p.325); the libretto of *The Rake's Progress*, their collaboration (p.353); and 'The Common Life' (p.395). Behind 'Dichtung und Wahreit' are three lovers: Kallman, Orlan Fox, and the Viennese known to us only as Hugerl (pp.395–6). A substantial part of 'September 1, 1939' is influenced by a remark in Nijinsky's diary, on Diaghilev (p.274).

3. 'A Day for a Lay', *Avant Garde* 11 (March 1970) pp.46–7. *The Platonic Blow* (N.Y., 1965), published by the carefully named Fuck You Press. For verification of this poem's authenticity, see Tom Driberg, *Ruling Passions* (London, 1977) pp.58–9; and Dorothy J. Farnan, *Auden in Love* (London, 1985) p.184.

4. Charles Osborne, *W.H. Auden: The Life of a Poet* (N.Y., 1979) p.256.

5. Anonymous review, 'The Queen is Dead', *Gay Star (Belfast Bulletin of the Northern Ireland Gay Rights Association)* 1, p.8.

6. W.H. Auden, *Forewords and Afterwords* (London, 1973) p.89. The context of this remark is a study of Shakespeare's sonnets. Of course, when a gay poet is still living, he may well

object to the release of biographical details, on the grounds of expediency. In 1945, when Robert Duncan wanted to write an essay on the homo-erotic patterns in Auden's poetry, Auden wrote to him: 'I must ask you not to publish the essay you propose. I'm sure you will realize that the better the essay you write, the more it will be reviewed and talked about, and the more likelihood there would be of it being brought publicly to my attention in a way where to ignore it would be taken as an admission of guilt. As you may know, I earn a good part of my livelihood by teaching, and in that profession one is particularly vulnerable. Further, both as a writer and as a human being, the occasion may always rise, particularly in these times, when it becomes one's duty to take a stand on the unpopular side of some issue. Should that ever occur, your essay would be a very convenient red herring for one's opponents.' – Ekbert Faas, *Young Robert Duncan: Portrait of the Poet as Homosexual in Society* (Santa Barbara, 1983) p.195.

7. Farnan, p.159.

8. Auden, pp.327, 453.

9. Among many essays which make no reference to Auden's homosexuality, and none to any homo-erotic element of his work, are the following: A. Alvarez, 'W.H. Auden', *Beyond All this Fiddle* (London, 1968) pp.91–93. Alvarez, 'W.H. Auden: Poetry and Journalism', *The Shaping Spirit* (London, 1958) pp.87–106. F.W. Bateson, 'Auden's Last Poems', *Essays in Criticism* 25, 3 (July 1975), pp.383–90. John Bayley, 'W.H. Auden', *The Romantic Survival* (London, 1957) pp.127–85. The nine essays in James Boatwright, ed., 'A Tribute to Wystan Hugh Auden on his Sixtieth Birthday', *Shenandoah* 18, 2 (Winter 1967). Edward Callan, 'Allegory in *The Age of Anxiety*', *Twentieth Century Literature* 10, 4 (Jan 1965) pp.155–65. R.G. Cox, 'The Poetry of W.H. Auden', *The Pelican Guide to English Literature* VII (Harmondsworth, 1973) pp.395–411. D.J. Enright, 'Reluctant Admiration: A Note on Auden and Rilke', *Essays in Criticism* 2, 2 (April 1952) pp.180–95. Lloyd Frankenberg, 'W.H. Auden', *Pleasure Dome* (Cambridge Mass., 1949) pp.301–15. George Fraser, 'Auden in

Midstream' and 'Auden's Later Manner', *Essays on Twentieth-Century Poets* (Leicester, 1977) pp.136–45, 146–51. Lillian Feder, 'W.H. Auden: "...homage by naming"', 'W.H. Auden: Myth as Analytic Instrument', and 'W.H. Auden: Unconscious Forces in History', *Ancient Myth in Modern Poetry* (Princeton, N.J., 1971) pp.243–69, 136–80, 317–43. G.S. Fraser, 'The Young Prophet', *New Statesman and Nation* 51, 1299 (28 Jan. 1956) pp.102–3. Frederick Grubb, 'English Auden and the 30's Ethos', *A Vision of Reality* (London, 1965) pp.137–57. John Haffenden, 'Early Auden', *P N Review* 5, 4 (1978) pp.11–13. Barbara Hardy, 'The Reticence of W.H. Auden' and 'W.H. Auden, Thirties to Sixties: A Face and a Map', *The Advantage of Lyric* (London, 1977) pp.84–94, 95–111. Philip Henderson, 'The Auden Age.' *The Poet and Society* (London, 1939) pp.202–31. Richard Hoggart, 'The Long Walk: The Poetry of W.H. Auden', *Speaking to Each Other* II (London, 1970) pp.56–94. Graham Hough, 'MacNeice and Auden', *Critical Quarterly* 9, 1 (Spring 1967) pp.9–17. Virginia M. Hyde, 'The Pastoral Formula of W.H. Auden and Piero di Cosimo', *Contemporary Literature* 14, 3 (1973), pp.332–46. Stanley Edgar Hyman, 'Poetics, Dogmatics, and Parabolics', *Standards* (N.Y., 1966) pp.108–12. Randall Jarrell, 'Freud to Paul: The Stages of Auden's Ideology', *Partisan Review* 12, 4 (1945), pp.437–57. David K. Kirby, 'Snyder, Auden, and the New Morality', *Notes on Contemporary Literature* 1, 1 (Jan.1971), pp.9–10. Lucy S. McDiarmid, 'Auden and the Redeemed City', *Criticism* 13, 4 (Fall 1971), pp.340–50. Moira Megaw, 'Auden's First Poems', *Essays in Criticism* 25, 3 (July 1975), pp.378–82. Edward Mendelson, 'The Auden-Isherwood Collaboration', *Twentieth Century Literature* 22, 3 (Oct.1976), pp.276–85. Gerald Moore, 'Luck in Auden', *Essays in Criticism* 7, 1 (Jan.1957), pp.103–8. Kathleen E. Morgan, 'The Analysis of Guilt: Poetry of W.H. Auden', *Christian Themes in Contemporary Poets* (London, 1965) pp.92–122. William H. Pritchard, 'Auden & Co.', *Seeing Through Everything* (London, 1977) pp.154–77.

D.S. Savage, 'The Strange Case of W.H. Auden', *The Personal Principle* (London, 1944) pp.155–82. Francis Scarfe, 'Aspects of Auden: The "Enfant Terrible" of the Thirties', *Auden and After* (London, 1942) pp.10–34. Michael Schmidt, 'W.H. Auden', *A Reader's Guide to Fifty Modern British Poets* (London, 1979) pp.233–43. Nathan A. Scott, Jr., 'The Poetry of Auden', *London Magazine* 8, 1 (Jan.1961), pp.44–63. Geoffrey Thurley, 'W.H. Auden: The Image as Instance', *The Ironic Harvest* (London, 1974) pp.54–78. Anthony Thwaite, 'W.H. Auden', *Contemporary English Poetry* (London, 1959) pp.65–78. John Wain, 'The Poetry of W.H. Auden', *Professing Poetry* (London, 1977) pp.72–102. A. Kingsley Weatherhead, 'The Good Place in the Latest Poems of W.H. Auden', *Twentieth Century Literature* 10, 3 (Oct.1964), pp.99–107. John Whitehead, 'The Auden Gravy Train,' *New Review* 3, 32 (Nov.1976), pp.60–2. Edmund Wilson, 'W.H. Auden in America,' *The Bit between my Teeth* (N.Y., 1966) pp.355–63. The omission is particularly glaring in the two Hardy essays, respectively on Auden's reticence and on his attitudes to love; in the Kirby essay, on modern attitudes to sex; and in the Morgan essay, on love and Auden's sense of sin and guilt.

Some of the full-length studies are not more forthright. The following contain no reference to homosexuality: John G. Blair, *The Poetic Art of W.H. Auden* (Princetown, N.J., 1965). Richard Hoggart, *Auden: An Introductory Essay* (London, 1951). Richard Johnson, *Man's Place: An Essay on Auden* (Ithaca, N.Y., 1973). Justin Replogle, *Auden's Poetry* (London, 1969) – apart from a dubious definition of 'camp' as 'originally homosexual slang meaning excessively feminine, precious', p.240. Each of the following has only one reference to homosexuality: George W. Bahlke, *The Later Auden* (N.Y., 1970), p.139, referring to one of the relationships in *The Age of Anxiety*. Ronald Carter, *W.H. Auden* (Milton Keynes, 1975), p.18, where Carter refers to Auden's homosexuality by giving a 17-line quotation from Arnold Kettle, at the centre of which is the brief mention, in parentheses. Barbara Everett, *Auden*

(London, 1964), p.87, referring to the homo- and heterosexual nature of desire in *The Age of Anxiety*. Herbert Greenberg, *Quest for the Necessary: W.H. Auden and the Dilemma of Divided Consciousness* (Cambridge, Mass., 1968), p.53, referring to the 'weakness' of the Airman in *The Orators*, which 'some commentators have identified with homosexuality'. Gerald Nelson, *Changes of Heart: A Study in the Poetry of W.H. Auden* (L.A., 1969), p.81, identifying Quant, in *The Age of Anxiety*, as 'an aging, homosexual widower'. George T. Wright, *W.H. Auden* (N.Y., 1969), p.52, referring to the 'homosexualism' of the Airman in *The Orators*.

10. François Duchêne, *The Case of the Helmeted Airman: A Study of W.H. Auden's Poetry* (London, 1972) p.12.

11. Clive James, 'Auden's Achievement', *Commentary* 56, 6 (Dec.1973) pp.53–4.

12. *Gay Sunshine* 36/37 (Spring/Summer 1978), p.20.

13. *The English Auden* (London, 1977) p.207; *Collected Poems* (London, 1976) p.131. Hereafter, in parenthetical page references, I shall abbreviate these two titles as EA and CP. It is Norman Pittenger who tells us 'Lay your sleeping head' was for Isherwood – 'Wystan and Morgan', *Gay News* 156 (Nov-Dec 1978) pp.22–4.

14. Greenberg and Wright have only one reference each to homosexuality, and both are to the Airman in *The Orators* (see note 9. above). Samuel Hynes suggests that the 'Letter to a Wound' is to a 'psychological abnormality', perhaps homosexuality; and characterises the Airman as 'a neurotic, a kleptomaniac, a homosexual'. But he fails to develop either reference – *The Auden Generation: Literature and Politics in England in the 1930s* (London, 1976) pp.92, 93. D.E.S. Maxwell mentions that the Airman has an uncle-fixation, 'perhaps associated with homosexuality', but he, too, fails to develop the idea – *Poets of the Thirties* (London, 1969) p.154.

15. Stephen Spender, *The Destructive Element* (London, 1935) p.268.

16. Duchêne, p.71.

17. John Fuller, *A Reader's Guide to W.H. Auden* (London, 1970) p.64.

18. Heinrich Kramer and James Sprenger, *Malleus Maleficarum* (London, 1928)

part 2, question 1, ch.7. Norman O. Brown, *Hermes the Thief* (N.Y., 1969) p.43. William Stekel, *Peculiarities of Behaviour: Wandering Mania, Dipsomania, Cleptomania, Pyromania and Allied Impulsive Acts* II (N.Y., 1924) p.11: 'I am inclined to claim . . . that in every case of cleptomania it is our duty to search for the homosexual root.' There is probably some such suggestion, too, in Dostoyevsky's story *The Honest Thief*.

19. However, Isherwood himself does not mention any such connection in *Christopher and his Kind*.

20. In the first edition of *The Orators* (1932), E was female; but when Auden prepared the book for its second edition, 'he did little more than drop two of the interpolated poems and re-sex the airman's lover from female to male' (Edward Mendelson, EA, p.xv, n.2). In fact, the second edition (1934) contains this curious slip: 'What would E say if he knew? Dare I tell her?' (p.61) This 'her' may be an oversight on Auden's part, or a conscious piece of campery. But, considering the very few changes he made for this edition, the pointlessness of the latter explanation makes it seem unlikely. For *The English Auden*, Mendelson claims to have used the second edition (p.xxi). But in this latest text of *The Orators*, all mentions of E are, indeed, male. The line quoted above now reads: 'What would E say if he knew? Dare I tell him?' (EA, p.86) Mendelson's alteration cannot be one of those he has made 'to avoid libel, obscenity or discourtesy' (EA p.xxii).

21. Wright, p.59.

22. Spender, p.268.

23. Fuller, p.63.

24. James G. Southworth, *Sowing the Spring* (Oxford, 1940) pp.135–6, 142.

25. Fuller, p.252.

26. Southworth, p.139.

27. James, p.54. Edward Mendelson, *Early Auden* (London, 1981) p.45, n.

28. Frederick Buell, *W.H. Auden as a Social Poet* (Ithaca, N.Y., 1973) p.37. Fuller, p.40.

29. Hynes, p.108. Southworth, p.137. Mendelson, pp.225–6.

30. James G. Southworth, *More Modern American Poets* (London, 1954) p.125.

31. Fuller, p.180.

32. Cyril Connolly, 'Remembering Auden',

Encounter 44, 3 (March 1975) pp.90–3; reprinted in Stephen Spender, ed., *W.H. Auden: A Tribute* (London, 1975).

33. Mendelson, p.228.
34. See Bayley, Callan, Greenberg, Hoggart, and Wright. On the other hand, Bahlke, Everett, and Nelson's books make only one reference each to homosexuality, and in each case the reference is to *The Age of Anxiety* (see note 9, above).
35. Southworth, *More Modern American Poets*, p.123.
36. Auden wrote that 'the sailor on shore is symbolically the innocent god from the sea who is not bound by the law of the land and can therefore do anything without guilt'. Although it is a *non sequitur*, this partly explains Emble's (or rather, his uniform's) allure – *The Enchafèd Flood* (London, 1985) p.123, n.
37. Callan, p.155.
38. But Stan Smith thinks Malin is homosexual – *W.H. Auden* (Oxford, 1985) p.166.
39. Dictionaries tend to offer only the other meaning of the phrase: a store-room or locker in the stern of a boat. This is not what Auden is talking about. In the afterword to his 'Ode', Mutsuo Takahashi provides an alternative, clumsier version of this poem, as recited to him 'by a former curator of the Museum of Modern Art in New York'. It has a title, 'Glory-Hole', and reads as follows:

Loneliness sits
In the toilet,
Waiting for
Reality
To enter through the
Glory-hole.

Takahashi has a metaphysical interpretation of the piece, to go with the sexual; but with it, justifiably, he illuminates his own poem more than Auden's – *Poems of a Penisist* (Chicago, 1975) pp.101–2. Both Auden and Takahashi may have associated the 'glory hole' with its near neighbour in English dictionaries, the 'gloriole,' a halo or nimbus.
40. Carpenter, p.299.

Chapter 7: Allen Ginsberg

1. See, for instance, the following: James Dickey, 'Allen Ginsberg', *Babel to Byzantium* (N.Y., 1973) pp.52–5. Gerrit Henry, 'Starting from Scratch', *Poetry* 124 (May 1974) pp.292–9. Richard Howard, 'Allen Ginsberg', *Alone with America* (London, 1970) pp.145–52. James F. Mersmann, 'Allen Ginsberg: Breaking Out', *Out of the Vietnam Vortex* (Lawrence, Kansas, 1974) pp.31–75. (But Mersmann does refer to Ginsberg's homosexuality on p.164, in an essay on Robert Duncan.) Geoffrey Thurley, 'Allen Ginsberg: The Whole Man In', *The American Moment* (London, 1977) pp.172–86. Diana Trilling, 'The Other Night at Columbia: A Report from the Academy', *Partisan Review* 26, 2 (Spring 1959) pp.214–30. A. Kingsley Weatherhead, *The Edge of the Image* (Seattle, 1967), of which pp.186–96 are on Ginsberg.
2. See, for instance, the following: Frederick Eckman, 'Neither Tame Nor Fleecy', *Poetry* 90, 6 (Sept.1957), pp.386–97, of which pp.391–3 review *Howl*: Eckman refers to homosexuality obliquely, once in a quotation from Stanley Kunitz (p.391), and once by quoting, without comment, Ginsberg's portrayal of Whitman, eyeing up grocery boys in a supermarket. Ihab Hassan, 'Allen Ginsberg', *Contemporary American Literature 1945–1972* (N.Y., 1973) pp.102–4: Hassan says Ginsberg learned about homosexuality, drugs, insanity, and other subjects during his youth, but does not suggest that this knowledge was of a practical sort, nor that it has had much lasting weight (p.103). Steven Stepanchev, 'Popular Poetry: Allen Ginsberg', *American Poetry Since 1945* (N.Y., 1965), pp.166–74; Stepanchev cites Ginsberg's putting his 'queer shoulder' to the wheel, and his bisexual foray into a bridal bed, both without comment. Other writers mention Ginsberg's homosexuality, but make no attempt to go beyond mere mention by examining its significance. See, for instance: Thomas F. Merrill, *Allen Ginsberg* (N.Y., 1969), which has glancing references on pp.19, 85, and 136 twice. Eric Mottram, *Allen Ginsberg in the Sixties* (Brighton & Seattle, 1972), with one reference on p.22.
3. Leslie Fiedler, *Waiting for the End* (London, 1965) p.242.
4. Paul O'Neil, 'The Only Rebellion

Around,' in Thomas Parkinson, ed., *A Casebook on the Beat* (N.Y., 1961) p.238.

5. There are important references to Rimbaud in 'Car Crash', 'Ignu', 'Manifesto', 'Memory Gardens', and 'Pertussin'; to Crane in 'Cleveland, the Flats', 'Death to Van Gogh's Ear', and 'Kansas City to Saint Louis'; and to Whitman in 'Love Poem on Theme by Whitman', 'A Supermarket in California', and on the dedicatory page of *The Fall of America*. Ginsberg has established, as a kind of Apostolic succession, his own homosexual descent from Whitman, by pointing out that he (Ginsberg) slept with Neal Cassady, who slept with Gavin Arthur, who slept with Edward Carpenter, who slept with Walt Whitman himself. Which is, as Ginsberg comments, 'an interesting sort of thing to have as part of the mythology' – Leyland, pp.106–7, 126–8. A similar theme was taken up in the play *Only Connect*, by Noel Greig and the late Drew Griffiths of London's Gay Sweatshop collective. The play was broadcast by BBC TV on 18 May 1979.

6. Allen Ginsberg, *Collected Poems 1947–1980* (Harmondsworth, 1985) pp.126–33. Hereafter, page references to this edition will appear in parentheses in the body of my text, with the abbreviation CP.

7. Winston Leyland, ed., *Gay Sunshine Interviews* I (San Francisco, 1978) pp.95–128, where Ginsberg is interviewed by Allen Young.

8. Fiedler, p.248. According to J.G. Ballard's *The Atrocity Exhibition* (London, 1970) pp.151–2, 'Results confirm the probability of Presidential figures being perceived primarily in genital terms; the face of L.B. Johnson is clearly genital in significant appearance – the nasal prepuce, scrotal jaw, etc. Faces were seen as either circumcised (J.F.K., Krushchev) or uncircumcised (L.B.J., Adenauer). In assembly-kit tests Reagan's face was uniformly perceived as a penile erection.'

9. In the *Gay Sunshine* interview, Ginsberg explains his deportation from Cuba, as follows: 'Well, the worst thing I said was that I'd heard, by rumor, that Raúl Castro was gay. And the second worst thing I said was that Che Guevara was cute' (p.113). While reaffirming his faith in the positive aspects of the Cuban revolution, Ginsberg goes on to criticise Castro's heavy-handed treatment of homosexuality, and the revolutionary establishment's tendency to denounce its political enemies as 'fairies' (pp.113–17).

10. Example: 'On one occasion in London, I was all but seduced by a very attractive policeman who came into the toilet at Shepherd's Bush dressed in black leather and started masturbating, his handcuffs at the ready to catch the queens.' Mario Mieli, *Homosexuality and Liberation* (London, 1980) pp.101–2.

11. Norman Mailer, *The Armies of the Night* (London, 1968) pp.38, 244, 271.

12. Fred Halstead, *Out Now! A Participant's Account of the American Movement against the Vietnam War* (N.Y., 1978) pp.611–12.

13. Halstead, p.613.

14. Mersmann, p.225.

15. Jane Kramer, *Paterfamilias: Allen Ginsberg in America* (London, 1970) p.95.

16. Halstead, p.204.

17. Allen Ginsberg, *Indian Journals March 1962–May 1963* (San Francisco, 1970), p.1. CP, pp.352, 553.

18. Rictor Norton describes how, in Renaissance love poems, the relationship concerned is often a 'slightly homoerotic' threesome, involving a man, a woman and Cupid. Norton continues: 'In one passage of Thomas Watson's *Hekatompathia or Passionate Centurie of Love* (1582), we find the lover, his mistress, and Cupid all in bed together: if this is merely a conventional way of saying that a man loved a maid, then the convention has certainly gotten out of hand.' *The Homosexual Literary Tradition* (N.Y., 1974) pp.259–60. Ginsberg's version of this loving intervention between bride and groom is, according to his *Gay Sunshine* interview (p.103), a fantasy about making love with Neal Cassady and his wife.

19. Mieli, p.138: 'The demand for the restoration of anal pleasure is one of the basic elements in the critique made by the gay movement of the hypostatising of the heterosexual-genital status quo by the dominant ideology.' Mieli, p.140: 'As a general rule, the more fear a man has of being fucked, the more he himself fucks badly, with scant consideration for the other person, who is reduced to a mere hole, a receptacle for his blind phallic egoism.'

Chapter 8: Thom Gunn

1. See, for instance: Dick Allen, 'The Gift
    to be Simple,' *Poetry* 124 (May 1974),
    pp.103–16; Kenneth Allott, 'Thom
    Gunn', *The Penguin Book of Contem-
    porary Verse* (Harmondsworth, 1962)
    pp.372–4; Sidney Bolt, 'Thom Gunn:
    Words in the Head', *Delta 43* (June
    1968) pp.12–16; Alan Brownjohn, 'The
    Poetry of Thom Gunn', *London Maga-
    zine* 2, 12 (March 1963) pp. 45–52;
    Peter Dale, reviews of FT and MSC,
    Agenda 2, 7 & 8 (May-June 1962)
    pp.21–5; James Dickey, 'Thom Gunn',
    Babel to Byzantium (N.Y., 1973)
    pp.120–3; Martin Dodsworth, 'Thom
    Gunn: Poetry as Action and Submiss-
    ion', *The Survival of Poetry* (London,
    1970) pp.193–215; Michael Fried, 'A
    Question of Form', *New Left Review* 12
    (Nov. 1961) pp.68–70; Richard
    Howard, 'Ecstasies and Decorum', *Par-
    nassus* 2, 2 (Spring/Summer 1974)
    pp.213–20; John Mander, 'In Search of
    Commitment: The Poetry of Thom
    Gunn', *The Writer and Commitment*
    (London, 1961) pp.153–78; Neil
    Powell, 'The Abstract Joy: 'Thom
    Gunn's Early Poetry', *Critical Quarterly*
    13, 3 (Autumn 1971) pp.219–227; Neil
    Powell, 'Thom Gunn: A Pierglass for
    Poets', *Carpenters of Light* (Manchester,
    1979) pp.19–59; M.L. Rosenthal,
    'Thom Gunn', *The New Poets* (N.Y.,
    1967) pp.251–7; Michael Schmidt,
    'Thom Gunn', *A Reader's Guide to Fifty
    Modern British Poets* (London, 1979)
    pp.376–82; Geoffrey Summerfield,
    'Thom Gunn', *Worlds: Seven Modern
    Poets* (Harmondsworth, 1974)
    pp.56–89; Julian Symons, untitled arti-
    cle in James Vinson, *Contemporary
    Poets* (London, 1975) pp.607–8; Patrick
    Swinden, 'Thom Gunn's Castle',
    Critical Quarterly 19, 3 (Autumn 1977)
    pp.43–61; Peter Thirlby, 'Thom Gunn –
    Violence and Tenderness,' *Delta* 8
    (Spring 1956) pp.16–21; John
    Thompson, 'A Poetry Chronicle', *Poetry*
    95, 2 (Nov.1959) pp.107–16.

2. See, for instance: Alan Bold, *Thom
    Gunn and Ted Hughes* (Edinburgh,
    1976): 'The Beach Head' is 'a verse epis-
    tle to a girl Gunn wants to possess',
    (p.22) and 'Tamer and Hawk' 'describes
    the poet under the control of a dominant
    mistress' (p.23). Frederick Grubb,

'Peacetime Conscript: Thom Gunn', *A
Vision of Reality* (London, 1965): 'The
Beach Head' 'compares a girl's body to a
Welfare State' (p.204) and in 'The Right
Possessor', 'The "nation" may be a
prevaricating girl' (p.204). B.J.C.
Hinton, *The Poetry of Thom Gunn*,
unpublished M.A. thesis (Birmingham,
1974): the loved one is female in
'Without a Counterpart' (p.52)
'Hungry' (p.67) 'Terms' (p.68) and
'Touch' (p.220); but on 'Light Sleeping',
Hinton comments: 'the poem seems to
be about homosexual love, although this
does not really affect its meaning' (p.72).
However, the reader is advised to take
care: for the homosexual or bisexual,
male poet can, and often does, write love
poems to the women in his life. With
reference to 'Carnal Knowledge', Gunn
has this to say: 'Now anyone aware that
I am homosexual is likely to misread the
whole poem, inferring that the thing
"known" is that the speaker would
prefer to be in bed with a man. But that
would be a serious misreading, or at least
a serious misplacement of emphasis. The
poem, actually addressed to a fusion of
two completely different girls, is not
saying anything as clear-cut as that.'
Thom Gunn, 'My Life Up to Now', in
Jack W.C. Hagstrom and George Bixby,
eds., *Thom Gunn: A Bibliography
1940–1978* (London, 1979) p.26, and
also in Thom Gunn, *The Occasions of
Poetry: Essays in Criticism and Autobio-
graphy* (London, 1982) p.188. Needless
to say, one must still read the poem, if
addressed to a woman, as a *gay man's*
address to a woman.

3. Roger Baker, 'Sorcery', *Gay News* 180
    (Nov–Dec.1979) p.23. Admittedly,
    Baker provides a facile definition of
    homo-eroticism in poetry: 'laments for
    elusive youths perhaps'.

4. The references occur in the following
    poems: 'Incident on a Journey' (*Fighting
    Terms*), 'On the Move', 'The Nature of
    an Action', 'The Unsettled Motorcylist's
    Vision of his Death', 'Lines from a
    Book', 'Market at Turk', 'The Allegory
    of the Wolf Boy', 'Julian the Apostate',
    'To Yvor Winters', 'Merlin in the Cave'
    (*The Sense of Movement*), 'Modes of
    Pleasure', and 'Claus von Stauffenberg'
    (*My Sad Captains*). Hereafter, page
    references to Gunn's main collections
    will be given parenthetically, in the body

of my text. The titles will be abbreviated as follows:

Fighting Terms (London, 1962): FT,
The Sense of Movement (London, 1957): SM,
My Sad Captains (London, 1961): MSC,
Touch (London, 1967): T,
Moly (London, 1971): M,
Jack Straw's Castle (London, 1976): JSC,
The Passages of Joy (London, 1982): PJ.

5. Tony Sarver, 'Thom Gunn', *Gay News* 134 (Jan 1978) p.16.
6. Gunn, *The Occasions of Poetry*, p.162.
7. See, for instance: 'The Secret Sharer' (FT, p.18), 'The Monster' (MSC, p.16), 'Bravery' (T, p.16), the epigraph to part 2 of *Jack Straw's Castle* (p.31), and 'Behind the Mirror' (JSC, p.68).
8. Michael J. Mitchell, 'Erotic S & M Amongst Gays,' *Gay News* 108 (Dec.1976) p.17.
9. Bold, p.30.
10. Bold, p.31.
11. Ekbert Faas, 'Ted Hughes and Crow', *London Magazine* 10, 10 (Jan.1971) p.7.
12. John Press, *Rule and Energy: Trends in British Poetry since the Second World War* (London, 1963) p.191.
13. Robert K. Martin, *The Homosexual Tradition in American Poetry* (Austin, Texas, 1979) p.183.
14. Colin Falck, 'Uncertain Violence,' *New Review*, 3, 32 (Nov.1976) p.40.
15. Bold, pp.19, 25.
16. Bold, pp.44, 34.
17. Martin, p.165.
18. Nicholas de Jongh, 'The Changing Face of the Brando Bard', *The Guardian* (14 Nov.1979), p.9.
19. I detect, perhaps unreasonably, an early whiff of this theme in 'At the Back of the North Wind' (SM, p.15), when Gunn describes the smells of a stable: 'Horses, leather, manure, fresh sweat, and sweet / Mortality'. These do not seem far removed from the odours of sadomasochism, and it seems logical (if possibly over-enthusiastic) to allow them to call the *equus eroticus* to mind. Shades of this game appear in stage versions of Peter Shaffer's *Equus*, while, in *East*, Steven Berkoff takes it a step further by having one man ride another, not as horse, but as motorbike *eroticus*. For quotidian reference, see Paul T. Brown, 'On the Differentiation of Homo- or Heteroerotic Interest in the Male: An Operant Technique Illustrated in a Case of a Motor-cycle Fetishist', *Behaviour Research and Therapy* 2, 1 (1964) pp.31–5.
20. Gunn, *The Occasions of Poetry*, pp.151–2.
21. Martin, p.180.
22. Bold, p.6.
23. Sarver, p.26.
24. Sarver, p.16. The first version of 'Jack Straw's Castle' lacks the later version's powerful ending in bed, and is appreciably weaker for that – *Manroot* 10 (Late Fall 1974/Winter 1975) pp.52–4.

BIBLIOGRAPHY

PRIMARY TEXTS

(Poetry written in English by men between 1914 and 1985. It is *from* these texts that I have gathered my primary material. Not all of these poems are homo-erotic, and not all homo-erotic poems appear here.)

Ashbery, John, *Self-Portrait in a Convex Mirror* (N.Y., 1975)

Auden, W.H., *The Age of Anxiety: A Baroque Eclogue* (London, 1948)

——, *Collected Poems* (London, 1976)

——, *Collected Shorter Poems 1930–1944* (London, 1950)

——, 'A Day for a Lay', *Avant Garde* 11 (March 1970) pp.46–7

——, *The English Auden: Poems, Essays and Dramatic Writings 1927–1939* (London, 1977)

——, *For the Time Being* (London, 1945)

——, *The Orators* (London, 1932; second edition, 1934)

——, *The Platonic Blow* (N.Y., 1965)

Barker, George, *Collected Poems 1930–1955* (London, 1957)

Bell, William, *Mountains Beneath the Horizon* (London, 1950)

Berryman, John, *Love and Fame* (London, 1971)

——, *Selected Poems 1938–1968* (London, 1972)

Betjeman, John, *Collected Poems, Enlarged Edition* (London, 1970)

Blakeston, Oswell, *How to Make Your Own Confetti* (London, 1965)

Blunden, Edmund, *Poems of Many Years* (London, 1957)

Brooke, Rupert, *1914, and Other Poems* (London, 1916)

Bunting, Basil, *Collected Poems* (London, 1978)

Campbell, Roy, *The Collected Poems of Roy Campbell* (London, 1949)

Coakley, William Leo, 'The Marriage of Dionysus and Apollo', *The Paris Review* 72 (Winter 1977) pp.111–12.

Cohen, Leonard, *Selected Poems 1956–1968* (London, 1969)

——, *The Spice-Box of Earth* (Toronto, 1961)

Cooper, Dennis, *Idols* (N.Y., 1979)

Corn, Alfred, *All Roads at Once* (N.Y., 1976)

Crane, Hart, *The Complete Poems and Selected Letters and Prose of Hart Crane* (London, 1968)

——, *White Buildings* (N.Y., 1972)

Creeley, Robert, *Poems 1950–1965* (London, 1966)

Day Lewis, C., *Poems of C. Day Lewis 1925–1972* (London, 1977)

Dillard, Gavin, *rosie emissions* (Seattle, 1975)

Dorn, Edward, *The Collected Poems 1956–1974* (Bolinas, Cal., 1975)

——, *Gunslinger 1 & 2* (London, 1970)

Douglas, Keith, *Complete Poems* (Oxford, 1978)

Duncan, Robert, *Bending the Bow* (London, 1971)

——, *Derivations: Selected Poems 1950–1956* (London, 1968)

——, *The First Decade: Selected Poems 1940–1950* (London, 1968)

——, *The Opening of the Field* (London, 1969)

——, *Roots and Branches* (London, 1970)

——, *The Years as Catches: First Poems (1939–1946)* (Berkley, Cal., 1966)

Dunn, Douglas, *Terry Street* (London, 1969)

——, *The Happier Life* (London, 1972)

Durrell, Lawrence, *Collected Poems* (London, 1960)

Eliot, T.S., *Collected Poems 1909–1935* (London, 1936)

——, *The Waste Land: A Facsimile and Transcript of the Original Drafts* (London, 1971)

Elmslie, Kenward, Kenneth Koch & James Schuyler, *Penguin Modern Poets 24: Kenward Elmslie, Kenneth Koch, James Schuyler* (Harmondsworth, 1974)

Fuller, Roy, *Collected Poems 1936–1961* (London, 1962)

Gardner, Brian, ed., *The Terrible Rain: The War Poets, 1939–1945* (London, 1966)

Gascoyne, David, *Collected Poems* (London, 1965)

Ginsberg, Allen, *Airplane Dreams: Compositions from Journals* (San Francisco, 1969)

——, *Ankor Wat* (London, 1968)

——, *Collected Poems 1947–1980* (Harmondsworth, 1985)

——, *Empty Mirror: Early Poems* (N.Y, 1970)

——, *The Fall of America: Poems of These States 1965–1971* (San Francisco, 1972)

——, *The Gates of Wrath: Rhymed Poems 1948–1952* (Bolinas, Cal., 1972)

——, *Howl, and Other Poems* (San Francisco, 1956)

——, *Iron Horse* (Toronto, 1972)

——, *Kaddish, and Other Poems 1958–1960* (San Francisco, 1961)

——, *Mind Breaths: Poems 1972–1977* (San Francisco, 1977)

——, *Planet News 1961–1967* (San Francisco, 1968)

——, *Poems All Over the Place, Mostly 'Seventies* (Cherry Valley, N.Y., 1978)

——, *Reality Sandwiches 1953–1960* (San Francisco, 1963)

Giorno, John, *Balling Buddha* (N.Y., 1970)

Goodman, Paul, *Collected Poems* (N.Y., 1973)

Graves, Robert, *Collected Poems 1975* (London, 1975)

Gunn, Thom, 'A Crab', *London Magazine* 1, 11 (Feb 1962) pp.6–7

——, *Fighting Terms* (London, 1962)

——, 'Four New Poems', *Gay News* 197 (Aug.1980) p.20

——, 'Interrogated to Interrogator', *London Magazine* 5, 3 (March 1958) pp.11–12

——, 'Jack Straw's Castle', *Manroot* 10 (Late Fall 1974/Winter 1975) pp. 52–4

——, *Jack Straw's Castle* (London, 1976)

——, 'Knowledge', *The Observer* 24 Sept.1961, p.28

——, *Moly* (London, 1971)

——, *My Sad Captains* (London, 1961)

——, 'Nice Thing' and 'Silence', *The Massachusetts Review* 23, 1 (Spring 1982) pp.132–3

——, *The Passages of Joy* (London, 1982)

——, *Poems 1950–1966: A Selection* (London, 1969)

——, *Selected Poems 1950–1975* (London 1979)

——, *The Sense of Movement* (London, 1957)

——, *Songbook* (N.Y., 1973)

——, *Sunlight* (N.Y., 1969)

——, *To the Air* (Boston, Mass., 1974)

——, *Touch* (London, 1967)

——, 'Two Poems', *London Magazine* 1, 4 (May 1954) pp.25–6.

Gunn, Thom and Ander, *Positives* (London, 1966)

Harwood, Lee, *The Man with Blue Eyes* (N.Y., 1966)

——, *The White Room* (London, 1970)

Henri, Adrian, Roger McGough and Brian Patten, *The Mersey Sound* (Harmondsworth, 1967)

Hill, Brian, *Collected Poems and Translations* (Southrepps, Norfolk, 1974)

Hill, Geoffrey, *Tenebrae* (London, 1978)

Housman, A.E., *The Collected Poems of A.E. Housman* (London, 1960)

Hughes, Langston, *Selected Poems* (N.Y., 1959)

Hughes, Ted, *The Hawk in the Rain* (London, 1957)

Humphries, Martin, *Mirrors* (London, 1980)

Humphries, Martin, ed., *Not Love Alone: A Modern Gay Anthology* (London, 1985)

Jarrell, Randall, *The Complete Poems* (N.Y., 1969)

Jones, David, *In Parenthesis* (London, 1963)

Joyce, James, *Pomes Penyeach, and Other Verses* (London, 1967)

Kirkup, James, *The Body Servant* (London, 1971)

——, *A Correct Compassion* (London, 1952)

——, *The Descent into the Cave* (London, 1957)

——, *The Drowned Sailor, and Other Poems* (London, 1947)

——, 'Elegy for Pier Paolo Pasolini', *Gay News* 93 (April 1976) p.15

——, 'The Love of Older Men,', *Gay News* 103 (Sept.1976) p.28

——, 'The Love that Dares to Speak its Name', *Gay News* 96 (June 1976) p.26

——, *Paper Windows: Poems from Japan* (London, 1968)

——, *The Prodigal Son: Poems 1956–1959* (London, 1959)

——, *Refusal to Conform: Last and First Poems* (London, 1963)

——, *A Spring Journey, and Other Poems of 1952–1953* (London, 1954)

——, *The Submerged Village, and Other Poems* (London, 1951)

——, *White Shadows, Black Shadows: Poems of Peace and War* (London, 1970)

Knight, G. Wilson, *Gold-Dust, with Other Poetry* (London, 1968)

Lacey, E.A., *Path of Snow: Poems 1951–1973* (Scarborough, Ontario, 1974)

Lawrence, D.H., *The Collected Poems of D.H. Lawrence* (London, 1932)

——, *The Complete Poems of D.H. Lawrence* (London, 1964)

Lehmann, John, *Collected Poems 1930–1963* (London, 1963)

——, 'Roman Life, Modern Times', *Gay News* 107 (Nov 1976) p.18

——, 'Thus Much and More', *Gay News* 114 (March 1977) p.18

Lewis, Alun, *Selected Poetry and Prose* (London, 1966)

Leyland, Winston, ed., *Angels of the Lyre: A Gay Poetry Anthology* (San Francisco, 1975)

——, *Orgasms of Light: The Gay Sunshine Anthology* (San Francisco, 1977)

Lindroos, Rubio Tapani, *Memories of Discreet Rooms* (London, 1977)

Logan, John *The Anonymous Lover: New Poems* (N.Y., 1973)

——, *Ghosts of the Heart* (Chicago, 1960)

Lowell, Robert, *Selected Poems* (N.Y., 1976)

Lucie-Smith, Edward, *Confessions and Histories* (London, 1964)

——, *Towards Silence* (London, 1968)

——, *The Well-Wishers* (London, 1974)

Macbeth, George, *Collected Poems 1958–1970* (London, 1971)

——, *In the Hours Waiting for the Blood to Come* (London, 1975)

MacDiarmid, Hugh, *Selected Poems* (Harmondsworth, 1970)

Macleish, Archibald, *New and Collected Poems 1917–1976* (Boston, 1976)

MacNeice, Louis, *Collected Poems 1925–1948* (London, 1949)

Mariah, Paul, *Personae Non Gratae* (San Lorenzo, Cal., 1971)

——, *This Light Will Spread: Selected Poems 1960–1975* (San Francisco, 1978)

McClure, Michael, *Dark Brown* (London, 1969)

McKuen, Rod, *Caught in the Quiet* (London, 1973)

Merrill, James, *Braving the Elements* (N.Y., 1972)

——, *The Country of a Thousand Years of Peace, and Other Poems* (N.Y., 1970)

——, *The Fire Screen* (London, 1970)

——, *Nights and Days* (London, 1966)

——, *Selected Poems* (London, 1961)

Meyer, Thomas, *The Bang Book* (N.Y., 1971)

Muir, Edwin, *Collected Poems 1921–1958* (London, 1960)

Muldoon, Paul, *Mules* (London, 1977)

——, *Why Brownlee Left* (London, 1980)

Nichols, Robert, *Ardours and Endurances; also, A Faun's Holiday, and Poems and Phantasies* (London, 1917)

——, *Aurelia, and Other Poems* (London, 1920)

——, *Such was my Singing* (London, 1942)

Norse, Harold, *Carnivorous Saint: Gay Poems 1941–1976* (San Francisco, 1977)

O'Hara, Frank, *Collected Poems* (N.Y., 1972)

Ondaatje, Michael, *The Collected Works of Billy the Kid* (Toronto, 1970)

Orlovsky, Peter, *Clean Asshole Poems and Smiling Vegetable Songs* (San Francisco, 1978)

Owen, Wilfred, *Collected Poems* (London, 1967)

Pitchford, Kenneth, *Color Photos of the Atrocities* (Toronto, 1973)

Plomer, William, *Celebrations* (London, 1972)

——, *Collected Poems* (London, 1973)

Poems from the Desert: Verses by Members of the Eighth Army (London, 1944)

Pound, Ezra, *The Cantos* (London, 1975)

Powell, Enoch, *Dancer's End and The Wedding Gift* (London, 1951)

Prince, F.T., *The Doors of Stone: Poems 1938–1962* (London, 1963)

Pudney, John, and Henry Treece, eds., *Air Force Poetry* (London, 1944)

Raine, Craig, *The Onion, Memory* (Oxford, 1980)

Read, Herbert, *Poems 1914–1934* (London, 1935)

——, *A World Within a War* (London, 1944)

Ronan, Richard, *Buddha's Kisses, and Other Poems* (San Francisco, 1980)

Rosenberg, Isaac, *The Collected Works of Isaac Rosenberg* (London, 1979)

Rottmann, Larry, Jan Barry & Basil T. Paquet, eds., *Winning Hearts and Minds:*

War Poems by Vietnam Veterans (N.Y., 1972)

Rowse, A.L., *Poems Chiefly Cornish* (London, 1944)

——, *Poems of Deliverance* (London, 1946)

——, *Poems Partly American* (London, 1959)

——, *The Road to Oxford* (London, 1978)

Sassoon, Siegfried, *Collected Poems 1908–1956* (London, 1961)

Scannell, Vernon, *The Loving Game* (London, 1975)

Shapiro, Karl, *Selected Poems* (N.Y., 1968)

Smith, David Emerson, *Queer Poet Lives* (San Francisco, 1979)

Southam, Barry, *Lovers and Other People* (Christchurch, New Zealand, 1973)

Spender, Stephen, *Collected Poems 1928–1953* (London, 1955)

Spicer, Jack, *The Collected Books of Jack Spicer* (L.A., 1975)

——, *Manroot 10: The Jack Spicer Issue* (Late Fall 1974/ Winter 1975)

Thomas, Dylan, *Collected Poems 1934–1952* (London, 1952)

Thomas, Edward, *Collected Poems* (London, 1965)

Thompson, Dunstan, *Lament for the Sleepwalker* (N.Y., 1947)

Trudgett, Richard, *Lost Soldier, Lost Town, and Other Poems* (London, 1945)

Tyler, Parker, *The Will of Eros: Selected Poems 1930–1970* (L.A., 1973)

Veryzer, Guy Summertree, *The Male Whore's Song* (Highland Park, Michigan, 1978)

Welch, Denton, *Dumb Instrument: Poems and Fragments* (London, 1976)

Whitmore, George, *Getting Gay in New York* (N.Y., 1976)

Wieners, John, *Behind the State Capitol: or Cincinnati Pike* (Boston, 1975)

——, *Nerves* (London, 1970)

——, *Selected Poems* (London, 1972)

Wilbur, Richard, *Poems 1943–1956* (London, 1957)

Williams, Charles, *Taliessin Through Logres* (London, 1938)

Williams, Jonathan, *An Ear in Bartram's Tree: Selected Poems 1957–1967* (Chapel Hill, 1969)

——, *The Loco Logodaedalist in Situ: Selected Poems 1968–1970* (London, 1971)

Woods, Gregory, 'The Coelacanth', *Square Peg* 14 (November 1986) p.36

Yeats, W.B., *The Collected Poems of W.B. Yeats* (London, 1950)

Young, Ian, *Common-or-Garden Gods* (Scarborough, Ontario, 1976)

——, *Double Exposure* (Trumansburg, N.Y., 1974)

——, *Year of the Quiet Sun* (Toronto, 1969)

Young, Ian, ed., *The Male Muse: A Gay Anthology* (Trumansburg, N.Y., 1973)

——, *Son of the Male Muse* (Trumansburg, N.Y., 1983)

LITERARY CRITICISM

Allen, Dick, 'The Gift to be Simple', *Poetry* 124 (May 1974) pp.103–16

Allott, Kenneth, 'Thom Gunn', *The Penguin Book of Contemporary Verse* (Harmondsworth, 1962) pp.372–4

Almansi, Guido, *L'estetica dell'osceno* (Torino, 1974)

——, 'Prefazione all'edizione italiana', Robert and Peggy Boyers, eds., *Omosessualità* (Milano, 1984) pp.7–16

Alvarez, A., *Beyond All This Fiddle: Essays 1955–1967* (London, 1968)

——, *The Shaping Spirit: Studies in Modern English and American Poets* (London, 1958)

Anonymous, 'The Queen is Dead', *Gay Star (Belfast Bulletin of the Northern Ireland Gay Rights Association)* 1, p.8

Auden, W.H., *The Dyer's Hand, and Other Essays* (London, 1963)

——, *The Enchafèd Flood* (London, 1985)

——, *Forewords and Afterwords* (London, 1973)

Austen, Roger, 'But for Fate and Ban: Homosexual Villains and Victims in the Military', *College English* 36, 3 (Nov 1974) pp. 352–9

Bahlke, George W., *The Later Auden: from 'New Year Letter' to About the House* (N.Y., 1970)

Baker, Roger, 'Sorcery', *Gay News* 180 (Nov.1979) p.23

Barthes, Roland. *Critical Essays* (Evanston, 1972)

——, *Image-Music-Text* (N.Y., 1977)

——, *A Lover's Discourse* (N.Y., 1978)

——, *Mythologies* (London, 1972)

——, *The Pleasure of the Text* (London, 1976)

——, *Roland Barthes* (London, 1977)

——, *Sade/Fourier/Loyola* (N.Y., 1976)

——, *Writing Degree Zero* (London, 1967)

Bataille, Georges, *L'Érotisme* (Paris, 1957)

——, *Les Larmes d'Eros* (Paris, 1964)

——, *Visions of Excess: Selected Writings, 1927–1939* (Manchester, 1985)

Bateson, F.W., 'Auden's Last Poems', *Essays in Criticism* 25, 3 (July 1975) pp.383–90

Bayley, John, *The Romantic Survival* (London, 1957)

Bedford, William, 'Necromantism and Masochism: An Interview with James Kirkup', *London Magazine* 18, 4 (July 1978) pp.58–63

Blackmur, R.P., *Language as Gesture: Essays in Poetry* (Westport, Connecticut, 1977)

Blair, John G., *The Poetic Art of W.H. Auden* (Princeton, N.J., 1965)

Bloomfield, B.C., and Edward Mendelson, *W.H. Auden: A Bibliography, 1924–1969* (Charlottesville, Virginia, 1972)

Boatwright, James, ed., 'A Tribute to Wystan Hugh Auden on his Sixtieth Birthday', *Shenandoah: The Washington and Lee University Review* 18, 2 (Winter 1967)

Bold, Alan, *Thom Gunn and Ted Hughes* (Edinburgh, 1976)

Bolsterli, Margaret, 'Studies in Context: The Homosexual Ambiance of Twentieth Century Literary Culture', *D.H. Lawrence Review* 6 (1973) pp. 71–85

Bolt, Sidney, 'Thom Gunn: Words in the Head', *Delta* 43 (June 1968) pp.12–16

Boyers, Robert, 'The Ideology of the Steambath', *Times Literary Supplement*, 30 May 1980, pp.603–4

Boyers, Robert, and George Steiner, eds., 'Homosexuality: Sacrilege, Vision, Politics', *Salmagundi* 58–9 (Fall 1982–Winter 1983)

Boyette, Purvis E., 'Shakespeare's *Sonnets*: Homosexuality and the Critics', *Tulane Studies in English* 21 (1974) pp.35–46

Branch, Douglas, *The Cowboy and his Interpreters* (N.Y, 1961)

Broadbent, J.B., *Poetic Love* (London, 1964)

Brooks, Cleanth, *The Well Wrought Urn: Studies in the Structure of Poetry* (London, 1949)

Brown, Susan Jenkins, *Robber Rocks: Letters and Memories of Hart Crane, 1923–1932* (Middletown, Connecticut, 1969)

Brownjohn, Alan, 'The Poetry of Thom Gunn', *London Magazine* 2, 12 (March 1963) pp.45–52

Buchen, Irving, ed., *The Perverse Imagination: Sexuality and Literary Culture* (N.Y., 1970)

Buell, Frederick, *W.H. Auden as a Social Poet* (Ithaca, N.Y., 1973)

Butterfield, R.W., *The Broken Arc: A Study of Hart Crane* (Edinburgh, 1969)

Callan, Edward, 'Allegory in *The Age of Anxiety*', *Twentieth Century Literature* 10, 4 (Jan.1965) pp.155–65

Cambon, Glauco, *The Inclusive Flame: Studies in Modern American Poetry* (Bloomington, Indiana, 1965)

Greene, Gayle, and Coppélia Kahn, eds., *Making a Difference: Feminist Literary Criticism* (London, 1985)

Carpenter, Humphrey, *W.H. Auden: A Biography* (London, 1981)

Carter, Ronald, *W.H. Auden* (Milton Keynes, 1975)

Cassity, Turner, 'Palo Alto and the Pampa', *Parnassus: Poetry in Review* 5, 2 (Spring/Summer 1977) pp.243–55

Cockshut, A.O.J., *Man and Woman: A Study of Love and the Novel, 1740–1940* (London, 1977)

Combs, Robert, *Vision of the Voyage: Hart Crane and the Psychology of Romanticism* (Memphis, 1978)

Cook, Bruce, *The Beat Generation* (N.Y., 1971)

Coombes, H., *D.H. Lawrence: A Critical Anthology* (Harmondsworth, 1973)

Cox, R.G., *The Pelican Guide to English Literature, Volume 7: The Modern Age* (Harmondsworth, 1973)

Crew, Louie, ed., *The Gay Academic* (Palm Springs, Cal., 1978)

Crew, Louie, and Rictor Norton, 'The Homosexual Imagination', *College English* 36, 3 (Nov, 1974)

Croft-Cooke, Rupert, *Feasting with Panthers: A New Consideration of Some Late Victorian Writers* (London, 1967)

Dale, Peter, '*Fighting Terms, My Sad Captains* by Thom Gunn', *Agenda* 2, 7 and 8 (May-June 1962) pp.21–5

d'Arch Smith, Timothy, *Love in Earnest: Some Notes on the Lives and Writings of the English 'Uranian' Poets from 1889 to 1930* (London, 1970)

Davidson, Mildred, *The Poetry is in the Pity* (London, 1972)

Davie, Donald, *Pound* (Glasgow, 1975)

de Jongh, Nicholas, 'The Changing Face of the Brando Bard', *The Guardian* (14 Nov.1979), p.9

Delavenay, Emile, *D.H. Lawrence and Edward Carpenter: A Study in Edwardian Transition* (London, 1971)

Dembo, L.S., *Hart Crane's Sanskrit Charge: A Study of* The Bridge (Ithaca, N.Y., 1960)

DeMott, Benjamin, ' "But He's a Homosexual" ', *New American Review* 1 (Sept.1967) pp.166–82

Dewan, George, 'Bourgeoisification Time', *The Guardian* (9 June 1979), p.13

Dickey, James, *Babel to Byzantium: Poets and Poetry Now* (N.Y., 1973)

Dix, Carol, *D.H. Lawrence and Women* (London, 1980)

Dodsworth, Martin, *The Survival of Poetry* (London, 1970)

Duchêne, François, *The Case of the Helmeted Airman: A Study of W.H. Auden's Poetry* (London, 1972)

Eberhart, Richard, *Of Poetry and Poets* (Urbana, Illinois, 1979)

Eckman, Frederick, 'Neither Tame nor Fleecy', *Poetry* 90, 6 (Sept 1957) pp.386–97

Ellmann, Richard, 'Getting to Know You', *New York Review of Books* 27, 16 (23 Oct. 1980) pp.35–7

Empson, William, *Seven Types of Ambiguity* (London, 1930)

Enright, D.J., 'Reluctant Admiration. A Note on Auden and Rilke', *Essays in Criticism* 2, 2 (April 1952) pp.180–95

Evans, P.J.D., *Robert Duncan and American Poetry Since the First World War* (unpublished M. Phil. thesis, King's College, London, 1975)

Everett, Barbara, *Auden* (Edinburgh, 1964)

Faas, Ekbert, 'Ted Hughes and Crow', *London Magazine* 10, 10 (Jan.1971) pp.5–20

——, *Young Robert Duncan: Portrait of the Poet as Homosexual in Society* (Santa Barbara, Cal., 1983)

Falck, Colin, 'Uncertain Violence', *New Review* 3, 32 (Nov.1976) pp.37–41.

Fawcett, Andrea P. Mudry, *Personal and Social Themes in W.H. Auden* (unpublished M.Litt. thesis, University of Bristol, 1972)

Feder, Lillian, *Ancient Myth in Modern Poetry* (Princeton, N.J., 1971)

Fiedler, Leslie A., *An End to Innocence: Essays on Culture and Politics* (N.Y., 1972)

——, *Love and Death in the American Novel* (N.Y., 1960)

——, *The Return of the Vanishing American* (London, 1972)

——, *Waiting for the End: The American Literary Scene from Hemingway to Baldwin* (London, 1965)

Fowlie, Wallace, *Love in Literature: Studies in Symbolic Expression* (Bloomington, Indiana, 1965)

Frankenberg, Lloyd, *Pleasure Dome: On Reading Modern Poetry* (Cambridge, Mass., 1949)

Fraser, George, *Essays on Twentieth-Century Poets* (Leicester, 1977)

Fraser, G.S., 'The Poetry of Thom Gunn', *Critical Quarterly* 3, 4 (Winter 1961) pp.359–67

——, 'The Young Prophet', *New Statesman* 51, 1299 (28 Jan.1956) pp.102–3

Fraxi, Pisanus, *Bibliography of Prohibited Books* (N.Y., 1962)

Freeman, Gillian, *The Undergrowth of Literature* (London, 1967)

Fried, Michael, 'A Question of Form', *New Left Review* 12 (Nov.–Dec. 1961) pp.68–70

Friedman, Paul, 'The Bridge: A Study in Symbolism', *The Psychoanalytic Quarterly* 21, 1 (1952) pp.49–80

Fuller, John, *A Reader's Guide to W.H. Auden* (London, 1970)

——, 'Thom Gunn', *The Review* 1 (April/May 1962) pp.29–34

Fussell, Paul, *The Great War and Modern Memory* (London, 1975)

Gass, William, *A Philosophical Inquiry on Being Blue* (Boston, 1976)

Gifford, Don, with Robert J. Seidman, *Notes for Joyce: An Annotation of James Joyce's Ulysses* (N.Y., 1974)

Gilbert, Sandra M., *Acts of Attention: The Poems of D.H. Lawrence* (London, 1972)

Gingerich, Martin E., *W.H. Auden: A Reference Guide* (London, 1977)

Gnerre, Francesco, *L'eroe negato* (Milano, 1981)

Green, Martin, *Children of the Sun: A Narrative of 'Decadence' in England after 1918* (N.Y., 1976)

Greenberg, Herbert, *Quest for the Necessary: W.H. Auden and the Dilemma of Divided Consciousness* (Cambridge, Mass., 1968)

Grubb, Frederick, *A Vision of Reality: A Study of Liberalism in Twentieth-Century Verse* (London, 1965)

Gunn, Thom, *The Occasions of Poetry: Essays in Criticism and Autobiography* (London, 1982)

Haffenden, John, 'Early Auden', *PN Review* 5, 4 (1978) pp.11–13

Hagstrom, Jack W.C., and George Bixby, *Thom Gunn: A Bibliography 1940–1978* (London, 1979)

Hamilton, Ian, 'Four Conversations', *London Magazine* 4, 8 (Nov.1964) pp.64–85

Hardy, Barbara, *The Advantage of Lyric: Essays on Feeling in Poetry* (London, 1977)

Hassan, Ihab, *Contemporary American*

Literature 1945–1972: An Introduction (N.Y., 1973)

Hayman, Ronald, 'The City and the House: On Recent Poetry', *Encounter* 34, 2 (Feb. 1970) pp.84–91

Hazo, Samuel, *Hart Crane: An Introduction and Interpretation* (N.Y., 1963)

Henderson, Philip, *The Poet and Society* (London, 1939)

Henry, Gerrit, 'Starting from Scratch', *Poetry* 124 (May 1974) pp.292–9

Hinton, B.J.C., *The Poetry of Thom Gunn* (unpublished M.A. thesis, Birmingham University, 1974)

Hoggart, Richard, *Auden: An Introductory Essay* (London, 1951)

——, *Speaking to Each Other, Volume 2: About Literature* (London, 1970)

Homberger, Eric, *The Art of the Real: Poetry in England and America since 1939* (London, 1977)

Horton, Philip, *Hart Crane: The Life of an American Poet* (N.Y., 1957)

Hough, Graham, 'MacNeice and Auden', *Critical Quarterly* 9, 1 (Spring 1967) pp.9–17

Howard, Richard, *Alone with America: The Art of Poetry in the United States since 1950* (London, 1970)

——, 'Ecstasies and Decorum', *Parnassus: Poetry in Review* 2, 2 (Spring/Summer 1974) pp. 213–20

Hyde, H. Montgomery, *A History of Pornography* (London, 1964)

Hyde, Virginia M., 'The Pastoral Formula of W.H. Auden and Piero di Cosimo', *Contemporary Literature* 14, 3 (1973) pp.332–46

Hyman, Stanley Edgar, *Standards: A Chronicle of Books for Our Time* (N.Y., 1966)

Hynes, Samuel, *The Auden Generation: Literature and Politics in England in the 1930s* (London, 1976)

James, Clive, 'Auden's Achievement', *Commentary* 56, 6 (Dec.1973) pp.53–8

Jarrell, Randall, 'Freud to Paul: The Stages of Auden's Ideology', *Partisan Review* 12, 4 (1945) pp.437–57

Johnson, Richard, *Man's Place: An Essay on Auden* (Ithaca, N.Y., 1973)

Johnson, Wendell Stacy, 'Auden, Hopkins, and the Poetry of Reticence', *Twentieth Century Literature* 20, 3 (July 1974) pp.165–71

Kermode, Frank, *The Genesis of Secrecy: On the Interpretation of Narrative* (Cambridge, Mass., 1979)

——, *Modern Essays* (London, 1971)

Kirby, David K., 'Snyder, Auden, and the New Morality', *Notes on Contemporary Literature* 1, 1 (Jan.1971) pp.9–10

Kramer, Jane, *Paterfamilias: Allen Ginsberg in America* (London, 1970)

Lawrence, D.H., *Phoenix II: Uncollected, Unpublished and Other Prose Works* (London, 1968)

Leibowitz, Herbert A., *Hart Crane: An Introduction to the Poetry* (N.Y., 1968)

Lewis, R.W.B., *The Poetry of Hart Crane: A Critical Study* (Princeton, N.J., 1967)

Longley, Edna, 'The British', *Times Literary Supplement* 4008 (18 January 1980) pp.64–5

Lowell, Amy, *Poetry and Poets* (N.Y., 1971)

Lutyens, David Bulwer, *The Creative Encounter* (London, 1960)

Lyon, Jr., George W., 'Allen Ginsberg: Angel Headed Hipster', *Journal of Popular Culture* (Winter 1969) pp.391–403

Mander, John, *The Writer and Commitment* (London, 1961)

Marshall, Tom, *The Psychic Mariner: A Reading of the Poems of D.H. Lawrence* (London, 1970)

Martin, Robert K., 'Crane's *The Bridge*, The Tunnel, 58–60', *The Explicator* 34, 2 (Oct, 1975) 16

——, 'Criticizing the Critics: A Gay Perspective', *Gay Sunshine* 35 (Winter 1978) pp. 24–5

——, *The Homosexual Tradition in American Poetry* (Austin, Texas, 1979)

Maxwell, D.E.S., *Poets of the Thirties* (London, 1969)

Mazzaro, Jerome, *Postmodern American Poetry* (Urbana, Illinois, 1980)

McDiarmid, Lucy S., 'Auden and the Redeemed City: Three Allusions', *Criticism* 13, 4 (Fall 1971) pp.340–50

Megaw, Moira, 'Auden's First Poems', *Essays in Criticism* 25, 3 (July 1975) pp.378–82

Mendelson, Edward, 'The Auden-Isherwood Collaboration', *Twentieth Century Literature* 22, 3 (Oct. 1976) pp.276–85

——, *Early Auden* (London, 1981)

Merrill, Thomas F., *Allen Ginsberg* (N.Y., 1969)

Mersmann, James F, *Out of the Vietnam Vortex: A Study of Poets and Poetry Against the War* (Lawrence, Kansas, 1974)

Meyers, Jeffrey, *Homosexuality and Literature, 1890–1930* (London, 1977)

Michell, John, *To Represent Our Saviour as 'that great cock' (Kirkup-Gay News) is not Blasphemy but Eternal and Christian*

Orthodoxy (London, 1977)

Middlebrook, Diane, 'Bound Each to Each', *Parnassus: Poetry in Review* (Spring/Summer 1974) pp.128–35

Miller, Casey, and Kate Swift, *Words and Women: New Language in New Times* (Harmondsworth, 1979)

Miller, Jr., James E., *T.S. Eliot's Personal Waste Land* (University Park, Pennsylvania, 1977)

Millett, Kate, *Sexual Politics* (N.Y., 1969)

Moore, Gerald, 'Luck in Auden', *Essays in Criticism* 7, 1 (Jan.1957) pp.103–8

Morgan, Kathleen E., *Christian Themes in Contemporary Poets: A Study of English Poetry of the Twentieth Century* (London, 1965)

Morrison, Blake, *The Movement: English Poetry and Fiction of the 1950s* (Oxford, 1980)

Mottram, Eric, *Allen Ginsberg in the Sixties* (Brighton/Seattle, 1972)

Muecke, D.C., *Irony and the Ironic* (London, 1970)

Murry, J. Middleton, *Son of Woman* (London, 1931)

Nelson, Gerald, *Changes of Heart: A Study in the Poetry of W.H. Auden* (L.A., 1969)

Norton, Rictor, *The Homosexual Literary Tradition: An Interpretation* (N.Y., 1974)

Nykl, A.R., *Hispano-Arabic Poetry and its Relations with the Old Provençal Troubadours* (Baltimore, 1946)

Osborne, Charles, *W.H. Auden: The Life of a Poet* (N.Y., 1979)

Owen, Guy, ed., *Modern American Poetry: Essays in Criticism* (DeLand, Florida, 1972)

Panahi, Mir Mohammad Hassani, *The Ethic of Love: The Philosophical Development of W.H. Auden's Poetry, 1922–1960* (Unpublished Ph.D. thesis, Exeter University, 1966)

Parini, Jay, 'Rule and Energy: The Poetry of Thom Gunn', *The Massachusetts Review* 23, 1 (Spring 1982) pp.134–51

Parkinson, Thomas, ed., *A Casebook on the Beat* (N.Y., 1961)

Partridge, Eric, *Shakespeare's Bawdy: A Literary and Psychological Essay and a Comprehensive Glossary* (London, 1968)

Paul, Sherman, *Hart's Bridge* (Urbana, Illinois, 1972)

Peter, John, 'A New Interpretation of *The Waste Land*', *Essays in Criticism* 19, 2 (April 1969) pp.140–75

Pinto, Vivian de Sola, *Crisis in English Poetry, 1880–1940* (London, 1951)

Pittenger, Norman, 'Wystan and Morgan', *Gay News* 156 (Nov.–Dec. 1978) pp.22–4

Powell, Neil, 'The Abstract Joy: Thom Gunn's Early Poetry', *Critical Quarterly* 13, 3 (Autumn 1971) pp.219–27

——, *Carpenters of Light: Some Contemporary English Poets* (Manchester, 1979)

Press, John, *Rule and Energy: Trends in English Poetry Since the Second World War* (London, 1963)

Pritchard, William H., *Seeing Through Everything: English Writers 1918–1940* (London, 1977)

Quinn, Sister M. Bernetta, *The Metaphoric Tradition in Modern Poetry* (N.Y., 1972)

Quinn, Vincent, *Hart Crane* (N.Y., 1963)

Ramsey, Roger, 'A Poetics for *The Bridge*', *Twentieth Century Literature* 26, 3 (Fall 1980) pp.278–93

Reeves, James, *Commitment to Poetry* (London, 1969)

Replogle, Justin, *Auden's Poetry* (London, 1969)

Rosenthal, M.L., *The Modern Poets: A Critical Introduction* (N.Y., 1960)

——, *The New Poets: American and British Poetry Since World War II* (N.Y., 1967)

Rowse, A.L., *Homosexuals in History: A Study of Ambivalence in Society, Literature and the Arts* (London, 1977)

Sarver, Tony, 'Thom Gunn', *Gay News* 134, pp.16, 26

Savage, D.S., *The Personal Principle: Studies in Modern Poetry* (London, 1944)

Scarfe, Francis, *Auden and After: The Liberation of Poetry, 1930–1941* (London, 1942)

Scheckner, Mark, 'The Survival of Allen Ginsberg', *Partisan Review* 46, 1 (1979) pp.105–12

Schmidt, Michael, *A Reader's Guide to Fifty Modern British Poets* (London, 1979)

Scobie, W.I., 'Gunn in America: A Conversation in San Francisco', *London Magazine* 17, 6 (Dec.1977) pp.5–15

Scott, Jr., Nathan A., 'The Poetry of Auden', *London Magazine* 8, 1 (Jan.1961) pp.44–63

Shurin, Aaron, and Steve Abbott, 'Interview: Robert Duncan', *Gay Sunshine* 40/41 (Summer/Fall 1979) pp.1–8

Smith, Elton Edward, *The Angry Young Men of the Thirties* (Carbondale, Illinois, 1975)

Smith, Stan, *W.H. Auden* (Oxford, 1985)

Sonnichsen, C.L., *From Hopalong to Hud: Thoughts on Western Fiction* (College Station, Texas, 1978)

Sontag, Susan, 'Notes on "Camp"', *Partisan Review* 31, 4 (Fall 1964) pp.515–30

——, 'The Pornographic Imagination', *Partisan Review* 34, 2 (Spring 1967) pp.181–212

Southworth, James, G., *Sowing the Spring: Studies in British Poets from Hopkins to MacNeice* (Oxford, 1940)

——, *More Modern American Poets* (London, 1954)

Spears, Monroe K., *The Poetry of W.H. Auden: The Disenchanted Island* (N.Y., 1963)

Spears, Monroe K., ed., *Auden: A Collection of Critical Essays* (Englewood Cliffs, N.J., 1964)

Spender, Stephen, *The Destructive Element: A Study of Modern Writers and Beliefs* (London, 1935)

——, 'W.H. Auden (1907–1973)', *Partisan Review* 40, 3 (1973) pp.546–8

Spender, Stephen, ed., *D.H. Lawrence: Novelist, Poet, Prophet* (London, 1973)

——, *W.H. Auden: A Tribute* (London, 1975)

Stambolian, George, and Elaine Marks, *Homosexualities and French Literature: Cultural Contexts/Critical Texts* (Ithaca, N.Y., 1979)

Steckmesser, Kent Ladd, *The Western Hero in History and Legend* (Norman, Oklahoma, 1965)

Steiner, George, *After Babel: Aspects of Language and Translation* (Oxford, 1975)

——, *Extraterritorial: Papers on Literature and the Language Revolution* (London, 1972)

——, *Heidegger* (London, 1978)

——, *In Bluebeard's Castle: Some Notes Towards the Re-definition of Culture* (London, 1971)

——, *Language and Silence: Essays 1958–1966* (London, 1967)

——, *On Difficulty, and Other Essays* (Oxford, 1978)

Stepanchev, Stephen, *American Poetry Since 1945: A Critical Survey* (N.Y., 1965)

Stimpson, Catharine R., 'Thom Gunn: The Redefinition of Place', *Contemporary Literature* 18, 3 (Summer 1977) pp.391–404

Sugg, Richard P., *Hart Crane's The Bridge: A Description of its Life* (University, Alabama, 1976)

Summerfield, Geoffrey, ed., *Worlds: Seven Modern Poets* (Harmondsworth, 1974)

Sutherland, John, *Offensive Literature: Decensorship in Britain, 1960–1982* (London, 1982)

Swinden, Patrick, 'Thom Gunn's Castle', *Critical Quarterly* 19, 3 (Autumn 1977) pp.43–61

Tate, Allen, ed., *Six American Poets from Emily Dickinson to the Present: An Introduction* (Minneapolis, 1966)

Thirlby, Peter, 'Thom Gunn – Violence and Tenderness', *Delta* 8 (Spring 1956) pp.16–21

Thody, Philip, 'Jean Genet and the Indefensibility of Sexual Deviation', *20th Century Studies* 2 (Nov.1969) pp.68–73

Thompson, John, 'A Poetry Chronicle', *Poetry* 95, 2 (Nov.1959) pp.107–16

Thurley, Geoffrey, *The American Moment: American Poetry in Mid-Century* (London, 1977)

——, *The Ironic Harvest: English Poetry in the Twentieth Century* (London, 1974)

Thwaite, Anthony, *Twentieth-Century English Poetry: An Introduction* (London, 1978)

——, *Contemporary English Poetry: An Introduction* (London, 1959)

Trilling, Diana, 'The Other Night at Columbia: A Report from the Academy', *Partisan Review* 26, 2 (Spring 1959) pp.214–30

Trudgill, Peter, *Sociolinguistics: An Introduction* (Harmondsworth, 1974)

Tytell, John, *Naked Angels: The Lives and Literature of the Beat Generation* (N.Y., 1976)

Unterecker, John, *Voyager: A Life of Hart Crane* (London, 1970)

Uroff, M.D., *Hart Crane: The Patterns of his Poetry* (Urbana, Illinois, 1974)

Vinson, James, ed., *Contemporary Poets* (London, 1975)

Vogler, Thomas A., *Preludes to Vision: The Epic Adventure in Blake, Wordsworth, Keats, and Hart Crane* (Berkeley, Cal., 1971)

Waggoner, Hyatt Howe, *The Heel of Elohim: Science and Values in Modern American Poetry* (Norman, Oklahoma, 1950)

Wain, John, *Professing Poetry* (London, 1977)

Weatherhead, A. Kingsley, *The Edge of the Image: Marianne Moore, William Carlos Williams and Some Other Poets* (Seattle, 1967)

——, 'The Good Place in the Latest Poems of W.H. Auden', *Twentieth Century Literature* 10, 3 (Oct. 1964) pp.99–107

——, 'Robert Duncan and the Lyric', *Contemporary Literature* 16, 2 (1975) pp.163–74

Weber, Brom, *Hart Crane: A Biographical and Critical Study* (N.Y., 1948)

Whitehead, John, 'Auden: An Early Poetical Notebook', *London Magazine* 5, 2 (May 1965) pp.85–93

——, 'The Auden Gravy Train', *New Review* 3, 32 (Nov.1976) pp.60–2

Wilson, Edmund, *The Bit Between My Teeth: A Literary Chronicle of 1950–1965* (N.Y., 1966)

Winters, Yvor, *On Modern Poets* (Cleveland, Ohio, 1959)

Woods, Gregory, *Functions of Sex in the Novels of William Burroughs* (unpublished M.A. thesis, University of East Anglia, 1975)

——, 'The Gay Sensibility in the Arts', *The European Gay Review* 1 (Nov.1986) pp.17–24

Wright, George T., *W.H. Auden* (N.Y., 1969)

Young, Ian, ed., *The Male Homosexual in Literature: A Bibliography* (Metuchen, N.J., 1975; second edition, 1982)

SEXUALITY

(Texts with cultural, historical, legal, political, psychological, sociological, or theological reference to sexuality in general, or to homosexuality in particular.)

Abbot, Sidney, and Barbara Love, *Sappho was a Right-on Woman: A Liberated View of Lesbianism* (N.Y., 1972)

Altman, Dennis, *Coming Out in the Seventies* (Boston, 1981)

——, *Homosexual: Oppression and Liberation* (London, 1974)

Anderson, Charles, 'On Certain Conscious and Unconscious Homosexual Responses to Warfare', *British Journal of Medical Psychology* 20, 2 (1944) pp.161–74

Aronson, Gerald J., 'Delusion of Pregnancy in a Male Homosexual with Abdominal Cancer', *Bulletin of the Meninger Clinic* 16, 5 (1952) pp.159–66

Bailey, Derrick Sherwin, *Homosexuality and the Western Christian Tradition* (London, 1955)

Beurdelay, Cecile, *L'Amour bleu* (N.Y., 1978)

Blamires, David, *Homosexuality from the Inside* (London, 1973)

Boswell, John, *Christianity, Social Tolerance, and Homosexuality: Gay People in Western Europe from the Beginning of the Christian Era to the Fourteenth Century* (Chicago, 1980)

Bourke, John G., *Scatologic Rites of All Nations* (Washington D.C., 1891)

Brain, Robert, *Friends and Lovers* (London, 1976)

Bronski, Michael, *Culture Clash: The Making of Gay Sensibility* (Boston, 1984)

Brown, Norman O., *Love's Body* (N.Y., 1966)

Brown, Paul T., 'On the Differentiation of Homo- or Heteroerotic Interest in the Male: An Operant Technique Illustrated in a Case of Motor-Cycle Fetishist', *Behaviour Research and Therapy* 2, 1 (1964) pp.31–5

Brownmiller, Susan, *Against Our Will: Men, Women and Rape* (London, 1975)

Bullough, Vern L., *Sexual Variance in Society and History* (N.Y., 1976)

Carpenter, Edward, *The Intermediate Sex: A Study of Some Transitional Types of Men and Women* (London, 1916)

——, *Intermediate Types Among Primitive Folk: A Study in Social Evolution* (London, 1919)

Carpenter, Edward, ed., *Ioläus: An Anthology of Friendship* (London, 1906)

Chesler, Phyllis, *About Men* (London, 1978)

Clarke, Lige, and Jack Nichols, *Roommates Can't Always Be Lovers: An Intimate Guide to Male-Male Relationships* (N.Y., 1974)

Cleugh, James, *Love Locked Out: A Survey of Love, Licence and Restriction in the Middle Ages* (London, 1964)

Cohen, Steve, Stephanie Green, Lesley Merryfinch, Gay Jones, Janet Slade and Maggie Walker, *The Law and Sexuality: How to Cope if You're not 100% Conventionally Heterosexual* (Manchester, 1978)

Cory, Donald Webster, *The Homosexual in America* (N.Y., 1951)

Cossolo, Felix, and Ivan Teobaldelli, *Cercando il paradiso perduto* (Milano, 1981)

Daly, Mary, *Gyn/Ecology: The Metaethics of Radical Feminism* (Boston, 1978)

D'Arcangelo, Angelo, *The Homosexual Handbook* (London, 1971)

De Becker, Raymond, *The Other Face of Love* (London, 1967)

Denneny, Michael, Charles Ortleb and Thomas Steele, *The View from Christopher Street* (London, 1984)

Dover, K.J., *Greek Homosexuality* (London, 1978)

Duvert, Tony, *Le Bon Sexe illustré* (Paris, 1974)
——, *L'Enfant au masculin* (Paris, 1980)
Dworkin, Andrea, *Pornography: Men Possessing Women* (N.Y., 1981)
Edwardes, Allen, *The Jewel in the Lotus: A Historical Survey of the Sexual Culture in the East* (London, 1965)
Edwardes, Allen, and R.E.L. Masters, *The Cradle of Erotica: A Study of Afro-Asian Sexual Expression and an Analysis of Erotic Freedom in Social Relationships* (N.Y., 1962)
Eglinton, J.Z., *Greek Love* (London, 1971)
Ellis, Havelock, *Psychology of Sex* (London, 1933)
——, *Studies in the Psychology of Sex* (Philadelphia, 1928)
Fischer, Hal, *Gay Semiotics: A Photographic Study of Visual Coding Among Homosexual Men* (San Francisco, 1977)
Foucault, Michel, *The History of Sexuality, Volume One: An Introduction* (Harmondsworth, 1981)
Frankl, George, *The Failure of the Sexual Revolution* (London, 1975)
Freud, Sigmund, *An Infantile Neurosis, and Other Works* (London, 1955)
——, *Leonardo da Vinci: A Memory of his Childhood* (London, 1957)
——, *On Sexuality: Three Essays on the Theory of Sexuality, and Other Works* (Harmondsworth, 1977)
——, *Three Contributions to the Theory of Sex* (N.Y., 1920)
Fromm, Erich, *The Forgotten Language: An Introduction to the Understanding of Dreams, Fairy Tales and Myths* (N.Y., 1957)
Gay Left Collective, *Homosexuality: Power and Politics* (London, 1980)
Gide, André, *Corydon: Four Socratic Dialogues* (London, 1952)
Goodman, Paul, 'The Politics of Being Queer', *Nature Heals: The Psychological Essays* (N.Y., 1977) pp.216–25
Greene, Gerald and Caroline, *S–M: The Last Taboo* (N.Y., 1974)
Heger, Heinz, *The Men with the Pink Triangle* (London, 1980)
Hocquenghem, Guy, *Homosexual Desire* (London, 1978)
Hodges, Andrew, and David Hutter, *With Downcast Gays: Aspects of Homosexual Self-Oppression* (London, n.d.)
Honoré, Tony, *Sex Law* (London, 1978)
Humphreys, Laud, *Out of the Closets: The Sociology of Homosexual Liberation* (Englewood Cliffs, N.J., 1972)
——, *Tearoom Trade: Impersonal Sex in Public Places* (Chicago, 1975)
Hyde, H. Montgomery, *The Other Love: An Historical and Contemporary Survey of Homosexuality in Britain* (London, 1970)
Jay, Karla, and Allen Young, *Lavender Culture* (N.Y., 1978)
Jung, C.G., *Symbols of Transformation: An Analysis of the Prelude to a Case of Schizophrenia* (London, 1967)
Katz, Jonathan, *Gay American History: Lesbians and Gay Men in the U.S.A.* (N.Y., 1976)
Kinsey, Alfred C., Wardell B. Pomeroy and Clyde E. Martin, *Sexual Behavior in the Human Male* (Philadelphia, 1948)
Knight, James A., 'False Pregnancy in a Male', *Psychosomatic Medicine* 22, 4 (1960) pp. 260–6
Krafft-Ebing, Richard von, *Psychopathia Sexualis* (N.Y, 1965)
Lacan, Jacques, *Écrits: A Selection* (London, 1977)
Lancini, Fiorenzo, and Paolo Sangalli, *La gaia musa* (Milano, 1981)
Lauritsen, John, and David Thorstad, *The Early Homosexual Rights Movement (1864–1935)* (N.Y., 1974)
Lawrence, D.H., *Sex, Literature and Censorship* (London, 1955)
Levi, Corrado, *New kamasutra: didattica sadomasochistica* (Milano, 1979)
Leyland, Winston, ed., *Flesh: True Homosexual Experiences from S.T.H., Volume 2* (San Francisco, 1982)
——, *Gay Sunshine Interview Anthology (Volume 1)* (San Francisco, 1978)
——, *Gay Sunshine Interviews II* (San Francisco, 1982)
Loovis, David, *Gay Spirit: A Guide to Becoming a Sensuous Homosexual* (N.Y., 1974)
Macourt, Malcolm, ed., *Towards a Theology of Gay Liberation* (London, 1977)
Magee, Bryan, *One in Twenty: A Study of Homosexuality in Men and Women* (London, 1966)
Marcus, Steven, *The Other Victorians: A Study of Sexuality and Pornography in Mid-Nineteenth Century England* (London, 1966)
Marcuse, Herbert, *Eros and Civilization* (London, 1969)
Masters, William Howell, and Virginia E. Johnson, *Homosexuality in Perspective* (N.Y., 1979)
——, *Human Sexual Response* (Boston,

1966)

McCaffrey, Joseph A., ed., *The Homosexual Dialectic* (Englewood Cliffs, N.J., 1972)

McDonald, Boyd, ed., *Cum: True Homosexual Experiences from S.T.H. Writers, Volume 4* (San Francisco, 1983)

——, *Sex: True Homosexual Experiences from S.T.H. Writers, Volume 3* (San Francisco, 1982)

Meat: How Men Look, Act, Walk, Talk, Dress, Undress, Taste, and Smell: True Homosexual Experiences from S.T.H. (San Francisco, 1981)

Mieli, Mario, *Homosexuality and Liberation: Elements of a Gay Critique* (London, 1980)

Miller, Leo, 'Il fiore nero', *FUORI!* 16 (autonno 1976) p.40

Milligan, Don, *The Politics of Homosexuality* (London, 1973)

Mitchell, Juliet, *Psychoanalysis and Feminism* (London, 1974)

Mitchell, Michael J., 'Erotic S & M Amongst Gays', *Gay News* 108 (Dec.1976) p.17

Money, John, and Geoffrey Hosta, 'Negro Folklore of Male Pregnancy', *Journal of Sex Research* 4, 1 (1968) pp.34–50

Morse, Benjamin, *The Homosexual* (Derby, Connecticut, 1962)

Nafzawi, Shaykh, *The Glory of the Perfumed Garden* (London, 1978)

Nichols, Jack, *Men's Liberation: A New Definition of Masculinity* (N.Y., 1975)

Ortega y Gasset, José, *On Love . . . Aspects of a Single Theme* (London, 1967)

Pešek-Marouš, Georgia, *The Bull: A Religious and Secular History of Phallus Worship and Male Homosexuality* (Rolling Hills, Cal., 1984)

Pezzana, Angelo, ed., *La politica del corpo: antologia del 'Fuori', movimento di liberazione omosessuale* (Roma, 1976)

Philska, Bernard, 'Les Chaînes du sexe: quelques questions à un *fist-fucké*', *Gai Pied* 31 (Oct.1981) pp.46–7

Plato, *The Symposium* (Harmondsworth, 1951)

Plutarch, *The Dialogue on Love*, in *Plutarch's Moralia* IX (London, 1969)

Policy Advisory Committee on Sexual Offences, *Working Paper on the Age of Consent in Relation to Sexual Offences* (London, 1979)

Praunheim, Rosa von, *Army of Lovers* (London, 1980)

Reade, Brian, ed., *Sexual Heretics; Male Homosexuality in English Literature from 1859 to 1900* (London, 1970)

Rechy, John, *The Sexual Outlaw: A Documentary. A Non-Fiction Account, with Commentaries, of Three Days and Nights in The Sexual Underground* (London, 1978)

Rector, Frank, *The Nazi Extermination of Homosexuals* (N.Y., 1981)

Reich, Wilhelm, *The Function of the Orgasm: Sex-Economic Problems of Biological Energy* (N.Y., 1942)

Reim, Riccardo, Laura di Nola and Antonio Veneziani, *Pratiche innominabili: violenza pubblica e privata contro gli omosessuali* (Milano, 1979)

Richards, Janet Radcliffe, *The Sceptical Feminist: A Philosophical Enquiry* (Harmondsworth, 1982)

Richmond, Len, and Gary Noguera, eds., *The Gay Liberation Book* (San Francisco, 1973)

Rodgers, Bruce, *The Queen's Vernacular: A Gay Lexicon* (London, 1972)

Rougemont, Denis de, *Passion and Society* (London, 1940)

Saslow, James, *Ganymede in the Renaissance: Homosexuality in Art and Society* (New Haven, Connecticut, 1986)

Severn, Bradley, *Intersexuality. Vol 1: The Bi-sexual Male* (Canoga Park, Cal., 1970)

Shuttle, Penelope, and Peter Redgrove, *The Wise Wound: Menstruation and Everywoman* (London, 1978)

Snodgrass, Jon, ed., *A Book of Readings for Men Against Sexism* (Albion, Cal., 1977)

Socialist Workers Party Gay Group, *The Word is Gay* (London, 1979)

Steinberg, Leo, 'The Sexuality of Christ in Renaissance Art and in Modern Oblivion', *October* 25 (Summer 1983)

Stendhal, *Love* (Harmondsworth, 1975)

Stopes, Marie Carmichael, *Married Love: A New Contribution to the Solution of Sex Difficulties* (N.Y., 1918)

Sutherland, Alistair, and Patrick Anderson, eds., *Eros: An Anthology of Friendship* (London, 1961)

Szasz, Thomas S., *The Manufacture of Madness: A Comparative Study of the Inquisition and the Mental Health Movement* (N.Y., 1970)

Tarnowsky, Benjamin, *Anthropological, Legal and Medical Studies on Pederasty in Europe* (N. Hollywood, Cal., 1967)

Taylor, G. Rattray, *Sex in History* (London, 1965)

Tiger, Lionel, *Men in Groups* (London, 1965)

Townsend, Larry, *The Leatherman's Handbook II* (N.Y., 1972)

Vātsyāyana, *The Kama Sutra of Vatsyayana* (London, 1963)

Walker, Benjamin, *Encyclopaedia of Esoteric Man* (London, 1977)

Walker, Mitch, *Men Loving Men: A Gay Sex Guide and Consciousness Book* (San Francisco, 1977)

Walter, Aubrey, ed., *Come Together: The Years of Gay Liberation (1970–73)* (London, 1980)

Webb, Peter, *The Erotic Arts* (London, 1983)

Weeks, Jeffrey, *Coming Out: Homosexual Politics in Britain, from the Nineteenth Century to the Present* (London, 1977)

Weinberg, Martin S., and Alan P. Bell, *Homosexuality: An Annotated Bibliography* (N.Y., 1972)

West, D.J., *Homosexuality* (London, 1955)

——, *Homosexuality* (Harmondsworth, 1960)

——, *Homosexuality* (Harmondsworth, 1968)

——, *Homosexuality Re-examined* (London, 1977)

Young, Wayland, *Studies in Exclusion I: Eros Denied* (London, 1965)

BACKGROUND POETRY

Alighieri, Dante, *Dante's Inferno* (London, 1933)

——, *Dante's Paradiso* (London, 1943)

——. *Dante's Purgatorio* (London, 1938)

Ariosto, Ludovico, *Orlando Furioso* (Harmondsworth, 1975)

Barnfield, Richard, *Poems 1594–1598* (London 1896)

Browne of Tavistock, William, *Poems of William Browne of Tavistock* (London, 1894)

Carpenter, Edward, *Towards Democracy* (London, 1892)

Catullus, Gaius Valerius, *The Poems of Catullus* (Harmondsworth, 1966)

Cavafy, C.P., *The Complete Poems of Cavafy* (London, 1961)

——, *Passions and Ancient Days: 21 New Poems* (London, 1972)

——, *The Poems of C.P. Cavafy* (London, 1951)

Cavafy, C.P., George Seferis, Odysseus Elytis and Nikos Gatsos, *Four Greek Poets* (Harmondsworth, 1966)

Cernuda, Luis, *The Poetry of Luis Cernuda* (N.Y., 1971)

——, *Selected Poems of Luis Cernuda* (Berkeley, Cal., 1977)

Chaucer, Geoffrey, *The Works of Geoffrey Chaucer* (London, 1966)

Cocteau, Jean, *Le Cap de Bonne-Espérance* (Paris, 1967)

——, *Poèmes 1916–1959* (Paris, 1956)

Coote, Stephen, ed., *The Penguin Book of Homosexual Verse* (Harmondsworth, 1983)

Crowley, Aleister, *White Stains* (London, 1973)

Dolben, Digby Mackworth, *The Poems of Digby Mackworth Dolben* (London, 1911)

Drummond of Hawthornden, William, *The Poetical Works of William Drummond of Hawthornden* (London, 1856)

Duffy, Maureen, *The Venus Touch* (London, 1971)

The Epic of Gilgamesh (Harmondsworth, 1970)

Faber, Frederick William, *Poems* (London, 1856)

Fletcher, Giles and Phineas, *Poetical Works* (Cambridge, 1970)

Genet, Jean, *Poèmes* (Paris, 1948)

George, Stefan, *Poems* (N.Y., 1967)

Goethe, J.W. von, *Poetical Works* (London, 1903)

Hesse, Hermann, *Poems* (London, 1971)

Holden, Anthony, ed., *Greek Pastoral Poetry: Theocritus, Bion, Moschus, the Pattern Poems* (Harmondsworth, 1974)

Hopkins, Gerard Manley, *Poems* (London, 1948)

Jay, Peter, ed., *The Greek Anthology and Other Ancient Greek Epigrams: A Selection in Modern Verse Translations* (London, 1973)

John of the Cross, Saint, *The Poems of St John of the Cross* (London, 1951)

Juvenal, *The Sixteen Satires* (Harmondsworth, 1967)

Kazantzakis, Nikos, *The Odyssey: A Modern Sequel* (London, 1959)

Klyuev, Nikolai, *Poems* (Ann Arbor, Michigan, 1977)

Kuzmin, Mikhail, *Wings: Prose and Poetry* (Ann Arbor, Michigan, 1972)

Lautréamont, *Oeuvres Complètes* (Paris, 1969)

Lorca, Federico García, *Selected Poetry* (Harmondsworth, 1960)

Lysohorsky, Ondra, *Selected Poems* (London, 1971)

Marlowe, Christopher, *The Complete Poems and Translations* (Harmondsworth, 1971)

Michelangelo, *The Sonnets of Michelangelo* (London, 1967)

Milton, John, *The Complete Poetical Works of John Milton* (London, n.d.)

Neruda, Pablo, *New Poems (1968–1970)* (N.Y., 1972)

——, *Twenty Love Poems and a Song of Despair* (London, 1969)

Newman, John Henry, *The Dream of Gerontius, and Other Poems* (London, 1914)

Ovid, *The Art of Love, and Other Poems* (Cambridge, Mass., 1969)

——, *The Metamorphoses* (N.Y., 1958)

Paris, Renzo, and Antonio Veneziani, eds., *L'amicizia amorosa: antologia della poesia omosessuale italiana dal XIII Secolo a oggi* (Milano, 1982)

Pasolini, Pier Paolo, *Roman Poems* (San Francisco, 1986)

——, *Selected Poems* (London, 1984)

Penna, Sandro, *Confuso sogno* (Milano, 1980)

——, *Tutte le poesie* (Milano, 1970)

Plath, Sylvia, *Ariel* (London, 1965)

——, *Crossing the Water* (London, 1971)

——, *Winter Trees* (London, 1971)

Radiguet, Raymond, *Collected Poems: Cheeks on Fire* (London, 1976)

Rimbaud, Arthur, *Complete Works, Selected Letters* (Chicago, 1966)

——, *Oeuvres* (Paris, 1960)

Rimbaud, Arthur, and Paul Verlaine, *A Lover's Cock, and Other Gay Poems* (San Francisco, 1979)

Ritsos, Yannis, *Selected Poems* (Harmondsworth, 1974)

——, 'Twelve Poems for Cavafy', *Modern Poetry in Translation* 4 (1968)

Rochester, John Wilmot, Earl of, *The Complete Poems of John Wilmot, Earl of Rochester* (New Haven, Connecticut, 1968)

Rolfe, Frederick, *Collected Poems* (London, 1974)

Santayana, George, *Poems of George Santayana* (N.Y., 1970)

Seferis, George, *Collected Poems 1924–1955* (London, 1969)

Shakespeare, William, *The Sonnets* (N.Y., 1965)

The Song of Roland (Harmondsworth, 1957)

Stone, Brian, ed., *Medieval English Verse* (Harmondsworth, 1964)

Takahashi Mutsuo, *A Bunch of Keys* (Trumansburg, N.Y., 1984)

——, *Poems of a Penisist* (Chicago, 1975)

Tasso, Torquato, *Gerusalemme Liberata* (London, 1806)

Tennyson, Alfred Lord, *Enoch Arden, and In Memoriam* (London, 1888)

Theognis, *Elegies*, in *Hesiod and Theognis* (Harmondsworth, 1973)

Thoreau, Henry, *Collected Poems of Henry Thoreau* (Baltimore, 1964)

Traherne, Thomas, *Centuries of Meditations* (London, 1908)

Ungaretti, Giuseppe, *Selected Poems* (Harmondsworth, 1971)

Verlaine, Paul, *Selected Poems* (Harmondsworth, 1974)

Waddell, Helen, *Medieval Latin Lyrics* (Harmondsworth, 1952)

Whitman, Walt, *Complete Poetry & Selected Prose and Letters* (London, 1938)

Wilde, Oscar, *Charmides, and Other Poems* (London, 1913)

——, *De Profundis, and Other Writings* (Harmondsworth, 1973)

PROSE FICTION

(The following three sections, on fiction, drama, and film, are not meant as exhaustive lists of works containing homo-erotic material. They only include items which were of use in the writing of this book.)

Aldiss, Brian, *The Hand-Reared Boy* (London, 1970)

——, *A Soldier Erect, or Further Adventures of the Hand-Reared Boy* (London, 1971)

Amory, Richard, *Frost* (London, 1972)

Anderson, Sherwood, *Horses and Men* (N.Y., 1923)

Andrzeyevski, George, *The Gates of Paradise* (London, 1962)

Anonymous, *Teleny, or the Reverse of the Medal: A Physiological Romance of Today* (London, 1966)

Apuleius, *The Golden Ass* (Harmondsworth, 1950)

Baldwin, James, *Another Country* (N.Y., 1962)

——, *Giovanni's Room* (N.Y., 1956)

Ballard, J.G., *The Atrocity Exhibition* (London, 1970)

Barr, James, *Quatrefoil* (N.Y., 1950)

Bassani, Giorgio, *Gli occhiali d'oro* (Torino, 1962)

Bataille, Georges, *Story of the Eye* (London, 1979)

Baxter, Walter, *Look Down in Mercy* (London, 1951)

——, *Look Down in Mercy* (N.Y., 1952)

Borges, Jorge Luis, *Ficciones* (London, 1962)

Bradbury, Ray, *The Illustrated Man* (London, 1952)

Bradford, Edwin Emmanuel, *Boris Orloff: A Christmas Yarn* (London, 1968)

Burns, John Horne, *The Gallery* (N.Y., 1947)

Burroughs, William, *The Naked Lunch* (N.Y., 1959)

——, *The Wild Boys: A Book of the Dead* (N.Y., 1971)

Campbell, Michael, *Lord Dismiss Us* (N.Y., 1968)

Capitanchik, Maurice, *Friends and Lovers* (London, 1971)

Capote, Truman, *Breakfast at Tiffany's* (N.Y, 1958)

——, *Other Voices, Other Rooms* (N.Y., 1948)

Chester, Alfred, *Behold Goliath* (N.Y., 1964)

[Cocteau, Jean,] *Le Livre blanc* (Paris, 1970)

Cohen, Leonard, *Beautiful Losers* (London, 1970)

Coleman, Lonnie, *Ship's Company* (Boston, 1955)

Dahl, Roald, *Someone Like You* (N.Y., 1954)

Dromgoole, Will Allen, *The Island of Beautiful Things* (Boston, 1912)

Duvert, Tony, *Journal d'un innocent* (Paris, 1976)

——, *Récidive* (Paris, 1976)

Firbank, Ronald, *The Complete Ronald Firbank* (London, 1961)

Flaubert, Gustave, *Three Tales* (Harmondsworth, 1961)

Forster, E.M., *The Life to Come, and Other Stories* (London, 1971)

——, *Maurice* (London, 1971)

——, *A Room with a View* (London, 1908)

Genet, Jean, *Journal du voleur* (Paris, 1949)

——, *Oeuvres complètes* (Paris, 1951)

George, Eliot, *The Leather Boys* (London, 1961)

Golding, William, *Rites of Passage* (London, 1980)

Gorham, Charles Orson, *McCaffery* (N.Y., 1961)

Grass, Günter, *The Flounder* (London, 1978)

Hemingway, Ernest, *The First Forty-Nine Stories* (London, 1962)

Herlihy, James Leo, *Midnight Cowboy* (N.Y., 1965)

——, *The Sleep of Baby Filbertson* (London, 1959)

Hill, Susan, *Strange Meeting* (London, 1971)

Holleran, Andrew, *Dancer from the Dance* (London, 1980)

Irving, John, *The World According to Garp* (London, 1978)

Isherwood, Christopher, *Lions and Shadows: An Education in the Twenties* (London, 1953)

——, *A Single Man* (London, 1964)

Joyce, James, *Ulysses* (London, 1960)

Kafka, Franz, *Metamorphosis, and Other Stories* (Harmondsworth, 1961)

Kazantzakis, Nikos, *The Last Temptation of Christ* (N.Y., 1960)

Kent, Nial, *The Divided Path* (N.Y., 1949)

Kerouac, Jack, *Desolation Angels* (N.Y., 1966)

King, Francis, *A Domestic Animal* (London, 1970)

Kleinberg, Seymour, ed., *The Other Persuasion* (N.Y., 1977)

Kosinski, Jerzy, *Cockpit* (London, 1975)

Kramer, Larry, *Faggots* (London, 1980)

Lawrence, D.H., *Aaron's Rod* (London, 1922)

——, *Kangaroo* (London, 1923)

——, *Lady Chatterley's Lover* (Harmondsworth, 1960)

——, *The Plumed Serpent* (London, 1926)

——, *The Prussian Officer, and Other Stories* (London, 1914)

——, *Sons and Lovers* (London, 1913)

——, *The White Peacock* (London, 1911)

——, *Women in Love* (London, 1921)

Lehmann, John, *In the Purely Pagan Sense* (London, 1976)

Little, Jay, *Somewhere Between the Two* (N.Y., 1956)

Madigan, Leo, *Jackarandy* (London, 1972)

Mailer, Norman, *The Armies of the Night: History as a Novel, the Novel as History* (N.Y., 1968)

Malaparte, Curzio, *Kaputt* (N.Y., 1946)

——, *La pelle* (Milano, 1978)

Mann, Thomas, *Death in Venice, Tristan, Tonio Kröger* (Harmondsworth, 1955)

Maugham, Robin, *The Last Encounter* (London, 1972)

——, *The Wrong People* (London, 1970)

McCullers, Carson, *Reflections in a Golden Eye* (Boston, 1941)

Melville, Herman, *Billy Budd, Sailor, and Other Stories* (Harmondsworth, 1967)

——, *Moby-Dick, or The Whale* (London, 1929)

Mishima Yukio, *Confessions of a Mask* (N.Y., 1958)

——, *Forbidden Colours* (London, 1968)

Moor, George, *The Pole and Whistle* (London, 1966)

Moorcock, Michael, *The Final Programme* (London, 1969)

Moravia, Alberto, *Two Adolescents* (London, 1952)

Murdoch, Iris, *An Accidental Man* (London, 1971)
——, *The Bell* (London, 1958)
——, *Henry and Cato* (London, 1976)
——, *The Sacred and Profane Love Machine* (London, 1974)
Murphy, Dennis, *The Sergeant* (N.Y., 1958)
Musil, Robert, *Young Törless* (London, 1955)
Peters, Fritz, *Finistère* (N.Y., 1949)
Petronius, *The Satyricon, and the Fragments* (Harmondsworth, 1965)
Peyrefitte, Roger, *Les Amitiés particulières* (Paris, 1943)
——, *L'Exilé de Capri* (Paris, 1959)
Proust, Marcel, *Time Regained* (London, 1970)
Purdy, James, *Eustace Chisolm and the Works* (London, 1968)
Pym, Barbara, *The Sweet Dove Died* (London, 1978)
Rabelais, François, *The Histories of Gargantua and Pantagruel* (Harmondsworth 1955)
Raven, Simon, *The Feathers of Death* (London, 1959)
——, *Fielding Gray* (London, 1967)
——, *Sound the Retreat* (London, 1973)
Rechy, John, *Bodies and Souls* (London, 1984)
——, *City of Night* (N.Y., 1963)
——, *Numbers* (N.Y., 1968)
Renault, Mary, *The Charioteer* (London, 1956)
——, *The Last of the Wine* (London, 1956)
Rolfe, Frederick, *The Desire and Pursuit of the Whole* (London, 1934)
Roth, Philip, *Portnoy's Complaint* (London, 1971)
Saba, Umberto, *Ernesto* (Torino, 1975)
Sade, Marquis de, *The Complete Marquis de Sade* (L.A., 1966)
——, *The 120 Days of Sodom, and Other Writings* (N.Y., 1966)
Soldati, Mario, *La confessione* (Milano, 1955)
Sontag, Susan, *The Benefactor* (London, 1964)
Stendhal, *Le Rouge et le Noir* (Paris, 1964)
Stewart, Angus, *Sandel* (London, 1968)
Storey, David, *Radcliffe* (London, 1963)
Thomas, Dylan, and John Davenport, *The Death of the King's Canary* (London, 1976)
Thomas, Ward, *Stranger in the Land* (Boston, 1949)
Tournier, Michel, *Gemini* (London, 1981)
——, *Le Roi des aulnes* (Paris, 1970)

——, *Vendredi, ou les limbes du Pacifique* (Paris, 1967)
Truscott, IV, Lucian K., *Dress Gray* (N.Y., 1979)
Vanden, Dirk, *All Is Well* (London, 1972)
Vidal, Gore, *The City and the Pillar* (N.Y., 1948)
——, *The City and the Pillar* (London, 1965)
——, *A Thirsty Evil* (London, 1956)
Wahl, Loren, *The Invisible Glass* (N.Y., 1950)
Warren, Patricia Nell, *The Front Runner* (N.Y., 1974)
Welch, Denton, *Maiden Voyage* (London, 1968)
White, Patrick, *Riders in the Chariot* (London, 1961)
——, *The Tree of Man* (London, 1956)
——, *The Vivisector* (London, 1970)
Wilde, Oscar, *The Picture of Dorian Gray* (London, 1891)
Williams, Tennessee, *Collected Stories* (London, 1986)
Willingham, Calder, *End as a Man* (N.Y., 1947)
Wilson, Angus, *As If By Magic* (London, 1973)
——, *The Wrong Set, and Other Stories* (London, 1949)
Windham, Donald, *Two People* (N.Y., 1965)
Woolaston, Graeme, *Stranger than Love* (London, 1985)

DRAMA

Aeschylus, *The Oresteian Trilogy: Agamemnon, The Choephori, The Eumenides* (Harmondsworth, 1956)
Albee, Edward, *The Zoo Story* (London, 1962)
Aristophanes, *The Knights, Peace, The Birds, The Assemblywomen, Wealth* (Harmondsworth, 1978)
Berkoff, Steven, *East, Agamemnon, The Fall of the House of Usher* (London, 1977)
Berman, Ed., ed., *Homosexual Acts: A Volume of Gay Plays* (London, 1975)
Crowley, Mart, *The Boys in the Band* (London, 1969)
Genet, Jean, *Deathwatch* (London, 1961)
Gilliatt, Penelope, *Sunday Bloody Sunday* (London, 1971)
Greig, Noel, and Drew Griffiths, *Only Connect*, BBC TV, 18 May 1979; producer, W. Stephen Gilbert
Hopkins, John, *Find Your Way Home* (Harmondsworth, 1971)

Lawrence, D.H., *The Complete Plays of D.H. Lawrence* (London, 1965)

Marlowe, Christopher, *The Complete Plays* (Harmondsworth, 1969)

Montherlant, Henry de, *La Ville dont le prince est un enfant* (Paris, 1957)

Ragni, Gerome, and James Rado, *Hair: The American Tribal Love-Rock Musical* (N.Y., 1969)

Rochester, John Wilmot, Earl of, *Sodom, or The Quintessence of Debauchery* (N. Hollywood, Cal., 1966)

Shaffer, Peter, *Equus* (London, 1973)

Shakespeare, William, *The Kingsway Shakespeare* (London, 1927)

Sherman, Martin, *Bent* (London, 1979)

Wilde, Oscar, *Plays* (Harmondsworth, 1969)

FILMS

Anderson, Lindsay, *If. . .*, 1968

Anger, Kenneth, *Fireworks*, 1947

——, *Inauguration of the Pleasure Dome*, 1954, recut 1966

——, *Invocation of my Demon Brother*, 1969

——, *Scorpio Rising*, 1962–1964

Cocteau, Jean, *Le Sang d'un poète*, 1930–2

——, *La Testament d'Orphée*, 1959

Costard, Helmuth, *Besonders Wertvoll*, 1968

Epstein, Rob, *The Times of Harvey Milk*, 1984

Fassbinder, Rainer Werner, *Fox and his Friends*, 1974

——, *Querelle*, 1982

Fellini, Federico, *Fellini-Satyricon*, 1969

Genet, Jean, *Un Chant d'amour*, 1950

Hazan, Jack, *A Bigger Splash*, 1974

Hurt, Harvey, *Fortune and Men's Eyes*, 1971

Huston, John, *Reflections in a Golden Eye*, 1967

Jarman, Derek, *The Angelic Conversation*, 1985

——, *Caravaggio*, 1986

——, *Jubilee*, 1978

——, *The Tempest*, 1979

Jarman, Derek, and Paul Humfress, *Sebastiane*, 1977

Lommel, Ulli, *Tenderness of the Wolves*, 1973

Mariposa Film Group, *Word is Out*, 1977

Minelli, Vincent, *Tea and Sympathy*, 1956

Morrissey, Paul, *Flesh*, 1968

Parker, Alan, *Midnight Express*, 1978

Pasolini, Pier Paolo, *Arabian Nights*, 1974

——, *The Canterbury Tales*, 1971

——, *The Decameron*, 1970

——, *Salò, or The 120 Days of Sodom*, 1975

Peck, Ron, *What Can I Do with a Male Nude?*, 1985

Peck, Ron, and Paul Hallam, *Nighthawks*, 1978

Penn, Arthur, *The Left-Handed Gun*, 1958

Praunheim, Rosa von, *Army of Lovers, or the Revolt of the Perverts*, 1978

Riefenstahl, Leni, *Olympia*, 1938

Ripploh, Frank, *Taxi Zum Klo*, 1981

Rosenthal, Jack, *The Naked Civil Servant*, 1975

Schiller, Greta, *Before Stonewall: The Making of a Gay and Lesbian Community*, 1984

Schlondorff, Volker, *Der Junge Törless*, 1966

Scott, Tony, *Top Gun*, 1986

Ustinov, Peter, *Billy Budd*, 1962

Vadim, Roger, *Barbarella*, 1967

Warhol, Andy, *Blow Job*, 1963

——, *Lonesome Cowboys*, 1967

Waters, John, *Pink Flamingos*, 1972

Wise, Robert, *The Sergeant*, 1968

MISCELLANY

Ackerley, J.R., *My Father and Myself* (London, 1968)

Allegro, John, *Lost Gods* (London, 1977)

——, *The Sacred Mushroom and the Cross: A Study of the Nature and Origins of Christianity within the Fertility Cults of the Ancient Near East* (London, 1973)

Auden, W.H., *A Certain World: A Commonplace Book* (London, 1971)

Babuscio, Jack, 'Military Masks', *Gay News* 86, p.18

Barber, Malcolm, *The Trial of the Templars* (Cambridge, 1978)

Beier, Ulli, ed., *The Origin of Life and Death: African Creation Myths* (London, 1966)

Bentley, Eric, *The Cult of the Superman* (Gloucester, Mass., 1969)

Billany, Dan, and David Dowie, *The Cage* (London, 1949)

Brown, Norman O., *Hermes the Thief: The Evolution of a Myth* (N.Y., 1969)

Burchett, George, *Memoirs of a Tattooist* (London, 1960)

Burroughs, William, and Allen Ginsberg, *The Yage Letters* (San Francisco, 1963)

Burton, Robert, *The Anatomy of Melancholy, What It Is, with All the Kinds, Causes, Symptoms, Prognostics, and Several Cures of It* (London, 1866)

Carpenter, Edward, *My Days and Dreams* (London, 1916)

Carter, Angela, *The Sadeian Woman* (London, 1979)

Chapman, Ronald, *Father Faber* (London, 1961)

Charters, Ann, *Kerouac: A Biography* (San Francisco, 1972)

Clark, Kenneth, *The Nude: A Study of Ideal Art* (London, 1956)

Cocteau, Jean, *A Call to Order* (London, 1926)

——, *The Journals of Jean Cocteau* (London, 1957)

Connolly, Cyril, *Enemies of Promise* (London 1973)

Crane, Hart, *The Letters of Hart Crane, 1916–1932* (Berkeley, Cal., 1965)

Crisp, Quentin, *The Naked Civil Servant* (London, 1968)

Crosby, Caresse, *The Passionate Years* (London, 1955)

Crossman, R.H.S., *Plato Today* (London, 1937)

Damase, Jacques, ed., *Saint Sébastien dans l'histoire de l'art depuis le XV° siècle* (Paris, 1979)

Davidson, Michael, *The World, the Flesh and Myself* (London, 1962)

Dickinson, G. Lowes, *After Two Thousand Years: A Dialogue between Plato and a Modern Young Man* (London, 1930)

——, *The Autobiography of G. Lowes Dickinson, and Other Unpublished Writings* (London, 1973)

——, *A Modern Symposium* (London, 1905)

——, *Plato and his Dialogues* (London, 1931)

Didron, Adolphe Napoléon, *Christian Iconography* (N.Y., 1965)

Diodorus Siculus, *Diodorus of Sicily, in Twelve Volumes* VIII (London, 1970)

Driberg, Tom, *Ruling Passions* (London, 1977)

Duncan, Robert, *The Truth and Life of Myth: An Essay in Essential Autobiography* (Fremont, Michigan, 1968)

Durgnat, Raymond, *Sexual Alienation in the Cinema* (London, 1972)

Ebenstein, H., *Pierced Hearts and True Love: An Illustrated History of the Origin and Development of European Tattooing and a Survey of its Present State* (London, 1953)

Fryer, Jonathan, *Isherwood* (London, 1977)

Ginsberg, Allen, *Indian Journals, March 1962–May 1963* (San Francisco, 1970)

——, *Journals, Early Fifties Early Sixties* (N.Y., 1977)

Giraud, Robert, 'The Skin Artists', *The Best of Olympia* (London, 1966) pp.70–5

Goodman, Paul, *Growing Up Absurd* (London, 1961)

Graves, Robert, *Good-bye to All That* (London, 1929)

——, *The Greek Myths* (Harmondsworth, 1960)

Greene, Graham, ed., *The Old School: Essays by Divers Hands* (London, 1934)

Halstead, Fred, *Out Now! A Participant's Account of the American Movement Against the Vietnam War* (N.Y., 1978)

Henderson, Philip, *Christopher Marlowe* (Brighton, 1974)

Hiscock, Eric, *The Bells of Hell Go Ting-a Ling-a Ling* (London, 1977)

Hitler, Adolf, *Mein Kampf* (London, 1939)

Howes, Keith, 'Designs on You', *Gay News* 139, p.21

Hughes, Patrick, and George Brecht, *Vicious Circles and Infinity: An Anthology of Paradoxes* (N.Y., 1975)

Hyde, H. Montgomery, *The Trials of Oscar Wilde* (London, 1948)

Isherwood, Christopher, *Christopher and his Kind, 1929–1939* (London, 1977)

——, *Exhumations: Stories Articles Verses* (London, 1966)

Julian of Norwich, *Revelations of Divine Love* (Harmondsworth, 1966)

Keene, Donald, ed., *Anthology of Japanese Literature to the Nineteenth Century* (Harmondsworth, 1968)

Kierkegaard, Søren, *Fear and Trembling, and The Sickness unto Death* (Garden City, N.Y., 1954)

Kramer, Heinrich, and James Sprenger, *Malleus Maleficarum* (London, 1928)

Lawrence, D.H., *The Collected Letters of D.H. Lawrence* (London, 1962)

Lawrence, T.E., *Seven Pillars of Wisdom: A Triumph* (London, 1935)

Leach, Edmund, *Lévi-Strauss* (London, 1970)

——, *Genesis as Myth, and Other Essays* (London, 1969)

Lehmann, John, *I Am My Brother* (London, 1960)

Lehner, Ernst and Johanna, *Folklore and Symbolism of Flowers, Plants and Trees* (N.Y., 1960)

Lévi, Eliphas, *L'Histoire de la magie* (London, 1969)

Lévi-Strauss, Claude, *L'Homme nu* (Paris, 1971)

——, *Structural Anthropology* (N.Y., 1963)

Longworth, T. Clifton, *The Worship of Love:*

A Study of Nature Worship Throughout the World (Hemel Hempstead, 1963)

Lowenfels, Walter, ed., *Walt Whitman's Civil War* (N.Y., 1960)

Lucretius, *On the Nature of the Universe* (Harmondsworth, 1951)

Mailer, Norman, *Cannibals and Christians* (N.Y., 1966)

——, *The Prisoner of Sex* (London, 1971)

Melly, George, *Rum, Bum and Concertina* (London, 1977)

Minucius Felix, M., *Octavius*, with Tertullian, *Apology* and *De Spectaculis* (London, 1966)

Mosley, Oswald, *The Greater Britain* (London, 1932)

Neville, Richard, *Playpower* (London, 1970)

Nin, Anais, *The Journals of Anais Nin, 1939–1944* (London, 1970)

Nuttall, Jeff, *Bomb Culture* (London, 1968)

Palmer, Tony, *The Trials of Oz* (London, 1971)

Paracelsus, *Selected Writings* (Princeton, N.J., 1958)

Pater, Walter, *Plato and Platonism: A Series of Lectures* (London, 1893)

——, *The Renaissance: Studies in Art and Poetry* (London, 1922)

Perloff, Marjorie, *Frank O'Hara: A Poet Among Painters* (N.Y., 1977)

Peyrefitte, Roger, *L'Enfant Amour* (Paris, 1969)

Pico della Mirandola, Gianfrancesco, *On the Dignity of Man, On Being and the One, and Heptaplus* (Indianapolis, N.Y., 1965)

Plato, *Phaedrus, and the Seventh and Eighth Letters* (Harmondsworth, 1973)

——, *Timaeus* (Harmondsworth, 1965)

Popper, K.R., *The Open Society and its Enemies, Volume 1: The Spell of Plato* (London, 1962)

Raven, Simon, *The English Gentleman: An Essay in Attitudes* (London, 1961)

Reid, Forrest, *Apostate* (London, 1926)

Rich, Adrienne, *Women and Honor: Notes on Lying* (London, 1979)

Rolfe, Frederick, *Venice Letters* (London, 1974)

Russell, Bertrand, *The Conquest of Happiness* (London, 1930)

——, *History of Western Philosophy, and its Connection with Political and Social Circumstances from the Earliest Times to the Present Day* (London, 1946)

Rycroft, Charles, *Reich* (London, 1971)

Schopenhauer, Arthur, *The Will to Live: Selected Writings of Arthur Schopenhauer* (N.Y., 1967)

Sinclair, Andrew, *Guevara* (London, 1970)

Smith, Don, *Early Christianity and 'the Homosexual': A Postscript to a Blasphemy Trial and a Challenge to Mrs Whitehouse (in 'Measured Tones')* (London, 1977)

Spender, Stephen, *World Within World: The Autobiography of Stephen Spender* (Berkeley, Cal., 1966)

Starkie, Enid, *Arthur Rimbaud* (London, 1973)

Steegmuller, Francis, *Cocteau: A Biography* (London, 1970)

Stekel, William, *Peculiarities of Behaviour: Wandering Mania, Dipsomania, Cleptomania, Pyromania and Allied Impulsive Acts* II (N.Y., 1924)

Swedenborg, Emanuel, *Heaven and its Wonders and Hell, from Things Heard and Seen* (London, 1920)

Szasz, Thomas, *Heresies* (Garden City, N.Y., 1976)

Taylor, F. Sherwood, *The Alchemists* (London, 1952)

Tom of Finland, *The Men* (N. Hollywood, Cal., 1976)

——, *The Best of Tom of Finland* (L.A., n.d.)

Tracey, Michael, and David Morrison, *Whitehouse* (London, 1979)

Tyler, Parker, *Screening the Sexes: Homosexuality in the Movies* (N.Y., 1972)

——, *Sex Psyche Etcetera in the Film* (Harmondsworth, 1971)

Umphlett, Wiley Lee, *The Sporting Myth and American Experience* (London, 1975)

Unamuno, Miguel de, *The Tragic Sense of Life* (London, 1962)

Vaughan, Keith, *Journal and Drawings 1939–1965* (London, 1966)

Vogel, Amos, *Film as a Subversive Art* (London, 1974)

Voltaire, *Philosophical Dictionary* (Harmondsworth, 1972)

Walter, Nicholas, *Blasphemy in Britain: The Practice and Punishment of Blasphemy, and the Trial of Gay News* (London, 1977)

Walters, Margaret, *The Nude Male: A New Perspective* (London, 1978)

Welch, Denton, *The Denton Welch Journals* (London, 1952)

White, Edmund, *States of Desire: Travels in Gay America* (N.Y., 1980)

Wildeblood, Peter, *Against the Law* (London, 1955)

Wiles, Bertha Harris, *The Fountains of Florentine Sculptors and their Followers from Donatello to Bernini* (N.Y., 1975)

Williams, Tennessee, *Memoirs* (London, 1976)

Willis, Paul E., *Profane Culture* (London, 1978)

Wilson, Colin, *Wilhelm Reich* (London, 1974)

Wolfenden, John, *Turning Points: The Memoirs of John Wolfenden* (London, 1976)

Worsley, T.C., *Flannelled Fool: A Slice of Life in the Thirties* (London, 1967)

'Y', *The Autobiography of an Englishman* (London, 1976)

PERIODICALS

(Two types of gay periodical: newspapers and arts magazines. I consulted those listed here more or less regularly throughout the period of my research. Some individual items which proved particularly useful are listed earlier in this bibliography.)

The Advocate (San Mateo, Cal.)
The Body Politic (Toronto)
Fag Rag (Boston, Mass.)
FUORI! (Torino)
Gai Pied (Paris)
Gay News (London)
Gay's the Word Review (London)
Gay Sunshine (San Francisco)
Mouth of the Dragon (New York)

INDEX